The Company Corporation®

Incorporating Businesses Since 1899

...introduces an online calendar and reminder service that notifies you when Incorporation or Limited Liability Company (LLC) documents and actions are due.....

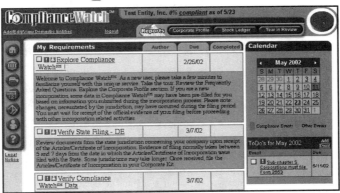

Let The Company Corporation® (TCC) help you manage the ongoing legal formalities associated with your LLC. ComplianceWatch® is an exclusive service of The Company Corporation®. It is designed to help protect your LLC in several important ways:

- access to a customized calendar and reminder service that can automatically notify you when it's time to hold your annual meeting, file annual reports, pay franchise taxes, and perform other duties to meet important deadlines

- access to sample documents and templates you can use to guide you through the preparation of your operating agreement

- the ability to record the official activities of your Limited Liability Company

To learn more about ComplianceWatch®, visit

www.compliancewatch.com

and take the tour.

Read This First

The information in this book is as up to date and accurate as we can make it. But it's important to realize that the law changes frequently, as do fees, forms and procedures. If you handle your own legal matters, it's up to you to be sure that all information you use—including the information in this book—is accurate.

We believe accurate and current legal information should help you solve many of your own legal problems on a cost-efficient basis. But this text is not a substitute for personalized advice from a knowledgeable lawyer. If you want the help of a trained professional, consult an attorney licensed to practice in your state.

The Company Corporation®
Incorporating Businesses Since 1899

Legal Forms for Starting & Running a Small Business

By Attorney Fred S. Steingold

Edited by Attorney Shannon Miehe

NOLO

SECOND EDITION	FEBRUARY 2001
Editor	SHANNON MIEHE
Cover Design	TONI IHARA
Book Design	TERRI HEARSH
Proofreading	ROBERT WELLS
CD-ROM Preparation	ANDRÉ ZIVKOVICH
Index	PATRICIA DEMINNA
Printing	CONSOLIDATED PRINTERS, INC.

For information on bulk purchases or corporate premium sales, please contact the Special Sales Department. For academic sales or textbook adoptions, ask for Academic Sales. Call 800-955-4775 or write to Nolo, 950 Parker Street, Berkeley, CA 94710.

Acknowledgments

Thanks to Jake Warner and Shannon Miehe for their superb editing as well as the energy and enthusiasm they brought to this project.

Thanks also to the other Nolo wizards who contributed their enormous skills to this book and the accompanying software—especially: Tony Mancuso, Barbara Kate Repa, Robin Leonard, Lisa Goldoftas and Ely Newman.

Finally, thanks to my colleague, Brook McCray Smith, for his many wise suggestions, and to my assistant, Jamie DeFlorio, for her help in preparing the manuscript.

About the Author

Fred S. Steingold practices law in Ann Arbor, Michigan. He represents and advises many small businesses, and frequently leads seminars on how to start and run a small business. He is the author of the *Legal Guide for Starting & Running a Small Business* (Nolo) and *The Employer's Legal Handbook* (Nolo), a bible for small business owners. His monthly column, *The Legal Advisor,* is carried by more than 30 trade publications around the country.

Table of Contents

4 Borrowing Money

5 Buying a Business

6 Leasing Space

7 Purchasing and Improving Real Estate

8 Buying, Selling, Manufacturing

9 Hiring Employees and Independent Contractors

Appendix A:
How to Use the CD-ROM

Appendix B:
Tear-Out Forms

Index

Introduction

How to Use This Book

The most important rule when making any business agreement is: Get it in writing.

In some situations—such as a contract to buy or sell real estate—only a written agreement is legally enforceable. Similarly, a contract that can't be carried out in one year, or a contract to sell goods exceeding a certain value set by state law (typically, $500), must be written.

But even in the situations where an oral contract is legal, there are many practical reasons to prefer writing your agreement down. Two years from now, you and the other people involved in any business transaction are likely to have significantly different recollections about what you collectively agreed to. So putting agreements in black and white is an important memory aid. But a well-drafted contract confers several other important benefits on its signers. For one, it serves as a framework within which to resolve disputes. And even if this proves impossible and a court contest ensues, it will be far easier to prove the terms of a written contract than an oral one.

Still another important benefit of drafting a written agreement is that the act of putting your contract together can help you and the other party(ies) focus on all key legal and practical issues, some of which might otherwise be overlooked. And by starting this process with a well-designed form—like those in this book—your chances of creating a thorough document are further enhanced.

To help you create sound legal agreements, this book provides convenient, ready-to-use forms for most of the common transactions your small business is likely to encounter. Whether you're borrowing money, buying a business, leasing an office or store, hiring employees, or contracting for goods or services, you'll find well-drafted contracts that are simple to customize to fit your needs.

Happily, the fill-in-the-blanks contracts in this book are a lot easier to use than most similar legal documents. Not only have we avoided legalese, we have also adopted a modern and easy-to-use layout. But don't let the lack of gobbledygook fool you: These forms cover all the important legal bases.

Because a legal form without good background information and instructions is almost valueless, each chapter provides the essential legal and practical information you'll need to create sound agreements. Unfortunately, even a book as chunky as this one doesn't have enough space to provide in-depth coverage of every practical and legal issue covered by every contract.

That's where other Nolo products come in. Throughout this book we'll refer you to other Nolo titles where you can learn even more about a specific topic, from hiring employees to choosing a domain name. If you need it, these books will provide you with detailed information and practical tips to get your business up and running—and keep it running. Some of the other small business titles Nolo offers are:

- The *Legal Guide for Starting & Running a Small Business*, by Fred S. Steingold. Everything you need to know about starting your business, from which business structure is best for you to hiring employees to tips on obtaining business insurance.

- *Tax Savvy for Small Business*, by Frederick W. Daily. An indispensable guide to tax deductions your small business shouldn't miss, as well as in-depth information on the taxation of different kinds of business entities.

- *How to Create a Buy-Sell Agreement & Control the Destiny of Your Small Business*, by Anthony Mancuso and Bethany K. Laurence. If you're starting a business with a co-owner, this book contains invaluable information on creating a buy-sell agreement and provides forms for you to create and customize your own agreement.

- *How to Form Your Own Corporation*, Anthony Mancuso (available for California, Texas and New York). If you're forming a corporation, this book gives you step-by-step instructions on reserving a corporate name, filing your articles of incorporation and lots of helpful information on corporate recordkeeping, taxation and issuing shares.

- *Hiring Independent Contractors: The Employer's Legal Guide*, by Stephen Fishman. If you're thinking of hiring independent contractors, this book is an invaluable resource. You'll learn the pros and cons of hiring independent contractors instead of employees, including the rules government agencies use to classify workers and the special tax issues associated with hiring independent contractors.
- *The Corporate Minutes Book: The Legal Guide to Taking Care of Corporate Business*, by Anthony Mancuso. This book contains all the minutes and resolutions you'll need to keep your corporate recordkeeping on track.
- *Form Your Own Limited Liability Company*, and *LLC Maker 1.0*, both by Anthony Mancuso. The former is a guide to forming your limited liability company in all 50 states and includes information and forms to help you reserve a name, file your articles of organization and create an operating agreement. The latter is an interactive Windows software program that helps you create, step-by-step, forms to reserve a name for your LLC, file your articles of organization and create an operating agreement.
- *The Partnership Book*, by Denis Clifford and Ralph Warner. If you want to form a partnership, this book is an indispensable guide to partnerships and contains forms to help you create your own partnership agreement.
- *Trademark: Legal Care for Your Business & Product Name*, by Stephen Elias and Kate McGrath. Everything you need to know about creating and protecting a trademark for your business or product name.

Look for this icon, which accompanies references to specific Nolo products where the related material is covered:

A. Four Practical Ways to Use the Forms in This Book

This book is a flexible resource that you can adapt to fit your needs and workstyle. There are at least four ways you can use the forms provided in this book.

- Since all forms are contained on the accompanying CD-ROM, perhaps the most efficient approach is to open, fill in and print out a form with your computer's word processor, customizing it as needed.
- Or, if you don't have a word processor, you can get the job done the old-fashioned way, by photocopying a form right out of the book and then filling it in with a typewriter, or by hand.
- In some instances, especially where a form will be used repeatedly, you may want to print out or photocopy a pile of blank forms, filling them in later (by hand or typewriter) as needed.
- If someone else has already prepared a proposed contract and presented it to you for signature, you can use the appropriate form in this book as a sort of checklist to make sure that the proposed contract has all the recommended ingredients. If it doesn't, you can have the preparer use the book's form as a model when making modifications or additions.

Think twice before using the only copy of a form. Although it's possible to tear out and use the forms directly from this book, this is a poor idea because you'll be left without a clean copy if you need a similar document in the future.

If you don't use the forms CD-ROM, photocopy the needed agreements.

Read over the explanatory materials in each chapter before filling out the forms. This book is designed to be used as needed, rather than read through in its entirety. Rather, if you want to perform a particular task (like borrow capital for your business), you'll go right to the appropriate form (for example, Form 4C: Promissory Note—Equal Monthly Installments). Just be sure to first read the introductory information at the beginning of the relevant chapter and at the beginning of the relevant section (in this case, Chapter 4, Section C) rather than jump directly to the form and its instructions.

B. Do You Need a Lawyer?

Most small business transactions are relatively straightforward. Just as you routinely negotiate business deals involving significant dollar amounts without formal legal help, you can usually just as safely complete the basic legal paperwork needed to record your understanding.

But like most generalizations, this one isn't always true. Creating a solid written agreement will occasionally mean seeking the advice of a lawyer to cope with a problematic issue. Fortunately, even when you decide to get a lawyer's help, the forms and information set out here should help you keep a tight rein on legal fees. You'll have gotten a running start by learning about the legal issues and perhaps drawing up a rough draft of the needed document, allowing you and your lawyer to focus on the few points that may not be routine.

Ideally, you should find a lawyer who's willing to serve as your small business legal coach—one who respects your ability to prepare drafts of routine paperwork and who stands ready to review and fine-tune your work when requested. A word of caution here: Some lawyers still subscribe to the old-fashioned notion that they and only they are the repository of all legal information and expertise. In their view, you should turn every legal question and problem over to them, and your participation should be limited to promptly paying their bills. It should

go almost without saying that even if this were an efficient way to run your business (it isn't—you clearly need to be involved in making all key decisions), you couldn't afford it.

To find a lawyer who's genuinely open to helping you help yourself and is sensitive to your need to keep costs down, talk to people who own or operate truly excellent small businesses. Ask them who they've chosen as their legal mentor. Speak as well to your banker, accountant, insurance agent and real estate broker—all of whom undoubtedly come into frequent contact with lawyers who creatively represent business clients.

 Of the approximately 650,000 American lawyers, probably fewer than 50,000 possess sufficient training and experience in small business law to be of real help to you. And even when you locate a lawyer skilled in small business law in

general, you need to make sure that he or she is knowledgeable about the specific job at hand. A lawyer who has a vast amount of experience in handling the sale and purchase of small businesses, for example, may have limited knowledge about the fast-changing world of commercial leases (not ideal if there's an unusual rent increase clause you want to discuss) and knows next to nothing about dealing with state or federal regulatory agencies (not good if you need to appeal the suspension of your liquor license). In short, always ask about the lawyer's background in the particular area of law that affects you.

 Chapter 24 of the *Legal Guide for Starting & Running a Small Business*, by Fred S. Steingold (Nolo), offers a strategy for finding the right lawyer, as well as explaining how lawyers charge for their work and how you can save money by doing your own legal research.

Icons Used in This Book

Throughout this book, these icons alert you to certain information.

 A legal or commonsense tip to help you understand or comply with legal requirements.

 A caution to slow down and consider potential problems.

 A suggestion to seek the advice of a lawyer, tax advisor or other professional.

 Refers you to a discussion of the topic or a related topic elsewhere in this book.

 Refers to the files on the forms CD-ROM in the back of the book.

 Refers you to other helpful publications.

Contract Basics

Most of the forms in this book are contracts —or promissory notes, which are just a special type of contract. As with any contract, you must understand what it says and make sure that it suits your needs. In addition, you face two other important issues:

- How do you properly identify the businesses and individuals who are parties to the contract?
- How do the parties sign the contract to make it legally binding?

Rather than repeat the instructions for dealing with these issues many times throughout the book, we discuss the legal context and give you our recommendations in this first chapter.

Similarly, in this chapter, we also explain two other basic contract concepts that appear throughout the book. The first involves the "disputes" clause, which establishes a structure to allow the parties to resolve any disputes that may later occur. The second deals with modifying or adding to a contract, which may occur any time.

But don't worry about having to memorize this basic information now in order to later complete a particular contract form. Along with the instructions for each form, we'll provide cross-references to the instructions in this chapter as needed.

A. Names Clause: Identifying the Parties to a Contract

At the beginning of most forms in this book, you'll need to fill in one or more names to identify the parties (individuals or businesses) who are agreeing to the contract. While this seems easy enough, it can sometimes be a little tricky, since how you identify the parties will vary somewhat depending on the type of business entities that are parties to the agreement.

For example, suppose you need to borrow money from your Uncle Al and want to put the loan in writing. First, you'll need a promissory note form (such as the ones in Chapter 4). Since both you and Uncle Al are individuals, you'll just need to include both your names—you as borrower, Al as lender—with no additional identification needed.

In a business context, however, a promissory note—or for that matter, any other contract—can be used by people owning or managing any of a half-dozen types of legal entities. (See "Types of Business Entities," below.) This means that determining the correct name format to use for a business is a little more complicated.

For a discussion of the different types of legal business entities, see Chapter 1 of the *Legal Guide for Starting & Running a Small Business*, by Fred S. Steingold (Nolo).

First, you need to make sure that you correctly name the business. Then you must designate its legal nature (partnership or corporation, for instance) and obtain the signature of the person or people with authority to legally bind the business. (Signatures are discussed below, in Section B.)

Assume, for example, that Mary Jones decides to go into the coin-operated laundry business as a sole

Types of Business Entities

- **Sole Proprietorship.** A one-owner business in which the owner is personally liable for all business debts.
- **General Partnership.** A business entity formed by two or more people, all of whom are personally liable for all partnership debts. When two or more people are in business together and haven't formed a limited partnership, corporation or LLC, they're treated as a general partnership by law even if they haven't signed a formal partnership agreement. A partnership doesn't pay federal incomes taxes; a partner's share of the profits or losses is reported on his or her personal tax return.
- **Limited Partnership.** A business entity formed by one or more general partners and one or more limited partners. Ordinarily, only the general partners are personally liable for the partnership debts.
- **Corporation.** A business entity formed by one or more shareholders. Ordinarily, a shareholder is not personally liable for the corporation's debts. This is so whether or not the corporation is organized for tax purposes as a regular (C) corporation or an S corporation; the two types of corporations differ only in terms of tax treatment. The big difference is that the undistributed income of a regular corporation is taxed at the corporate level. That's not true with an S corporation; for tax purposes, income and losses pass through to the individual shareholders as if they were partners in a partnership.
- **Limited Liability Company (LLC).** A business entity formed by one or more members. Ordinarily, a member is not personally liable for the LLC's debts and is taxed in the same way as if he or she were a partner (unless the LLC chooses to be taxed as a corporation).

proprietor and to buy the assets of a laundry owned by Clean Times Inc., a corporation, using Form 5B (in Chapter 5). The corporation's shareholders are Alice Appleby and Richard Reardon, who are respectively the president and secretary-treasurer. How do you state the buyer's and seller's names in the first clause of the contract to purchase the business?

As a sole proprietor, Mary Jones can just fill in her own name as the borrower. Alternatively, if she's using a fictitious name to operate the business —like Mary's Clean-O-Mat—she can add after her name the phrase "doing business as Mary's Clean-O-Mat" or "dba Mary's Clean-O-Mat."

What about the seller? For a corporation, you'll need to (1) include the official corporate name, and (2) identify the state of incorporation. Thus, the correct form is "Clean Times Inc., a New York Corporation." So the first clause of the contract would be as follows:

1. NAMES

Clean Times Inc., a New York Corporation, Seller, and Mary Jones, Buyer, agree to the following sale.

 Use the official corporate name even if a business uses a different name. Sometimes a corporation does business using a name that's different from its official corporate name—for example, an assumed name, fictitious name or trademarked name. We recommend that in preparing legal forms, you stick to the official corporate name. To return to the Clean Times example, there can be only one corporation organized under New York law with the name Clean Times Inc. By using this name in a legal document, you avoid any possible confusion about what business is signing the paper.

We've included a "names" chart, below, to consult whenever you need to fill in the names clause in any form. The chart gives the recommended format for completing the names clause.

 The recommended formats for names are in the file NAMES.

Formats for Names in Legal Forms	
Type of Entity	**Identification**
Individual	John Smith
Two or More Individuals	John Smith and Mary Jones
Sole Proprietor (Either style can be used)	John Smith [or] John Smith, doing business as John's Diner
General Partnership	Smith & Jones, a Michigan Partnership
Limited Partnership	Professional Management Limited Partnership, a New York Limited Partnership
Corporation	Modern Textiles Inc., a Texas Corporation
Limited Liability Company	Games and Such LLC, a Michigan Limited Liability Company

B. Signature Clause: Signing a Contract

For a contract to be legally binding, all parties must sign it. Signing a document might seem like a simple and obvious task, but it does involve a few important legal subtleties. Let's consider what format should be used to sign the contract between Mary Jones and Clean Times. As sole proprietor, Mary Jones must begin with (1) the name of her business, followed by (2) the type of business entity it is—here, a sole proprietorship—followed by (3) her signature, (4) her name printed out, (5) her title in the business—in this case Mary's the owner—and (6) her address. Like so:

BUYER

Mary's Clean-O-Mat

A Sole Proprietorship

By: _____

    Mary Jones

    Owner

    1234 Lucky St.

    White Plains, New York

The selling corporation includes the same information, except that the president of the corporation must sign on behalf of the business.

SELLER

Clean Times Inc.

A New York Corporation

By: _____

    Alice Appleby

    President

    123 Chesterfield Boulevard

    White Plains, New York

We've included a "signature" chart, below, to show you how to deal with signatures in all common business contexts.

 The signature formats are in the file SIGNING.

1. Who Signs Contracts for a Corporation?

A corporation determines which of its officers have authority to sign agreements and other legal documents on behalf of the corporation. The authority to sign can usually be found in the corporation's bylaws or in a resolution of the directors.

In a small incorporated business, the president almost always has that authority, and this reality is reflected in our chart. But the bylaws or a directors'

Signature Lines on Legal Forms

Individual	*John Smith* John Smith
Two or More Individuals	*John Smith* John Smith *Mary Jones* Mary Jones

Sole Proprietor (Either style can be used)	*John Smith*
	 John Smith
	 [or]
	 John's Diner
	 A Sole Proprietorship
	 By: *John Smith*
	     John Smith
	     Owner

General Partnership	Smith & Jones
	 A Michigan Partnership
	 By: *Mary Jones*
	     Mary Jones
	     Partner

Limited Partnership	Professional Management Limited Partnership
	 A New York Limited Partnership
	 By: *Mary Jones*
	     Mary Jones
	     General Partner

Corporation	Modern Textiles Inc.
	 A Texas Corporation
	 By: *Mary Jones*
	     Mary Jones
	     President

Limited Liability Company	Games and Such LLC
	 A Michigan Limited Liability Company
	 By: *Mary Jones*
	     Mary Jones
	     Member/Manager

resolution may empower other officers to sign as well—for example, a vice president or corporate secretary. If a lot is at stake in a transaction, and the corporation you're dealing with intends to have someone other than its president sign a legal document on behalf of the corporation, it makes sense to ask to see the bylaw or directors' resolution authorizing the other officer to sign.

However, where you're buying all or almost all of the assets of a corporation (as in our example), it's a good idea to go a step farther and make sure that even the president has the necessary authorization to make the sale under the terms of a specific resolution of the shareholders. The resolution should include approval of the purchase price and the terms of payment (for example, a 20% down payment with the balance to bear interest at 10% a year and to be paid in equal monthly installments over a five-year period). Obtaining such a resolution gives you a high degree of assurance that the corporation will be legally bound by the contract.

Bypass the need to examine corporate paperwork by asking that all shareholders sign the contract of sale. Not only does getting the signatures of all shareholders on a contract of sale leave no doubt as to the president's authority to sell you the business, but the accompanying consent language can also bind the shareholders personally to carry out the contract terms.

In the few forms where such consent is advised, like Form 5B: Contract for Purchase of Business Assets From a Corporation, we've included the recommended language in the form itself.

2. A Business Owner's Personal Liability

How a business is legally organized is critical to determining whether or not a business owner who signs a contract or other document is personally liable if things go wrong. Obviously, this is an important issue: when you're the person signing, you definitely want to know if you're putting your personal (nonbusiness) assets at risk. And when someone on the other side of a transaction is signing, you need to know if you can go after his or her personal assets if the business fails to meet its obligations.

If a business is organized as a sole proprietorship or general partnership, an owner is automatically personally liable for meeting the terms of all business contracts. (In a limited partnership, only the general partner(s) would be liable.) If the contract terms aren't met, the person or business on the other side of the deal can sue and get a judgment (a court determination that a sum of money is owed) against not only the business but its owner as well, and the owner's assets can be taken by the creditor to satisfy (pay) the judgment amount.

However, if a corporation or LLC fails to meet the terms of a contract, only the business is liable. This means that the person or business on the other side of the deal is only able to get a judgment against the business (not the owner) and can only collect from the business's assets (not the owner's)—unless an owner of a corporation or LLC voluntarily waives this barrier to personal liability by personally guaranteeing the contract, as explained in Section 3, below.

EXAMPLE 1: Harold signs a five-year lease for a car repair shop he plans to run under the name of Hal's Garage. Since he doesn't incorporate or form an LLC and no one else owns the business with him, the law describes his business as a sole proprietorship. Harold's business never takes off and, after six frustrating months, he closes. The landlord sues for unpaid rent and gets a judgment against Harold personally. The landlord can collect not only from the few paltry dollars left in the business's bank account, but can go after Harold's personal bank account, his car and his house (although Harold may be eligible to invoke debtor's exemption laws to limit what the landlord can take).

EXAMPLE 2: Spencer forms a corporation called Spencer Enterprises Inc. The corporation then leases space for five years to run a car repair shop; Spencer signs the lease as president of Spencer Enterprises Inc. After six months, the business closes. The landlord can only get a judgment from the corporation and collect from its meager assets. Although Spencer loses all the money he put into the business, his car, bank account and other personal assets are safe.

3. A Business Owner's Personal Guarantee

When an owner of shares in a corporation or a member of an LLC signs a contract or promissory note using the signature format recommended in our chart for a corporation or LLC, he or she does not become personally liable. That's because the format makes it clear that the owner is signing on behalf of the business, not as an individual.

Sometimes, however, people agree that one or more corporate shareholders or LLC members will assume personal responsibility (liability) for the terms of the contract, lease or promissory note. This commonly occurs, for example, when a corporation borrows money and the lender requires a shareholder to sign a promissory note as president of the corporation and also as an individual to personally guarantee payment of the note. If the parties agree that a personal guarantee is appropriate, the language you can add at the end of a contract or promissory note to provide that guarantee is shown below.

These optional guarantee clauses are in the file SIGNING. If you decide to use one of the guarantees, copy the appropriate form and paste it into your document.

Personal Guarantee of a Contract—Single Guarantor

In consideration of _____ *[name of other party]* _____

signing the above contract with _____ *[name of corporation or LLC]* _____

_____, I personally guarantee the performance of all obligations of

___ *[name of corporation or LLC]* _____

in the above contract.

Dated: _____

Signature: _____

Printed Name: _____

Address: _____

_____

Personal Guarantee of a Contract—
Two or More Guarantors

In consideration of _____ *[name of other party]* _____

signing the above contract with _____ *[name of corporation or LLC]* _____

_____, we jointly and individually guarantee the performance of all obligations of

___ *[name of corporation or LLC]* _____

in the above contract.

Dated: _____

Signature: _____

Printed Name: _____

Address: _____

_____

Dated: _____

Signature: _____

Printed Name: _____

Address: _____

_____

Personal Guarantee of a Lease—Single Guarantor

In consideration of _____ *[name of landlord]* _____

signing the above lease with _____ *[name of corporation or LLC]* _____

_____, I personally guarantee the performance of all obligations of

[name of corporation or LLC] _____

in the above lease.

Dated: _____

Signature: _____

Printed Name: _____

Address: _____

_____

Personal Guarantee of a Lease—Two or More Guarantors

In consideration of _____ *[name of landlord]* _____

signing the above lease with _____ *[name of corporation or LLC]* _____

_____, we jointly and individually guarantee the performance of all obligations of

[name of corporation or LLC] _____

in the above lease.

Dated: _____

Signature: _____

Printed Name: _____

Address: _____

_____

Dated: _____

Signature: _____

Printed Name: _____

Address: _____

_____

Personal Guarantee
of a Promissory Note—Single Guarantor

In consideration of _____ *[name of lender]* _____

lending funds to _____ *[name of corporation or LLC]* _____,

I personally guarantee the timely payment of the above promissory note.

Dated: _____

Signature: _____

Printed Name: _____

Address: _____

_____

Personal Guarantee
of a Promissory Note—Two or More Guarantors

In consideration of _____ *[name of lender]* _____

lending funds to _____ *[name of corporation or LLC]* _____,

we jointly and individually guarantee the timely payment of the above promissory note.

Dated: _____

Signature: _____

Printed Name: _____

Address: _____

_____

Dated: _____

Signature: _____

Printed Name: _____

Address: _____

4. Customized Guarantees

Sometimes a guarantor will agree to be liable for only a certain amount of money or for only a limited period of time. You can tailor the guarantee accordingly, for example:

GUARANTEE FOR A LIMITED AMOUNT:

In consideration of _____*[name of lender]*_____ lending funds to _____*[name of corporation or LLC]*_____, I personally guarantee the timely payment of the above promissory note. The maximum amount of my liability, however, is $5,000.

GUARANTEE FOR A LIMITED TIME:

In consideration of _____*[name of landlord]*_____ signing the above lease with_____*[name of corporation or LLC]*_____, I personally guarantee the performance of all obligations of _____*[name of corporation or LLC]*_____ for the first twelve months of the above lease.

⚠ Pre-printed guarantees may be more complicated. The forms in this book are more straightforward than some forms you may encounter in the commercial world. A bank's form for a loan guarantee may, for example, contain a sentence like the following, which asks the guarantor to: "waive notice of acceptance, notice of nonpayment, protest and notice of protest with respect to the obligation covered hereunder." Lying behind this linguistic fog are statutory rights that may allow a guarantor to stall—or even prevent—a lender from collecting on a guarantee. For obvious reasons, a commercial lender will want you to waive, or give up, these rights. It's often okay to waive these statutory rights, and it may be difficult to obtain a loan from a commercial lender if you don't. But as with any legal document you're asked to sign, if you don't fully understand the terms, it's best to consult a lawyer.

5. Requiring a Spouse's Signature

If one party is signing a document in a capacity that makes him or her personally liable for a business debt or other business obligation, the other party may ask that his or her spouse sign as well. This is most likely to happen, for example, if you're personally borrowing money that you'll use in your business or if you're personally guaranteeing a debt or other obligation of a corporation in which you own shares or of an LLC in which you're a member.

Similarly, you may find yourself in a situation in which you'd like to have the spouse of the other party sign a document. In addition to the situation just mentioned, this could happen if you're lending money to or entering into an agreement with an individual whose spouse is financially well-off and could repay the debt if the borrower defaulted.

Not surprisingly, having a spouse sign a document can substantially increase the other party's legal rights. For example, in most states if you alone sign for a loan or agree to be liable for any other obligation, the creditor can get a judgment for nonpayment against you but not your spouse. This means that, ordinarily—except in community property states where all marital, or community, property can be taken to pay for the debts of both spouses—a creditor will be able to reach the property that you own in your own name, but not the property that you and your spouse own in both your names. But if you and your spouse both sign a contract and then don't abide by its terms, the other party will be able to sue and get a judgment against both of you. In addition, the creditor can then enforce the judgment by seizing your joint bank account or jointly owned real estate as well as property you own in your name alone. The creditor will also be able to go after property that's in your spouse's name alone, and even be able to garnish your spouse's paycheck.

If the parties agree that a spouse's personal guarantee is appropriate, you can use one of the personal guarantee clauses referred to in Section 3.

Both Spouses Are Liable for Most Debts in Community Property States

Nine states follow the community property system: Arizona, California, Idaho, Louisiana, Nevada, New Mexico, Texas, Washington and Wisconsin. In these states, a married couple's property tends to be primarily community (joint) property regardless of the names in which it's held. Each spouse may also own separate property, but—especially in longer marriages—most property tends to be owned by both. In most instances, the rights of creditors to grab property after getting a judgment for nonpayment of a debt varies considerably, depending on whether it's legally classified as community or separate.

- **Community Property.** Usually, property earned or acquired by either spouse after marriage—except by gift or inheritance or covered by a premarital agreement in which the parties agree to keep property separate—is at risk for a debt incurred by either spouse. A creditor can go after the community property of you and your spouse to pay off a debt, even if you alone signed for the loan.

- **Separate Property.** This usually is property a spouse owned before getting married, acquired after marriage by gift or inheritance, or agreed in writing to be kept separate. It's also property —such as investments or even a business— acquired using separate assets. If, for example, someone gets married owning a piece of real estate, sells it and uses the proceeds to buy securities, the securities are also separate property. If your spouse has separate property and signs for a loan or other legal obligation, his or her separate property will be at risk if you default, but if your spouse declines to sign, his or her separate property (but not his or her portion of any community property) will normally be beyond the creditor's reach. Of course, as long as you sign on the bottom line, your own separate property will be at risk whether or not your spouse signs.

6. Witnesses and Notaries

Notarization means that a person authorized as a notary public certifies in writing that:

- you're the person you claim to be, and
- you've acknowledged under oath signing the document.

Very few legal documents need to be notarized or signed by witnesses. In fact, only one form in this book needs to be notarized (Form 5F: Affidavit—No Creditors, in Chapter 5), and in some states notarization isn't even required for that form. Notarization and witnessing are usually limited to documents that are going to be recorded at a public office charged with keeping such records (usually called the county recorder or register of deeds). Occasionally—but very rarely—state laws require witnesses or notaries to sign other types of documents.

⚠ **Having a document notarized doesn't guarantee that the person signing the document has the authority to do so.** When a notary public witnesses a signature and enters that information into her record book, she's only certifying that the person signing the document is who he claims he is. Whether that person has the authority to sign a document on behalf of a business is another matter entirely. Consider asking for resolutions from the business's shareholders, members or partners approving the transaction and granting the person the authority to bind the business to the contract. For more information on these kinds of resolutions, see *The Corporate Minutes Book: The Legal Guide to Taking Care of Corporate Business*, and *Your Limited Liability Company: An Operating Manual*, by Anthony Mancuso (Nolo).

C. Standard Clauses

If you were to look at a handful of various business contracts—loan agreements, sales contracts or leases—you'd find that many of them include identical clauses, often found at the end of the contracts. These clauses address issues that often come up in any contract, such as

- whether the parties intend the contract to be modified in writing only
- how each party will communicate with the other regarding the contract, and
- what will happen to the rest of the contract if a judge decides that one part of it is not legal.

Instead of writing clauses to address these issues from scratch, lawyers find it quicker to consult form books, where they find them already written and ready to drop into almost any contract. These clauses are known as "boilerplate" clauses (boilerplates are sheets of steel that can be cut to form the shell of any boiler). The essence of a boilerplate clause is that no one is likely to argue much about the precise language of the clause—but whether you and the other side want to include the clause is, of course, a matter of negotiation.

That said, the clauses that follow should elicit little, if any, resistance from the other party to your contract. That's because most of the time, the ones we've chosen will benefit both of you. For example, one boilerplate clause we recommend allows you and the other party to specify which state's law will apply in the event of a disagreement over the meaning or implementation of your contract. Without that clause, if you and the other side get into a dispute over the contract, you may spend time and money arguing over that preliminary issue—*before* you even get to the heart of your dispute!

Let's look at each clause and see why it's useful to have it in your contract. Each of these clauses is included in most contracts in the book, generally at the end.

1. Entire Agreement

Before you sign your agreement, you and the other party will negotiate certain points. Hopefully, the points you and the other party agree on will end up in your contract. But sometimes you and the other party will talk about a point or an issue, not reach a conclusion and leave it out of the final agreement. The language in this section, sometimes called an "integration clause," means that only what is written in the agreement (not what you discussed) is part of the contract between you and the other party. Although it's not foolproof, including an integration clause in your agreement can help prevent the other party from claiming that you agreed to something that's not in (or conflicts with something in) the contract, and use those prior conversations to prove that you did agree to it.

Similarly, sometimes you and the other party will have negotiated your contract by writing letters back and forth, or will have written up a temporary agreement to govern your relationship until you have time to create a more formal contract. This clause also prevents those previous writings from being considered part of your contract if, somewhere along the line, the terms of your contract conflict with what's written in those other documents.

2. Successors and Assignees

After you sign the contract, you may decide to sell or merge your company. And—heaven forbid—it's possible that the contract will outlive you. Will the new company or your heirs gain your rights under the contract? Or, suppose you'd simply to like to get someone else to take over your rights and obligations under the contract—can you do so without having to get the other party's permission? The "successors and assignees" clause attempts to address these issues. As we've drafted it, this clause allows either you or the other party to assign your rights under the contract without having to get the other party's permission, and also provides that your heirs and successors will automatically succeed to your rights and duties under the contract.

You should note, however, that some people will object to this clause because, for whatever reason, they will be uncomfortable allowing you to assign your rights and obligations under the contract to someone else without their permission. For instance, if you contract with someone to customize or manufacture goods, the buyer understandably may not want you to be able to assign your duty to manufacture or customize those goods to someone else. If that's the case, you can delete this clause, or modify the clause a bit to provide that the contract can only be assigned with the written permission of the other party.

3. Notices

Since you and the other party might not be seeing each other frequently, it makes sense to exchange mailing addresses and agree on how you'll send written communications about the contract to each other. Generally, you'll fill in your address by your signature at the end of the contract. Also, if you need to deliver an important legal notice to the other party, such as a warning that the other party is in breach of the contract, or notice to a landlord that you're terminating your tenancy, you should make sure you deliver notice in one of the ways set out in this paragraph, since this is how you and the other party have agreed to get in touch with each other.

4. Governing Law

Although you and the other party to your contract probably won't end up in court over your contract, it makes sense to designate which state's law will apply to it before you get into a dispute. Usually, you and the other party to the contract will be in the same state, so just fill in that state.

While it might take a bit more negotiation, if you and the other party *are* located in different states, designating the governing law is even more important. If you don't choose a law to govern your agreement, you could spend precious time fighting over the law that will apply to your contract, instead of the actual dispute. If you can negotiate it,

it's usually advantageous for you to have the laws of your home state govern an agreement, since every state has different laws regarding general contract interpretation, and this is the law you and any attorney you hire will probably be most familiar with.

5. Counterparts

Sometimes, parties to a contract will need to be in different places when they sign an agreement and won't be able to sign it on the same page. In this case, parties usually sign separate signature pages and put them together to create one agreement. To prevent the parties from getting into a dispute over whether an agreement signed this way is valid (believe it or not, people have tried to argue that an agreement wasn't properly signed because they didn't sign on the same page), the counterparts clause allows each party to sign the contract on a separate signature page, yet still have it considered one agreement.

6. Modification

After you've signed your agreement, from time to time you and the other party to the contract may discuss various aspects of your agreement and even talk about changing some of its provisions. However, to prevent a casual conversation with the other party from turning into a full-scale amendment of the agreement, the modification clause requires any amendment to the contract to be in writing and signed by both of you. That way, you and the other party can make sure you've thought about the changes and agreed to them.

7. Waiver

Occasionally, the other party to your contract may slip a little on one of their obligations to you, such as by paying you a few days late or failing to complete a project on time. Even if you only let it happen once, the other party might try to argue that by not enforcing the right, you've forfeited the ability to enforce that right forever. (Lawyers call this "waiver.") The waiver clause attempts to prevent the other party from doing this, and should allow you to be flexible and let a few things slide without giving up important rights under the contract.

> ⚠ **Clauses like this don't always work.**
> Although this paragraph can help prevent the other party from claiming that you've permanently waived a right, it's not foolproof. To ensure that no one could infer from your behavior that you've permanently waived a right, make sure you at least send a letter to the other party if they haven't fulfilled one of their obligations. The letter should state clearly that while you're willing to overlook the missed obligation once, you're definitely going to enforce the right in the future (make sure you keep a copy of this correspondence). This way, the other party will have a more difficult time arguing that you've permanently waived the right.

8. Severability

There's always a possibility, however remote, that you'll get into a dispute with the other party and a judge will need to interpret your agreement. And, although it's very unlikely, there's also a possibility that one or more of the provisions of your agreement could be unenforceable or invalid. Some courts, upon discovering an unenforceable or invalid clause in a contract, will void the entire contract—which is probably not what either of you intended.

This clause says that if a court is called upon to interpret your agreement and finds that any part of it is void or unenforceable, the court may "sever" the unenforceable clause from the rest of the contract, while the enforceable provisions will remain intact.

D. Resolving Disputes

Sooner or later, even the most conscientious business is likely to run into a legal dispute involving a contract. One way to resolve it is through a court fight. This approach is usually a poor one, since trials are typically expensive, prolonged, emotionally draining and, in some instances, even threatening to the survival of the business. It usually makes far more sense to attempt to resolve disputes through other means, such as:

- **Negotiation.** The parties to the dispute try to voluntarily work out their differences through open discussions which often result in each compromising a little to put the matter to rest.
- **Mediation.** The parties try to achieve a voluntary settlement with the help of a neutral third party (the mediator) who helps disputants craft their own solution. Mediation is inexpensive, quick, confidential, and effective about 80% of the time.
- **Arbitration.** The parties allow a neutral third party (the arbitrator) to arrive at a binding decision in order to resolve the dispute. Normally, the decision is solely up to the arbitrator. In some situations, however, the parties establish certain limits in advance of the arbitration—for example, X employee can

be awarded anywhere between $25,000 and $100,000 if the supervising personnel of Y employer have sexually harassed her. Where limits are set by the parties, the arbitrator is bound by them. Arbitration is almost always speedier and usually much less expensive than litigation.

Ideally, you'd like to be able to settle disputes through negotiations conducted by you and the other parties involved. This is usually a speedy, inexpensive way to put disagreements behind you and move on with your business. Unfortunately, however, even when everyone tries in good faith to negotiate a settlement, they don't always succeed. Recognizing this, the dispute resolution paragraph set out below, and used in contracts throughout this book, lets the parties agree in advance on a framework mandating noncourt alternatives such as mediation and arbitration for resolving disputes.

 This clause is in the file DISPUTE.

Disputes

(Choose One)

☐ **Litigation.** If a dispute arises, any party may take the matter to court.

☐ **Mediation and Possible Litigation.** If a dispute arises, the parties will try in good faith to settle it through mediation conducted by

    ☐ _____ .

    ☐ a mediator to be mutually selected.

The parties will share the costs of the mediator equally. Each party will cooperate fully and fairly with the mediator and will attempt to reach a mutually satisfactory compromise to the dispute. If the dispute is not resolved within 30 days after it is referred to the mediator, any party may take the matter to court.

☐ **Mediation and Possible Arbitration.** If a dispute arises, the parties will try in good faith to settle it through mediation conducted by

    ☐ _____ .

    ☐ a mediator to be mutually selected.

The parties will share the costs of the mediator equally. Each party will cooperate fully and fairly with the mediator and will attempt to reach a mutually satisfactory compromise to the dispute. If the dispute is not resolved within 30 days after it is referred to the mediator, it will be arbitrated by

    ☐ _____ .

    ☐ an arbitrator to be mutually selected.

Judgment on the arbitration award may be entered in any court that has jurisdiction over the matter. Costs of arbitration, including lawyers' fees, will be allocated by the arbitrator.

As you see, this dispute resolution system allows the parties to make one of three choices:

- **Litigation.** You go to court and let a judge or jury resolve the dispute. Although this is the traditional method, as mentioned, it's also usually the most expensive, time-consuming and emotionally draining.

- **Mediation and possible litigation.** The parties agree to let a mediator help them reach a voluntary settlement of the dispute. If mediation doesn't accomplish this goal, any party can take the dispute to court. You can name the mediator when you prepare the form or agree on one when the need arises.

- **Mediation and possible arbitration.** This is similar to the previous choice: the parties start by submitting the dispute to mediation. Here, however, if mediation doesn't lead to a settlement, the dispute is submitted to arbitration. The arbitrator makes a final decision which will be enforced by a court, if necessary. You can name the arbitrator when you prepare the form or agree on one when the need arises.

For a comprehensive and practical discussion of mediation and other methods of resolving disputes, see *How to Mediate Your Dispute*, by Peter Lovenheim (Nolo).

E. Modifying a Contract: Attachments and Amendments

No legal form is likely to be a perfect fit for every transaction it's used for. You'll sometimes need to tinker with one of our forms to make it work for you. Fortunately, there are several easy ways to modify and customize the forms in this book.

Large chunks of material can best be added to a contract *before it's signed* by using an attachment to the form. To add material by mutual agreement *after the original document has been signed,* use an amendment.

How to Make Your Modifications

There are a couple of ways you can modify a contract:

With your word processor. If you're creating a form on your computer using the CD-ROM supplied with this book, you can of course use your word processing program to change or add to it to suit your needs.

Make small changes by hand. After a form is typed (or even handwritten), it's often necessary to make changes. It's both practical and perfectly legal to make small changes by crossing out language that doesn't apply and using a pen to add new material. After you do this, have all parties initial and date the changes to show that they agree. This can be done next to the changed wording, if there's room, or in the margin.

---

1. Attachments

An attachment is the routine place to put lengthy material that doesn't easily fit in the form we provide. As long as the attachment clearly refers to the contract to which it is being attached, this approach is as legal as it is sensible. For example, a lengthy legal description of real estate you're buying, the specifications for the remodeling of your business space or a list of parts for a machine you are ordering would all appropriately go in an attachment.

To effectively attach material to a contract, simply identify the original document (state the type of document and the names of the parties and its date). When preparing two or more attachments, number them consecutively—that is, Attachment Number 1, Attachment Number 2, etc.

We've provided specific forms for an attachment to a lease (Form 6J) and an attachment to a real estate purchase contract (Form 7F). For attachments to other types of contracts, you can use the general form shown below.

Attachment to Contract

Attachment Number _____

1. Names

This attachment is made by _____

and _____ .

2. Terms of Attachment

We agree to the following Attachment to the ____ *[insert title of document]* _____

_____ dated _____ concerning

[state in general terms the subject of the contract]: _____

_____

_____

[insert the specific terms of the attachment] _____

_____

_____

_____

Dated: _____

Name of Business: _____

a _____

By: _____

Printed Name and Title: _____

Address: _____

_____

Dated: _____

Name of Business: _____

a _____

By: _____

Printed Name and Title: _____

Address: _____

_____

All the forms in this book are provided as tear-outs in Appendix B and on the accompanying forms CD-ROM. As you read the instructions for Attachments, you may want to either tear out the form or open the form's file on the CD-ROM so you can follow along. This general attachment is in the file ATTACH on the CD-ROM. (For more information on using the forms CD-ROM, see Appendix A, "How to Use the CD-ROM.") If you don't use the forms CD-ROM, be sure to photocopy the agreement so you'll have a clean copy to use later.

All parties to the main document should also sign each attachment.

2. Amendments

Once a contract has been signed, it can be changed only if all the parties agree and sign an amendment. Amendments should be numbered consecutively and should refer not only to the contract being amended but also to the specific paragraph being amended.

Don't use amendments for major changes. Amendments to existing contracts work fine when a couple of items are being changed (for example, a completion date is being extended or a dollar amount raised or lowered), but can cause confusion when lots of items in the original contract will be changed. Where changes will be extensive, it often makes sense to redo the entire document to avoid the possibility of confusion.

We've provided specific forms for an amendment of a lease (Form 6I) and an amendment of a real estate purchase contract (Form 7G). For amendments to other types of contracts, you can use the general form shown below. This form is in the file AMEND on the CD-ROM and a tear-out copy is provided in Appendix B. (For more information on using the forms CD-ROM, see Appendix A, "How to Use the CD-ROM.") If you don't use the forms CD-ROM, be sure to photocopy the agreement so you'll have a clean copy to use later.

A sample filled-in amendment is also shown below.

Amendment of Contract

Amendment Number _____

_____ and

_____

agree to the following amendment of the _____ *[insert title of document]* _____

dated _____ concerning:

___ *[state in general terms the subject of the contract]* _____

_____

_____

___ *[insert the specific terms of the amendment]* _____

_____

_____

   In all other respects, the terms of the original contract and any earlier amendments will remain in effect. If there is a conflict between this amendment and the original contract or any earlier amendment, the terms of this amendment will prevail.

Dated: _____

Name of Business: _____

a _____

By: _____

Printed Name and Title: _____

Address: _____

_____

Dated: _____

Name of Business: _____

a _____

By: _____

Printed Name and Title: _____

Address: _____

_____

Amendment of Contract

Amendment Number ___1___

Village Rentals, LLC, a Limited Liability Company, Owner and Claudia Redgrave, doing _____ and business as Sunnyside Café.

agree to the following amendment of the _____ Equipment Rental Contract _____

dated _____ October 17, 2000 _____ concerning:

the rental of two Sun Ray Model space heaters.

Paragraph 4 is amended to reduce the rent from $120 per week to $100 per week beginning December 1, 2000.

In all other respects, the terms of the original contract and any earlier amendments will remain in effect. If there is a conflict between this amendment and the original contract or any earlier amendment, the terms of this amendment will prevail.

Dated: _____ November 25, 2000 _____

Name of Business: _____ Village Rentals LLC _____

a _____ New York Limited Liability Company _____

By: _____ Louis Dickens _____

Printed Name and Title: _____ Louis Dickens, President _____

Address: _____ 125 State Street, Ithaca, New York _____

Dated: _____ November 25, 2000 _____

Name of Business: _____ Sunnyside Café _____

a _____ Sole Proprietorship _____

By: _____ Claudia Redgrave _____

Printed Name and Title: _____ Claudia Redgrave, Owner _____

Address: _____ 1020 University Avenue, Ithaca, New York _____

Forming Your Business

When you start a new business, you must choose a legal format. For most small businesses, the choices come down to these:

- sole proprietorship
- general partnership
- regular corporation (sometimes called a C corporation)
- S corporation, or
- limited liability company (LLC).

Other legal formats—limited partnership, professional corporation and nonprofit corporation—are unlikely to meet the needs of the typical small business.

If you start a one-person business, your business will automatically be treated as a sole proprietorship unless you establish a corporation or LLC. Similarly, if you start a business with two or more people, your business will automatically be treated as a general partnership unless you form a corporation, LLC or limited partnership.

The most important factors in deciding which way to go are:

- **Personal liability.** Will you be personally liable for business debts? (Personal liability means that a business creditor can get a judgment against you for a business debt—then, collect the judgment out of your personal assets such as a personal bank account or your home.) The fast answer is that as a sole proprietor or a partner, you'll face personal liability for business debts. But as the owner of shares in a corporation or as a member of an LLC, you'll generally face no personal liability—unless, of course, you voluntarily agree to assume it by signing a personal guarantee (such as for a business loan).

Limited liability isn't a big deal for many micro businesses. A great many small service and retail businesses simply don't subject their owners to significant debt or lawsuit risk. And often even in the few cases where they do, a good insurance policy will provide needed protection.

This means that there's often really no compelling need to form a corporation or LLC.

- **Taxes.** Will you and the other business owners simply report your portion of profits and losses on your own income tax returns, or will the business itself be taxed on its profits? Sole proprietors, partners, owners of S corporation stock and members of LLCs need only contend with one level of taxation: the tax paid by the owners on their individual returns. By contrast, a regular or "C" corporation pays taxes on its corporate earnings in addition to the taxes paid by the shareholders who receive dividends.

Sometimes being taxed twice is cheaper. Although you'd think that being subject to the income tax at both the corporate and personal levels would be more expensive than being taxed once on all business income on your personal return, you'd sometimes be wrong. Because the initial federal income tax rates are lower for incorporated businesses than for individuals, and because businesses often prefer not to pay out all earnings to owners, but instead want to keep money in the business from one year to the next (for example, to pay for future expansion), operating as a regular corporation—or as an LLC that has elected to be taxed as a corporation—can result in tax savings. For more detailed information, see the eGuide *Save Taxes With Corporate Income Splitting*, by Anthony Mancuso, available for purchase at http://www.nolo.com.

- **Time and expense.** Will it be time-consuming and costly to form and maintain the business? Sole proprietorships and partnership are relatively easy and inexpensive to start and keep up. Corporations and LLCs typically require more time and effort and cost a bit more—but the cost needn't be a tremendous burden. You can handle all or most of the paperwork yourself by using one of the Nolo books listed below.

- **Fringe benefits.** Will the business be able to provide fringe benefits (health insurance, retirement plans and the like) to the owners and deduct the cost of those benefits as a business expense? Of course, this question is only relevant to businesses with enough income to pay fairly generous fringe benefits in the first place. But if your business is lucky enough to be in this category, the regular C corporation offers the best tax-saving opportunities.

 For in-depth information on choosing a legal format for your business, see Chapter 1 of the *Legal Guide for Starting & Running a Small Business*, by Fred S. Steingold (Nolo). For specifics and useful forms to create various types of business entities, see the following publications from Nolo:

- *Form Your Own Limited Liability Company,* by Anthony Mancuso, shows you how to establish an LLC in all 50 states.
- *How to Form Your Own Corporation,* by Anthony Mancuso, available for California, New York and Texas.
- *The Partnership Book: How to Write a Partnership Agreement,* by Denis Clifford and Ralph Warner
- Nolo's *LLC Maker*, Windows software, by Anthony Mancuso.

It's often smart to start with the simplest legal format and convert later if necessary. It can be eminently sensible to start out as a simple, inexpensive sole proprietorship or partnership. Later you can convert to a corporation or LLC if your risk of personal liability increases or there are compelling tax reasons to do so. Fortunately, changing a partnership or sole proprietorship to a corporation or LLC is usually quick and easy.

Because more than 90% of businesses are organized as sole proprietorships or partnerships, the first two forms (2A and 2B) presented here should meet most start-up needs.

Because only you are involved, no formal document is required to create a sole proprietorship.

However, there are several practical and legal steps you must take to put your business on the right track.

Use Form 2A: Checklist for Starting a Sole Proprietorship, to guide you through the start-up phase.

You can start a partnership by simply doing business with other people. In other words, you don't need a written partnership agreement. But as you might guess, following this seat-of-the-pants approach is a poor idea. Preparing a written partnership agreement allows you to provide a sound footing for your legal relationship with your partners and helps prevent or resolve disputes that may later arise. Use Form 2B: Partnership Agreement, for this purpose.

The paperwork for starting a corporation or LLC is somewhat more extensive, involving articles of incorporation and bylaws (for a corporation) or articles of organization and an operating agreement (for an LLC) and often other forms that must be customized to meet each state's requirements. Although these state-specific forms are beyond the scope of this book, we do offer three useful forms for those starting a corporation, and one form for those starting an LLC.

When you create a small corporation, it's sensible to have all the shareholders agree in advance on the basic elements of the business, including the name and purpose of the corporation, how many shares of stock will be issued and authorized, how many shares each owner will acquire and who will serve on the board of directors. Use Form 2C: Pre-Incorporation Agreement, to do this.

Every incorporated business needs bylaws to lay out the legal rules for running the corporate legal entity. The bylaws cover such matters as how many people will serve on the board of directors, when and where regular meetings will be held, who may schedule a special meeting and what officers the corporation will have. Form 2D: Corporate Bylaws, is a good starting point.

By law, a shareholder can freely transfer shares of stock, unless all shareholders agree to restrict the sale or transfer of shares. Free transfer is okay for General Motors or any other publicly traded stock, but can create havoc in a small corporation where the shareholders usually run the business. If you're in business with two other shareholders, for example, you probably wouldn't want owner #3 to sell his or her stock to a complete stranger, since the new person may have a completely different vision than you do about how the company should be run. Accordingly, Form 2E: Stock Agreement, allows you to provide in advance what will happen if a shareholder (or the shareholder's estate) wants to sell his or her shares.

If you want to limit your personal liability as the owner of a small business, you have two good choices: the tried-and-true corporation or the new-and-streamlined limited liability company (LLC). These days, many business owners prefer the simplicity and flexibility of the LLC. While, strictly speaking, a single-member LLC usually doesn't require an operating agreement, it can be a useful legal tool when dealing with banks, title insurance companies and other businesses. Form 2F, LLC Operating Agreement for Single-Member LLC, shows you how to create one.

A. Form 2A: Checklist for Starting a Sole Proprietorship

When you start a sole proprietorship, you and the business are the same. Unlike a new partnership, corporation or limited liability company (LLC), you don't have to agree with business associates (partners, shareholders or LLC members) on the structure of your legal entity. It follows that there's no form for you to complete analogous to a partnership agreement, pre-incorporation agreement or LLC operating agreement. But because you still need to keep track of a number of legal and practical requirements for putting your business on a sound footing, we recommend you use Form 2A: Checklist for Starting a Sole Proprietorship.

A full explanation of all checklist items is beyond the scope of this form-driven book. However, the following instructions tell you which Nolo products will provide any additional information you might need.

Instructions for Form 2A: Checklist for Starting a Sole Proprietorship

All the forms in this book are provided as tear-outs in Appendix B and on the accompanying forms CD-ROM. As you read the instructions for Form 2A, you may want to either tear out the form or open the form's file on the CD-ROM so you can follow along. Form 2A is in the file FORM2A.RTF on the CD-ROM. (For more information on using the forms CD-ROM, see Appendix A, "How to Use the CD-ROM.") If you don't use the forms CD-ROM, be sure to photocopy the agreement so you'll have a clean copy to use later.

Business Name

Before using a business name, it's wise to conduct a name search to avoid a possible conflict with a business already using the same name or a similar one. Typically, if your sole proprietorship is a small local business, you can feel reasonably secure if you've searched for conflicts at the state and local level. Check the records of the state office where corporations and LLCs are registered and those of the state, county or local offices where assumed or fictitious business names are filed. Also check the phone books and city directories covering your area.

In most states, you'll need to register your business name as a fictitious or assumed name—generally by filling out and filing a printed form at a designated county office. You may also need to publish your business name in a local newspaper. A sample Certificate of Assumed Name (sometimes also called a Fictitious Business Name Statement) is included below. Many counties and municipalities provide forms on the Web. See http://www.piperinfo.com for a comprehensive list of state and local government on the Internet.

If you plan to do business regionally or nationally and will use your business name to identify a product or service, look into registering your trademark or service mark at the state or federal level.

BN-15-0198   ♻ printed on recycled paper

PEGGY M. HAINES
WASHTENAW COUNTY CLERK/REGISTER

THIS IS A LEGAL DOCUMENT
TYPE OR PRINT CLEARLY
USE BLACK OR BLUE INK

M.C.L.A. 445.1 et seq.
M.C.L.A. 445.2B
FILING FEE $10.00

REMIT PAYMENT / MAIL TO:
WASHTENAW COUNTY CLERK
P.O. BOX 8645
ANN ARBOR, MI 48107-8645

TELEPHONE (734) 994-2501

WASHTENAW COUNTY — CERTIFICATE OF ASSUMED NAME
THIS CERTIFICATE EXPIRES FIVE (5) YEARS FROM THE DATE OF FILING
THE UNDERSIGNED, hereby certifies that the following persons now owns (or) intends to own, conduct or transact business in the County of Washtenaw, State of Michigan, under the designation, name or style stated below:

1. AN ORIGINAL___X___ RENEWAL_____ CHANGE OF LOCATION_____ DISSOLUTION_____

2. NAME OF BUSINESS___Aardvark   Café_____

3. PRINCIPAL ADDRESS OF BUSINESS____555   State   St.,   Dexter,   MI   44444___
                                            street   city   state   zip code

4. (PRINT) FULL LEGAL NAME(S) OF PERSON(S)   RESIDENCE ADDRESS(ES)

Edward ____ F. ____ Jones ____   111 Adam St. _____
first   middle   last   number and street

                                             city   state   zip code
_____   Dexter,   MI   44444

5. IF ANYONE LISTED IN #4 **IS NOT** AN INDIVIDUAL PERSON, PLEASE EXAMINE REVERSE SIDE BEFORE SIGNING.

6. NON-RESIDENTS OF MICHIGAN, MUST FILE A "CONSENT TO SERVICE" (BN-05). FILING FEE $2.00.

7. SIGNATURE(S) OF ALL PERSON(S) LISTED ABOVE — ACKNOWLEDGED BEFORE A NOTARY PUBLIC.

(Signature) *Edward F. Jones* _____

STATE OF MICHIGAN   )ss.
COUNTY OF WASHTENAW)

(Signature)_____

Subscribed and sworn to before me this

(Notary Signature) *Sidney Smith* _____

day, __May____ __15,___ __20XX___
      month   day   year

Notary Public, ___Washtenaw_____ County, MI

Commission expires___June 1, 20XX_____

FOR OFFICE USE ONLY — DO NOT WRITE BELOW THIS LINE

Counter ☐   Mail ☐   Franchise   Yes ☐   No ☐   Approved _____ / _____

CERTIFICATION OF RECORD
STATE OF MICHIGAN   )
                          SS
COUNTY OF WASHTENAW)
I, PEGGY M. HAINES, CLERK/REGISTER OF SAID COUNTY OF WASHTENAW DO HEREBY CERTIFY that the foregoing is a true and exact copy of the original document on file in my office.

Dated: _____

Peggy M. Haines

PEGGY M. HAINES,
WASHTENAW COUNTY CLERK/REGISTER

FILE #

PREVIOUS FILE #

For more information on naming your business and products, see *Trademark: Legal Care for Your Business & Product Name*, by Stephen Elias and Kate McGrath (Nolo).

Licenses and Permits

You may need one or more licenses or permits for your business. In some locations, every business needs a basic business license. Beyond that, you may need a specialized business license (or several of them)—especially if you sell food, liquor or firearms or work with hazardous materials.

As a sole proprietor, you normally needn't worry about getting a federal license or permit unless you're an investment advisor or starting a trucking company or meat product business.

States require licensing of people practicing the traditional professions such as lawyers, physicians, pharmacists and architects, and may require licenses for other occupations such as barbers, auto mechanics, pest control specialists and insurance agents—the list varies from state to state.

You'll probably need a special license or permit from state or local authorities to run a business such as a restaurant, bar, taxi service or waste removal company. Again, the list varies so you'll need to inquire further.

 To learn more about licenses and permits, see *The Small Business Start-Up Kit*, by Peri Pakroo (Nolo).

Insurance

There's no substitute for establishing a good working relationship with a knowledgeable insurance agent or broker. Basically, you want the peace of mind of knowing that you have liability coverage in case someone is physically injured on your premises or because of your business operations (car accidents, for example) or their property is damaged, destroyed or lost.

You also want to be sure there's adequate liability coverage for your business if an employee—driving his or her own car—injures someone in an accident while on the job.

It's almost always sensible to carry insurance to replace or repair your own property if it's stolen or damaged by fire, flood, windstorm, earthquake, vandalism—or any of dozens of other hazards.

If you'll be manufacturing a product—or selling dangerous items—look into product liability insurance so you're covered if a product you've made or sold injures someone.

Finally, review your business operations with an experienced insurance agent or broker to learn what other coverage may be appropriate.

 Chapter 12 of the *Legal Guide for Starting & Running a Small Business* covers insuring your business.

Taxes

This checklist alerts you to two IRS publications (both free) that tell you what you need to know about federal taxes. Basically, you'll report your business income (or loss) on Schedule C each year, which becomes part of your individual Form 1040. Your income is added to (or subtracted from) your income from other sources—a salaried job, investment income or your spouse's earnings, for example.

Pay estimated taxes, if necessary. When your sole proprietorship starts to generate income, the taxes withheld from any salaried job and from your spouse's earning may be insufficient to cover your tax obligation to the IRS—which includes not only a tax on your income but also the Social Security and Medicare tax. You need to estimate your business income and your likely tax bill so you can pay the extra taxes in quarterly installments. If you underpay, you face interest and penalties. (See IRS Publication 505, *Tax Withholding and Estimated Tax.*)

Because tax practices vary widely around the country, you'll need to inquire with your state, county and local governments to learn if your business is subject to nonfederal income tax, property tax or other business tax.

You'll spare yourself a load of grief if your keep your sole proprietorship's financial affairs separate from your personal financial affairs—and it's best to do this right from the start. The task is simple if you use Intuit's *QuickBooks* or other accounting software geared toward small business.

Depending on the volume and complexity of your business finances, you may benefit from hiring a part-time bookkeeper or consulting an accountant who can show you how to set up a simple bookkeeping system.

To find out more about tax basics for small business, see *Tax Savvy for Small Business*, by Frederick W. Daily (Nolo).

Home-Based Business

Many a sole proprietor starts by working at home—and may continue using his or her home as the base of operations indefinitely. If you'll be working out of your home, a few precautions will help you avoid unexpected legal difficulties.

First, make sure you have adequate liability and property damage insurance. Your homeowner's policy may not cover you if a UPS delivery person trips on your porch step while delivering a business package to you or your dog bites a visiting client. Similarly, you may find that homeowner's coverage won't pay for a business computer that gets stolen.

An insurance agent or broker can probably extend your coverage for a modest additional premium.

Be aware that even though your home may be your castle, you may not have an unlimited right to do business there. If you're in a rented unit, your lease may prohibit business operations. In a private home, you may be bound by covenants, conditions and restrictions—rules that apply to all owners in your subdivision, condo or planned unit development. And then there are local zoning ordinances that may not allow businesses in the district where you live.

First, learn what the restrictions are. You may be able to abide by the strict letter of them. If, however, your business will technically violate the restrictions, see if you can meet their spirit. It's highly unlikely that a neighbor or municipal zoning ordinance will try to stop your business use if you keep a low profile. Limit your signage, keep deliveries to a minimum and don't see too many customers or clients at your home. Neighbors are unlikely to complain if you run a quiet, low-traffic business that doesn't affect them.

Taxes—especially the rules on deductions and depreciation—are another concern for a home-based business. Form 2A: Checklist for Starting a Sole Proprietorship, lists a helpful, free IRS publication.

 More and more government forms and publications are available on the Internet. Although we've provided some of them for you, most of the IRS publications and forms referenced in this book are also available for free on the IRS website at http://www.irs.gov. Most of the forms are in PDF format, which means you'll have to download Adobe Acrobat software in order to read and print them. Adobe Acrobat is available free at http://www.adobe.com. Always check an agency's website to make sure you have the most current version of any government form—most agencies will print the date the form was last revised in the lower right-hand corner of the document.

Hiring People

Being a sole proprietor doesn't mean you have to do all the work yourself. Chances are you'll be hiring employees or independent contractors early in the game.

Start by completing IRS Form SS-4, *Application for Employer Identification Number,* which you then mail or fax to the IRS to get a tax number for your business. (If you're in a hurry, you can obtain an EIN over the phone—see the instructions for Form SS-4 on the forms CD-ROM for more information.) We've included a sample completed SS-4 for you to refer to, and a blank Form SS-4 is included on the forms CD-ROM, along with instructions. This form is also available at http://www.irs.gov. You'll need the number when you pay the employer's and employees' share of income taxes, and Social Security and Medicare levies. (You may want to apply for a tax number even if you don't plan to hire employees immediately. Using a federal tax number instead of your Social Security number for business tax reporting can help you separate your business and personal financial affairs—a good habit to get into.)

Look into the workers' compensation insurance requirements in your state. You'll need this coverage in case a worker suffers an on-the-job injury. Such injuries aren't covered by normal liability insurance.

If you hire employees, you'll have to make payments to your state's unemployment compensation fund, which provides short-term relief to workers who are laid off.

We've also included employee tax withholding forms (Form W-4) from the IRS and employment eligibility verification forms (Form I-9) from the Immigration and Naturalization Service (INS) on the forms CD-ROM, along with the instructions. You'll need the first one for keeping track of how many dependents each employee is claiming for tax purposes, and the second one to establish that you've properly checked to see that each employee is legally eligible to work in this country.

If you hire independent contractors, you want to make sure the IRS won't reclassify them as employees —which could result in penalties being assessed against you. In close cases, the IRS prefers to see workers treated as employees (you withhold and pay their income taxes) rather than as independent contractors (they take care of their own taxes). To qualify as an independent contractor under IRS rules, a worker must control both the outcome of a project and the means of accomplishing it. (See Form 9G: Contract with Independent Contractor, and the accompanying instructions in Chapter 9.)

 For more information on employees and independent contractors, see *The Employer's Legal Handbook,* by Fred S. Steingold (Nolo).

 Form W-4 is in the file FW4.PDF. Form SS-4 is in the file FSS4.PDF. And Form I-9 is in the file I-9.PDF. These forms are also provided as tear-outs in Appendix B.

B. Form 2B: Partnership Agreement

Use this form to establish a general partnership—a business with two or more owners, each of whom is personally liable for business debts. Although the law recognizes oral partnerships, there are huge benefits to putting yours in writing. For one, the process of creating a written agreement forces you and your partners to confront and talk through many important decisions, such as how much money each partner will invest in the business, how profits and losses will be allocated, how the partnership will be managed and what happens if a partner withdraws from the business. What's more, a written partnership agreement can provide an invaluable framework to handle later misunderstandings and disagreements, which of course are likely to be part—hopefully a small part—of any business.

Another benefit of creating a formal agreement is that it allows the partners to adjust the operating rules of the partnership to suit their needs instead of simply being bound by the "default" rules that state law imposes in the absence of an agreement. For example, suppose you and another partner get

Form **SS-4**	**Application for Employer Identification Number**	EIN	
(Rev. April 2000)	(For use by employers, corporations, partnerships, trusts, estates, churches, government agencies, certain individuals, and others. See instructions.)		
Department of the Treasury Internal Revenue Service	▶ Keep a copy for your records.	OMB No. 1545-0003	

Please type or print clearly.

1 Name of applicant (legal name) (see instructions)
Photobiz, LLC

2 Trade name of business (if different from name on line 1) **3** Executor, trustee, "care of" name

4a Mailing address (street address) (room, apt., or suite no.)
555 Jackson Ave.

5a Business address (if different from address on lines 4a and 4b)

4b City, state, and ZIP code
Anytown, CA 99999

5b City, state, and ZIP code

6 County and state where principal business is located
Jefferson County, California

7 Name of principal officer, general partner, grantor, owner, or trustor—SSN or ITIN may be required (see instructions) ▶ 123-12-1234
Liz Barton (Member)

8a Type of entity (Check only one box.) (see instructions)

Caution: If applicant is a limited liability company, see the instructions for line 8a.

☐ Sole proprietor (SSN) _____
☐ Partnership   ☐ Personal service corp.
☐ REMIC   ☐ National Guard
☐ State/local government   ☐ Farmers' cooperative
☐ Church or church-controlled organization
☐ Other nonprofit organization (specify) ▶ _____
☒ Other (specify) ▶ sole proprietor and disregarded

☐ Estate (SSN of decedent) _____
☐ Plan administrator (SSN) _____
☐ Other corporation (specify) ▶ _____
☐ Trust
☐ Federal government/military
_____ (enter GEN if applicable) _____

8b If a corporation, name the state or foreign country (if applicable) where incorporated | State | Foreign country

9 Reason for applying (Check only one box.) (see instructions)
☒ Started new business (specify type) ▶
Limited Liability company
☐ Hired employees (Check the box and see line 12.)
☐ Created a pension plan (specify type) ▶
☐ Banking purpose (specify purpose) ▶ _____
☐ Changed type of organization (specify new type) ▶ _____
☐ Purchased going business
☐ Created a trust (specify type) ▶ _____
☐ Other (specify) ▶ _____

10 Date business started or acquired (month, day, year) (see instructions)
February 1, 20XX

11 Closing month of accounting year (see instructions)
December

12 First date wages or annuities were paid or will be paid (month, day, year). **Note:** If applicant is a withholding agent, enter date income will first be paid to nonresident alien. (month, day, year) . . . . ▶ March 1, 20XX

13 Highest number of employees expected in the next 12 months. **Note:** If the applicant does not expect to have any employees during the period, enter -0-. (see instructions) . . . . ▶

Nonagricultural	Agricultural	Household
1	0	0

14 Principal activity (see instructions) ▶ Advertising Agency

15 Is the principal business activity manufacturing? . . . . ☐ Yes ☒ No
If "Yes," principal product and raw material used ▶

16 To whom are most of the products or services sold? Please check one box. ☐ Business (wholesale)
☐ Public (retail)   ☒ Other (specify) ▶ Businesses   ☐ N/A

17a Has the applicant ever applied for an employer identification number for this or any other business? . . . . ☐ Yes ☒ No
Note: If "Yes," please complete lines 17b and 17c.

17b If you checked "Yes" on line 17a, give applicant's legal name and trade name shown on prior application, if different from line 1 or 2 above.
Legal name ▶   Trade name ▶

17c Approximate date when and city and state where the application was filed. Enter previous employer identification number if known.
Approximate date when filed (mo., day, year) | City and state where filed | Previous EIN

Under penalties of perjury, I declare that I have examined this application, and to the best of my knowledge and belief, it is true, correct, and complete.

Business telephone number (include area code)
(555) 123-4567
Fax telephone number (include area code)
(555) 123-4568

Name and title (Please type or print clearly.) ▶ Liz Barton, Member

Signature ▶ *Liz Barton*   Date ▶ 2-1-XX

Note: Do not write below this line. For official use only.

Please leave blank ▶	Geo.	Ind.	Class	Size	Reason for applying

For Privacy Act and Paperwork Reduction Act Notice, see page 4.   Cat. No. 16055N   Form **SS-4** (Rev. 4-2000)

into a dispute about the business and one of you sues the other. If you don't have a written partnership agreement, the judge will decide the case based on your state's partnership statute—which may be different from what you and the other partner would like to happen. By contrast, if you have provided your own way of handling things in a written agreement, it will normally control and determine the judge's decision.

EXAMPLE: Al, Barbara and Carl start a partnership business. Since they're old friends and don't like paperwork, they never actually agree on the formula for allocating profits, let alone put it in writing. Because Al will be working full-time in the business and Barbara and Carl will be working only part-time, their joint assumption seems to be that Al will get 50% of the profits and Barbara and Carl will each get 25%. However, a year later, after a bitter falling out among the partners followed by a lawsuit, a judge is forced to consider this issue. Because there's no written agreement and the oral evidence is inconclusive, the judge must follow state law and rule that each partner is entitled to one-third of the profits. As part of her written order, the judge points out that had the partners agreed in writing to a 50%-25%-25% split, she would have enforced it.

What Is a Limited Partnership?

The fill-in-the-blanks form in this book is for a general partnership and not a limited partnership—a very different legal animal that combines some attributes of a partnership with some attributes of a corporation.

Most limited partnerships are formed for real estate or other investment ventures where one or more active partners will run a business financed by the investments of a number of silent partners. A limited partnership must have at least one general partner who has the same rights and responsibilities (including unlimited liability) as does a partner in a general partnership. It also must have at least one limited partner (and usually has more) who is typically a passive investor. A limited partner isn't personally liable for the debts of the partnership—as long as he or she doesn't participate in managing the business.

Because setting up a limited partnership is complicated, you should see a lawyer if you're going to start one.

For more on partnerships, see Chapter 2 of the *Legal Guide for Starting & Running a Small Business*, by Fred S. Steingold (Nolo), and *The Partnership Book*, by Denis Clifford and Ralph Warner (Nolo).

Filing Paperwork With State or Local Government

One advantage of a partnership over a corporation or limited liability company is that your partnership agreement doesn't have to be filed with a public agency along with a hefty fee. However, in some states, you will need to file a partnership certificate giving the names of the partners. And in a few states, you may also need to publish a notice in the newspaper informing the public that you've formed the partnership. Check with the county clerk or the secretary of state's office for details on your state's requirements.

Instructions for Form 2B: Partnership Agreement

All the forms in this book are provided as tear-outs in Appendix B and on the accompanying forms CD-ROM. As you read the instructions for Form 2B, you may want to either tear out the form or open the form's file on the CD-ROM so you can follow along. Form 2B is in the file FORM2B.RTF on the CD-ROM. (For more information on using the forms CD-ROM, see Appendix A, "How to Use the CD-ROM.") If you don't use the forms CD-ROM, be sure to photocopy the agreement so you'll have a clean copy to use later.

1. Partners

Insert the names of all partners.

2. Partnership Name

Insert the name of the partnership. If you're going to use a business name for your partnership that's different from the names of the partners, it's wise to make at least a local name search to determine if some other business is already using the name. Check state and local business directories and Yellow Pages for possible conflicts. Especially if your partnership plans to do business regionally or nationally and your business name will be used to identify your products or services, you'll want to broaden your search—and consider registering your trademark (or service mark) at the state or federal level.

 For in-depth information on this subject, see *Trademark: Legal Care for Your Business & Product Name*, by Stephen Elias and Kate McGrath (Nolo).

3. Partnership Duration

Insert the date the partnership began or when it is to begin. Then check one of the boxes to indicate when the partnership will end. If you check the second box, insert a date for the end of the partnership.

4. Partnership Office

Insert the address where partnership records will be kept. Usually this will be the partnership's main business location. If the partnership's mailing address is the same as the partnership office, check the first box. If you have a separate mailing address—a post office box, for example—check the second box and fill in the mailing address.

5. Partnership Purpose

Insert the purpose of the partnership.

SAMPLES:

- to operate one or more retail stores for the sale of computer software.
- to manufacture and distribute equipment for the preparation of espresso, cappuccino and other coffee-based beverages.
- to design websites for computer users.
- to cater banquets, picnics and other social and business functions requiring food service, and to rent equipment to be used in connection with such catering services.

6. Capital Contributions

Insert the date when the partners are to contribute their start-up capital—the funds or property given to the partnership to enable it to begin operations.

    A. If partners will be contributing cash, fill in their names and the amount each will contribute.

    B. If partners will contribute property, insert the partners' names. Then describe the property and what value it will be given on the partnership's books.

7. Capital Accounts

You don't need to insert anything here. A capital account is a bookkeeping technique for keeping track of how much of the partnership assets each partner owns. Your capital account starts out with the amount you invest in the partnership. To that figure you add your share of the profits and deduct your share of the losses.

Get help setting up your books. If you're unfamiliar with business bookkeeping, see an accountant to help you get started, including an explanation of how capital accounts work. The accountant can also brief you on how to meet your federal and state business tax obligations. But first, see *The Partnership Book*, by Denis Clifford and Ralph Warner (Nolo), which explains the basics.

8. Profits and Losses

A. Check the first box if you want partners' shares of profits and losses to be proportionate to the capital they put into the partnership. Here are two examples of what occurs if you make this choice.

> **EXAMPLE 1:** Three partners put in the same amount of capital—$10,000 each. All profits will be added equally to each partner's capital account and losses will be equally subtracted.

> **EXAMPLE 2:** One partner puts in $20,000 and two partners put in $10,000 each. The profits and assets will be allocated 50%/25%/25%.

Check the second box and insert a different formula if you don't want profits to be divided according to capital contributed. For example, if you agree that one partner will be spending more time than the others working on the partnership business, you may decide to allocate more profits to that partner than would be true if you simply divvied them up in proportion to how much capital each partner contributed.

> **EXAMPLE:** Since Linda Smith will be handling bookkeeping duties for the partnership in addition to her other partnership duties, 40% of the net profits will be credited to her capital account and 30% of the net profits will be credited to the capital account of each of the other two partners. Net losses will be charged equally against the partners' capital accounts.

Of course, this isn't the only way to recognize the contribution of the partner who's doing extra work. You could, for example, agree to pay her a salary for keeping the books, making it fair to simply allocate profits in proportion to contributions.

B. You don't need to insert anything here. Partnership assets won't be distributed to partners unless all the partners agree.

9. Salaries

You don't need to insert anything here. Generally, a partner's reward for doing work for the partnership is a share of the partnership profits. But as suggested in the instructions for paragraph 8, there's no legal or tax reason why the partners can't agree to hire one or more partners as employees who will receive a salary for their services. If you decide to follow such an arrangement, spell out the details in the partnership agreement.

10. Interest

You don't need to insert anything here. Again, the benefit a partner receives from investing money in a partnership is a share of partnership profits. If you agree that a partner is to receive interest, it's better to have the partner lend money to the partnership. Document the loan with a promissory note. (See Chapter 4.)

11. Management

Approach this section with a healthy dose of skepticism. The reality is that for a small partnership to succeed, the partners need to have both shared goals and confidence in one another's judgment. If those elements don't exist, pages of rules as to how decisions should be made won't help. Or put more bluntly, if you don't trust your partners and enjoy working with them, don't bother creating a partnership in the first place.

It's difficult to define how day-to-day decisions will be made in a partnership. Certainly when it comes to important decisions, it's smart to talk over the matter with all the partners and respect each other's opinion. But unanimity on everything may be as unnecessary as it is hard to achieve—making it impractical to select the first option in this paragraph (agreement of all partners on all partnership decisions).

Checking the second box and the appropriate requirements allows you more flexibility by requiring unanimity on just the major business decisions that you specify.

12. Partnership Funds

Insert the name of the financial institution where you'll keep the partnership funds.

Then check a box to indicate who will be able to sign partnership checks. If you check the last box, insert the number of partners who must sign. In a three-person partnership, for example, you may want to require that checks be signed by two partners.

The financial institution where you have the account will have a form of its own for you to fill out.

13. Agreement to End Partnership

You don't need to insert anything here. This paragraph makes it clear that the partnership can be ended if all the partners agree.

14. Partner's Withdrawal

Here there are two major legal points to think about. First, if you don't have an agreement on the subject, the law says your partnership will end if any partner decides to leave the partnership. Second, if there's no agreement to the contrary, a partner isn't free to transfer his or her partnership interest to someone else. In short, unless you agree in writing to a different plan, if one partner leaves, the partnership assets will be liquidated, bills will be paid and the partners will be cashed out. Check the first box if this scenario is what you want.

Check the second box if you want to give the remaining partners the chance to keep the partnership alive by buying out the interest of the withdrawing partner. Technically, this means the remaining partners will create a new partnership, but the business will continue as if there was no change.

15. Partner's Death

As with a partner's withdrawal, a partner's death will end the partnership—unless you agree to another outcome. After liquidation of the partnership assets, the dead partner's share of the assets will be paid to that partner's estate. Check the first box if that's the result you want.

Check the second box if you want to give the remaining partners the chance to keep the partnership alive by buying out the interest of the deceased partner. (Technically, the remaining partners will have a new partnership.)

16. Buy-Out

Complete this optional paragraph only if you've provided for a buy-out of a withdrawing partner's interest (paragraph 14) or a deceased partner's interest (paragraph 15). Check one of the first two boxes if it contains an acceptable formula for fixing the buy-out price. If not, check the third box and fill in the method of setting the buy-out amount.

If you haven't provided for a buy-out in paragraph 14 or 15, either cross out this paragraph (in which case, all partners should initial the deletion) or insert the words, "Not Applicable." (CD-ROM users can just delete it and renumber the paragraphs that follow.)

Determining how much the remaining partners should pay for a deceased or retiring partner's share is a complicated subject. For example, you might want to treat a partner who retires because of age or illness differently than one who leaves to take up ultimate snowboarding. For a thorough discussion, see *How to Create a Buy-Sell Agreement & Control the Destiny of Your Small Business*, by Anthony Mancuso and Bethany K. Laurence (Nolo).

Standard Clauses

The remainder of the agreement contains the standard clauses we discussed in Chapter 1, Section C. The only thing you'll need to fill in here is the name of the state whose law will apply to the contract in the paragraph called "Governing Law."

Date and Signatures

Fill in the date the agreement is signed. Each of the partners must sign his or her name, and their respective names and addresses should be typed in.

C. Form 2C: Pre-Incorporation Agreement

This pre-incorporation form is designed for people who plan to incorporate a small business owned by a handful of shareholders, each of whom will actively take part in the day-to-day operations of the business. Although not legally required, a pre-incorporation agreement can be a very useful aid to starting a new corporation. The process of drawing up an agreement can be of crucial help to allow you and other owners to focus on key business issues. Sometimes doing this may even cause you to abandon the idea of starting the business. If so, this should be seen as a positive development. It's much better to confront tough management issues early rather than after everyone has invested money, time and energy in a business enterprise.

A pre-incorporation agreement is just the first step you take in starting a corporation. Among the other important things you must do are:

- prepare and file the articles of incorporation (known in some states by other names—see instruction below for paragraph 2)
- select a board of directors
- adopt bylaws
- issue stock, and
- decide whether or not you want to elect S corporation tax status.

Nolo publishes *How to Form Your Own California Corporation*, *How to Form Your Own New York Corporation* and *How to Form Your Own Texas Corporation*, all by Anthony Mancuso. If you live in one of these states, the book for your state will provide first-class guidance. In other states, look at the Secretary of State's or Corporation Commissioner's website; many of these websites have helpful incorporation information and forms.

Instructions for Form 2C: Pre-Incorporation Agreement

All the forms in this book are provided as tear-outs in Appendix B and on the accompanying forms CD-ROM. As you read the instructions for Form 2C, you may want to either tear out the form or open the form's file on the CD-ROM so you can follow along. Form 2C is in the file FORM2C.RTF on the CD-ROM. (For more information on using the forms CD-ROM, see Appendix A, "How to Use the CD-ROM.") If you don't use the forms CD-ROM, be sure to photocopy the agreement so you'll have a clean copy to use later.

1. Shareholders' Names

Insert the names of all shareholders.

2. Incorporation

Insert the state in which you plan to incorporate. Corporations are created under state law rather than federal law. Each state has its own rules for how to start a corporation. The best place to form your corporation is the state in which you and the other incorporators live and intend as your primary place to do business. Disregard suggestions that there are advantages for a small business to incorporate in Delaware or some other state. By and large, this is malarkey, since in most cases you'll also have to pay fees to the state where your business is located.

Usually, a state office—such as the Secretary of State—can provide a form for the articles of incorporation. Many Secretary of State offices provide incorporation forms and a list of filing fees on their website. Check http://www.piperinfo.com for a list of state government agencies on the Web. Plan to attach a copy of the articles of incorporation to the pre-incorporation agreement as an attachment (and label it, for example, as Attachment 1).

 Legal jargon for basic incorporation documents differs from state to state. In some states, the articles of incorporation may be called something else: certificate of incorporation, charter of incorporation or articles of association are common variants. But no matter what your state calls the forms necessary to register your incorporated business, one thing is true everywhere: you'll have to file it along with a fee at your state's incorporation office. You won't, however, need to file your pre-incorporation agreement.

In some states, the signature of just one person is required on the articles of incorporation. If that's permitted in your state and you want to have one of you sign that form, check the first box and fill in the name of the designated signer. If the law requires or if you want other shareholders to sign, check the second box.

3. Corporate Name

Fill in the name of the new corporation. Be sure the name complies with corporation laws of your state. For example, you may be required to include one of the following words or abbreviations in the name of the corporation: Corporation, Incorporated, Company, Limited, Corp., Inc., Co. or Ltd.

 Check in advance on name availability. Every state prevents two or more corporations from registering or using the same name, or even names that are very similar. Accordingly, you should check in advance to see if the name you want to use is available. Contact the state office that handles corporate filings. Usually they'll be able to tell you by phone if there's a potential conflict and, if there isn't, explain how you can reserve your proposed name for a month or two to give you a chance to file your formal incorporation papers. Unfortunately, finding that a name is available in your state doesn't guarantee that you can use it. Especially if you will use the name to identify goods and services, you also need to see if your name violates another business's trademark. (*Trademark: Legal Care for Your Business & Product Name*, by Stephen Elias and Kate McGrath (Nolo), explains how to do this.)

Check the second box if you're planning to use a secondary business name that's different from the official corporate name. Then fill in the name.

EXAMPLES:
- Apollo Furniture Inc. wants to do business as Apollo—a shortened form of its official name. It inserts the name Apollo in the space.
- Apollo Furniture wants to do business as Contemporary Studio—a name completely different from its official name. It inserts the name Contemporary Studio in the space.

You'll need to make your secondary name a matter of public record. State law will probably require you to file an assumed name certificate with a state or county office. And in some states, you'll need to publish a notice in the newspaper supposedly informing the public of your fictitious name. This will let the public know that the business called Contemporary Studio, for example, is just another name for Apollo Furniture Inc. See Section A for an example of a fictitious business name statement.

4. Corporate Purpose

Insert the purpose of the corporation. Use simple language and describe the purpose broadly enough to cover all your intended and possible activities.

SAMPLES:

- to operate one or more retail stores for the sale of computer software.
- to manufacture and distribute equipment for the preparation of espresso, cappuccino and other coffee-based beverages.
- to design Web sites for computer users.
- to cater banquets, picnics and other functions requiring food service, and to rent equipment to be used in connection with these catering services.

5. Corporate Stock

Insert the total number of shares the corporation will be issuing to the shareholders signing the agreement.

⚠️ **There's a difference between authorized stock and issued stock.** Your new corporation will be authorized under state law to issue a certain number of shares of stock. The number is usually established at the time you incorporate and in some states will be tied to the fees you pay the state for incorporating. Just the same, it's a good idea to have plenty of stock authorized so that you'll have some in reserve after you issue shares to the initial shareholders—although if you run out, you can always get authority later for more stock.

This paragraph of the shareholders' agreement deals only with the shares you'll be issuing to the initial shareholders and not with the total number of shares authorized.

This paragraph also assumes that all your shares will be common stock, meaning that there's no guarantee that dividends will be paid. No problem. As a practical matter, because income tax laws tax money paid out in dividends twice (once at the corporate level and once when paid to the shareholders), most small businesses instead compensate their owners through salaries, bonuses and fringe benefits which are taxable to the shareholders, but tax deductible business expenses to the corporation. And even if it might be a good idea to issue preferred stock (under which owners receive a fixed dividend before dividends are paid to common stock owners), doing so is simply too complex for most small businesses.

6. Stock Subscriptions

Here, each shareholder makes a commitment to buy a certain number of shares.

Fill in the name of each person signing the agreement, the number of shares each is buying and the total price each is paying. Most new corporations charge $1.00 per share—a simple and common-sense approach that simplifies bookkeeping.

After you've incorporated and the shareholders have paid for their shares, the corporation will issue a stock certificate to each shareholder making it official that the person named has a designated number of shares in the corporation. It's usually signed by the corporation's president and secretary. You can buy blank forms at an office supply store.

7. Tax Status

The reference to Section 1244 of the Internal Revenue Code means that if the corporation fails, the shareholders can write off their stock purchase as an ordinary tax loss. This means the loss can be used to offset ordinary income that a shareholder has from other sources. If, for example, a shareholder invests $1,000 in the corporation and loses that entire investment, he or she can use that loss to reduce by $1,000 the amount of salary income that would otherwise be subject to income tax.

Check the optional paragraph if all shareholders want the corporation to elect S corporation status. (CD-ROM users can just delete it.) If so, shareholders will be taxed as if they are partners. Each shareholder's share of the corporation's profit or loss will be reported on his or her personal tax return. The corporation itself will pay no income tax.

If shareholders don't elect S corporation status, the corporation will be a regular corporation and will have to pay income taxes on its earnings.

Should You Elect S Corporation Status?

The several pros and cons of electing S corporation status are covered in Chapter 1, Section D, of the *Legal Guide for Starting & Running a Small Business*, by Fred S. Steingold (Nolo). Many new corporations elect S corporation status so that the shareholders can use possible corporate losses to offset their personal income. However, choosing to be an S corporation isn't always the best course of action—especially if the corporation is likely to be profitable and intends to retain some of its profits for future expansion. A regular corporation (one that hasn't elected S corporation status) will pay taxes on the retained earnings at the corporate rate, which often is lower than the rate that shareholders would have to pay if the earnings were taxed to the shareholders. Another point worth considering is that the IRS lets a regular C corporation have a fiscal year that's different than the calendar year. This generally isn't allowed for an S corporation. If your business will be seasonal and you would like to adopt a non-calendar fiscal year, consider forming a C corporation. After thoroughly reading up on this subject, you may still need help from a tax advisor in deciding between forming an S corporation or a regular corporation.

If you like the idea of having the profits and losses of your business pass through to the owners for tax purposes, you should also know that this can be accomplished by forming a limited liability company (LLC). LLC owners automatically receive partnership tax treatment unless they elect to be taxed as a corporation. Again, consider talking to a tax advisor if you need help in choosing which way to go.

For more information on small business taxation, see *Tax Savvy for Small Business*, by Frederick W. Daily (Nolo).

8. Board of Directors

You don't need to insert anything here. The board of directors makes the important policy decisions for the corporation and elects the corporate officers.

In a small business in which the owners actually run the business, it usually makes sense for everyone to serve on the board of directors. In many states, the number of required directors is tied to the number of shareholders. For instance, a corporation with one shareholder would need only one director, while a corporation with two shareholders would need at least two directors and a corporation with three or more shareholders would need at least three directors.

9. Officers

Insert the names of the officers. One person can hold more than one office. The same person can be the president and treasurer, for example. This is often done where there are only two or three shareholders.

10. Place of Business

Insert the address of your main location. This is the address where the records of the corporation will be kept and where official notice will be sent.

11. Bylaws

Attach bylaws as an attachment and fill in an addendum number. Form 2D, the next form in this chapter, can be the basis for your bylaws.

Standard Clauses

The remainder of the agreement contains the standard clauses we discussed in Chapter 1, Section C. The only thing you'll need to fill in here is the name of the state whose law will apply to the contract in the paragraph called "Governing Law."

Signatures

Each shareholder must sign his or her name, and their addresses should be typed in.

D. Form 2D: Corporate Bylaws

Bylaws are detailed rules for operating a corporation. You should prepare and follow bylaws for two reasons.

First, every corporation needs an orderly way to handle the legalities of corporate life. You need rules, for example, on how to elect the board of directors and corporate officers, how to hold meetings and the number of votes required for shareholders and directors to take action. Bylaws deal with these and related issues.

Second, as you know, one big reason to do business as a corporation is to limit your personal liability. But to be sure you maintain limited liability status, you need to act like a real corporate entity—which means creating a paper trail that demonstrates your corporation is following traditional business formalities. Doing this not only means adopting bylaws when your corporation is established but also keeping ongoing corporate records such as minutes of regular and special shareholders, and directors, meetings. (See Chapter 3.) In short, good corporate recordkeeping will help protect you if the IRS or a creditor insists that your corporation is just a sham and tries to go after your house, car, bank accounts and other property that you own personally.

The bylaws in this chapter are designed for a small corporation—one in which a handful of people own all the stock and are actively involved in the day-to-day operations of the business. At first they may look complicated and even a little over-whelming. True, there are a lot of details, but these bylaws are sensible, written in clear language and easy to put into practice.

You may need more customized bylaws. Our bylaws give you a reasonable measure of flexibility, but you may have other ideas about running your business that don't easily fit into this mold. Chances are your creative ideas will affect only, one or two areas of corporate management. If so you can use these bylaws for most provisions, but see a lawyer for help with appropriate wording to cover the troublesome areas.

Incorporators should formally adopt bylaws as soon as the incorporation papers have been signed and filed with the required state office. But the ideal time to prepare them is when the incorporators are putting together a pre-incorporation agreement (Form 2C). This helps all shareholders learn whether they have really achieved a meeting of the minds on many of the key aspects of starting and running the corporation. Unless the answer is a fairly enthusiastic yes, think at least twice before going forward.

Instructions for Form 2D: Corporate Bylaws

All the forms in this book are provided as tear-outs in Appendix B and on the accompanying forms CD-ROM. As you read the instructions for Form 2D, you may want to either tear out the form or open the form's file on the CD-ROM so you can follow along. Form 2D is in the file FORM2D.RTF on the CD-ROM. (For more information on using the forms CD-ROM, see Appendix A, "How to Use the CD-ROM.") If you don't use the forms CD-ROM, be sure to photocopy the agreement so you'll have a clean copy to use later.

Heading

In the first blank, insert the name of your corpora-tion. In the second blank, fill in the state in which you filed your incorporation papers.

Article I: Meetings of Shareholders

Article I covers the procedures for annual and special meetings of shareholders.

1. First insert when annual meetings will take place.

> **SAMPLE:**
> The first Wednesday in September.

Next insert the year when the first annual meeting will be held. This will usually be in the year after the corporation is formed. Finally, insert the time when annual meetings will start.

2. Insert the number of people who will serve on the board of directors. Typically in a small

corporation, all of the shareholders will want to serve on the board of directors.

3. A special meeting of shareholders is simply one called and held between the scheduled annual meetings.

   Check a box to indicate whether one shareholder can call a special meeting of shareholders or whether it takes several shareholders. If you check the second box, insert the number of shareholders required to call a special meeting. Check the third box if the president also can call a special meeting of shareholders.

4. You don't need to fill in anything here. This section sets out the notice requirements for annual and special meetings.

 For a notice, see Chapter 3, Section A, Form 3A: Notice of Shareholders' Meeting.

5. You don't need to fill in anything here. This section provides the minimum number of votes that have to be present for a meeting to be valid.

6. You don't need to fill in anything here. Each share of stock constitutes one vote.

7. You don't need to fill in anything here. Proxies need to be in writing.

 For a proxy form, see Chapter 3, Section C, Form 3C: Shareholder Proxy.

8. You don't need to fill in anything here. For shareholders to take action, the action must normally be supported by a majority of the shares the corporation has issued. There are two exceptions. First, although it's rare, state law occasionally mandates a two-thirds or even three-fourths vote on some issues such as a corporate merger or a dissolution of the corporation. Consult the corporation statute in your state to learn if any actions require more than a majority vote. Second, and far more commonly, shareholders themselves may use their bylaws to require a supermajority vote

for certain significant actions such as purchasing or selling real estate, borrowing significant sums of money or selling all or nearly all of the corporation's assets. You can do it by modifying this paragraph.

SAMPLE:

Approval of the sale or purchase of real estate by the corporation requires the assent of two-thirds of the corporate shares that have been issued. All other shareholders' actions require the assent of a majority of the corporate shares that have been issued, but if state law requires a greater number of votes, that law will prevail.

9. You don't need to fill in anything here. This section allows shareholders to take action by signing written consents. As fully explained in Chapter 3, written consents are a way for shareholders to take action without holding a meeting. A meeting, documented in formal minutes, is still the best way to deal with controversial issues, but for routine matters or actions that all shareholders agree with, written consents are a convenient way to proceed.

Article II: Stock

1–4. Nothing needs to be filled in here. These sections tell who must sign stock certificates, and the requirements for keeping track of and transferring shares of stock.

Article III: Board of Directors

1. This makes it clear that the board of directors will run the corporation. But it's worthy of note that since the shareholders and directors are

often the same in a small corporation, the shareholders aren't typically delegating management to others. Insert the name of the state in which you filed your incorporation papers.

2. You don't need to fill in anything here. This section sets out a procedure for filling vacancies on the board of directors.

3. Check a box to indicate who can call a special meeting of the directors—the president, any directors or several directors. If you check the last box, insert the number of directors required to call a special meeting.

   Then, insert the number of days required for a notice of a meeting of the directors.

4. Insert the number of directors required for a quorum at directors' meetings. A quorum is the minimum number of directors who must be present for the meeting to be valid.

5. Check one box to indicate the type of vote required for actions to be taken by the board of directors. If you check the last box, insert the minimum number of directors' votes required.

6. You don't need to fill in anything here. Typically, directors of a small corporation aren't paid for those duties but, of course, may get paid for the other work they do for the corporation. Suppose, for example, that you, Joe and Alice each own one-third of the shares of a corporation and you each work in the business each day. The corporation will pay you each a salary for your work and may pay you each a bonus as well—but probably won't pay you something additional for the time you spend serving on the board of directors.

7. You don't need to fill in anything here. This allows directors to take actions in writing (in legal jargon, "by written consent") so they don't have to hold a formal meeting.

8. You don't need to fill in anything here. Holding a meeting by conference call can be a great convenience.

Article IV: Officers

The officers of a corporation are responsible for running the business on a day-to-day basis.

1. Check a box for each officer your corporation will have. You can check more than one box. (CD-ROM users should just delete the unused officer choices.)

2. You don't need to fill in anything here. This section provides for the president to preside at directors' meetings.

3. Check a box to indicate whether the vice president or the secretary takes over if the president can't act. The vice president is the appropriate officer if there is one, but not every corporation has a vice president.

4–5. You don't need to fill in anything here. This section defines the roles of the secretary and treasurer.

6. You don't need to fill in anything here. This section gives the board of directors the authority to set salaries for the corporation's officers.

Article V: Fiscal

1. Check whether the corporate books will be kept on a cash basis or accrual basis. Most small corporations use the cash basis. Consult an accountant or do some of your own research for advice on which is best for you.

2. You don't need to fill in anything here. This section requires the treasurer to give financial statements to the shareholders annually.

Article VI: Amendments

You don't need to fill in anything here. The shareholders can amend the bylaws.

 For in-depth help in calling and holding special meetings and adopting corporate resolutions, see *The Corporate Minutes Book*, by Anthony Mancuso (Nolo). Also see Chapter 3 of this book for several additional useful forms.

Date and Signatures

Fill in the date the bylaws are adopted. Each of the shareholders must sign his or her name, and their respective names and addresses should be typed in.

E. Form 2E: Stock Agreement

Owners of a small corporation usually want to maintain some control over who can become fellow shareholders. For this reason, it makes sense to limit the ability of current shareholders to sell their stock to outsiders.

This form is designed to deal with those concerns. The basic idea is that before an outsider can come aboard as a shareholder, the corporation will have a chance to buy the shares. If the corporation itself declines to do so, the other existing shareholders will have a chance to buy the stock. The selling shareholder may sell his or her shares to an outsider only if the corporation and the nonselling shareholders decline to buy the stock.

The form also deals with what happens to the shares of a shareholder who dies.

There Are Many Ways to Draft a Shareholders' Agreement—and Many Ways to Fund a Buy-out

Be aware that this is a very basic form that provides just one way to address shareholder issues. You may want to deal with the reality that the owner of a minority of the shares may find no outside buyer for his or her stock—so you may want to use another way of putting a value on the stock if there's to be a buy-out.

Similarly, you may want to provide a source of funds for the corporation to buy the shares of a shareholder who has died. A common and sensible way is for the corporation to buy life insurance for this purpose.

In practical terms, dealing with owners' interests in most types of business entities is very similar. For an in-depth look at buy-outs and how to structure them, including forms for creating your own buy-sell agreement, see *How to Create a Buy-Sell Agreement & Control the Destiny of Your Small Business*, by Anthony Mancuso and Bethany K. Laurence (Nolo).

Instructions for Form 2E: Stock Agreement

All the forms in this book are provided as tear-outs in Appendix B and on the accompanying forms CD-ROM. As you read the instructions for Form 2E, you may want to either tear out the form or open the form's file on the CD-ROM so you can follow along. Form 2E is in the file FORM2E.RTF on the CD-ROM. (For more information on using the forms CD-ROM, see Appendix A, "How to Use the CD-ROM.") If you don't use the forms CD-ROM, be sure to photocopy the agreement so you'll have a clean copy to use later.

1. Names

In the first set of blanks, insert the name of the shareholders. Then fill in the corporation's name.

2. Restrictions on Sale of Stock

Again, insert the name of the corporation.

3. Offer to Corporation

You don't need to insert anything here. This section says if a shareholder receives a good faith offer for his or her shares, the corporation gets first crack at purchasing them at that price. A good faith offer is one that's freely negotiated and not rigged to artificially boost the price.

4. Offer to Shareholders

You don't need to insert anything here. This section lets the other shareholders buy the stock at the good faith offer price if the corporation declines.

Pro rata means that if, for example, there are three nonselling shareholders and they each own 1,000 shares of stock, they can each buy one-third of the stock being offered for sale.

5. Remaining Shares

You don't need to insert anything here. This gives the selling shareholders 30 days to sell any shares to the original offeror if the corporation and shareholders don't buy all the shares being offered.

6. Continuing Effect

Insert the date that the agreement is signed.

7. Death of Shareholder

Check the box to the left of the paragraph heading if you wish to include this optional paragraph in the agreement. It provides for the corporation to carry insurance on the lives of the shareholders so it will have readily available funds to buy the shares of a shareholder who dies.

Check the first box within the paragraph if you want the corporation's accountant to determine the value of the deceased shareholder's shares. Check the second box if you want to provide a different method of determining how much the corporation will pay the deceased shareholder's estate for those shares. You may wish to consult a CPA or lawyer about alternative methods of valuation, or see *The Partnership Book*, by Denis Clifford and Ralph Warner (Nolo), for valuation language that can be adapted for corporate shareholders.

⚠ Jointly owned shares need further attention. Paragraph 7 of this form is based on the usual situation in which each shareholder owns the shares of stock in his or her name alone, meaning that the shares will become part of the shareholder's estate if he or she dies. Much less commonly in a small incorporated business, a shareholder may own shares jointly with his or her spouse; in that situation, the shares of the first spouse to die will belong to the surviving spouse rather than the estate of the spouse who has died. This paragraph won't work for jointly owned shares unless it's substantially modified—a task that will probably require professional assistance.

Standard Clauses

The remainder of the agreement contains the standard clauses we discussed in Chapter 1, Section C. The only thing you'll need to fill in here is the name of the state whose law will apply to the contract in the paragraph called "Governing Law."

Date and Signatures

Fill in the date the agreement is signed. Each shareholder must sign his or her name, and their respective names and addresses should be typed in.

F. Form 2F: LLC Operating Agreement for Single-Member LLC

If you're forming a small business and wish to limit your personal liability, consider setting up a limited liability company (LLC). It will limit your personal liability for business debts the same way a corporation would—a benefit you won't have if you do business as a sole proprietorship or partnership. Faced with a choice, many entrepreneurs favor the LLC format over the corporate format. The reason: creating and maintaining an LLC can be simpler and requires less paperwork.

Normally, an LLC is taxed like a partnership. The business itself pays no federal income tax. Instead, the profits and losses pass through to the members (owners) who report their share on their individual tax returns. Most small business owners prefer this arrangement. You can, however, elect to have your LLC taxed as a corporation. In that case, the business itself would be taxed. To do so, you file IRS Form 8832, Entity Classification Election. Your tax advisor can give you further guidance on this issue.

The LLC allows wide latitude in how you structure its management. For example, it can be run by all the members, by some members who are selected as managers, by outside managers or by a team of members and outside managers. You also don't need to have a board of directors like a corporation does. Another attractive feature of LLCs is that you may allocate profits, losses and distributions to members in different proportions than their respective ownership interests, which you may not do in an S corporation.

Investigate other types of business structures. While the LLC is a very appealing choice for a small business, there are some instances in which a corporation may have a slight edge. For more details, see Chapter 1 of the *Legal Guide for Starting & Running a Small Business*, by Fred S. Steingold (Nolo).

Corporations and LLCs Use Different Terms

Although there are many similarities between corporations and LLCs, there are many differences as well—especially when it comes to terminology, as shown in the following chart:

Term	Corporation	LLC
What an Owner Is Called	Shareholder	Member
What an Owner Owns	Shares of Stock	Membership Interest
What Document Creates the Entity	Articles of Incorporation	Articles of Organization
What Document Spells Out Internal Operating Procedures	Bylaws	Operating Agreement

In virtually every state (except, at this writing, Massachusetts and the District of Columbia), you can form an LLC with only one member and, of course, multi-member LLCs are permitted in all states. Typically, to set up an LLC, you must prepare just two basic legal documents: the articles of organization (a public document you file with the state) and the operating agreement (an internal agreement you enter into with the other LLC members which defines your rights and responsibilities to each other as well as how profits, losses and distributions will be allocated). Although we will refer to these documents as articles of organization and operating agreements, the exact names are different in a few states.

In most states, preparing your articles of organization is surprisingly simple, especially if your LLC is a typical small business consisting of a handful of owners. Most states provide a printed form for the articles of organization—just fill in the blanks, sign the form and file it with the LLC filing office. The task is even easier in states that include instructions for filling in the blanks. Other states don't provide the actual articles of organization form but do furnish something almost as convenient: sample articles with instructions. You can prepare your own articles of incorporation by following the format and contents of the sample.

If your state is one of the few that provides neither fill-in-the-blank forms nor sample forms with instructions, you'll need to check your state's LLC statute to learn what to put into the articles of organization.

 Other resources. For step-by-step instructions on preparing articles of organization and other organizational documents for your LLC, consult *Form Your Own Limited Liability Company*, and *LLC Maker*, an interactive Windows software program that provides forms and information for setting up an LLC in all 50 states, both by Anthony Mancuso (Nolo).

The other document most LLCs need is an operating agreement. This is the document that defines members' day-to-day duties, how profits and losses will be shared and what happens if a member retires or dies. It's absolutely necessary for you to have one if you have two or more members. Although an operating agreement is usually optional for a one-member LLC, it's often a good idea to have one. This is particularly true if you will be borrowing money from a commercial lender—many banks want to make sure you are observing the legal formalities of operating a limited liability entity. Form 2F is an example of such a form.

 You need a different agreement for two or more members. For help in preparing an operating agreement for an LLC with two or more members, see *Form Your Own Limited Liability Company* and *LLC Maker*, both by Anthony Mancuso (Nolo), cited above.

Instructions for Form 2F: LLC Operating Agreement for Single-Member LLC

All the forms in this book are provided as tear-outs in Appendix B and on the accompanying forms CD-ROM. As you read the instructions for Form 2F, you may want to either tear out the form or open the form's file on the CD-ROM so you can follow along. Form 2F is in the file FORM2F.RTF on the CD-ROM. (For more information on using the forms CD-ROM, see Appendix A, "How to Use the CD-ROM.") If you don't use the forms CD-ROM, be sure to photocopy the agreement so you'll have a clean copy to use later.

1. Names

Insert the name of the LLC in the first space. Your LLC name will have to comply with state legal requirements. This usually means including an LLC designator such as "Limited Liability Company" or "Limited Company" in the LLC name. Many states allow abbreviations such as LLC or LC.

> **EXAMPLE:** You choose Andover Services as the name of your business. Depending on the state in which your business is located, one or more of the following names may be appropriate ways to indicate that your business is an LLC:
> - Andover Services Limited Liability Company
> - Andover Services L.L.C.
> - Andover Services LLC
> - Andover Services Limited Liability Co.
> - Andover Services Ltd. Liability Co.
> - Andover Services Limited Company
> - Andover Services Ltd. Co.
> - Andover Services L.C.
> - Andover Services LC.

Insert the state in the second blank. Insert your name in the third blank.

2. Formation

Each state has its own law covering the creation and operation of a limited liability company. Insert the name of the state in which your LLC is being formed, which will almost always be the state in which you live. Your articles of organization will describe the purpose of your LLC; you needn't repeat it here.

3. Offices

Your state law typically will require you to give an address for your registered office—the place where lawsuits and legal notices can be delivered. This usually will be your normal place of business or your home. Insert the address here.

Your state law will also require you to designate a resident agent—the person to whom lawsuits and legal notices can be delivered. The form assumes that you'll be the resident agent of your LLC.

4. Management

Most owners of single-member LLCs want to manage the business themselves. This form takes it a step further and specifically provides that you can delegate some authority to someone else.

There's also an optional paragraph in which you can name someone to run the business if you die or are unable to act—because you're in the hospital, for example. If want to include this paragraph, check the box and then insert the name of a trusted friend, relative or business colleague.

5. Capital Contributions

You'll need to put some money or other property into the LLC in exchange for your member's interest. If you're contributing money, check the first box and then insert the amount. It's best to put in just a token amount such as $1,000 as your capital contribution. You can always lend additional funds to the business. You'll probably open an LLC bank account and put the start-up contribution into that account, along with any other funds you're lending to the LLC.

 Have the LLC give you a promissory note for any funds you lend to the company. See Chapter 4 for forms and details about promissory notes.

 Document major LLC events. Although most state laws don't require limited liability companies to keep the same kinds of detailed records as a corporation, it's often a good idea to get the members' written consent to certain events anyway. Documenting major events, such as taking out a large loan, selling LLC property or acknowledging the contribution of property from a member to the LLC, can prevent later misunderstandings among the members. For a comprehensive guide to running a limited liability company, see *Your Limited Liability Company: An Operating Manual*, by Anthony Mancuso (Nolo).

If you're going to contribute property—such as a computer or real estate—check the second box and describe the property. (Of course, you may contribute both money and property. It's not either/or.)

 You'll need additional paperwork to transfer property to your LLC. You should use a Bill of Sale to transfer tangible personal property—such as a computer—to the LLC. Form 8C can be modified for this purpose. You should use a deed to transfer real estate to the LLC.

6. Taxes

Normally, you'll want your single-member LLC to be taxed as a sole proprietorship. This means the profits and losses will pass through to you and you'll report them on Schedule C as part of your annual Form 1040. The LLC will not pay any federal income tax. If you and your tax advisor agree that this is best for you, then check the first box.

An alternative is to have your LLC be taxed as a corporation, in which case the LLC will be taxed on its income and you will be taxed on any distributions you receive from the LLC. Because of some quirks in the tax laws, this option may reduce your taxes by allowing you to split the LLC's income between the LLC and yourself, especially if you're going to hold some profits in reserve for future use by the LLC. This might happen, for example, if your LLC is saving up to buy a new building or buy some expensive equipment. If you and your tax advisor conclude that this is the better way to go, then check the second box.

 If you choose corporate taxation, you need to file a special IRS form right after you start your LLC. As mentioned above, it's IRS Form 8832, Entity Classification Election.

7. Funds

Nothing needs to be filled in here. This paragraph simply authorizes you to decide where you'll deposit LLC funds and provides who can sign checks.

8. Additional Members

Nothing needs to be filled in here. This paragraph simply recognizes that you may want to bring in other members someday. In that case, you'll want to amend your articles of organization and operating agreement to fit the new situation.

9. Distributions

Nothing needs to filled in here. You'll be the sole judge of when to distribute cash and other LLC assets.

Signatures

Date the agreement. Then sign the agreement twice: once on behalf of the LLC and once as the owner. For more on signatures, see Chapter 1, Section B. ■

Running Your Corporation

To fulfill its legal and practical obligations, an incorporated small business needs to hold key corporate meetings and keep a written record of important corporate decisions. Failure to do this can have seriously negative consequences. For example, the lack of good corporate records makes you vulnerable if a creditor or the IRS challenges the legitimacy of your corporation. In a worst case scenario, a judge may even decide that your failure to act and keep records like a corporation means you and other shareholders lose the limited personal liability shield the corporation normally provides, leaving you to face personal liability for the corporation's debts.

Don't despair if you've missed a meeting or two. A small lapse in corporate record-keeping needn't have dire consequences. If you've missed holding and recording a few meetings, you can repair much of the damage by holding them later or by taking action through consent forms and then putting the documentation in your record book.

To follow legal procedures necessary to document that your corporation really exists, all formal actions taken by the shareholders and directors should be written in the form of minutes or consents and kept in a corporate record book. Your record book needn't be fancy; an ordinary loose-leaf notebook will do the job. Day-to-day decisions made by officers and employees are not documented in the corporate record book. What does need to be recorded are the minutes of corporate meetings. Meetings fall into three general categories:

- **Annual meetings.** Shareholders should always hold them; directors typically should—usually at the same time as or immediately following the shareholders' meeting. Any topic raised at an annual meeting can be voted upon. While it may not be technically required (since the meeting date is in the bylaws), it's a good idea to send advance notice of the annual meetings to everyone involved, listing all subjects you think may be covered. And it's especially smart to do this if unexpected

or unusual business will be addressed at the meeting. The main item of business at the shareholders' annual meeting is usually the election of directors, following rules set out in the corporation's bylaws. There may also be a discussion of the company's finances and the plans for the coming year. Directors who hold annual meetings use them primarily as an occasion to elect the corporate officers.

- **Regular meetings.** Directors may find it makes sense to set up a schedule of periodic meetings—to be held quarterly, for example—which take place on certain fixed dates. Shareholders may do the same but, especially where most or all are also directors, have no real need to do so. This is because shareholders don't directly manage the business, but by law and under the terms of the corporation's bylaws delegate that responsibility to the directors. At regular meetings, action can be taken on any subject.

- **Special meetings.** Usually the corporation's president or a majority of directors or shareholders may call special meetings between annual meetings or regular meetings. A majority of shareholders might do this, for example, to fill a vacancy on the board of directors caused by death or resignation or perhaps to approve a sale of the corporation's major assets. Directors might hold a special meeting to pass a resolution needed to deal with important corporate business such as approving a bank loan, an employment contract or the sales of real estate. At special meetings, the bylaws will normally provide that the participants can vote only on the topics listed in the notice of the meeting, which must be mailed a set number of days in advance.

This chapter provides a quick survey of the requirements for holding and running corporate meetings, along with the basic forms to accomplish the job. For a much more comprehensive treatment of this subject, see *The Corporate Minutes Book: The Legal Guide to Taking Care of Corporate*

How Is a Corporation Organized?

As you think about keeping up with ongoing corporate paperwork responsibilities, it helps to keep in mind the essential elements of the corporate structure. Here is a brief review of the material discussed in this chapter.

- Articles of incorporation, signed by one or more incorporators, are filed with the secretary of state or other designated state office to create the corporation. In some states the document is called a certificate of incorporation, charter or articles of association.

- Bylaws, adopted by the incorporators or directors, provide detailed rules for running the corporation, including when meetings will be held, how many directors or shareholders constitute a quorum so that official votes can be taken, and so on.

- Shareholders (often referred to as stockholders) own the corporation's stock. They elect directors and make (or ratify) essential decisions such as whether to merge with another business, dissolve the corporation, amend the articles of incorporation or sell the bulk of the corporation's assets.

- Directors manage the corporation, elect the officers (such as president, secretary and treasurer) and make major policy decisions such as establishing employee benefit plans, approving the leasing of real estate and authorizing the borrowing of money by the corporation.

- Officers carry out the corporation's day-to-day business operations. Most corporations have a president, secretary and treasurer.

- Minutes, signed by the corporate secretary, are a written summary of actions taken at a shareholders' or directors' meeting.

- Annual reports, containing information required by state law, are filed with the state's corporate filing office (often the Secretary of State or Corporations Commissioner) whose main office is at the state capital.

Most small business corporations are owned by just a few people who each play several roles in the corporate structure as shareholders and directors as well as holding all of the corporate offices. Indeed, it's common (and perfectly legal) to have a corporation in which one person serves as the sole director, holds all of the offices and is the corporation's sole shareholder and employee.

Business, by Anthony Mancuso (Nolo). This book gives detailed, step-by-step instructions on how to set up and run shareholder and director meetings and provides a number of fill-in-the-blank legal and tax resolutions designed to document important corporate actions (buying or selling real estate or borrowing money, for example) for inclusion in corporate minutes or written consents. This book contains a computer CD-ROM with many ready-to-use corporate forms.

When shareholders and directors will hold a scheduled meeting, the best practice is for the corporate secretary to notify the shareholders or directors well in advance of the time and place of the meeting.

To give written notice of various corporate meetings, you can use one of the first two forms: Form 3A: Notice of Shareholders' Meeting, or Form 3B: Notice of Directors' Meeting.

The corporate bylaws may allow a shareholder to sign a proxy giving another person the authority to appear and vote the signer's shares at a shareholder meeting. A shareholder may wish to do this if he or she is going to be out of town or otherwise unable to attend the meeting in person. You can use Form 3C: Shareholder Proxy, for this purpose.

At a shareholders' or directors' meeting, the participants discuss the issues and approve or reject motions put before them. The corporate secretary prepares minutes recording significant actions and keeps them in the corporate record book. Form 3D: Minutes of Shareholders' Meeting, and Form 3E: Minutes of Directors' Meeting, can be used to do this.

Corporate bylaws may permit meetings to be held through a telephone conference call. Form 3F: Minutes of Telephone Conference Directors' Meeting, shows how minutes may be written for such a meeting.

An even more streamlined and convenient way for shareholders or directors of a small company to take action is by signing written consents—that is, written approval of corporate actions with no actual meeting being held. Written consents are commonly used in place of a meeting in a situation where no controversial issues are outstanding and all share-holders or directors agree on whatever action will be taken. In this context, they offer a good way for directors and shareholders—especially those in corporations that have very few owners—to take care of required paperwork without ever having to convene a formal meeting. For examples of written consents, see Form 3G: Consent of Shareholders, and Form 3H: Consent of Directors.

When you've completed the forms in this chapter and obtained the needed signatures, place them in your corporate record book along with the corporation's articles of incorporation, bylaws and other important corporate legal documents.

A. Form 3A: Notice of Shareholders' Meeting

Corporate bylaws, following the dictates of state law, usually require that the corporation hold an annual meeting of shareholders and specify the date, time and location. Bylaws also typically permit the president and a certain percentage of shareholders to call special meetings and sometimes—but less commonly—bylaws establish a schedule of regular shareholder meetings (held more frequently than yearly) as well.

Form 3A is designed to give shareholders notice of an annual, regular or special meeting. Even if—as is common—your bylaws already establish the date, time and place of the annual meeting or regular meetings and don't require that further notice of such meetings be given, it's still good practice to send a notice. A shareholder who forgets the meeting date and misses the meeting may nevertheless resent the fact that he or she was not reminded that an important action was to be taken. In short, the courtesy of sending a notice, even if it's not required, will help a small corporation run more smoothly.

If your bylaws require that shareholders be sent notice of annual or regular meetings, check to see how far in advance you must give the notice. Your bylaws may also contain special rules as to how the notice is sent (certified rather than regular mail, for example).

A notice is always required for a special meeting. And unlike a regular meeting, notice of a special meeting must specify the topics to be covered. Check your bylaws to learn how far in advance and by what means the notice is to be given. Your by-laws will also state who can call for a special meeting of shareholders. Often the president or another officer is given such authority or a specified number of shareholders can require that such a meeting be held.

For annual meetings, a notice can do double duty. Where the shareholders and the directors are the same people—a common situation in small businesses—you can combine the annual meetings of both and send a single notice.

Guidelines for Notices to Shareholders

To be in compliance with all states' legal notice requirements for shareholders' meetings, follow these rules:

Rule 1. Provide written notice of all shareholders' meetings.

Rule 2. Mail the notice at least ten business days prior to shareholders' meetings—unless your bylaws require a longer notice or a different type of delivery.

Rule 3. State the purpose of the meeting in the notice.

Source: The Corporate Minutes Book: The Legal Guide to Taking Care of Corporate Business, by Anthony Mancuso (Nolo).

Instructions for Form 3A: Notice of Shareholders' Meeting

All the forms in this book are provided as tear-outs in Appendix B and on the accompanying forms CD-ROM. As you read the instructions for Form 3A, you may want to either tear out the form or open the form's file on the CD-ROM so you can follow along. Form 3A is in the file FORM3A.RTF on the CD-ROM.

(For more information on using the forms CD-ROM, see Appendix A, "How to Use the CD-ROM.") If you don't use the forms CD-ROM, be sure to photocopy the agreement so you'll have a clean copy to use later.

Name of Corporation

In the first blank, fill in the name of the corporation. Then check a box to indicate if this is to be an annual, regular or special meeting. (CD-ROM users can just delete the unused text.)

1. Date

Insert the date the meeting will be held.

2. Time

Insert the time the meeting will start.

3. Place

If your bylaws specify that shareholders' meetings are to be held at the business's principal place of business, list that location. Otherwise, insert the place where the meeting will be held.

4. Purposes

You're usually not required to state in advance the matters that will be covered at an annual or regular meeting of shareholders. At such a meeting, shareholders are free to propose and vote on any matters that are brought up. As noted earlier, however, if an unusual or possibly controversial item will be considered, it's both courteous and a good business practice to list the agenda items.

With a special meeting, you usually are legally required to list all items that will be voted on in the notice of the meeting. Topics not listed can't be legally approved unless, of course, all shareholders agree.

In a notice of an annual meeting of shareholders, election of the board of directors is always an agenda item, so you'll want to include it in the notice.

SAMPLE:

To elect the board of directors of UpTown Inc.

All issues that affect the basic character or structure of the corporation should also be addressed at a shareholders' meeting. For example, shareholders would appropriately consider a proposal to merge with another business, amend the articles of incorporation or bylaws or fill a vacancy on the board of directors. In preparing the notice of the meeting, you can describe these topics briefly in your own words:

SAMPLES:

- To consider the proposed merger of UpTown Inc. with Tempo Associates Inc.
- To consider amending the Articles of Incorporation to change the name of UpTown Inc. to Chipco Inc.
- To consider amending the bylaws of UpTown Inc. to increase the number of directors from four to five.
- To fill the vacancy on the board of directors of Uptown Inc. created by the resignation of Barbara Jones.

By law, if this will be an annual or regular meeting, any topic may be raised and voted on. Even so, it's a good idea to check the box indicating that other business may be transacted.

5. Special Meetings

If the notice is for a special meeting, include this optional paragraph by checking the box and indicating which authorized corporate officer (often the president) or which shareholders have called for the meeting. (CD-ROM users can just delete this paragraph.) Your bylaws should tell you who has the legal authority to call special meetings.

Date and Signature

Notices are usually signed by the corporate secretary. Insert the date, the name of the corporate secretary and the name of the corporation.

B. Form 3B: Notice of Directors' Meeting

Corporate bylaws often establish a date, time and location for an annual meeting of directors. In small, closely held companies, in which the shareholders typically serve as directors, it usually makes sense to combine the shareholders' and directors' annual meetings into a single meeting or, if you prefer, to schedule the directors' annual meeting for immediately after that of the shareholders. In either situation, it's fine to use one meeting notice for both meetings.

Your bylaws—or perhaps the directors themselves acting through a resolution—may also establish a schedule of regular meetings to be held more frequently than once a year, perhaps as often as quarterly. Bylaws also typically permit the president or a certain number of directors to call special meetings as needed.

Form 3B is designed to give directors notice of any of these types of meeting. As is true for shareholders' meetings, bylaws usually establish the time and place of the annual meeting, and the bylaws or the directors may set the time and place for regular meetings, with no further notice required. But it's still a good idea and courteous to always send a notice.

If your bylaws do require you to notify directors of annual or regular meetings, there may also be requirements for how far in advance notice must be given and for the manner of giving notice—certified rather than regular mail, for example.

A notice is always required for a special meeting and that notice must specify the topics to be covered.

Again, check your bylaws for details on when and how notice is to be given. Your bylaws will also state who can call for a special meeting of directors. Often the president or another officer is given such authority or a specified number of directors can require that such a meeting be held.

Guidelines for Notices to Directors

To comply with every state's legal notice requirements for directors' meetings, follow these rules:

Rule 1. Provide written notice of all directors' meetings.

Rule 2. Mail the notice at least five business days prior to directors' meetings—unless your by-laws require a longer period or a different type of delivery.

Rule 3. State the purpose of the meeting in the notice.

Source: *The Corporate Minutes Book: The Legal Guide to Taking Care of Corporate Business,* by Anthony Mancuso (Nolo).

Instructions for Form 3B: Notice of Directors' Meeting

All the forms in this book are provided as tear-outs in Appendix B and on the accompanying forms CD-ROM. As you read the instructions for Form 3B, you may want to either tear out the form or open the form's file on the CD-ROM so you can follow along. Form 3B is in the file Form3B.RTF on the CD-ROM. (For more information on using the forms CD-ROM, see Appendix A, "How to Use the CD-ROM.") If you don't use the forms CD-ROM, be sure to photocopy the agreement so you'll have a clean copy to use later.

Name of Corporation

In the first blank, fill in the name of the corporation.

Then check a box to indicate if this is to be an annual, regular or special meeting. (CD-ROM users can just delete the unused text.)

1. Date

Insert the date the meeting will be held.

2. Time

Insert the time the meeting will start.

3. Place

If your bylaws specify that directors' meetings be held at the business's principal place of business, list that location. Otherwise, insert the place the meeting will be held.

4. Purposes

Technically you aren't required to state in advance the purposes of an annual or regular meeting of directors. At such a meeting, directors are free to propose and vote on any issues anyone brings up. However, it's a good business practice to list the business to be transacted if you know about it in advance. This is particularly helpful if some surprising or possibly controversial topic is likely to be discussed and acted on.

A special meeting is another matter: you're usually required by your bylaws to list the topics to be discussed. If you don't and the directors vote on a nonlisted item, the vote won't be valid unless all the directors are present and the vote is unanimous.

One frequently asked question is, "How closely do directors have to manage a corporation?" There is no precise answer. The job of the directors is to determine the business policies of the corporation. How much the directors themselves do and how much they delegate to the corporation's officers will vary from business to business, but often the directors' approval is sought for such items as signing major contracts, leasing or buying space, borrowing money and hiring top managers and setting their salaries. You can state the agenda items briefly and in plain language:

SAMPLES:
- To consider exercising the corporation's option to extend its lease for an additional three years.
- To consider offering to Gene Baker the position of Research Director of RacaFrax Inc. with a two-year contract.

• To consider borrowing $50,000.00 from First Thrift Bank to be used for renovation of the RacaFrax Inc. corporate offices.

If this will be an annual or regular meeting, check the box indicating that other business may be transacted—to cover the possibility that new topics may come up that aren't presently anticipated.

5. Special Meetings

If the notice is for a special meeting, include this optional paragraph by checking the box and indicating which authorized corporate officer or which directors have called for the meeting. (CD-ROM users can just delete this paragraph.) Your bylaws should tell you who can call special meetings.

Date and Signature

Meeting notices are usually signed by the corporate secretary. Insert the date, the name of the corporate secretary and the name of the corporation.

C. Form 3C: Shareholder Proxy

This form can be used by a shareholder to give another shareholder the authority to vote the owner's shares of stock at a shareholders' meeting. It's unusual to use proxies in the world of small corporations because the shareholders typically make it a point to be present at all important shareholders' meetings or, alternatively, if a meeting really isn't necessary, handle business using written consents as discussed below (Form 3G). And, of course, it's also common for other shareholders to willingly reschedule an important meeting to make it possible for everyone to attend.

But if you're going to be out of town, for example, when the scheduled meeting will be held and you can't get the meeting date changed, you may wish to give someone else the right to vote your shares—especially if you expect that action will be taken on a controversial matter and the vote will be close. By

giving another shareholder your proxy, you'll be sure your vote will be counted.

Instructions for Form 3C: Shareholder Proxy

All the forms in this book are provided as tear-outs in Appendix B and on the accompanying forms CD-ROM. As you read the instructions for Form 3C, you may want to either tear out the form or open the form's file on the CD-ROM so you can follow along. Form 3C is in the file FORM3C.RTF on the CD-ROM. (For more information on using the forms CD-ROM, see Appendix A, "How to Use the CD-ROM.") If you don't use the forms CD-ROM, be sure to photocopy the agreement so you'll have a clean copy to use later.

Name of Person Authorized to Vote

Fill in the name of the person who will hold your proxy—the person who will have the right to vote your stock at a meeting.

Name of Corporation

Insert the name of the corporation.

Type of Meeting

Check the box to indicate whether the proxy is for either a regular, special or annual meeting. In the blank, fill in the scheduled meeting date.

Signature

The shareholder must sign his or her name, and his or her name and address should be typed in.

D. Form 3D: Minutes of Shareholders' Meeting

Use this form to record actions taken at a shareholders' meeting. These minutes are streamlined to meet the minimum needs of an incorporated small business consisting of just a few shareholders—

typically, the same people who serve on the board of directors and operate the company from day to day. These simplified minutes, for example, do not recite the traditional parliamentary procedures such as naming the shareholders who propose and second a resolution or motion, nor do they indicate the number of votes cast on each issue. This reflects the fact that shareholders in small corporations often do not strictly follow formal "Roberts Rules of Order" type procedures in conducting meetings, preferring to make most decisions by consensus.

Corporations wishing a higher degree of documented formality should consult *The Corporate Minutes Book: The Legal Guide to Taking Care of Corporate Business*, by Anthony Mancuso (Nolo). It contains excellent forms for minutes, as well as examples of wording for a large number of the most used corporate resolutions.

Instructions for Form 3D: Minutes of Shareholders' Meeting

All the forms in this book are provided as tear-outs in Appendix B and on the accompanying forms CD-ROM. As you read the instructions for Form 3D, you may want to either tear out the form or open the form's file on the CD-ROM so you can follow along. Form 3D is in the file FORM3D.RTF on the CD-ROM. (For more information on using the forms CD-ROM, see Appendix A, "How to use the CD-ROM.") If you don't use the forms CD-ROM, be sure to photocopy the agreement so you'll have a clean copy to use later.

Opening Paragraph

In the first blank, insert the name of the corporation and then check a box for the type of meeting—annual, special or regular. Next, insert the date and place of the meeting and the time the meeting began and the time it ended. Remember to indicate "a.m." or "p.m."

Notice

Insert the date the notice of the meeting was sent, check a box indicating the type of delivery and attach a photocopy of the notice. (Form 3A above can be used for the notice.)

Quorum

A quorum is the minimum number of votes that must be present for shareholders to hold a meeting at which action is taken. You'll usually find your corporation's quorum requirements in the corporate bylaws. Most typically, each share of stock gets one vote and the holders of a majority of the shares must be present at a meeting to form a quorum. Insert the names of shareholders who attended the meeting, either in person or by proxy. In the case of shareholders who attended by proxy, insert the name of the proxy.

SAMPLE:

Constance Baker by Joseph Chen, her proxy.

Actions Taken

1. If the minutes of the last meeting were approved, check the box indicating if the last meeting was an annual or special meeting and fill in the date of that meeting.

2. Describe any actions taken at the shareholders' meeting.

SAMPLE 1:

The following people were elected to serve as directors until the next annual meeting or until their successors take office:

Barry Baker

Elaine Epifano

John Simpson

Kim Santiago

SAMPLE 2:

The shareholders of Racafrax Inc. voted unanimously to approve the sale of the building at 127 Main Street, Arkadelphia, Arkansas, to Venture Enterprises in accordance with the proposed contract presented by the corporate president.

A majority vote of those shareholders present at a meeting may not be enough. The bylaws of some corporations may require a yes vote of a supermajority of shares—two-thirds, three-fourths or even more—to approve certain shareholder actions. Have the bylaws handy at every meeting so you know exactly how many votes a particular action requires for passage.

Date and Signature

Minutes are usually signed by the corporate secretary. Insert the date, the name of the corporate secretary and the name of the corporation.

E. Form 3E: Minutes of Directors' Meeting

Use these minutes to record actions taken at a directors' meeting. As with Form 3D: Minutes for Shareholders' Meeting, this form is streamlined for use by small businesses that want to keep things simple. It should work well to record what went on at most routine directors' meetings. However, you may need more specialized information if the directors plan to take unusual or highly specialized actions. The best source of the sample minutes needed to accomplish this is *The Corporate Minutes Book: The Legal Guide to Taking Care of Corporate Business*, by Anthony Mancuso (Nolo), which contains wording for most kinds of directors' resolutions.

Instructions for Form 3E: Minutes of Directors' Meeting

All the forms in this book are provided as tear-outs in Appendix B and on the accompanying forms CD-ROM. As you read the instructions for Form 3E, you may want to either tear out the form or open the form's file on the CD-ROM so you can follow along. Form 3E is in the file FORM3E.RTF on the CD-ROM. (For more information on using the forms CD-ROM, see Appendix A, "How to Use the CD-ROM") If you don't use the forms CD-ROM, be sure to photocopy the agreement so you'll have a clean copy to use later.

Opening Paragraph

In the first blank, insert the name of the corporation and then check a box for the type of meeting—annual, special or regular. Next, insert the date and place of the meeting and the time the meeting began and the time it ended. Remember to insert "a.m." or "p.m."

Notice

Insert the date the notice of the meeting was sent, check a box indicating the type of delivery and attach a photocopy of the notice. (Form 3B, above, can be used for the notice.)

Quorum

A quorum is the minimum number of directors who must be present for directors to hold a valid meeting and take action. Commonly, a corporation's bylaws require that at least a majority of the directors be present to constitute a quorum. Insert the names of directors who attended the meeting.

Actions Taken

If the minutes of the last meeting were approved, fill in the date of that meeting.

Insert any other actions taken. Again, remember the bylaws of a good many incorporated small businesses require as many as two-thirds or three-quarters of all directors to vote yes for certain types of issues, such as authorizing the corporation to borrow money.

SAMPLES:

- The directors of Round Stone Inc. voted unanimously to hire Gene Baker as its director of research under the proposed two-year employment contract presented by the president, a copy of which is attached.

- The directors of Round Stone Inc. unanimously approved the exercising of the corporation's option to extend its lease for the building at 27 Barksdale Street, Galveston, Texas, for an additional three years and authorize the president to send the appropriate notice to the landlord, Rypan Holding Inc. of Fort Worth, Texas.

If your corporation's bylaws require more than a simple majority of the directors to approve certain actions—perhaps loans over $50,000—be careful to specify the number of directors who voted in favor of the action.

SAMPLE:

The following four directors of Square Z Inc. voted in favor of authorizing the president to arrange for a $75,000.00 loan from First Thrift Bank of Larchmont, New York, to be used for renovation of the corporate offices at 1002 Boston Post Road, Larchmont, New York: Joe Jacob, Karl Koch, Lawrence Lamont and Mindy Maxwell. Director Ned Norris voted no.

 You don't need director action for day-to-day business decisions. Directors are in charge of the overall management of the corporation —not the nitty-gritty details of everyday business decisions which are best left to the corporation's officers and employees (some or all of whom may also be directors). Typically, a corporation will delegate considerable authority to the company president or other officers or employees, with the result that there will be many, many business decisions you're not required to document in directors' minutes. You might, for example, empower the president to hire and fire all employees except where an employee will be offered a contract of more than one year or a salary of more than $75,000, in which case the issues must be bought to the board for prior approval.

Date and Signature

Minutes are usually signed by the corporate secretary. Insert the date, the name of the corporate secretary and the name of the corporation.

F. Form 3F: Minutes of Telephone Conference Directors' Meeting

Use this form if, as authorized by your bylaws, you hold a directors' meeting by telephone. Such meetings are just as legal as a face-to-face meeting held in one room. However, especially if you have more than two directors, it makes sense to document for each meeting that a meeting by conference call is agreeable to all. One convenient way to do this is to have each director fax or mail in a consent form before the phone meeting. Keep these forms in the corporate record book along with the minutes of the meeting.

The same quorum requirements—generally found in the bylaws—apply to telephone conference meetings as to any other type of directors' meeting. Your president or secretary can begin the meeting by polling the group to be sure the required number of directors are on the line. Your corporate bylaws or the law in your state may provide that if the number of directors participating in a meeting falls below the number required for a quorum, no further action can be taken. This means that if a director leaves the conference call by hanging up and less than a quorum of directors remain on the line, you won't be able to take action until a quorum is reestablished.

Cyberspace meetings are also fine unless a director objects. For technophiles familiar with the many cyberoptions now available for corporate meetings—including video conferencing and computer bulletin boards—holding a directors' meeting by telephone may seem almost quaint. But are these virtual meetings legal? Most state's statutes governing corporate meetings are broad enough to allow meetings through just about any type of telecommunications. But until the legal rules for cybermeetings are better established, if a director objects to using one of the newer methods of holding a meeting where important issues will be discussed and decided, it's still best to meet in person.

Instructions for Form 3F: Minutes of Telephone Conference Directors' Meeting

All the forms in this book are provided as tear-outs in Appendix B and on the accompanying forms CD-ROM. As you read the instructions for Form 3F, you may want to either tear out the form or open the form's file on the CD-ROM so you can follow along. Form 3F is in the file FORM3F.RTF on the CD-ROM. (For more information on using the forms CD-ROM, see Appendix A, "How to Use the CD-ROM.") If you don't use the forms CD-ROM, be sure to photocopy the agreement so you'll have a clean copy to use later.

In the first paragraph, insert the name of the corporation. In the following blank, insert the date of the telephone conference.

In the next paragraph, fill in the starting and ending times.

Next, fill in the actions taken during the meeting.

Date and Signature

Minutes are usually signed by the corporate secretary. Insert the date, the name of the corporate secretary and the name of the corporation.

G. Form 3G: Consent of Shareholders

As explained above, there's more than one way for shareholders to take action. The most familiar way is for shareholders to meet and vote in person, but other ways of recording shareholders' votes are growing in popularity, especially the use of signed consents by shareholders in the absence of a meeting.

Consents are most commonly used when the only purpose of a meeting is to document routine and noncontroversial actions such as reelecting existing directors and especially where one or more shareholders live or work a fair distance from the others. And even if an action is unusual—for example, changing the name of a corporation—if all shareholders (and, of course, most small corporations have fewer than ten) have already discussed and agreed to such a change, a written consent will work fine. In short, using a consent form such as Form 3G: Consent of Shareholders, instead of holding a meeting can often be a convenient and non-controversial alternative to holding a face-to-face meeting.

> **EXAMPLE:** Following the traditional practice, the shareholders of Racafrax Inc. would hold an annual meeting at which they reelect the directors and vote to amend the articles of incorporation to change the name of the corporation. The corporate secretary would then write up those actions in minutes (see Form 3D: Minutes of Shareholders' Meeting) and place the minutes in the corporate record book.

But there's an easier way for Racafrax shareholders to make and document their actions: signed consents without a meeting. If the needed number of Racafrax shareholders sign a consent form sent to them by mail agreeing to these actions, they have the same legal effect as if the shareholders had adopted them at a face-to-face meeting.

Using a written consent in place of minutes makes especially good sense in the following situations:

- **A meeting was missed.** If your corporation failed to hold an annual meeting of shareholders (or several of them) or missed another regularly scheduled meeting, you can fill the gap in your corporate records by having all shareholders sign a consent form that approves the routine actions that would have been taken at an in-person meeting. If, for example, the shareholders missed their December 15, 2000, annual meeting, they might all sign a written consent on February 15, 2001, approving the election of the board of directors, effective as of December 15, 2000. The consent resolution would be dated February 15, 2001—the date the shareholders actually signed it.
- **A one-person corporation.** If you're the only shareholder, there's no sensible way you can hold a meeting with yourself. At the same

time, you still want to observe the traditional corporate formalities in case someone later claims your corporation is a legal sham. Using written consents for your actions as sole shareholder helps establish a paper trail should the validity of your corporation ever be challenged by the IRS or a business creditor.

- **A small family-owned business.** If you own a corporation with your spouse, your kids or a brother or sister, it's likely that you and these family business colleagues agree 100% on all the important corporate issues. Holding a formal meeting to vote on business issues can feel awkward—perhaps ludicrous—and can almost always be avoided by using written consents instead to meet the corporation's legal recordkeeping needs.

 Make sure all shareholders are fully informed of all actions in the absence of a meeting. Actions taken using written consents don't necessarily require the signature of all shareholders. For example, state law may say that a corporation can amend its articles of incorporation if those who own 80% or more of the corporate shares approve such a change. So if a corporation has five shareholders who each own 20% of the stock, four could approve this action by signing a consent form. But if you do take action by written consent rather than by holding a meeting, your bylaws may require you to send prompt notice of the consent action to any shareholders who didn't sign the consent form. Even if the bylaws don't require such a notice, it's a good idea to do so to avoid giving the impression that sneaky things are going on.

Instructions for Form 3G: Consent of Shareholders

All the forms in this book are provided as tear-outs in Appendix B and on the accompanying forms CD-ROM. As you read the instructions for Form 3G, you may want to either tear out the form or open the form's file on the CD-ROM so you can follow along. Form 3G is in the file FORM3G.RTF on the CD-ROM. (For more information on using the forms CD-ROM, see Appendix A, "How to Use the CD-ROM.") If you don't use the forms CD-ROM, be sure to photocopy the agreement so you'll have a clean copy to use later.

Name of Corporation

Insert the name of the corporation.

Actions Taken

Insert the actions agreed to.

SAMPLE:

1. **Amendment of Bylaws:**

   Article I, Section 2, of the corporate bylaws is amended to read as follows:

   "At the annual meeting, shareholders will elect a board of five directors."

2. **Election of Directors:** The following people are elected to serve as directors of the corporation:
   Alice Andreas
   Bill Bonfield
   Connie Carter
   Donna Dowright
   Elena Ellis

3. **Assumed Name:** Beginning April 1, 20___, the corporation will do business under the assumed name of Zanzibar Technologies. The president of the corporation is authorized and directed to file an appropriate Certificate of Assumed Name with the Secretary of State's office.

You should place the signed consent form in your corporate record book along with minutes of meetings.

For more information about using consent forms for taking shareholder action and for examples of language to use, see *The Corporate Minutes Book: The Legal Guide to Taking Care of Corporate Business*, by Anthony Mancuso (Nolo).

Signatures

The consent should be dated and signed by each shareholder.

H. Form 3H: Consent of Directors

As explained in the introduction to this chapter, directors may document their actions by signed consents instead of holding meetings, voting on issues and recording the votes in minutes. Because the legal and practical considerations for the use of such consents by directors are very similar to those governing the use of consents by shareholders, see the introduction to the instructions for Form 3G: Consent of Shareholders.

If fewer than all the directors sign the consent, send a copy to those who didn't sign so they know what's happened and can ask for a meeting to re-open the issue if they disagree. Notifying the non-signers is often required by a corporation's bylaws. As with shareholder consents, it's usually a poor idea to use written consents of directors as a mechanism for avoiding open discussion of controversial issues. Cutting off even one dissenting voice can be a recipe for a lawsuit in any small corporation.

See the instructions for Form 3G for information on why written consents can be especially useful if yours is a one-person corporation.

Instructions for Form 3H: Consent of Directors

All the forms in this book are provided as tear-outs in Appendix B and on the accompanying forms CD-ROM. As you read the instructions for Form 3H, you may want to either tear out the form or open the form's file on the CD-ROM so you can follow along. Form 3H is in the file FORM3H.RTF on the CD-ROM. (For more information on using the forms CD-ROM, see Appendix A, "How to Use the CD-ROM.") If you don't use the forms CD-ROM, be sure to photocopy the agreement so you'll have a clean copy to use later.

Name of Corporation

Insert the name of the corporation.

Actions Taken

Insert the actions taken.

> **SAMPLE:**
>
> 1. **Election of Officers.** The following people were elected to serve in the offices listed next to their names:
>
> | | |
> |---|---|
> | Barbara Alden | President |
> | Jeff Barton | Secretary |
> | Laura Crain | Treasurer |
>
> 2. **Negotiation of Lease.** The president of RacaFrax Inc. is authorized to negotiate and sign a two-year lease for the first floor of 12 Texas Street, Fort Worth, Texas, at a gross rent not to exceed $2,000 a month.
>
> 3. **Corporate Bank Accounts.** The bank accounts of RacaFrax Inc. will be transferred from State Bank to First Thrift Bank (Fort Worth Branch), and the president and treasurer are authorized to sign all documents necessary to make this transfer.

Date and Signatures

Fill in the date. Each consenting director needs to sign.

You should place the signed consent form in your corporate record book along with minutes of meetings. ■

Borrowing Money

Many small businesspeople need more funds than they currently have to buy or expand a small business. And of course, extra cash may be necessary in an emergency to cover extensive unforeseen expenses. No matter what the reason, if you need to tap outside sources for a loan, you essentially have two choices: to borrow the money privately from friends or family members or to apply for loan from a bank or other institution.

Whether you borrow money from a bank or someone you know, you'll sign a promissory note to document your assurance that you'll repay the money. A promissory note says, in effect, "I promise to pay you $_____ plus interest of ____%" and then describes how and when you're to make payments.

This chapter contains four promissory notes designed for use when your business borrows money from a friend or relative. Banks and other commercial lenders write up their own forms for you to sign, so there's no reason to include those forms here.

 Chapter 7 of the *Legal Guide for Starting & Running a Small Business*, by Fred S. Steingold (Nolo), contains in-depth coverage on raising money for your business.

A. Understanding Promissory Notes in General

A promissory note is a binding legal contract. As with all contracts, something of value is exchanged between two parties. In this case, you (the borrower) receive money. The lender receives your promise to repay the money—usually with interest—at specified dates. If you don't meet the repayment terms, the lender can sue and get a judgment against you for the amount you owe plus court costs and possibly lawyers' fees. With a judgment in hand, the lender can then collect the money owed from your bank accounts and other assets.

Before borrowing money and signing a promissory note, you need to fully understand the terms and details.

1. Interest

Unless otherwise specified in the note, interest is paid at the end of the borrowing interval—not in advance. For example, if you borrow money on January 1 and agree to pay interest each month on the first day of the month, your February payment will cover the interest for your use of the money in January.

State usury laws cap the rate of interest a lender can charge—often in the range of 10% to 20% for business loans. A lender who charges more is not allowed to go to court to collect the excess amount and may face other financial penalties. As long as the interest rate doesn't exceed your state's usury law, you and the lender can negotiate any rate that's acceptable to both of you.

State laws generally allow a lender to charge a higher interest rate when a business borrows money than when an individual does—in fact, some states put no limit on the rate of interest a business may be charged. But in several states the borrowing business must be a corporation before a lender can charge the higher rate or be free from interest rate limits.

In the real world, the interest rate charged is rarely a problem. Friends and relatives aren't likely to charge you an excessive interest rate—or, in most instances, sue you if you take too long to pay—so usury laws are rarely a problem. The sensible way to approach interest is to choose a rate that's fair to and benefits everyone involved—slightly lower than you'd pay a commercial lender and slightly more than the lender would earn in a safe investment (such as a money market fund). Check the usury law of your state only if the rate exceeds 10%.

2. Personal Guarantee

If your business is organized as a sole proprietorship or general partnership, by definition you'll be personally liable for repaying the business loan. On the other hand, if your business is organized as a corporation or limited liability company, and you sign a promissory note on behalf of the corporation or the LLC, you are not personally liable for repayment. The lender can look only to your business's assets for repayment. For this reason, a bank or other commercial lender usually requires you to personally guarantee repayment of a loan to your corporation or LLC, in which case you make yourself personally liable. If your business doesn't repay the loan, the lender can sue you and go after your personal assets, as if you hadn't organized as a corporation or LLC in the first place.

 Personal guarantees are discussed in Chapter 1, Section B3.

Of course, commercial lenders aren't the only ones who want to be repaid. A financially savvy friend or relative may also ask you to personally guarantee the repayment of a loan to your corporation or LLC. Chapter 1 contains language you can add to a promissory note to personally guarantee a loan.

If your spouse is asked to guarantee repayment of a loan, be aware of the possible consequences. Your spouse's personal liability added to your own will place at risk any property you and your spouse own jointly, as well as your spouse's separate property and wages. Generally, a lender is more likely to require your spouse's guarantee if you're borrowing money for a sole proprietorship than if the loan is being made to a partnership, corporation or limited liability company.

Others may guarantee repayment. If you're starting a new business, a lender may conclude that the business is not sufficiently creditworthy to qualify for a loan, even if you and your spouse personally guarantee repayment. The solution may be to ask a parent, aunt, uncle or close friend —someone with greater financial resources than you—to guarantee repayment. If you do that, however, be sure to fully disclose all the risks you're aware of to your friend or relative. A co-guarantor (often called a co-signer) must be told that he or she is on the hook to repay the loan if you and your business can't. And a co-guarantor should understand that guaranteeing your loan could impair his or her ability to borrow money.

3. Get Permission to Borrow

If your business is a corporation, the board of directors should adopt a corporate resolution approving not only the borrowing of money but also the pledging of corporate assets as security for the loan. And, even though it's probably not required by your bylaws or state law, it's a good idea to get written permission from any shareholders who are not also directors. This will forestall shareholder grumbling if the corporation can't repay the loan and corporate assets are liquidated by the lender. A commercial lender will want to see the board of directors' resolution authorizing the loan. A friend or relative who lends you money is less likely to insist on seeing it. Similarly—and for the same reasons—if your business is an LLC, get written permission from all the members before borrowing money or pledging LLC assets as collateral for a loan. A commercial lender may have its own form that you can use for this purpose.

4. Security Interest

In addition to having you personally guarantee a loan, a bank or other commercial lender may want to obtain a security interest in (have a lien on) business property—or possibly nonbusiness property such as your house. If you default on the loan, the lender will have the right to seize and sell the property to pay off the loan, without having to sue you first. By contrast, if you default on a loan for which you're personally liable but haven't granted a security interest, the lender will have to sue you, get a judgment, locate your available assets and seize them to collect what you owe.

A friend or relative who lends you money for your business isn't as likely as a commercial lender to ask for the loan to be secured. Still, you may decide that it's a fair feature or enticement to offer the lender—or you may simply want to give a cautious lender some additional peace of mind about full repayment.

The promissory notes in this chapter can be used for secured loans. Use Form 4G: Security Agreement, to supplement a promissory note where tangible personal property—furniture and equipment, for example—is being pledged as security. For further protection, a commercial lender may also ask you to sign a Uniform Commercial Code (UCC) Financing Statement, which can be filed with a designated state or county official to provide notice to the public that the lender has a security interest in the pledged property. While a friend or relative isn't likely to insist that you sign a Financing Statement, you may feel it's appropriate to offer this extra measure of legal protection.

⚠ **Don't pledge more property than necessary.** When you pledge assets to secure the repayment of money you're borrowing, pledge only enough property to cover the loan. You want be free to sell your other assets or possibly to use them to secure additional loans.

💼 **Pledging real estate as security requires professional assistance.** If you pledge your home or other real estate as security for a business loan, a security agreement won't be adequate to protect the lender. A well-informed lender will ask you to sign a mortgage or a deed of trust to be recorded (filed) with the county records office to establish the lender's interest in your real estate. Procedures for preparing and recording mortgages and deeds of trust are somewhat technical and vary from state to state; it's wise to seek the assistance of a real estate lawyer.

5. Acceleration Clause

The promissory notes in this chapter contain what is commonly called an acceleration clause. This bit of legal jargon simply means that if you don't make a required payment within a specified number of days after it becomes due, the lender can demand payment of the entire loan amount. If you still don't pay, the lender can sue you for the entire amount owed. Without an acceleration clause, the lender would have to sue each time you missed a payment or wait until you missed all installments to sue for the whole amount. Either choice would be unfairly burdensome.

6. Late Fee

A lender may want to include a clause in the promissory note tacking on a late charge for payments not made on time. Resist this one. If a payment is late, interest continues to run on the principal balance owed, meaning the lender is already being compensated for your use of the money over more time. A late charge means the lender is double-dipping.

7. Prepayment

The promissory notes in this chapter allow you to pay off the loan early. You can do this by increasing each installment payment, increasing some installment payments or making occasional additional payments. If you have the money to pay early, doing so reduces the overall amount of interest you'll pay. Some states guarantee borrowers this right. In other states, however, lenders can charge a penalty amounting to a portion of future interest when you pay back a loan early unless the promissory note states that prepayment will be allowed without penalty.

⚠️ Even if you prepay some of the loan, you still must make your regular monthly installment payments. Suppose that on June 1 you make your normal monthly installment payment of $200. To reduce the principal amount, you pay $1,000 extra. Even though you may think you've paid five months in advance, you haven't. On July 1—and on the first day of each month after that—you still must make your normal monthly payment of $200 until the loan is paid off. In short, if you make extra payments, be sure you'll still have enough cash on hand to make regular payments as they become due.

8. Fees and Costs

The promissory notes in this chapter require you to pay the lender's costs and lawyers fees if the lender must sue to collect on the note.

9. Signing and Storing Your Promissory Note

Sign only the original promissory note and give it to the lender to keep. Keep a photocopy of the signed note (marked "COPY") for your records. The lender should return the original to you when you've paid the note off.

 For more information on getting approval from corporate directors and shareholders for borrowing money and pledging assets, see *The Corporate Minutes Book: The Legal Guide to Taking Care of Corporate Business*, by Anthony Mancuso (Nolo).

10. Amending a Promissory Note

Occasionally, you and the lender may want to change the terms of an existing promissory note. The best way to do this is to prepare and sign a new promissory note containing the new terms. Include the following language in the new promissory note:

> This promissory note replaces the $_____ promissory note signed by Borrower on _____, 20___, and payable to Lender.

Remember, you should never rely on oral understandings about your rights or obligations under an agreement, particularly with a promissory note, where your good credit is at stake. This means that everything that you and your lender agree on should be clearly written into the note itself, and every change you agree on should be taken care of in a written amendment. Fortunately, the promissory notes in this chapter contain an integration clause and a modification clause. For more information on how these standard clauses work, see Chapter 1, Section C.

Be sure the lender returns the original promissory note to you in exchange for the new note.

⚠️ **Somebody else may be collecting on your promissory note.** As you may know, it's quite common for a commercial lender to assign a promissory note to some other lending institution. When that happens, you must make any remaining payments to the new owner of the note. Now if the lender is a friend or family member, assigning a promissory note is much less common—but it can happen. An assignment shouldn't change your obligations under the note, just who you are supposed to pay.

B. The Promissory Notes in This Chapter

The main differences among the four promissory notes in this chapter concern how you'll pay back the loan.

- **Form 4C: Promissory Note (Equal Monthly Payments; All Principal and Interest Paid).** This note requires you to pay the same amount each month for a specified number of months. Part of each payment goes toward interest and the rest goes toward principal. When you make the last payment, the loan and interest are fully paid. In legal and accounting jargon, this type of loan is said to be fully amortized over the period that the payments are made.

- **Form 4D: Promissory Note (Equal Monthly Payments; Large Final Balloon Payment).** This note requires you to make equal monthly payments of principal and interest for a relatively short period of time. These payments do not pay off (or amortize) the loan, however. Instead, after you make the last installment payment, you'll still owe a balance—and you must pay that balance in one payment, called a balloon payment. This type of promissory note offers definite benefits to the borrower—primarily lower monthly payments during the course of the loan, thus keeping cash available for other needs.

EXAMPLE: Phil needs some start-up money for his new business. Cousin Edna is willing to lend him $20,000 at 7% interest, but she'd like to have all the money back in two years when she plans to modernize her kitchen and bathroom. Phil and Edna agree that Phil will pay back $200 a month for two years. At the end of two years, Phil will have reduced the loan balance from $20,000 to $17,589.94. (The rest of his payments will have gone toward interest.) Phil will owe this balance to Edna in one balloon payment. Phil is comfortable with this arrangement. If he doesn't have the cash to pay the balloon payment, he knows he can refinance his house with the bank to pay off Edna.

- **Form 4E: Promissory Note (Payments of Interest Only; Large Final Balloon Payment of Principal).** With this type of note, you repay the lender by making payments of interest at specified intervals such as monthly. At the end of the loan term, you must make a balloon payment to cover all the principal and any remaining interest.

- **Form 4F: Promissory Note (Single Payment of Principal and Interest).** With this type of promissory note, you pay off the loan at a specified date in one payment that includes the entire principal amount and the accrued interest.

EXAMPLE: Renee borrows $15,000 from her former college roommate for her graphic design business. The loan is at 8% and is to be repaid in one payment in seven years. Unless Renee pays back the loan early, she will owe $23,400.

 Promissory notes can help preserve friendships and family harmony. It's smart to sign a promissory note even if the friend or relative from whom you're borrowing assures you that such formality isn't necessary. Think of it this way: documenting the loan can do no harm—and it can head off misunderstandings about whether the money is a loan or gift, when it is to be repaid and how much interest is owed.

Equity Investments: Another Way to Raise Money

New or expanding businesses that need cash some-times seek equity investors who will buy a piece of the business. Investors stand to make money if your business succeeds and to lose money if it fails. The advantage to this arrangement is that unlike borrowing money, you normally make no commitment to investors that they'll get their money back if things go poorly. Of course, in exchange for this freedom from debt worries, there is a significant disadvantage—you relinquish (sell) a share of your business in exchange for the investment. If your business flourishes, your investors will own part of your success.

Depending on the arrangements you make, equity investors may or may not be entitled to participate in making business decisions. Almost surely they will be entitled to share in any profits your business earns. And if your business prospers and you sell it someday, the investors will be entitled to a chunk of what you receive in proportion to their share in the business.

Special state and federal securities laws govern the sale of interests to these equity investors. If you're interested in pursuing this route, consult a small business expert to make sure you comply with these often complicated laws.

C. Form 4C: Promissory Note (Equal Monthly Installments; All Principal and Interest Paid)

If you've ever taken out a mortgage or car loan, you're familiar with how repayment works. You pay off the loan in equal monthly payments over a set

time, usually a number of years. Each of your monthly payments is partly applied to interest and partly to principal. As the amount you owe declines, the amount of each payment that goes to principal and interest changes (the principal portion gradually goes up while the interest portion goes down). This is called amortizing the loan.

If you know the amount you plan to borrow (the principal amount) the interest rate and the number of years over which you'll make payments, you can consult an amortization schedule in a book or on computer software to arrive at the monthly payment. With software such as *Quicken, Lotus 1-2-3, Microsoft Excel* or *Banker's Secret,* you can print out a schedule showing how much of each payment will go toward interest and how much toward principal.

If you don't have immediate access to computer software to calculate the amortization, the chart below can help you determine what amount needs to be paid each month to pay off a loan over time. Here's how to use it:

Step 1. In the left-hand column of the chart, find your interest rate.

Step 2. At the top of the chart, find the period of time you'll have to repay the loan—the period between the making of the loan and the date all principal will be paid.

Step 3. Find the figure where the two columns intersect. For instance, if the interest rate is 10% and the loan will be paid over five years, the figure at the intersection point is .0212.

Step 4. Multiply that figure by the principal amount of the loan. The product is the monthly payment, which includes principal and interest.

EXAMPLE: Vladimir makes a loan of $10,000 at 10% interest. The loan is payable in monthly installments over five years. Vladimir multiplies .0212 by $10,000 to get $212, the amount of each monthly payment.

Amortization Chart for Monthly Payments

Interest Rate	\multicolumn{9}{Number of Years}								
	1	**1.5**	**2**	**2.5**	**3**	**4**	**5**	**6**	**7**
3.0%	0.0847	0.0569	0.0430	0.0346	0.0291	0.0221	0.0180	0.0152	0.0132
3.5%	0.0849	0.0571	0.0432	0.0349	0.0293	0.0224	0.0182	0.0154	0.0134
4.0%	0.0851	0.0573	0.0434	0.0351	0.0295	0.0226	0.0184	0.0156	0.0137
4.5%	0.0854	0.0576	0.0436	0.0353	0.0297	0.0228	0.0186	0.0159	0.0139
5.0%	0.0856	0.0578	0.0439	0.0355	0.0300	0.0230	0.0189	0.0161	0.0141
5.5%	0.0858	0.0580	0.0441	0.0358	0.0302	0.0233	0.0191	0.0163	0.0144
6.0%	0.0861	0.0582	0.0443	0.0360	0.0304	0.0235	0.0193	0.0166	0.0146
6.5%	0.0863	0.0585	0.0445	0.0362	0.0306	0.0237	0.0196	0.0168	0.0148
7.0%	0.0865	0.0587	0.0448	0.0364	0.0309	0.0239	0.0198	0.0170	0.0151
7.5%	0.0868	0.0589	0.0450	0.0367	0.0311	0.0242	0.0200	0.0173	0.0153
8.0%	0.0870	0.0591	0.0452	0.0369	0.0313	0.0244	0.0203	0.0175	0.0156
8.5%	0.0872	0.0594	0.0455	0.0371	0.0316	0.0246	0.0205	0.0178	0.0158
9.0%	0.0875	0.0596	0.0457	0.0373	0.0318	0.0249	0.0208	0.0180	0.0161
9.5%	0.0877	0.0598	0.0459	0.0376	0.0320	0.0251	0.0210	0.0183	0.0163
10.0%	0.0879	0.0601	0.0461	0.0378	0.0323	0.0254	0.0212	0.0185	0.0166
10.5%	0.0881	0.0603	0.0464	0.0380	0.0325	0.0256	0.0215	0.0188	0.0169
11.0%	0.0884	0.0605	0.0466	0.0383	0.0327	0.0258	0.0217	0.0190	0.0171
11.5%	0.0886	0.0608	0.0468	0.0385	0.0330	0.0261	0.0220	0.0193	0.0174
12.0%	0.0888	0.0610	0.0471	0.0387	0.0332	0.0263	0.0222	0.0196	0.0177

Interest Rate	\multicolumn{9}{Number of Years}								
	8	**9**	**10**	**11**	**12**	**13**	**14**	**15**	**20**
3.0%	0.0117	0.0106	0.0097	0.0089	0.0083	0.0077	0.0073	0.0069	0.0055
3.5%	0.0120	0.0108	0.0099	0.0091	0.0085	0.0080	0.0075	0.0071	0.0058
4.0%	0.0122	0.0110	0.0101	0.0094	0.0088	0.0082	0.0078	0.0074	0.0061
4.5%	0.0124	0.0113	0.0104	0.0096	0.0090	0.0085	0.0080	0.0076	0.0063
5.0%	0.0127	0.0115	0.0106	0.0099	0.0092	0.0087	0.0083	0.0079	0.0066
5.5%	0.0129	0.0118	0.0109	0.0101	0.0095	0.0090	0.0085	0.0082	0.0069
6.0%	0.0131	0.0120	0.0111	0.0104	0.0098	0.0092	0.0088	0.0084	0.0072
6.5%	0.0134	0.0123	0.0114	0.0106	0.0100	0.0095	0.0091	0.0087	0.0075
7.0%	0.0136	0.0125	0.0116	0.0109	0.0103	0.0098	0.0094	0.0090	0.0078
7.5%	0.0139	0.0128	0.0119	0.0111	0.0106	0.0101	0.0096	0.0093	0.0081
8.0%	0.0141	0.0130	0.0121	0.0114	0.0108	0.0103	0.0099	0.0096	0.0084
8.5%	0.0144	0.0133	0.0124	0.0117	0.0111	0.0106	0.0102	0.0098	0.0087
9.0%	0.0147	0.0135	0.0127	0.0120	0.0114	0.0109	0.0105	0.0101	0.0090
9.5%	0.0149	0.0138	0.0129	0.0122	0.0117	0.0112	0.0108	0.0104	0.0093
10.0%	0.0152	0.0141	0.0132	0.0125	0.0120	0.0115	0.0111	0.0107	0.0097
10.5%	0.0154	0.0144	0.0135	0.0128	0.0122	0.0118	0.0114	0.0111	0.0100
11.0%	0.0157	0.0146	0.0138	0.0131	0.0125	0.0121	0.0117	0.0114	0.0103
11.5%	0.0160	0.0149	0.0141	0.0134	0.0128	0.0124	0.0120	0.0117	0.0107
12.0%	0.0163	0.0152	0.0143	0.0137	0.0131	0.0127	0.0123	0.0120	0.0110

Instructions for Form 4C: Promissory Note (Equal Monthly Installments; All Principal and Interest Paid)

All the forms in this book are provided as tear-outs in Appendix B and on the accompanying forms CD-ROM. As you read the instructions for Form 4C, you may want to either tear out the form or open the form's file on the CD-ROM so you can follow along. Form 4C is in the file FORM4C.RTF on the CD-ROM. (For more information on using the forms CD-ROM, see Appendix A, "How to Use the CD-ROM.") If you don't use the forms CD-ROM, be sure to photocopy the agreement so you'll have a clean copy to use later.

1. Names

In the first blank, insert the name of the borrower's business. In the second blank, insert the lender's name.

See the introduction to this chapter for a discussion of the situations when you may be putting your personal assets as well as your business at risk in borrowing money.

2. Promise to Pay

In the first blank, insert the principal amount of the loan. Next fill in the annual interest rate.

The phrase "For value received" is legal jargon meaning that you have received something—in this case, money—from the lender in exchange for your promise to pay money. It's there because the law requires that for your promise to pay to be binding, you must receive something of value from the other party.

3. Monthly Installments

Insert the number of monthly payments you'll make to repay the loan and the amount of each installment. As noted, the accompanying amortization chart allows you to quickly calculate the amount of each installment.

4. Date of Installment Payments

Insert the day of the month when payments will be made and the date the first payment is due. For example, if you borrow money on January 15, 2001, you might provide for payments to be made on the 15th of each month, with the first payment due on February 15, 2001.

5. Application of Payments

You don't need to insert anything here. Each payment automatically goes to pay accrued interest first. The rest goes toward the remaining principal. These allocations are easily handled by number-crunching software such as *Quicken* or a spreadsheet program. Basically, here's how it works. Assume that the annual interest rate is 8% on a $5,000 loan and that the promissory note calls for monthly installment payments. To determine the interest portion of the payment, you'd divide the annual interest by 12. To illustrate:

Loan balance	$5,000.00
Interest rate	x .08
Annual interest	$ 400.00
Payments per year	÷ 12
Interest for first month	$ 33.33

If you're making payments of $200.00 each month, your payment for the current month would be applied as follows:

Interest	$ 33.33
Principal	$ 166.67
Total	$ 200.00

That would leave a principal balance of $4,833.33 ($5,000.00 less $166.67) remaining on the loan. So next month, since the principal is less, the interest portion of your $200.00 payment will be a bit less and the principal portion will be a bit more.

6. Prepayment

This paragraph allows you to prepay the money you've borrowed—that is, pay all or part of the principal in advance. As discussed in the introduction to this chapter, by prepaying, you cut down on the total amount of interest you pay. You don't need to insert anything here.

7. Loan Acceleration

It's typical in a promissory note to provide that if a payment is late by more than a specified number of days, the lender can declare the entire unpaid balance due. As discussed in the introduction to this chapter, this is called an "acceleration clause." All you need do is fill the number of days that will trigger acceleration. Thirty days is often appropriate when the lender is a friend or relative.

8. Security

Check the first box if the note is unsecured, meaning that the lender does not have a lien on or security interest in any property.

Check the second box if you're giving the lender a security interest in business property. Insert the name of the business. You can use Form 4G: Security Agreement. You should also sign a Uniform Commercial Code Financing Statement which the lender can record (file) with the appropriate state or county office. When you pay off the loan, the lender must give you an official discharge of the financing statement which you should then file at the same place where the financing statement was filed.

Check the third box if you're giving the lender a lien on real estate owned by you or the business. Check the box indicating whether this will be done by a mortgage or deed of trust. The practice varies from state to state. Finally, insert the legal description of the real estate as found in your deed or title insurance policy.

 Have a lawyer prepare the mortgage or deed of trust. Because of the technical intricacies of real estate titles, it's best to have an expert draft the mortgage or deed of trust that will secure the loan. After the loan is made, it's the job of the lender to see that the mortgage or deed of trust gets recorded at the appropriate county records office. When the loan is paid, the lender should remove the lien (security interest) by giving

you a discharge of the mortgage or deed of trust that you can record where the original document was recorded.

9. Collection Costs

Nothing needs to be filled in here. This paragraph requires you to pay the lender's reasonable costs and lawyer's fees if the lender takes you to court to collect on the note and wins the lawsuit.

Standard Clauses

The remainder of the note contains the standard clauses we discussed in Chapter 1, Section C. The only thing you'll need to fill in here is the name of the state whose law will apply to the note in the paragraph "Governing Law."

Signature and Guarantee

If you're a sole proprietor or partner and sign the note, you'll be personally liable for repaying it. This means that if the payments aren't made, the lender can get a court judgment against you and collect it not only out of business assets but from your personal assets as well.

By contrast, if you sign as a member or manager of a limited liability company or as an officer of a corporation, you'll not be personally liable for repayment; the lender can only get a court judgment against the LLC or corporation and collect from its assets. For that reason, the lender may want you to add a personal guarantee to the loan, in which case you'll be personally liable for repayment. If this is the case, add the appropriate guarantee language from the file SIGNING at the end of the promissory note. See the introduction to this chapter and Chapter 1, Section B3, for more information about personal guarantees.

Only the borrower and guarantors, if any, sign the note. The lender does not sign it. (See Chapter 1, Section B, on signing contracts.)

 Guarantee language that you can copy and paste into these promissory notes is included in the file SIGNING.

D. Form 4D: Promissory Note (Equal Monthly Payments; Large Final Balloon Payment)

Suppose you borrow money and would like to spread out the repayment over four years, but the burden of making installment payments sufficient to pay it off in that time would be too great. To allow you to conserve cash, the lender might agree to compute the monthly payments based on an eight-year amortization period—making the monthly payments substantially lower. You'd also agree that at the end of the four years, you'd pay off whatever was still owing on the loan by making a lump-sum or balloon payment. Form 4D is designed for this type of loan.

> **EXAMPLE:** Phyllis is arranging to borrow $20,000 from her uncle Ted to start a transcription service for doctors who dictate their medical charts. They agree that Phyllis will repay the loan by making monthly payments over a four-year period and that the yearly interest rate will be 8%. Using *Quicken's* amortization feature, Phyllis and Ted determine that it would take monthly payments of $488.26 to pay off the loan in full by the end of the fourth year. But this worries Phyllis, since in the first few months making payments of that size would pinch the tiny cash flow of her new business. To make things easier for Phyllis, she and Ted agree to the following: Phyllis will pay $282.73 a month—the amount it would take to amortize the loan over an eight-year period. At the end of four years, Phyllis will make a lump-sum payment of $11,864.27 to pay off the remaining principal balance.

Amortization computations may vary.
The figures in the above example were derived using Quicken's amortization feature. If you use the chart provided earlier in this chapter, you'll find that the computations are rounded off: the monthly installments for the four-year period are calculated at $488; the eight-year figure is $283, with the balloon payment of $11,900.

Instructions for Form 4D: Promissory Note (Equal Monthly Payments; Large Final Balloon Payment)

All the forms in this book are provided as tear-outs in Appendix B and on the accompanying forms CD-ROM. As you read the instructions for Form 4D, you may want to either tear out the form or open the form's file on the CD-ROM so you can follow along. Form 4D is in the file FORM4D.RTF on the CD-ROM. (For more information on using the forms CD-ROM, see Appendix A, "How to Use the CD-ROM.") If you don't use the forms CD-ROM, be sure to photocopy the agreement so you'll have a clean copy to use later.

1. Names
In the first blank, insert the name of your business. In the next blank, insert the lender's name.

See the introduction to this chapter for a discussion of when you may be putting your personal assets as well as your business at risk in borrowing money.

2. Promise to Pay
In the first blank, insert the amount of the loan. Next fill in the annual interest rate. For information on interest rates and usury laws, see the introduction to this chapter. To understand the legal meaning of the phrase, "For value received," see the instructions for paragraph 2 of Form 4C.

3. Monthly Installments
Insert the number of installment payments you'll make and the amount of each installment. As noted above, an amortization schedule—from a book or software—can help you figure out the amount of the installments.

4. Date of Payments

Insert the day of the month when the regular monthly payments will be made and the due date of the first payment. For example, if you borrow money on January 15, 2001, you might provide for payments to be made on the 15th day of each month, with the first payment due on February 15, 2001.

In the final space, insert the date by which you'll make the balloon payment covering the entire balance of principal and interest.

5. Application of Payments

You don't need to insert anything here. Each payment pays the accrued interest first. The rest goes toward the principal.

See the instructions for paragraph 5 of Form 4C.

6. Prepayment

See the instructions for paragraph 6 of Form 4C. You don't need to insert anything here.

7. Loan Acceleration

See the instructions for paragraph 7 of Form 4C.

8. Security

See the instructions for paragraph 8 of Form 4C.

9. Collection Costs

Nothing needs to be filled in here. See the instructions for paragraph 9 of Form 4C.

Standard Clauses

The remainder of the note contains the standard clauses we discussed in Chapter 1, Section C. The only thing you'll need to fill in here is the name of the state whose law will apply to the note in the paragraph "Governing Law."

Signature and Guarantee

See the instructions for Form 4C.

E. Form 4E: Promissory Note (Payments of Interest Only; Large Final Balloon Payment)

You and the lender may agree that you'll make monthly payments of interest, and then pay off the entire principal in one lump sum at a date some months or years down the line. Form 4E is designed for this purpose. The advantage of this method is that the periodic payments you make will be lower than if you were to make payments that included both interest and principal. The disadvantage is that since you're borrowing the principal for a longer time, you'll be paying more interest.

> **EXAMPLE:** Peter borrows $20,000 at 8% interest from a family friend, Tracy, to expand his used CD business. Tracy will need the entire amount back by the end of four years to make a down payment on a vacation cabin she plans to buy. Using an amortization book, Peter figures out that if he pays back the debt in equal installments each month for four years, each payment will need to be $488.26—a bit more than he can handle right now. But if he pays interest only, his payments will be only $133.33 a month.

Peter and Tracy agree to this arrangement, giving Peter four years to raise the $20,000 that will be needed to pay back the entire principal. Peter isn't worried because he firmly believes his business will be strong enough by then that he'll have no problem refinancing through a bank loan, if necessary.

Note the higher cost to Peter of doing it this way. He'll be making 48 payments of interest totaling $6,400 plus the repayment of the $20,000 —which adds up to $26,400. If, instead, he amortizes the loan over four years by making 48 monthly payments of $488.26 each, his total cost will be $23,436.48, which is nearly $3,000 less. Of course, the interest on business loans is a tax deductible expense which cushions the impact a bit.

 Interest-only payments afford the borrower maximum flexibility. If a borrower gets a lender to agree to the interest-only method and then finds herself in the happy position of having a lot of cash on hand, she can prepay some of the principal, thus reducing the interest payments. But if cash flow isn't so great, she's under no pressure to pay any part of the principal until the end of the loan period, at which point she may have other alternatives, such as borrowing the necessary payback amount from a commercial lender.

Instructions for Form 4E: Promissory Note (Payments of Interest Only; Large Final Balloon Payment)

All the forms in this book are provided as tear-outs in Appendix B and on the accompanying forms CD-ROM. As you read the instructions for Form 4E, you may want to either tear out the form or open the form's file on the CD-ROM so you can follow along. Form 4E is in the file FORM4E.RTF on the CD-ROM. (For more information on using the forms CD-ROM, see Appendix A, "How to Use the CD-ROM.") If you

don't use the forms CD-ROM, be sure to photocopy the agreement so you'll have a clean copy to use later.

1. Names

In the first blank, insert the name of your business. In the next blank, insert the lender's name.

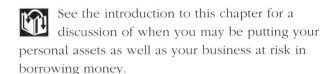 See the introduction to this chapter for a discussion of when you may be putting your personal assets as well as your business at risk in borrowing money.

2. Promise to Pay

In the first blank, insert the amount of the loan. Next fill in the annual interest rate. See the introduction to this chapter and the instructions for paragraph 2 of Form 4C.

3. Interest Payments

Here you provide the repayment schedule you and your lender agree on. Check only one box. (CD-ROM users should delete the unused text.)

Check the first box if you'll pay interest annually and insert the date of each annual payment—for example, "January 1." In the next blank, fill in the year you'll make the first interest payment.

Check the second box if you'll make regular monthly interest payments. In the first blank, insert the day of the month and when you'll begin—for example, the 15th day of each month. Then fill in the month interest payments will begin—for example, January 15, 2001.

Check the third box if you plan to pay interest at intervals other than annually or monthly, such as the 15th day of January, April, July and October beginning April 15, 2001. Use the blanks to specify the details.

The lender may prefer monthly payments. From the lender's point of view, requiring monthly payments can make good sense, since it gets the borrower in the habit of paying regularly.

4. Principal Payment

Insert the date by which you'll repay the principal. Even if it's several years in the future, you need to set a date so that interest payments don't go on indefinitely.

5. Prepayment

This paragraph allows you (but doesn't require you) to prepay—that is, pay in advance—on the principal. By prepaying principal, you cut down on the overall amount of interest you pay. You don't need to insert anything here. See the discussion of prepayments in the introduction to this chapter.

6. Loan Acceleration

Insert how many days the borrower will have before owing late charges. See the introduction to this chapter for information about late charges.

7. Security

See the instructions for paragraph 8 of Form 4C.

8. Collection Costs

Nothing needs to be filled in here. See the instructions for paragraph 9 of Form 4C.

Standard Clauses

The remainder of the note contains the standard clauses we discussed in Chapter 1, Section C. The only thing you'll need to fill in here is the name of the state whose law will apply to the note in the paragraph "Governing Law."

Signature and Guarantee

See the instructions for Form 4C.

F. Form 4F: Promissory Note (Single Payment of Principal and Interest)

If you and the lender prefer to keep things really simple, Form 4F may fit your needs. Here you agree to pay off the money you borrowed plus interest in one single payment. This works best for a short-term loan or possibly a loan from an affluent parent or grandparent to a child where the promise to repay is seen as an expression of the younger person's intent—not something that the lender would ever really enforce in court if the payment were delayed.

A will or trust can address fairness issues within a family. A large loan from a parent to a child can cause friction among siblings—especially if the parent dies before the child fully repays it. One solution is for the parent to provide in a will or living trust that any unpaid loan will be treated as a partial advance payment of that child's inheritance.

Instructions for Form 4F: Promissory Note (Single Payment of Principal and Interest)

All the forms in this book are provided as tear-outs in Appendix B and on the accompanying forms CD-ROM. As you read the instructions for Form 4F, you may want to either tear out the form or open the form's file on the CD-ROM so you can follow along. Form 4F is in the file FORM4F.RTF on the CD-ROM. (For more information on using the forms CD-ROM, see Appendix A, "How to Use the CD-ROM.") If you don't use the forms CD-ROM, be sure to photocopy the agreement so you'll have a clean copy to use later.

1. Names

In the first blank, insert the name of your business. In the next, insert the lender's name.

See the introduction to this chapter for a discussion of when you may be putting your personal assets as well as your business at risk in borrowing money.

2. Promise to Pay

In the first blank, insert the amount of the loan. Next fill in the annual interest rate. See the instructions to Form 4C.

3. Payment Date

Insert the date by which you'll repay the entire amount of the loan plus interest.

4. Prepayment

This paragraph allows you to prepay—that is, pay in advance—on the principal. By prepaying, you cut down on the overall amount of interest you pay. You don't need to insert anything here. For a discussion of prepayments, see the introduction to this chapter.

5. Security

See the instructions for paragraph 8 of Form 4C.

6. Collection Costs

Nothing needs to be filled in here. See the instructions for paragraph 9 of Form 4C.

Standard Clauses

The remainder of the note contains the standard clauses we discussed in Chapter 1, Section C. The only thing you'll need to fill in here is the name of the state whose law will apply to the note in the paragraph "Governing Law."

Signature and Guarantee

See the instructions for Form 4C.

G. Form 4G: Security Agreement (For Tangible Personal Property)

Someone lending money to your business may feel more confident about the loan if he or she is given a security interest in the assets of the business. Then, if you don't repay the loan as promised, the lender can take the property you've pledged, sell it and use the proceeds to at least partially repay the borrowed amount. Providing security, of course, is just what you do when you borrow money to help finance a house purchase and give the lender a mortgage or deed of trust empowering the lender to take and sell the house if you default on the loan.

Before completing and signing a security agreement for a business loan, it helps to know how the law classifies property.

Real estate or **real property** refers to land and the buildings attached to land. To grant a lender a security interest in (or lien on) real estate you own, you'd sign a mortgage or deed of trust. The lender would then record (file) the mortgage or deed of trust with a county land records office where it would become a matter of public record.

Personal property includes all property that's not real estate. It can be property you use for personal purposes, such as your car, boat, clothes and saxophone, as well as property used in or owned by your business, such as a business truck, machinery, a copy machine, a computer or furniture. Personal property is of two types:

- **Tangible personal property**—property you can actually see and touch such as a car or desk.
- **Intangible personal property**—property that's an abstract legal right, often represented by a document or certificate. It includes a bank account, certificate of deposit, stock in a corporation, the right to collect rent under a lease, accounts receivable and a copyright, trademark or patent.

While it's possible for a business or an individual to pledge intangible personal property as security for a loan, it's far more common—and legally simpler—to pledge real estate or tangible personal property. Form 4G can be used where you're pledging some or all of your business's tangible personal property as security.

Get help if you're using real estate as security for a loan. This form is intended only for tangible personal property. As explained in the introduction to this chapter, if you pledge your home or other real estate as security for a business loan, a security agreement won't be adequate to protect the lender. A well-informed lender will ask you to sign a mortgage or a deed of trust which can then be recorded (filed) with a designated county official to establish the lender's security interest in the real estate. Because title to real estate is a highly technical matter beyond the scope of this book, you should seek the assistance of a real estate lawyer before signing a mortgage or deed of trust.

For similar reasons, you should consult an intellectual property lawyer for help in pledging intangible personal property such as a copyright, trademark or patent as security for a loan. You should also consult a small business expert if you want to pledge your ownership interest in your business, such as your shares of stock in your corporation, as collateral for the loan.

Instructions for Form 4G: Security Agreement (For Tangible Personal Property)

All the forms in this book are provided as tear-outs in Appendix B and on the accompanying forms CD-ROM. As you read the instructions for Form 4G, you may want to either tear out the form or open the form's file on the CD-ROM so you can follow along. Form 4G is in the file FORM4G.RTF on the CD-ROM. (For more information on using the forms CD-ROM, see Appendix A, "How to Use the CD-ROM.") If you don't use the forms CD-ROM, be sure to photocopy the agreement so you'll have a clean copy to use later.

1. Names
In the first blank, fill in your name. In the second, fill in the lender's name.

 Get permission from directors, shareholders and members before pledging assets. As explained in the introduction to this chapter, if your business is a corporation or an LLC, the board of directors or members should adopt a resolution approving not only the borrowing of money but also the pledging of company assets as

security for the loan. And it's a good idea to get written permission from shareholders who are not directors or members who are not managers as well.

2. Grant of Security Interest
You may need to check more than one box.

You'll almost certainly check the first box, which refers to the tangible personal property listed in the Attachment. (See the explanation of the term tangible personal property in the introduction to these instructions.) Typically, you'll list in the Attachment the items that your business currently owns—or some of them. When you check the first box, also fill in the name by which your business is known.

The lender may also want a security interest in any other property you add to the business, including replacement inventory. In that case, check the second box as well.

Check the third box if you're going to pledge tangible personal property that you own or a single item of business property—a car, for example—and then describe the item you're pledging.

As noted in the introduction to this chapter, you should pledge enough property to cover the loan, but not more.

3. Security for Promissory Note
Fill in the amount borrowed under the promissory note and the interest rate.

4. Financing Statement
You don't need to insert anything in this paragraph. It confirms that you'll sign a financing statement—a Uniform Commercial Code form (called Form UCC-1) that's filed with a governmental agency in your state to let the public know that the property you're using in your business is subject to the lender's lien. Anyone checking the public records—a bank's loan department, for example—will learn that your friend or relative who's lending money to your business has a prior lien on the property described in the notice.

A sample UCC-1 is included below. Some states now accept a national, standardized form, but not

THIS SPACE FOR USE OF FILING OFFICER

FINANCING STATEMENT — FOLLOW INSTRUCTIONS CAREFULLY
This Financing Statement is presented for filing pursuant to the Uniform Commercial Code and will remain effective, with certain exceptions, for 5 years from date of filing.

A. NAME & TEL. # OF CONTACT AT FILER (optional)	B. FILING OFFICE ACCT. # (optional)
Edward Brown 555-123-5555	

C. RETURN COPY TO: (Name and Mailing Address)

Olde Lighting, Inc.
555 Eastern Drive
Berkeley, CA 99999

D. OPTIONAL DESIGNATION (if applicable):   LESSOR/LESSEE   CONSIGNOR/CONSIGNEE   NON-UCC FILING

1. DEBTOR'S EXACT FULL LEGAL NAME - insert only one debtor name (1a or 1b)

1a. ENTITY'S NAME			
New Lighting, LLC			
1b. INDIVIDUAL'S LAST NAME	FIRST NAME	MIDDLE NAME	SUFFIX

1c. MAILING ADDRESS	CITY	STATE	COUNTRY	POSTAL CODE
555 Jefferson Ave.	Berkeley	CA	USA	99999

1d. S.S. OR TAX I.D.#	OPTIONAL ADD'NL INFO RE ENTITY DEBTOR	1e. TYPE OF ENTITY	1f. ENTITY'S STATE OR COUNTRY OF ORGANIZATION	1g. ENTITY'S ORGANIZATIONAL I.D.#, if any
38-6666666		LLC	CA	NONE

2. ADDITIONAL DEBTOR'S EXACT FULL LEGAL NAME - insert only one debtor name (2a or 2b)

2a. ENTITY'S NAME			
2b. INDIVIDUAL'S LAST NAME	FIRST NAME	MIDDLE NAME	SUFFIX

2c. MAILING ADDRESS	CITY	STATE	COUNTRY	POSTAL CODE

2d. S.S. OR TAX I.D.#	OPTIONAL ADD'NL INFO RE ENTITY DEBTOR	2e. TYPE OF ENTITY	2f. ENTITY'S STATE OR COUNTRY OF ORGANIZATION	2g. ENTITY'S ORGANIZATIONAL I.D.#, if any
				NONE

3. SECURED PARTY'S (ORIGINAL S/P or ITS TOTAL ASSIGNEE) EXACT FULL LEGAL NAME - insert only one secured party name (3a or 3b)

3a. ENTITY'S NAME			
Olde Lighting, Inc.			
3b. INDIVIDUAL'S LAST NAME	FIRST NAME	MIDDLE NAME	SUFFIX

3c. MAILING ADDRESS	CITY	STATE	COUNTRY	POSTAL CODE
555 Eastern Drive	Berkeley	CA	USA	99999

4. This FINANCING STATEMENT covers the following types or items of property:

All furniture, fixtures, equipment and inventory of Debtor. Also, any tangible personal property (including replacement inventory) that Debtor now owns or later acquires in connection with Debtor's business known as Star Lighting located at 555 Jefferson Ave., Berkeley, CA. Also the proceeds of all insurance policies that now or later cover the secured property.

5. CHECK BOX (if applicable)   This FINANCING STATEMENT is signed by the Secured Party instead of the Debtor to perfect a security interest (a) in collateral already subject to a security interest in another jurisdiction when it was brought into this state, or when the debtor's location was changed to this state, or (b) in accordance with other statutory provisions (additional data may be required)

7. If filed in Florida (check one)   Documentary stamp tax paid   Documentary stamp tax not applicable

6. REQUIRED SIGNATURE(S)

New Lighting, LLC

By: *Laura White*, Member

8. This FINANCING STATEMENT is to be filed (for record) (or recorded) in the REAL ESTATE RECORDS   Attach Addendum   (if applicable)

9. Check to REQUEST SEARCH CERTIFICATE(S) on Debtor(s) (ADDITIONAL FEE) (optional)   All Debtors   Debtor 1   Debtor 2

(1) FILING OFFICER COPY — NATIONAL FINANCING STATEMENT (FORM UCC1) (TRANS) (REV. 12/18/95)

all. Check your state's Secretary of State website or call their office to obtain the proper forms and filing fees. A good place to start is http://www.piperinfo. com, a directory of state and local government websites.

Remember to get a discharge. When you've paid off the loan, you're entitled to get a document from the lender verifying that there's no longer a security interest in the pledged property. If you forget to get this document and record it at the same office where the financing statement was filed, you can run into a snag when you go to sell the property or your entire business. That's because to a potential purchaser prudently doing a UCC search, it will appear that the property is still subject to the lender's lien.

5. Use and Care of the Secured Property

Fill in the location where you'll keep the secured property that's owned by the business.

> **SAMPLE:**
> Keep at 555 High Street, Dallas, Texas, the Secured Property owned by the Borrower's business and use it only in the operation of the business.

6. Borrower's Default

In the first blank, fill in the number of days after which you're in default on your promissory note. This should be the same number of days stated in the promissory note itself. In the second blank, fill in the number of days you have to correct a violation of paragraph 5 before you're in default on the security agreement.

7. Lender's Rights

This summarizes the lender's rights under the Uniform Commercial Code if you default on your obligations under this security agreement.

Fill in the name of the state where the property is located.

8. Notice to Borrower

Fill in the location where the lender should send you a notice if you've defaulted and the lender plans to sell, lease or otherwise dispose of the property.

Standard Clauses

The remainder of the agreement contains the standard clauses we discussed in Chapter 1, Section C. The only thing you'll need to fill in here is the name of the state whose law will apply to the contract in the paragraph called "Governing Law."

Signature

Fill in the required information. See Chapter 1, Section B, on signing contracts.

Attachment to Security Agreement

Typically you'll list in the attachment the items that your business currently owns—or some of them. If you check the first box in paragraph 2, you must fill this in and attach it to the security agreement.

1. Names

Insert the names of the borrower and the lender.

2. Terms of Attachment

Insert the date of the security agreement. Then list the tangible personal property which the borrower is pledging as security for repayment of the loan. ∎

Buying a Business

f you want to go into business, you have three basic choices:

- start a business from scratch
- buy an existing business, or
- buy a franchise.

Buying an existing business can be a good middle course between the risk of starting a completely new enterprise and the high costs, forced uniformity and other often-reported problems of operating a franchise. If you choose wisely, you have the opportunity to purchase a business that's already solidly profitable and has an excellent opportunity to do even better with your infusion of new savvy and energy. Unfortunately, finding a profitable business that's not beset by hidden problems at a price you can afford isn't always easy.

 Chapter 10 of the *Legal Guide for Starting & Running a Small Business*, by Fred S. Steingold (Nolo), offers an extended discussion of the legal and practical issues of buying a business. It takes you through the purchase process step-by-step, including information on how to value the business and how to draft a solid purchase contract.

Once you locate a business that may be suitable for purchase, inquire about how the business is legally structured—the main alternatives being a sole proprietorship, partnership, corporation or limited liability company (LLC). However, once a business is yours, you can fairly easily change its structure. You might, for example, buy a business that was a sole proprietorship but decide to operate it through a new corporation or LLC you form.

From a legal standpoint, buying a business from a sole proprietor is relatively simple because you're dealing with only one person. Buying from a partnership, LLC or corporation with more than one shareholder is a bit more complex—mainly because you'll usually be dealing with two or more people whose interests will never be exactly the same. For this reason, it's wise to insist that all the partners, LLC members or corporate shareholders—not just those who own a majority stake—sign all the documents involved.

 Both spouses must sign in community property states. Nine states follow the community property system: Arizona, California, Idaho, Louisiana, Nevada, New Mexico, Texas, Washington and Wisconsin. In those states and absent a marriage contract providing otherwise, a married couple's property accumulated after marriage is usually community (or jointly owned) property regardless of the names in which it's held (exceptions include property received by inheritance or gift). This normally includes at least a partial interest in a business (even one that was owned by one spouse prior to marriage). Generally in a community property state, if you buy a business from a sole proprietor whose spouse plays no role in running the business and you pay a fair price, the law doesn't absolutely require you to get the spouse's written consent. But because of the likelihood that the business is jointly owned, the far better approach is to always obtain the signature of the spouse of the sole proprietor who's selling you the business. That way, you avoid the possibility of a later dispute between the spouses threatening to affect your purchase.

When you buy a business from a sole proprietorship, a partnership or an LLC, you never acquire the old legal structure, only the assets (and depending on how the business is structured, possibly the liabilities) of the business. Form 5A: Contract for Purchase of Business Assets From a Sole Proprietorship, Partnership or Limited Liability Company, is designed for such a purchase.

It's best to avoid assuming business liabilities. A major issue in buying any business is whether you'll be purchasing only its assets or if, as part of the deal, you'll also be taking on responsibility for its liabilities. You'll avoid many potential legal and debt entanglements if you insist on buying the assets only (even if this means you pay a higher price). But whatever you and the seller decide, it's key to clearly record your understanding in the purchase documents.

Things get somewhat more complicated when you buy a business from a corporation. Now there are two ways to structure the purchase: By buying the corporate stock from its existing shareholders, you can purchase the corporation itself. Or you can buy only its assets (and possibly take over some of its liabilities), in which case the selling shareholders will still own the corporate shell minus the assets you've purchased. It's almost always better to buy the corporate assets rather than the corporate stock because, among other things, it helps you avoid the liabilities of the existing business and it gives you significant tax advantages. Form 5B: Contract for Purchase of Business Assets From a Corporation, is designed for this purpose.

Environmental concerns. If you're the buyer and the assets you're buying include real estate—either vacant land or a building—you want to make sure that you're not going to run up against environmental protection laws. For more information on this subject, see Chapter 7, Section A.

Get the Consent of Shareholders When You Purchase Corporate Assets

Remember that a corporation is a separate legal entity from its owners—the shareholders. When you purchase the assets of a small corporation, you want to avoid the possibility of having to deal with disgruntled minority owners. Even though the corporation's bylaws or shareholders' agreement may permit the sale of its assets with the consent of a majority of the shareholders (or some higher number), it's legally far safer for you if you insist that all shareholders agree with the sale of the corporation's assets. Get this consent in writing by following a two-step process:

- Require that all shareholders sign the Contract for Purchase of Business Assets from a Corporation (Form 5B).
- Ask that all of the corporation's shareholders and directors sign and give you a copy of an official Corporate Resolution Authorizing Sale of Assets (Form 5C).

A big bonus for insisting that all shareholders sign the contract is that it makes them personally liable for the warranties and representations in the contract. Without their signatures, should things go wrong, your only recourse would be against the corporation, which by that time would probably be without funds. You can also include language committing each shareholder to any noncompetition clause in the agreement—but, as with other noncompete covenants, you must pay the signer something to make the covenant legally binding.

In some situations you may not be able to swing a deal in which you buy only corporate assets. This can occur, for example, if the seller insists on a stock sale—perhaps because he or she believes there's a tax advantage in going this route. If you agree to this, you'll need to conduct an in-depth investigation of the corporation's financial affairs. You should also try to get a strong personal guarantee from the shareholders that things are as stated.

In a few instances, you may actually prefer to buy the corporation rather than its assets. This can occur, for example, if the corporation has a valuable long-term lease that can't be transferred (assigned) to another tenant such as a new corporation you plan to form. If you buy the corporate stock, the existing corporation will probably be able to continue on as a tenant, enabling you to enjoy the benefits of the lease. Form 5D: Contract for Purchase of Corporate Stock, is designed for such situations.

After you and the seller have signed a contract covering your purchase of business assets, there will need to be a formal transfer of the ownership. Called a "closing," this event is similar to what happens when a house is sold; legal paperwork transferring ownership is signed and the sellers receive their money. Form 5E: Bill of Sale is the usual way a seller transfers ownership to a buyer of tangible personal property—legal jargon for objects such as machinery, inventory, supplies and office equipment that you can touch. Real property (land and buildings) is not included in a bill of sale, nor are intangible assets such as accounts receivable or contracts. Title to real property is transferred by a deed which you record (file) at a designated county office to make it a matter of public record. Intangible assets are transferred through various legal documents—the most common being an assignment. In addition, the seller won't use a bill of sale to transfer ownership of any vehicles included in the sale, but instead will simply authorize the title to the vehicles to be changed to the new owner on the records of the appropriate state agency, a process you've doubtless become familiar with when you've sold a car.

Your legal headaches will be vastly reduced if the business you're buying doesn't owe money, since there will be no creditors to deal with. But even if the seller tells you that all creditors have been paid, you'll want to use Form 5F: Affidavit—No Creditors to get this assurance in writing and under penalty of perjury. Another advantage of having such a declaration in hand is that you won't have to worry about whether you've complied with your state's creditor notification law (bulk sales law), since this procedure is unnecessary if no money is owed.

What Are Bulk Sales Laws?

Creditor notification or bulk sales laws swept the country at the end of the 19th century, and most remain on the books today. To avoid the possibility that a business owner will order lots of goods on credit, quickly unload the business on an unsuspecting purchaser and then disappear without using the money to pay off the business debts, these laws require that creditors be notified before business assets are transferred to a new owner. These laws apply to transfers where a major part of the seller's assets consists of materials, supplies, merchandise or other inventory. Generally, they don't apply to transfers where the seller's business consists primarily of selling personal services.

In most states, a seller covered under the bulk sales law must give a buyer a list (sworn to under penalty of perjury) of all business creditors and the amount each is owed. Then, several days before the sale is closed —the exact number of days is specified in the state law—the buyer must send a notice to creditors so they know the business is changing hands and can arrange to have their claims paid at or before closing. If a proper notice is sent, the buyer knows that, after the closing, the goods being purchased are free from old claims by creditors of the seller.

Although bulk sales notices are not conceptually difficult, their preparation is governed by fussy state laws and the notices must be sent (and in some states, published) in very precise ways. Because the details differ from state to state, you'll need to get your rules and forms locally, either at a law library or legal newspaper, in the many states where notices must be published.

Extra paperwork is needed if the business still owes money. If the business you purchase will still have unpaid debts after the closing, Form 5F: Affidavit—No Creditors, won't work. To comply with your state's creditor notification law (called the bulk sales law), which requires that creditors be notified of a sale, you'll either need to do some research (see "What Are Bulk Sales Laws," below) or hire a lawyer to help you.

In buying any business, it's rare to pay the full purchase price up front. Most often, the buyer agrees to pay only a portion of the total at closing, relying on the seller to finance the rest. You might, for example, agree to buy a business for $150,000 by paying the seller $30,000 as down payment and the balance of $120,000 in monthly installments over a five-year period.

Whenever a portion of the sales price will be paid in the future, the seller will probably expect you to sign a promissory note for the balance of the purchase price (see Forms 4C, 4D and 4E in Chapter 4). In addition, the seller will want to retain a security interest—or lien—in the assets you're purchasing. In concept, this is similar to the mortgage that a bank holds on a homeowner's home. If the homeowner defaults on paying the bank, the bank can take (foreclose on) the home. Similarly, in the sale of a business, the seller wants to be able to take back the business if you don't make the promised payments. In this connection, Form 5G: Security Agreement, acknowledges that the business assets can be seized if you don't keep up your payments.

A. Form 5A: Contract for Purchase of Business Assets From a Sole Proprietorship, Partnership or Limited Liability Company

As explained in the beginning of this chapter, when you buy a business from a sole proprietorship, a partnership or an LLC, you never acquire the old legal structure, only the assets (and depending on how the business is structured, possibly the liabilities) of the business. You can do this with Form 5A.

Instructions for Form 5A: Contract for Purchase of Business Assets From a Sole Proprietorship, Partnership or Limited Liability Company

All the forms in this book are provided as tear-outs in Appendix B and on the accompanying forms CD-ROM. As you read the instructions for Form 5A, you may want to either tear out the form or open the form's file on the CD-ROM so you can follow along. Form 5A is in the file FORM5A.RTF on the CD-ROM. (For more information on using the forms CD-ROM, see Appendix A, "How to Use the CD-ROM.") If you don't use the forms CD-ROM, be sure to photocopy the agreement so you'll have a clean copy to use later.

1. Names

Insert the names of the seller and buyer. The seller will be the sole proprietorship, partnership or limited liability company (LLC) that is selling its assets to you.

If the seller is a sole proprietorship, insert the seller's own name. If the seller is a partnership, insert the name of the partnership. If the seller is an LLC, insert the name of the LLC. Consult the chart in Chapter 1, Section A, for more information about how to identify a business.

The different formats for the names clause are in the file NAMES on the form CD-ROM.

Remember that only the name of the seller is inserted in the seller's slot even though others having some relationship to the seller may be signing the contract. As discussed in Chapter 1, Section A, these additional signers may include, for example, a sole proprietor's spouse (in a community property state), the individual partners in a partnership, or the individual members of an LLC. Technically, they are not the sellers but are signing to agree to the terms of the contract.

2. Sale of Business Assets

In the first blank, insert the name that the seller's business uses. In the second blank, fill in the business's address. Include the street address, city and state.

SAMPLE:

Seller is selling to Buyer and Buyer is buying from Seller the assets of the business known as Red's Rite Spot, located at 123 Main Street, Berkeley, California.

If the business has several locations and you're buying the assets used at more than one location, list all those locations.

SAMPLE:

Seller is selling to Buyer and Buyer is buying from Seller the assets of the business known as Bagels & Baguettes, located at 456 State Street and 789 North Liberty, Atlanta, Georgia.

3. Assets Being Sold

Specify exactly what you're buying by checking all the boxes that apply to your purchase. If you're using the forms CD-ROM, delete the paragraphs that don't apply to your purchase and renumber, if necessary. Unless you fill this in completely, you may be in for costly disagreements later on.

Check box A if you're purchasing the goodwill of the business, which includes the right to use the business name and phone number. If you consider the business name to be a particularly valuable asset, you should verify that the name has been properly protected as a trademark.

For information on legal protection for business names, see *Trademark: Legal Care for Your Business & Product Name*, by Stephen Elias and Kate McGrath (Nolo).

Check box B if you're going to continue to occupy the same business premises. Fill in the required information about the seller's current lease.

Before you buy any business, you should always ask for copies of all leases and contracts. If you plan to occupy the space where the business is presently located, or take over the business's existing contracts (such as a supply agreement or an equipment lease), ask for copies of these documents. Here's why: If you're taking over a lease, you'll obviously need to know how much the rent is, how long the lease runs and all other key terms. If you're assuming a contract, you'll need to know the key terms and assess whether they're acceptable to you.

Also make sure the leases and contracts can legally be assigned to you. Many real estate leases contain clauses prohibiting the tenant from assigning the lease—that is, letting a new tenant take over the new space—without the landlord's permission. Similarly, many business contracts prohibit one party from assigning the contract to someone else without the other party's consent. You'd hate to buy a business with the idea of staying at the same location and then have to face an eviction action or a landlord trying to shake you down for a fee to approve the assignment. And if the seller has favorable contracts with vendors or equipment leasing companies, you'd hate to lose the benefits of these contracts and have to negotiate new contracts from scratch.

Whether a provision requiring the other party's consent to assign the contract is present or not, to avoid any unpleasant surprises, it's best to ask the seller to get the landlord's or other party's written consent to your taking over the lease or the contract before you buy a business. See paragraph 13 in Form 5A for language that accomplishes this.

Check box C if you'll be acquiring the inventory of the business.

Check box D if you're buying furniture, fixtures and equipment from the seller. List the specific items on a separate page or schedule.

Check box E if you'll be taking over an existing equipment lease, as would often be the case if the business doesn't own all of its equipment. This could include phone systems, copiers, computers, warehouse equipment (such as forklifts), vehicles and large outdoor trash containers. Make sure that if you do check this box, you also attach a list of the specific equipment leases being assigned. Remember, as we mentioned, you should ask to see copies of the equipment leases and make sure that the equipment leases can be assigned to you.

Use box "F. Other" to cover any assets not already clearly defined, including things like proprietary software or a patent, trademark or copyright.

SAMPLE:
- All rights to the StarCo trademark.
- All rights to the proprietary accounting software developed for the seller.

⚠️ **A covenant not to compete is not an asset of the business.** If as part of the sale the seller will give you a "covenant not to compete," you may be tempted to list it here. Don't. A noncompete agreement isn't considered a business asset; that's why paragraph 16 covers this issue separately.

4. Purchase Price

In the first blank, insert the total purchase price. Your task in order to take maximum advantage of favorable tax depreciation rules (see "Allocate Your Purchase Dollars to Get Tax Benefits," below) is to allocate the purchase price among the various items you're buying rather than simply stating a lump sum, since doing this can have favorable tax consequences. Fill in the constituent amounts.

SAMPLE:
The purchase price of $42,000 is allocated as follows:
A.	Goodwill	$ 8,000
B.	Assignment of lease	$4,000
C.	Furniture, fixtures and equipment	$30,000
D.	Other	$0

Allocate Your Purchase Dollars to Get Tax Benefit

You'll get more favorable tax treatment if you assign most of the purchase price to assets that are eligible to be written off quickly through depreciation or expense allowances. The price you pay for inventory, for example, can be written off as merchandise is sold. Furniture, fixtures and equipment can be written off in five to seven years. The write-off of amounts you pay for a trade name or goodwill must be stretched out over 15 years; the same is true for the seller's covenant not to compete (which is listed separately in paragraph 16).

 Chapter 10 of the *Legal Guide for Starting & Running a Small Business*, by Fred S. Steingold (Nolo), contains a more thorough discussion of the best legal and tax-saving strategies for allocating your purchase price. Also consider having your plan reviewed by a tax pro.

Note that the purchase price doesn't include any inventory held for sale. Assuming the business you're interested in has inventory, it's customary to provide that a physical count of the inventory will be taken just before closing. If the inventory will be bought, check the box and include paragraph 5, Price of Inventory.

5. Price of Inventory (Optional)

This is an optional paragraph. If you're going to be buying the seller's current inventory of merchandise, check the first box. (CD-ROM users who won't be buying the inventory should delete the whole paragraph and renumber all that follow.) Then use this paragraph to indicate how the price of these goods will be determined.

If you and the seller are going to physically count the merchandise yourselves, check the box before the words "Seller and Buyer."

If you plan to hire an inventory service company to do it, check the next box instead.

Then, insert the number of days before the closing when the merchandise will be physically counted. Ideally, this should occur as close to the closing date as possible—certainly not longer than a week before.

You may want to put a cap on the amount you'll have to pay for the inventory of the business. If so, check the last box and fill in the agreed-on amount.

⚠ **Some inventory may not be readily salable.** Consider modifying this paragraph if the inventory is damaged, obsolete or otherwise not worth what the seller paid for it. In this situation, it is appropriate to pay for some or all of the inventory at a reduced price—or even to omit some of the inventory from the purchase because it's worthless. After you work out the terms with the seller, modify this paragraph accordingly. Incidentally, if you have any doubts about whether the seller has really paid for the inventory—even though the seller gives you Form 5F, stating under oath that there are no creditors—ask for proof.

6. Accounts Receivable

When you buy a business, it's usually best to agree that money owed to the business ("accounts receivable") will remain the seller's property. Otherwise, you have a problem. Since you lack experience with the customers who owe money, it's hard for you to know if a given account can be easily collected and thus impossible to assign it a realistic value. By contrast, the seller knows his or her customers and has experience in getting them to pay up. Far better from your point of view to leave the accounts receivable—and the headaches of

collection—in the seller's hands. In this paragraph, select one of the two alternatives.

Check the first box if you won't buy the seller's accounts receivable.

Check the second box if for some reason (perhaps the seller has substantially discounted them or you've assured yourself that most accounts will be paid on time) you're willing to acquire the seller's accounts receivable. Fill in the age of the accounts you're acquiring (old ones usually aren't worth much). But even for current accounts receivable, it's always sensible to pay a discounted amount; after all, you'll probably expend some effort in collecting the accounts and even with a well-run business, a small but not insignificant percentage won't be collectable.

7. Deposit

The seller will usually expect you to pay a deposit (in legal jargon, an "earnest money deposit") to bind the deal. If your purchase falls through because the seller can't deliver as promised or a contingency can't be satisfied (for example, the landlord won't consent to assigning the lease to you as called for in the contract), you get this money back. If you back out without a good reason, the seller keeps the money. If, as expected, the deal proceeds, the money is applied toward the purchase price.

Fill in the amount of the deposit you're giving the seller to bind the deal. Obviously, from the buyer's point of view, the lower the amount, the better.

8. Payments at Closing

In this paragraph, you can check more than one box. Check the first box and insert the amount you'll be paying the seller at closing. Remember to deduct the amount of the deposit.

Also, check the second box if you're buying the business's inventory.

Also, check the third box if you're buying the business's accounts receivable.

9. Promissory Note

In more than 90% of business purchases, the buyer makes a down payment at closing and pays the balance in installments over a number of years. This paragraph applies in such situations.

First, check the appropriate box for the buyer's type of business.

 Forms for promissory notes are covered in Chapter 4.

Buying As a Sole Proprietor: If you're buying the business as a sole proprietor and you alone will be responsible for the payments on the promissory note, you needn't check any of the boxes in paragraph 9 of the contract. However, if you're buying the business as a sole proprietor and you've agreed to have your spouse or another person be fully responsible (along with you) for payment, check the first box and insert the name of the other person. See also Chapter 1, Section B.

 If two or more people sign a promissory note, each is 100% responsible to pay it. What happens if two or more people sign the promissory note and a default occurs? Almost always, the contract provides that all signers will be "jointly and individually liable" (or sometimes, "jointly and severally liable"). These words mean that if the promised payments aren't made, the seller can sue and collect the full amount from any one of signers.

Buying As a Partnership: If you're buying the business as a partnership, check the second box to make you and the other partners each fully responsible for the payments.

Buying As a Corporation or LLC: One advantage of forming a corporation or LLC to run a business is that shareholders and LLC members are not ordinarily personally liable for business debts (in legalese, they enjoy "limited liability"). This means if you're going to be operating the business through a corporation or LLC and one of these entities is the only signer of the promissory note, you and the other shareholders or LLC members won't be personally liable for making the payments. Unfortunately, in the real world, the seller is unlikely to agree to let your corporation or LLC be solely responsible for payments, but will

instead insist that some or all of the corporate shareholders or some or all of the members of the LLC personally guarantee payment of the promissory note (that is, waive their limited liability status by signing personally). If so, check the third box and insert the names of the people who are agreeing to be personally responsible for payment.

Get a firm commitment early from multiple signers. If several people agree to be personally responsible for payments on the promissory note, they should either all sign the purchase contract itself or agree in writing that they will co-sign the promissory note. Otherwise, if one or more suffer buyer's remorse and try to renege on their commitment, there will be no way to compel them to sign the promissory note at closing, in which case the deal may fall through.

A. Fill in the annual interest rate.

B. Insert the amount of your monthly payment. This contract assumes you'll make the same payment each month, as most people do with a home mortgage. To determine the amount of the monthly payment, use the table in Chapter 4 found in the introduction to Form 4C: Promissory Note (Equal Monthly Installments; All Principal and Interest Paid). If you need to do a computation for a payment plan not covered by the chart or if you wish to see how each payment will be allocated between interest and principal, you can use computer software such as *Quicken* or a spreadsheet program to crunch the numbers.

C. Insert the date by which the entire balance is to be paid off. This may involve a big payment at the final payoff date. For example, you may use a 15-year amortization schedule to figure out the monthly amounts, but may agree to pay off the balance within five years with the remaining balance to be paid in one big "balloon" payment.

D. Nothing needs to be filled in.

E. Nothing needs to be filled in.

F. Insert how many days the buyer has before seller can declare that the entire balance is due on a late payment.

10. Security for Payment

If you're a homeowner, you probably signed a mortgage when you bought your house, giving the lender a security (ownership) interest in the real property until the loan is paid off. If you don't pay the principal or interest on schedule, or if you fall behind in paying property taxes or let the house insurance lapse, the lender has the legal right to foreclose and sell the property. Similarly, whoever is selling you a business will probably want to retain an ownership or security interest in the assets you're buying until you've made your last payment. If in the meantime you default on making installment payments, the security interest allows the seller to take back the assets.

By checking the first box, you agree to sign Form 5G: Security Agreement, giving the seller a security interest in the assets. You also agree to sign a second document called a Uniform Commercial Code (UCC) Financing Statement, which is filed ("recorded") at a public office to let third parties such as lenders or purchasers know about the security interest. See Chapter 4 for more information about financing statements and forms.

⚠️ **Think twice before using your house as security.** If you're buying a small business, especially one that primarily sells services and doesn't own much property, there may not be many tangible business assets to pledge as security for the portion of the purchase price you borrow from the seller. In that situation, the seller may suggest that you pledge some nonbusiness asset as security— your car or boat, perhaps. Fair enough. But if the seller asks for a mortgage on or a deed of trust to your house, think long and hard about it. Putting your house at risk for a business debt is often a poor choice, if for no other reason than if the business has a few slow months, your anxiety level will be sky high.

If the existing lease is being assigned to you as part of the purchase price, the seller may want to take back a property or security interest in the lease so as to be eligible to become the tenant again and

resume business at the same location if you default on your obligations. If the seller wants that kind of protection, check the second box.

11. Seller's Debts

As a buyer, you don't want to be responsible for the seller's debts. This paragraph makes it clear that the seller will pay all business debts that may affect or be tied to the assets you're purchasing. For good measure, this paragraph requires the seller to sign an affidavit (statement under oath) at closing confirming that all debts and liabilities of the business have been paid. See Form 5F: Affidavit—No Creditors.

⚠️ **Make sure preexisting business debts get paid—or fully understand what you're getting into.** Sometimes a seller will need to use the money you pay at closing to take care of all business debts and liabilities (often this is to fulfill a contract provision requiring the seller to pay all debts prior to purchase). Fine, as long as you don't leave anything to chance. To make sure outstanding bills really do get paid, one good approach is to pay them yourself at closing out of the seller's proceeds; then when you're sure there are no more, give the seller a check for the amount that's left over.

In some instances, despite your desire to buy business assets without becoming responsible for the seller's debts, you may run across a situation where you can pick up a business at a very reasonable price, but only if you agree to take over some debts of the seller. Beware! Make sure you know the full extent of the debts and that you understand the technical details of your state's "bulk sales law," which requires creditors to be notified of a business sale. (See sidebar earlier in this chapter.) Also check the public records to see if anyone has a lien (UCC Financing Statement) on any of the assets you plan to purchase. Depending on the state, these financing statements are then filed at a governmental office, either at the state or county level or both (a commercial loan officer at your bank should be able to tell you). A sample UCC-1 financing statement is included in Chapter 4.

To further protect yourself from undisclosed creditors, consider including a contract provision that allows you to hold back a chunk of the purchase price for 90 days. Also realize that since creditors come in many shapes and sizes, and no one tactic will completely protect you against all of them, this is one area where getting some help from a lawyer who specializes in small business issues can definitely be worth the money.

12. Closing

At a closing, you meet with the seller to sign and exchange all the documents needed to complete the purchase. You pay whatever money and sign any promissory note required for the ownership of the assets to be transferred to you; the seller then signs over the assets to you.

Insert the date, time and location of the closing.

> **SAMPLE:**
> The closing will take place:
> Date: Wednesday, May 2, 2001
> Time: 1:00 p.m.
> Location: 123 Washington Street, Ethic, New York.

Check the box if you live in a community property state. As noted in the beginning of this chapter, in a community property state, it's desirable to have the spouse of a sole proprietor sign the closing documents.

13. Documents for Transferring Assets

Check all appropriate boxes. (CD-ROM users should delete the language that does not apply.)

Check A if you're buying tangible assets—for example, furniture, equipment or inventory.

Check B if you're taking over an existing lease of business space.

Check C if you're taking over any other contracts.

Check D if you're acquiring any trademarks, patents or copyrights.

14. Seller's Representations

In this paragraph, you get the seller's written word ("warranty") as to various conditions affecting the assets you're buying so that you can have legal recourse against the seller if problems later arise. You also receive the seller's "representations"—factual statements you can rely on. In combination, these legal guarantees give you a broad basis for taking legal action against the seller if key promises are not honored or statements he or she has made as part of your purchase contract turn out not to be true. If, for example, the seller states in writing that he or she has given you accurate information about the earnings of the business and that later turns out to be untrue, you may use this representation as a basis for getting your money back or reducing the purchase price to offset losses caused by the misstatement.

In G, you may want to add additional items to fit your transaction.

> **SAMPLE:**
> Seller will have the compressor in the 15-foot Polar Bear freezer (serial no. 17411) replaced with an equivalent new model before closing and warrants that it will remain in good operating condition for 24 months following closing. Seller will be responsible for all parts or labor need to repair the freezer if it fails to operate properly during the 24-month period.

 Get something called a "certificate of good standing" before you buy a business. If you're buying a business from an LLC, corporation or even a partnership, you can usually get something called a "Certificate of Good Standing" from your state's Secretary of State's office or the agency that monitors business entities. A certificate of good standing can help you verify that the seller has met its filing responsibilities, and in some cases will even tell you whether the seller has paid the requisite state taxes. (In some states, you may have to check with the state treasury department to verify that a business has paid its taxes.) Obtaining a good standing certificate is fairly inexpensive and is one way of making sure you're buying a reputable business.

15. Buyer's Representations

In paragraph A, insert the appropriate language if you're not satisfied with the condition of some tangible assets. If you're satisfied, insert "Not applicable."

SAMPLE:

… except for the Polar Bear freezer (serial no. 17411) which Seller has agreed to repair.

If you're not paying the full price for the assets at the closing but giving the seller a promissory note for the unpaid balance, the seller will want to know if you're creditworthy and will probably ask you for a financial statement or other information about your financial situation.

16. Covenant Not to Compete

You may not want to buy a business unless the seller agrees not to compete with you for a certain period after the sale. However, you should realize that even if the seller signs such an agreement, it's possible that later on in a court proceeding, she may challenge its validity, claiming that it's unreasonably restrictive. You may have heard that when noncompete agreements are made between an employer and an employee—particularly a lower-echelon employee—courts have often invalidated or modified the agreements because they unreasonably limited the employee's right to earn a livelihood. Fortunately, when a noncompetition agreement is tied to a sale of a business, an adverse court ruling is much less likely to occur, since the seller presumably is being adequately compensated for agreeing not to compete. Still, to help ensure enforcement by a court if necessary, it's prudent to ask for those

restrictions that are really necessary to protect your business interests, but no more.

Check the box that states the kind of seller you're buying from—sole proprietor, partnership or LLC. (In the case of a partnership or LLC, it's reasonable to require that all of the business owners agree to the covenant not to compete. And where spouses of business owners have business know-how and pose a competitive threat, consider requiring that they agree as well.) Then, fill in the blanks; they're the same for all the alternative paragraphs. Remember that each person committed to signing a covenant not to compete should also sign this contract.

 CD-ROM users should simply select the paragraph you need and delete the ones that don't apply.

In the first blank, insert the number of years that the noncompetition clause applies. Ordinarily, you'd want the clause to apply for at least one year. Restricting the seller's ability to compete for up to three to five years is common, but anything more than that is likely to be vulnerable to legal challenge.

The noncompetition clause applies to business which is similar to the one you're buying. This is because a noncompete should be broad enough to include logical extensions of the existing business, but not so extensive that the seller is restricted from opening a business in a different field. For example, if you're buying a business that helps companies set up and maintain internal computer networks or intranets, there is no need to use noncompete language that's so broad it prevents the seller from operating a business that helps design web sites for selling products directly to the public.

The geographical area of protection from competition will vary, of course, depending on the geographical scope of the business activities. To maximize your chances of creating an enforceable agreement, the geographic scope should be reasonable—and the most reasonable thing to do is limit the former owner's ability to compete with you only in areas where you actually conduct business.

17. Risk of Loss

Nothing needs to be inserted here.

18. Disputes

See Chapter 1, Section D, for more information about dispute resolution clauses.

19. Additional Agreements

Insert any other terms that apply to your purchase.

20. Required Signatures

If you're buying from a partnership or LLC, have all the partners or LLC members sign this contract so they'll all be bound by the covenant not to compete. Check the appropriate boxes.

If the seller is a sole proprietor in a community property state, see the beginning of this chapter for a discussion of getting the signature of a sole proprietor's spouse in the nine community property states. If you choose to do so, check the appropriate box.

Standard Clauses

The remainder of the agreement contains the standard clauses we discussed in Chapter 1, Section C. The only thing you'll need to fill in here is the name of the state whose law will apply to the contract in the paragraph called "Governing Law."

 For more on signing contracts, see Chapter 1, Section B.

B. Form 5B: Contract for Purchase of Business Assets From a Corporation

As discussed above, there are two ways to structure the purchase of a corporation: You can purchase the corporation itself or you can buy only its assets. It's almost always better to buy the corporate assets rather than the corporate stock because, among other things, it helps you avoid the liabilities of the existing business and it gives you significant tax advantages. You can do this with Form 5B: Contract for Purchase of Business Assets From a Corporation.

Instructions for Form 5B: Contract for Purchase of Business Assets From a Corporation

All the forms in this book are provided as tear-outs in Appendix B and on the accompanying forms CD-ROM. As you read the instructions for Form 5B, you may want to either tear out the form or open the form's file on the CD-ROM so you can follow along. Form 5B is in the file FORM5B.RTF on the CD-ROM. (For more information on using the forms CD-ROM, see Appendix A, "How to Use the CD-ROM.") If you don't use the forms CD-ROM, be sure to photocopy the agreement so you'll have a clean copy to use later.

1. Names

Insert the name of the corporation that's selling the assets you're buying and the state in which it's incorporated. Then insert the buyer's name.

2. Sale of Business Assets

In the first blank, insert the name that the seller's business actually uses. In the second blank, fill in the business's address. Include the street address, city and state.

> **SAMPLE:**
> Seller is selling to Buyer and Buyer is buying from Seller the assets of the business known as Red's Rite Spot, located at 123 Main Street, Sacramento, California.

 Find out if the business and corporate names are different. A business may actually use a different name than that of the corporation. For example, a corporation called Red's Rite Spot, Inc., may operate a restaurant called The Rite Spot Cafe, The Cafe Rouge or maybe even Main Street Restaurant. You'll use the corporation's name in the first paragraph and the business's day-to-day name here.

Environmental concerns. If you're the buyer and the assets you're buying include real estate—either vacant land or a building—you want to make sure that you're not going to run up against environmental protection laws. For more information on this subject, see Chapter 7, Section A.

3. Assets Being Sold

See instructions for paragraph 3 of Form 5A.

4. Purchase Price

See instructions for paragraph 4 of Form 5A.

5. Price of Inventory (Optional)

See instructions for paragraph 5 of Form 5A.

6. Accounts Receivable

See instructions for paragraph 6 of Form 5A.

7. Deposit

See instructions for paragraph 7 of Form 5A.

8. Payments at Closing

See instructions for paragraph 8 of Form 5A.

9. Promissory Note

See instructions for paragraph 9 of Form 5A.

10. Security for Payment

See instructions for paragraph 10 of Form 5A.

11. Seller's Debts

See instructions for paragraph 11 of Form 5A.

12. Closing

See instructions for paragraph 12 of Form 5A.

13. Documents for Transferring Assets

See instructions for paragraph 13 of Form 5A.

14. Seller's Representations

See instructions for paragraph 14 of Form 5A.

15. Buyer's Representations

See instructions for paragraph 15 of Form 5A.

16. Covenant Not to Compete

In a small business, the seller's shareholders are likely to be closely involved in the operation of the business. If so, you may want all of them to agree in writing not to compete with you for a certain period after you buy the business assets. To make the shareholders' commitment binding, you should make some payment to each of them as individuals.

This is an important distinction, since technically the money you pay for the business assets goes to the corporation and not directly from you to the individuals who own the stock of the corporation. So if you're going to pay a total of $100,000 for a business, you might list the purchase price for the corporate assets as $98,000 and pay the remaining $2,000 in equal portions to the two shareholders in return for their covenants not to compete.

See instructions for paragraph 16 of Form 5A for information about how to make a noncompete agreement stand up if it's challenged in court.

In the first blank, insert the number of years that the noncompetition clause applies (you'd want the clause to apply for at least one year). Restricting the seller's or shareholders' ability to compete for up to three to five years is common, but anything more than that is likely to be vulnerable to legal challenge.

The noncompetition clause applies to business which is similar to the one you're buying. This is because a noncompete should be broad enough to include logical extensions of the existing business, but not so broad that it unnecessarily limits the shareholders' new business ventures.

The geographical area of protection from competition will vary, of course, depending on the geographical scope of business activities.

In the second blank, insert the amount you'll pay each shareholder for agreeing not to compete.

 Consider requiring covenants from shareholders' family members. In buying a small business from a closely held corporation, you may face a situation in which a shareholder's spouse or adult child does not own stock in the corporation, but nevertheless possesses insider's know-how about how to run such a business. If so, the spouse or child may pose a competitive threat, meaning you should consider requiring the spouse or child to join in the covenant not to compete. As with other noncompete covenants, you must pay the signer something so that the covenant is legally binding.

If you are going to require a noncompete covenant from the spouses, be sure to get their signatures on the purchase contract.

17. Risk of Loss

Nothing needs to be inserted here.

18. Disputes

See Chapter 1, Section D, for more information about dispute resolution clauses.

19. Additional Agreements

Insert any other terms that apply to your purchase.

20. Required Signatures

In addition to having the corporate seller sign the contract, have all of the shareholders (and family members, if necessary) acknowledge that they consent to the sale and to the terms of the covenant not to compete (paragraph 16).

Standard Clauses

The remainder of the agreement contains the standard clauses we discussed in Chapter 1, Section C. The only thing you'll need to fill in here is the name of the state whose law will apply to the contract in the paragraph called "Governing Law."

 For more on signing contracts, see Chapter 1, Section B.

C. Form 5C: Corporate Resolution Authorizing Sale of Assets

Corporate bylaws usually require the written consent of shareholders and directors before the corporation may sell all or substantially all of its assets. Traditionally, corporations have acted by having in-person meetings of shareholders or directors at which votes are taken and recorded in the form of resolutions, which are part of the minutes of the meetings. However, these days, because it's more convenient (and just as legal), the shareholders of many corporations act through the use of written agreements (often called consents). To be valid, these consents must be signed by shareholders or directors with a majority (or, if required by corporate documents, a supermajority) of voting power.

As explained in the beginning of this chapter, if you're buying the assets of a corporation (using Form 5B: Contract for Purchase of Business Assets From a Corporation), it makes sense to have all the shareholders and directors approve the sale of assets, even if unanimous consent isn't required under either the corporation's bylaws or state law. Use Form 5C: Corporate Resolution Authorizing Sale of Assets, to do this.

Instructions for Form 5C: Corporate Resolution Authorizing Sale of Assets

All the forms in this book are provided as tear-outs in Appendix B and on the accompanying forms CD-ROM. As you read the instructions for Form 5C, you may want to either tear out the form or open the form's file on the CD-ROM so you can follow along. Form 5C.RTF is in the file FORM 5C on the CD-ROM. (For more information on using the forms

CD-ROM, see Appendix A, "How to Use the CD-ROM.") If you don't use the forms CD-ROM, be sure to photocopy the agreement so you'll have a clean copy to use later.

In the first blank on the resolution, insert the name of the corporation. In the second blank, insert the state in which it's incorporated. Then, insert the number that identifies which attachment the purchase agreement is—usually Attachment 1. Finally, insert the date. Following the signature lines, the signers should indicate their status—shareholder, director or both—by crossing out whichever doesn't apply.

D. Form 5D: Contract for Purchase of Corporate Stock

As noted in the beginning of this chapter, when you buy a business from a corporation, it's almost always better to buy the corporate assets rather than the corporate stock. Use Form 5B: Contract for Purchase of Business Assets From a Corporation, to do this. But in some situations (for example, the seller offers you a significantly better price) you may wish to deviate from this general rule and buy corporate stock. Use Form 5D: Contract for Purchase of Corporate Stock, to accomplish this.

Environmental concerns. If you're buying the stock of a corporation and the corporate assets include real estate—either vacant land or a building—you want to make sure that you're not going to run up against environmental protection laws. For more information on this subject, see Chapter 7, Section A.

Instructions for Form 5D: Contract for Purchase of Corporate Stock

All the forms in this book are provided as tear-outs in Appendix B and on the accompanying forms CD-ROM. As you read the instructions for Form 5D, you may want to either tear out the form or open the form's file on the CD-ROM so you can follow along. Form 5D is in the file FORM5D.RTF on the CD-ROM. (For more information on using the forms CD-ROM, see Appendix A, "How to Use the CD-ROM.") If you don't use the forms CD-ROM, be sure to photocopy the agreement so you'll have a clean copy to use later.

1. Names

Insert the names of the sellers—the shareholders who are selling their stock to you. If shareholders live in a community property state, check the appropriate boxes and list the names of their spouses; as they are usually co-owners of the stock, it's wise to have them join in the sale. See the beginning of this chapter for information on a spouse's property rights in community property states.

Insert the name of the buyer who is buying the stock from the present shareholders.

If the shareholders live in a community property state and are listed in this paragraph, check the box before "Spouses."

For you to fully own the business, you'll need to buy the shares of all existing shareholders. Of course, this may be easy since it's common for a small company to have only one or two shareholders.

It's best to buy all the stock. Generally, you and your business associates will want complete control over the business you're buying. Especially in a small business, there can often be problems if you inherit minority shareholders who aren't part of your team. If you can't get all the existing shareholders to sell their stock, my advice is to look for another business to buy.

2. Sale of Corporate Stock

Fill in the name of the corporation and the state of incorporation.

SAMPLE:

Triad and True, Inc., a New Jersey corporation.

Next, fill in the total number of shares the corporation has issued, the name of each shareholder and the number of shares of stock that the shareholder owns.

3. Purchase Price

In the first blank, fill in the price you are paying for each share of stock.

In the second blank, fill in the total amount you are paying for all the stock.

Check box A if you and the seller agree that a part of the purchase price will be placed in escrow with an outside person for 90 days to cover undetermined tax liabilities of the corporation. You can then either fill in the name of the escrow agent or check the box indicating that you'll agree on an escrow agent later.

 See the instructions for Form 5F in this chapter for more on escrow arrangements and sample language for an escrow agreement.

Check box B if you and the seller agree that you'll simply withhold the money for taxes instead of placing this money with an escrow agent.

 Consider withholding money to cover unknown debts. Later in this form (paragraph 6C) the seller states that all the debts and liabilities of the corporation are listed in an attached schedule. If you have any doubts about the accuracy and completeness of the list, consider adding a paragraph here placing a portion of the purchase price in escrow (or simply allowing you to withhold it) for 90 days to pay any unlisted debts that may surface. At the end of the 90 days, if no debts surface, the money is turned over to the seller. For more information on checking with state agencies to make sure the corporation's property isn't subject to any liens, see the instructions for paragraph 11 of Form 5A.

4. Closing

At a closing, you meet with the seller to sign and exchange all the documents needed to complete the purchase. You pay (often in the form of a cashiers' check) whatever money is required for the ownership of the stock to be transferred to you and you receive stock certificates and other corporate documents.

 It's your show now. As the new owner of all shares, you'll want to immediately take legal charge by choosing a new board of directors. The new directors will then elect new officers. For guidance, see *The Corporate Minutes Book: The Legal Guide to Taking Care of Corporate Business,* by Anthony Mancuso (Nolo), a book that explains how to handle most details of small corporation governance and provides all the forms necessary to accomplish the job.

Insert the date, time and location of the closing.

SAMPLE:
The closing will take place:
Date: Thursday, May 2, _____
Time: 1:00 p.m.
Location: 123 Washington Street, Essex, New York.

Watch for "change of control" provisions in the corporation's leases and contracts.
Even when you're buying the stock of a corporation instead of its assets, you may need to get permission to take over a lease or other contracts to which the corporation is a party. This is because many savvy landlords and businesspeople have put "change of control" provisions in their leases and contracts. These provisions usually provide that if the corporation sells more than a certain percentage of its stock, this transfer is really an assignment of the lease or contract—and requires the landlord's or other party's consent before the buyer can assume the seller's or the tenant's rights and benefits. To make sure your new business will benefit from these leases and contracts, ask to see copies of these documents. And if you discover one of these provisions, ask the seller to get the landlord's or other party's permission to assign the lease or the contract before you buy the business. See paragraph 5 of Form 5D for language that will accomplish this.

5. Documents for Buyer

This paragraph assures that you'll get the documents you need to be in full charge of the business you're buying. If the sellers live in a community property state, check the box.

6. Sellers' Representations

In this paragraph, you want the current shareholders' assurances regarding key issues affecting the corporation and the stock you're buying. By getting these representations in writing, you'll have legal recourse against these people if the representations turn out to be false. (See the instructions to paragraph 14 of Form 5A for additional information.) Be sure to attach a schedule listing the corporation's debts and liabilities, as called for in paragraph 6B.

7. Covenant Not to Compete

See instructions for paragraph 16 of Form 5B.

Where a shareholder's spouse or adult child has been active in the business but may not be a shareholder, consider having the spouse or child (as well as the shareholder) sign a covenant not to compete. This will protect against the possibility of unwanted competition from the family member. As with other noncompete covenants, you must pay each signer something so that the covenant is legally binding. Remember, each person agreeing to give a covenant not to compete must join in signing the contract.

8. Risk of Loss

See instructions for paragraph 17 of Form 5A.

9. Disputes

See Chapter 1, Section D, for more information about dispute resolution clauses.

10. Additional Agreements

Insert any other items that apply to your purchase.

11. Required Signatures

Insert the name of the corporation whose shares you're buying. All shareholders of the corporation should sign the contract. In addition, in community property states, it's recommended that the spouses of shareholders named in paragraph 1 also sign.

Standard Clauses

The remainder of the agreement contains the standard clauses we discussed in Chapter 1, Section C. The only thing you'll need to fill in here is the name of the state whose law will apply to the contract in the paragraph called "Governing Law."

E. Form 5E: Bill of Sale

When you purchase business assets from a sole proprietor, partnership or limited liability company (Form 5A: Contract for Purchase of Business Assets From a Sole Proprietorship, Partnership or Limited Liability Company) or from a corporation (Form 5B: Contract for Purchase of Business Assets From a Corporation), you'll want the seller to give you a bill of sale—a document that transfers to you the title to the business's tangible personal property. Usually, this will consist of the furniture, fixtures and equipment and, in some cases, the inventory of goods sold. The seller should give you the bill of sale at closing.

As noted in the beginning of this chapter, some business assets you may be buying cannot be transferred through a bill of sale, but will require other documents instead. This includes land and buildings, which must be transferred by a deed that you record (file) at a designated county office to make it a matter of public record. It also includes intangible assets such as accounts receivable, contracts, trademarks, copyrights and patents, which must be transferred using various legal documents—the most common being an assignment. In addition, the seller won't use a bill of sale to transfer ownership of any vehicles included in the sale, but instead will simply authorize the title to the vehicles to be changed to the new owner on the records of the appropriate state agency—a process you're likely familiar with if you've ever sold a car.

If you're buying the stock of a corporation rather than its assets (Form 5D: Contract for Purchase of Corporate Stock), you won't need a bill of sale. The corporation itself will continue to own the business assets. By buying the stock of the corporation, you'll automatically own the corporation and all its assets.

Instructions for Form 5E: Bill of Sale

All the forms in this book are provided as tear-outs in Appendix B and on the accompanying forms CD-ROM. As you read the instructions for Form 5E, you may want to either tear out the form or open the form's file on the CD-ROM so you can follow along. Form 5E is in the file FORM5E.RTF on the CD-ROM. (For more information on using the forms CD-ROM, see Appendix A, "How to Use the CD-ROM.") If you don't use the forms CD-ROM, be sure to photocopy the agreement so you'll have a clean copy to use later.

1. Names

Fill in the names of the seller and buyer. If the seller is a business, use the correct name format, as discussed in Chapter 1, Section A. The individual partners, LLC members or corporate shareholders will need to sign the bill, however. (See instructions for signatures, below.) Include an attachment clearly identifying the property the seller is transferring to you.

A bill of sale doesn't guarantee the condition of the property. It's your job to inspect the business assets carefully before you sign the contract for purchase (Form 5A or Form 5B). Use paragraph 15A of the purchase contract to list any repairs or replacements that the seller is agreeing to make. If you don't specify the repairs or replacements in the contract, you must accept the assets in "as is" condition. To make sure the property hasn't deteriorated between the time you signed the contract and the time of closing, consider a final walk-through inspection just before the closing.

2. Acknowledgment of Payment

If you're buying the business assets in a single, lump-sum payment, check the first box.

If—as is more likely—you'll be making installment payments, check the second box.

3. Warranty of Ownership

This paragraph contains a warranty (guarantee) that the seller owns the assets you're buying.

Check the first box if you're paying the purchase price in full at closing.

Check the second box if you'll pay for the assets in part by a promissory note payable to the seller with the seller retaining a security interest in the assets.

Signatures

Both buyer and seller must sign.

If the seller is a partnership, LLC or corporation, have each partner, LLC member or corporate shareholder sign the bill of sale to personally accept responsibility for the warranty of ownership. See Chapter 1, Section B.

Community Property States: In a community property state, the spouse of a sole proprietor may have a property interest in the assets of a sole proprietor's business. In such states, you should have the spouse as well as the sole proprietor sign the bill of sale so that legal ownership of the tangible personal property is fully transferred to you.

Attachment to Bill of Sale

Insert the names of the seller and buyer. Next, clearly describe the property the seller is transferring to you. The seller should date and sign the attachment.

F. Form 5F: Affidavit— No Creditors

Use Form 5F: Affidavit—No Creditors, if you're buying business assets (Form 5A: Contract for Purchase of Business Assets From a Sole Proprietorship, Partnership or Limited Liability Company or Form 5B: Contract for Purchase of Business Assets From a Corporation). By having the seller put in writing at the closing that all debts and liabilities have been paid, you won't have to worry about giving notice to creditors to comply with the bulk sales requirements of your state's laws.

 See the beginning of this chapter for a discussion of bulk sales requirements.

There's some variation from state to state regarding the degree of formality that's needed when a seller verifies in writing at the closing that all debts and liabilities of the business have been paid. By getting the statement in the form of an affidavit—a written statement signed under oath in the presence of a notary public—you'll meet the formal requirements of every state.

Instructions for Form 5F: Affidavit— No Creditors

All the forms in this book are provided as tear-outs in Appendix B and on the accompanying forms CD-ROM. As you read the instructions for Form 5F, you may want to either tear out the form or open the form's file on the CD-ROM so you can follow along. Form 5F is in the file FORM5F.RTF on the CD-ROM. (For more information on using the forms CD-ROM, see Appendix A, "How to Use the CD-ROM.") If you don't use the forms CD-ROM, be sure to photocopy the agreement so you'll have a clean copy to use later.

Introduction

At the beginning of the form, fill in the state and county where it will be signed and the name of the person who will sign it:

If the seller is a sole proprietor, insert his or her name.

If the seller is a partnership, a partner should sign.

If the seller is a limited liability company, a member should sign.

If the seller is a corporation, the president should sign.

1. Entity Selling Assets

Check the box that describes whether the seller is a sole proprietor, a partnership, a limited liability company or a corporation. If the seller is a sole proprietor, fill in the name of the business. If the seller is a partnership, an LLC or a corporation, fill in the name of the seller.

Finally, fill in the name of the buyer.

2. No Security Interests

Nothing needs to be inserted. The seller is affirming that the assets you're buying are not subject to any security interests or other liens.

3. No Creditors

The seller is affirming that all debts and liabilities of the business have been paid and the business owners have no debts or liabilities that affect the assets or the right of the seller to transfer the assets. Check the appropriate box, depending on the legal structure of the seller.

💡 **Arrange for payment of utility bills.** At closing, the seller won't have an up-to-the-minute phone bill and probably won't have final bills for gas, electricity or water either. While lawyers can endlessly debate whether these undetermined utility bills do or do not amount to a debt or liability of the business, there's almost always a common-sense, practical way to deal with the issue. For example, if a third party such as a lawyer, accountant or title company representative is assisting with the closing, you and the seller can agree that the seller will leave a few hundred dollars with the third party to pay the utility bills. In legal jargon, the money is left in escrow and the third party who's helping out is the escrow agent. Put your agreement in writing.

ESCROW AGREEMENT

Abigail Bernstein, Seller, and Carlos Diaz, Buyer, agree as follows with Annette Miller, Escrow Agent.

1. Seller is depositing $200 with Escrow Agent.
2. Escrow Agent will use these funds to pay the telephone and other utility charges for Abby's Cafe for the period ending May 31, ___.
3. After 60 days, Escrow Agent will return any excess funds to Seller.

Abigail Bernstein
Abigail Bernstein, Seller

Annette Miller
Annette Miller, Escrow Agent

Carlos Diaz
Carlos Diaz, Buyer

If there's no third party to take care of paying the bills, the seller should be willing to let you keep a few hundred dollars of the seller's money to pay the bills, with the understanding that you'll refund any excess. The important point here is that the undetermined final utility bills needn't trigger the cumbersome notice requirements of your state's bulk sales law.

4. No Claims

The seller is affirming that there are no claims against the seller, the assets or the business owners that affect the assets. Check the appropriate box, depending on the legal structure of the seller.

5. Indemnification

If the statements in the Affidavit prove to be inaccurate, the seller will make sure you won't suffer any loss.

Signature

The seller should sign, using the proper signature format for its type of business (sole proprietorship, partnership, LLC or corporation), as discussed in Chapter 1, Section B.

Notarization

The form contains notarization language to assure that it's truly an affidavit. Official notarization wording differs a bit from state to state. A local notary should be able to assist you with completing this section of the form and making any slight changes needed to comply with local law and practice.

💡 **Notarization isn't always required.** In a number of states, the seller can simply sign this document "under penalty of perjury" and it will be the same as if notarized. The exact wording can vary.

SAMPLE:

I certify (or declare) under penalty of perjury that the foregoing is true and correct.

_____
Signature

_____
Date

Source: California Code of Civil Procedure Section 2015.5

G. Form 5G: Security Agreement

If you're buying business assets (Form 5A: Contract for Purchase of Business Assets From a Sole Proprietorship, Partnership or Limited Liability Company or Form 5B: Contract for Purchase of Business Assets From a Corporation) and not paying the purchase price in full at closing, the seller will want you to sign a promissory note for the unpaid balance. (See Chapter 4 for examples of promissory notes.)

Along with the promissory note, the seller will surely require you to sign a security agreement that gives the seller what amounts to a continuing ownership interest in the property until you have made the final payment. If you don't keep up your payments, this security agreement allows the seller to take back the business assets. If you do make all the payments, the seller will no longer have a lien (security interest)—but, as noted below, if you've signed a UCC financing statement in addition to a security agreement, when you've fully paid the debt, remember to have the seller sign a discharge that you can record at the proper public office to officially cancel the security interest.

⚠️ **Be careful about putting nonbusiness assets at risk.** As noted in the instructions to Form 5A, if you're buying a service business, the seller may seek to secure payment of the promissory note by getting a mortgage or a deed of trust on your house. Putting your house at risk to buy a business is usually a poor idea.

Instructions for Form 5G: Security Agreement

All the forms in this book are provided as tear-outs in Appendix B and on the accompanying forms CD-ROM. As you read the instructions for Form 5G, you may want to either tear out the form or open the form's file on the CD-ROM so you can follow along.

Form 5G is in the file FORM5G.RTF on the CD-ROM. (For more information on using the forms CD-ROM, see Appendix A, "How to Use the CD-ROM.") If you don't use the forms CD-ROM, be sure to photocopy the agreement so you'll have a clean copy to use later.

1. Names

Insert names of buyer and seller.

You'll almost always check the first box, which refers to the property you're buying. This is probably the same list the seller used for the bill of sale (Attachment 1 to Form 5E).

Check the second box as well if you agree to give the seller a security interest in any property you add to the business, such as replacement inventory.

2. Security for Promissory Note

Fill in the date of the promissory note, the amount owed and the interest rate.

3. Financing Statement

You don't need to insert anything here. This paragraph confirms that you'll sign a financing statement —a UCC notice that's filed with a governmental agency to let the public know that the property you're using in your business is subject to the seller's legal claim (lien). The reason the seller wants you to sign a financing statement is that it limits your practical ability to fraudulently resell the business assets to someone else pretending they're 100% yours. Once the UCC financing statement has been signed and filed, anyone who buys the major business assets from you will buy them subject to the lien of the person you're buying from—whether or not this new buyer actually looked at public records. This doesn't apply, however, to ordinary customers who buy items from an inventory of sale goods; they can buy merchandise without having to worry about a lien because the seller's lien only applies to the inventory as a whole—not to individual items you sell in the normal course of doing business.

⚠️ **Remember to get a discharge when you've paid off the debt.** Once you've paid for the business assets, there's no longer a need for the seller to retain a security interest in them. You're entitled to receive a signed discharge form from the seller verifying that the lien is no longer in effect, which you should then record (file) at the same state or county office where the seller has recorded the UCC financing statement that you originally signed.

4. Use and Care of the Secured Property

Check all appropriate boxes. (CD-ROM users should delete the language they don't want to include.)

If you check box A, fill in the location where you'll keep the secured property and the type of business for which you'll use it.

> **SAMPLE:**
> Keep the Secured Property at 555 High Street, Dallas, Texas, and use it only in the operation of the computer repair and sales business.

5. Buyer's Default

Nothing needs to be filled in here.

6. Seller's Rights

This summarizes the seller's rights under the Uniform Commercial Code if you default on your obligations under this security agreement. Fill in the name of the state where the property is located. Check the boxes that describe the rights you want to include.

7. Notice to Buyer

Fill in the location where the seller should send you a notice if you've defaulted and the seller is going sell, lease or otherwise dispose of the property.

Standard Clauses

The remainder of the agreement contains the standard clauses we discussed in Chapter 1, Section C. The only thing you'll need to fill in here is the name of the state whose law will apply to the contract in the paragraph called "Governing Law."

Signature

Both parties should sign, and the contract should be dated. See Chapter 1, Section B.

Attachment to Security Agreement

Describe the secured property referred to in paragraph 1. ∎

CHAPTER

6

Leasing Space

Commercial leases are usually long and complicated—and often tilted heavily in favor of the landlord. By contrast, the leases in this chapter are comparatively short and simple, and more balanced from both the landlord's and tenant's point of view. But if you're a tenant looking to rent commercial space, be forewarned: many landlords have developed their own leases and may insist that you use their form. Still, especially with a smaller landlord—someone who owns only a single building or two, for example—you should have a good shot at having the landlord agree to use your lease form.

Even where a landlord insists on using the ten-page, fine-print monster that they have paid a law firm big bucks to tilt in their favor, a careful reading of this chapter should equip you to spot unfair clauses and insist on reasonable modifications. In this context, it's key to understand that everything is negotiable (and in many instances landlords present biased clauses precisely because they expect tenants to negotiate).

Chapter 11 of the *Legal Guide for Starting & Running a Small Business*, by Fred S. Steingold (Nolo), contains more information on negotiating a favorable lease and an explanation of the basic law that applies to leases.

This chapter contains three leases—and seven additional forms associated with the leasing process. Using Form 6A: Gross Lease, you make one, all-inclusive rental payment each month and it's up to the landlord to pay all property-related expenses including taxes and insurance. However, in many real estate markets, especially for newer buildings, it's more common to use a "net" lease—one in which you pay a fixed rent but also have to pay for some or all of the building's operating expenses such as real estate taxes, building maintenance and landlord's insurance. In that case, use Form 6B: Net Lease, if you'll be occupying the entire building or Form 6C: Net Lease, if you'll be occupying only part of the building.

Make Sure You Know How the Landlord Is Measuring the Space

Instead of stating the rent as an inclusive figure for the entire commercial space you're considering (for example, $2,000 a month for the first floor of the building), it's common for a landlord to quote a rate based on square footage (for example, $12 per square foot per year or $1.00 per square foot per month). If the landlord uses one of the square footage methods, be sure you understand how the square footage will be computed. Perhaps surprisingly, in the world of commercial leases, some landlords begin their measurements at the center of exterior walls and others even start at the outside of the walls. In either of these situations, you'll be paying for a good deal of unusable space. To be sure you are really leasing the space you need, first, physically measure it and then carefully determine if your furniture and equipment will fit without crowding. Measuring the interior space will also allow you to determine how much the landlord will be charging you. For example, if it turns out that the landlord is measuring from the outside of the walls, the $12 per square foot per year price he quotes you may actually translate into $14 per square foot of usable space. That's not necessarily bad if your total monthly rent bill is competitive with the rent you'd pay for comparable space elsewhere. The point is that you can't make valid comparisons unless you know all the facts.

Be aware that another typical landlord practice—especially in an office building—is for the landlord to charge you rent for a percentage of the building's common areas even though you don't enjoy exclusive use of those areas. So, for example, if you rent 10% of the office space in a building, the landlord may add in 10% of the common area space in determining the square footage you're renting.

Net Leases vs. Gross Leases

How can you decide whether to use a gross lease (like Form 6A) or a net lease (like Form 6B or 6C)? First, be aware that you may not have the opportunity to choose between a net lease, where you pay rent plus additional amounts for operating expenses—typically, utilities, insurance, real property taxes, common area maintenance, janitorial services, snow removal and lawn care—and a gross lease, where you pay one monthly rent check to the landlord who in turn takes care of these other expenses. In many situations, the landlord will simply insist on one method rather than the other.

Given a choice, you of course care far more which type of lease will be cheaper in the long run than you do who actually pays bills such as taxes and insurance. As a general rule, expect the initial monthly rent on a net lease plus the extra charges for such things as insurance and taxes to come to less than the rent on a gross lease for the same space. That's because in agreeing to a gross lease, the landlord will often want to charge a little extra to protect against possible increases in property taxes, insurance and other operating costs he may experience during the lease term. Reasoning backward, this means you should also understand that while a net lease may be cheaper at the start (even after you pay all the extra items), you rather than the landlord bear the risk of increases in taxes, insurance and maintenance bills during the lease term.

The length of the lease is obviously a key factor in determining whether a cheaper net lease or a more expensive gross lease is better. The shorter the lease period, the more likely you are to prefer a cheaper net lease, since costs will have less time to go up. Of course, the reverse is also true. If a lease is for more than three years—and certainly if it's for more than five years—a gross lease where you don't bear the risk of tax, insurance and maintenance cost increases becomes an excellent idea, even if it's slightly more expensive to begin with.

After you've leased space for your business, you may discover at some point that you can't or don't want to occupy the space—or some part of it—for the full term of the lease. This can occur because your business is wildly successful and you need to move to larger quarters, because it's just limping along, requiring you to economize by cutting back on the amount of space you occupy, or for many other reasons. Depending on the circumstances, the process of transferring occupancy rights to another tenant is referred to in legal jargon as subletting or assignment.

But what if your lease says you can't sublet or assign the space without the landlord's consent? Start by understanding that a fair lease should provide that if you wish to assign or sublet, "the landlord won't unreasonably withhold consent." But even if your lease doesn't say this, the law of many states reads this language in. This is great news, since it can often mean that if you find a suitable new tenant to take over your lease at the same or a higher amount, you're off the hook to pay future rent whether or not the landlord decides to rent to this person.

What's the legal difference between a sublease and assignment? While some of the technicalities can be daunting, basically, if you transfer just some of the leased space to another tenant or transfer all the space for only part of the remainder of the lease period, it's called a sublease. Typically, with a sublease—such as Form 6D: Sublease—the subtenant pays rent to you and you continue to pay the landlord under the terms of your lease. If your lease, like most leases, requires you to obtain the landlord's consent to a subletting of your space, you can use Form 6E: Landlord's Consent to Sublease, for this purpose.

By contrast, an assignment occurs if you transfer all the space to someone else for the entire remaining term of the lease. In this situation, the new tenant deals directly with (pays rent to) the landlord. This can be done using Form 6F: Assignment of Lease.

⚠ You're still on the hook. Don't assume that because you've sublet part or all of your space or assigned the entire lease to another tenant, you're relieved of your responsibility to pay rent and meet other obligations in the lease. On the contrary, in most states, under either arrangement, you're still responsible for making good on any unpaid rent the subtenant or assignee fails to pay. Although there are some subtle legal differences between subletting and assigning (you have less obligation to pay for damages caused by a new tenant under an assignment, for example), under either you are only free of future financial obligations if the landlord releases you in writing. The landlord may be willing to do this, especially if you're able to find a substitute tenant who's financially strong and willing to pay a higher rent.

It's common to negotiate a lease with an option to extend the lease beyond its original duration. For example, you may have a three-year lease that gives you the option to extend the lease for another three years. Generally, a lease with an option to renew requires the tenant to notify the landlord in writing if the tenant decides to extend the lease (exercise the option). Form 6G: Notice of Exercise of Lease Option, allows you to do this.

If your lease doesn't include an option to extend, you and the landlord may still agree to an extension at any time before the original lease term runs out. Form 6H: Extension of Lease, allows you and the landlord to lengthen the lease with perhaps a few modifications, without starting from scratch.

When conditions change during the life of your lease, you and the landlord may mutually agree to change some of the terms. If so, you can accomplish this with Form 6I: Amendment of Lease.

Finally, sometimes you need to add material to a lease that doesn't fit within a prepared form or doesn't adapt easily to word processing—a diagram, for example. You can add this material by using Form 6J: Attachment to Lease.

A. Form 6A: Gross Lease

As discussed in the beginning of this chapter, in a gross lease you pay the landlord a fixed monthly rent and it's up to the landlord to pay for all expenses of operating the building, including real estate taxes, real estate insurance, building maintenance and repairs and utilities—except for any utilities that are separately metered and for which you agree to pay. If you've ever rented a house or an apartment unit, chances are excellent that you signed what amounts to a gross lease, even though it didn't carry that name.

A gross lease gives you the certainty of knowing exactly what you'll be paying for your space during the entire lease term. If real estate expenses go down, your landlord makes more money on the lease; conversely, if expenses go up, your landlord does less well financially. It follows that on a long-term gross lease, a landlord may seek to buffer the impact of possible future increases in operating expenses by providing that the rental amount you are obligated to pay will step up periodically. Assuming you have negotiated a favorable rental in the first place and the step-up is modest, you may find this acceptable, since you still have the certainty of knowing what the rent will be during each year of the lease. But remember, America as a whole or your industry or entire region could hit an economic downdraft tomorrow with the result that rents in your area might actually drop. In short, don't just assume it makes sense to agree to a series of built-in increases.

There are at least two other common ways that a landlord can try to deal with the possibility of increasing operating costs. The first is to provide that if expenses go up during the lease term, you must pay for them. For example, if the property tax starts out at $3,000 and then jumps to $3,300 you'd be responsible for the additional $300. Another popular method is tied to increases in the Consumer Price Index or other inflation-sensitive indicator. Under either of these methods, you won't know exactly how much your total rent bill will be in future years unless you insist on a cap or upper limit on the amount of the increase. It makes sense to do this; otherwise, if your landlord's lease costs or the overall inflation index spike upwards, you might find yourself with a lease that suddenly presents the risk of bankrupting you.

Estoppel Letters

Although we haven't included them in the lease forms in this chapter, you may come across a clause in other lease forms entitled "Estoppel Letters" or "Estoppel Certificates." You could read the clause over and over without having a clue as to what it's all about. And, depending on what happens during your lease, you might never encounter this clause in practice. Still, it's a good idea to know what you're signing.

Estoppel letters often come up when your landlord wants to sell the property or needs a loan. Since a buyer will get the building along with its tenants and their leases, he or she will want an assurance that the tenants are living up to the terms of their leases and are not owed any money from the landlord, such as money for tenant improvements. If the landlord needs a loan, a lender will be more willing to make the loan if it knows that the rent money is clear of any claims by the tenants. As a condition of the sale or the loan, these buyers and lenders may ask the landlord for an "estoppel letter" or "estoppel certificate" from each tenant. The letter is simply a statement signed by each tenant certifying that, to the best of the tenant's knowledge, the tenant and the landlord are following the lease.

Tenants sometimes need an estoppel letter, too. If you want to sell your business, take out a loan, merge, sublease or assign, you too will need to convince the person you're dealing with that the situation they're about to walk into is a good one, without hidden problems.

If you're a tenant, there's nothing wrong with a clause requiring you to provide an estoppel letter. But when you're negotiating your lease, it's perfectly okay for you to suggest that the estoppel letter clause be mutual, and to insist on fair consequences if you refuse to sign an estoppel letter for some reason (some clauses state that if you refuse to sign an estoppel, you will be in default under the lease, which would give the landlord the right to terminate the lease). Obviously, it makes sense for both of you to craft a more rational consequence.

Above all, when you receive an estoppel letter prepared by the landlord, be sure to read it carefully and compare it with the terms of your lease. For example, the landlord may provide an estoppel letter stating that you have no renewal right when you do indeed have one in your lease. Obviously, the landlord was devious or careless in preparing the letter. To avoid future problems, fix the letter to reflect the true state of affairs before you sign it, because the consequences of signing an estoppel that you know is inaccurate could be significant—you could end up unintentionally waiving a right or getting involved in a fight between your landlord and a lender.

Bargain to have no rent increase for at least the first two years. When you bargain to rent a business space, I recommend that you insist that rent not go up one penny for at least 24 months. Before you sign on the bottom line is the time when you have maximum bargaining power, in most instances. Simply say no to a landlord who proposes raising the rent after only one year—after all, your bargaining power will never be better than it is before you sign on the bottom line.

Instructions for Form 6A: Gross Lease

All the forms in this book are provided as tear-outs in Appendix B and on the accompanying forms CD-ROM. As you read the instructions for Form 6A, you may want to either tear out the form or open the form's file on the CD-ROM so you can follow along. Form 6A is in the file FORM6A.RTF on the CD-ROM. (For more information on using the forms CD-ROM, see Appendix A, "How to Use the CD-ROM.") If you don't use the forms CD-ROM, be sure to photocopy the agreement so you'll have a clean copy to use later.

1. Names

Insert the landlord's name and the name of your business. See Chapter 1, Section A, for a discussion of how to use names in legal documents.

2. Premises Being Leased

Fill in a description of what you're leasing.

SAMPLES:
- The building at 320 North Main Street, Ann Arbor, Michigan.
- The entire first floor of the building at 320 North Main Street, Ann Arbor, Michigan.
- The portion of the building at 320 North Main Street, Ann Arbor, Michigan, that is outlined in blue ink on the drawing in Attachment #2.
- The west 3,000 square feet of the second floor of the building at 320 North Main Street, Ann Arbor, Michigan, as shown on the drawing in Attachment #2.

If you're renting an entire building, be sure to describe not only the building but also any accompanying features such as parking areas, driveways and outbuildings.

SAMPLE:
The building at 320 North Main Street, Ann Arbor, Michigan, and the entire 400-square foot parking lot on the north side of the building.

If you're renting part of a building and will be sharing some facilities with other tenants, check the box before the words "Shared Facilities" and then check the items that apply. Pay attention to the fact that the broad categories listed on our form may not be sufficiently specific to really define what you are leasing. If so, check "other" or create a more detailed attachment. (You can use Form 6J for this.) For example, if your lease gives you the right to park in an adjacent parking lot that's shared with other tenants, you should reach a clear understanding with the landlord about whether you're entitled to a certain number of spaces or whether parking is on a first-come, first-served basis.

Identify your parking spaces and conference room rights. If you're getting a certain number of spaces, it's good practice to attach a drawing to the lease that identifies them and requires the landlord to clearly mark them with signs or pavement paint. Similarly, if your lease gives you the right to use a conference room, you need to agree on how often you can use it and the procedures for reserving the room.

3. Term of Lease

Fill in the number of years that the lease runs, as well as the date the lease starts and ends.

4. Rent

Insert the day of the month on which rent is due.

If your rent will remain constant throughout the lease, check the first box and then insert the amount of monthly rent. (To avoid confusion, you can cross out the rest of the paragraph since it doesn't apply.)

Some Optional Rent Clauses

Here are some clauses you might consider adding:

Optional cost-of-living clause: The following language can be used if you and the landlord agree on annual cost-of-living increases in the rent beginning after the first two years of the lease and further agree on an upper limit on these increases:

SAMPLE:

On the second anniversary of the beginning of the lease term and on each anniversary after that, the rent will be adjusted based on any increase in the Consumer Price Index of the Bureau of Labor Statistics (all-items index for all urban consumers, U.S. city average, 1982-84 = 100) or any replacement index. The adjusted rent for the lease year succeeding any adjustment (payable in monthly installments) will be the product arrived at by multiplying the rent for the year just prior to adjustment by a fraction, the numerator of which will be the Index number for the month immediately preceding the adjustment and the denominator of which will be the Index number for the month used in the numerator of the previous adjustment (or, on the second anniversary of the beginning of the lease term, the Index number for the month immediately preceding the beginning of the lease term). In no event, however, will the rent exceed $_____ per month.

Optional rent abatement clause: In rent negotiations, it's fairly common for commercial landlords to provide one to three months of free rent at the beginning of the first lease term to cushion the tenant's moving expenses. In legal jargon, this is sometimes called a rent abatement. If you've successfully negotiated a rent-free period, you'll need to slightly modify wording of the lease, as shown below.

SAMPLE (Rent constant throughout the lease)

Tenant will pay rent of $_____ per month for the entire term of the lease, except for the first three months of the lease which will be rent free.

SAMPLE (Rent changes during lease term)

Tenant will pay the following rent:

$_____ per month during the 12-month period beginning September 1, _____, except for the first three months of the lease which will be rent free.

SAMPLE:

Tenant will pay rent of $2,500 per month for the entire term of the lease.

If your rent will increase during the term of the lease, check the second box and fill in the monthly amounts for each year of the lease, inserting the date that each lease year begins.

SAMPLE:

Tenant will pay the following rent:

- $2,500 per month during the 12-month period beginning January 1, 2001.
- $2,500 per month during the 12-month period beginning January 1, 2002.
- $2,600 per month during the 12-month period beginning January 1, 2003.
- $2,700 per month during the 12-month period beginning January 1, 2004.
- $2,800 per month during the 12-month period beginning January 1, 2005.

5. Option to Extend Lease

Getting an option to extend gives you the choice of whether to keep renting the space beyond the original lease term. For example, you might bargain for a two-year lease with an option clause giving you the right to continue (renew) the lease for an additional three years. Insisting on an option clause often makes sense because if your business thrives, you know you can stay at the same location and pay a predetermined rent. Conversely, if your business isn't doing well at the end of the initial lease period and you need to scale down or close down—or if it's doing super-well and you need larger space—you can decline to exercise the option and leave the original location.

Insert the number of years that the lease will be extended if you exercise your option. Then put in any changes in the terms that will apply during the extension period.

SAMPLE:

- During the extension period, the rent will be
  $_____ per month.
- During the extension period, the rent will be
  $_____ per month for the first year;
  $_____ per month for the second year; and
  $_____ per month for the third year.

Finally, insert your deadline for notifying the landlord that you're exercising the option. A date 60 days before the expiration of the original lease would be reasonable, but the landlord may bargain for a longer notice period of somewhere between 90 and 180 days.

If you're able to negotiate an additional option period, check the box before the words "Additional Option" and fill in the blanks as you did with the original option period.

⚠ **Rent for an option period should not be open-ended.** The lease should define the amount of rent you'll pay during any option period. Normally, this should either be the same amount of rent you paid for the original lease term, a stated new rental amount or an amount readily established by a mechanism (current rent plus an increase based on the Consumer Price Index, for example) stated in the option clause. Absolutely avoid a statement that the rent for the option period will be negotiated later on. While this type clause defers the sometimes difficult task of focusing on what will constitute a reasonable rent in the future, accepting it means you run the obvious risk that the landlord will demand an unaffordable increase.

A Move-In Checklist Can Help Prevent Disputes

The leases in this book—and most other lease forms as well—say that in order to get back your security deposit, you must return the leased space to the landlord in good condition, except for reasonable wear and tear. As you know, this general language can open the door to disputes over a number of issues—one of which is what shape the space was in when you rented it. To reduce the likelihood of a disagreement, it makes sense for you and the landlord to walk through the space together at the time you take possession and write down the condition of each component. Obviously, the items to be checked will vary depending on the building, but the following list is a good starting point:

- ☐ Roof
- ☐ Ceilings
- ☐ Foundation and Structural Components
- ☐ Floors and Floor Coverings
- ☐ Window Coverings
- ☐ Light Fixtures
- ☐ Electrical System
- ☐ Water System
- ☐ Sewage Disposal System
- ☐ Sprinkler System
- ☐ Alarm System
- ☐ Windows and Doors
- ☐ Walls
- ☐ Bathroom Fixtures
- ☐ Heating, Ventilating and Air-Conditioning System
- ☐ Outside Spaces (Walkways, Parking Lot, Landscaping)
- ☐ Equipment

You and the landlord should make and sign two copies of the move-in checklist and each of you should keep one. Then, when you move out, conduct another walk-through inspection with the landlord to check the condition of the space. If you and the landlord observe, for example, that the light fixture inside the entry hall is dented but the dent was noted on your move-in checklist, it will be clear that you're not responsible for fixing or replacing it.

6. Security Deposit

Insert the amount of any security deposit that you and the landlord agree on. Typically, the amount will be equal to one or two months rent.

Many residential landlords prepare a pre-printed form to ease the task of documenting the move-in and move-out inspections. See, for example, the Landlord/Tenant Checklist in *Leases & Rental Agreements*, by Marcia Stewart, Ralph Warner and Janet Portman (Nolo). Commercial landlords should consider doing the same.

7. Improvements by Landlord

If you're taking the premises as is, check the first box. Otherwise, check the second box; then prepare a separate sheet called an Attachment (see Form 6J: Attachment to Lease) to give the details of any repairs and improvements (often called buildouts) the landlord will make. Before you rent the space, you may want to hire an experienced contractor to help you decide what changes are needed. And if the repairs and improvements will be extensive, consider having an architect or a contractor prepare detailed specifications so that they can be added to the lease in the form of an attachment.

 Don't be shy about asking for improve- ments. If you're leasing space for at least three or five years, it's routine for the landlord to agree to upgrade it to meet your needs. The extent of the improvements (or buildouts) is, of course, a matter of negotiation and depends on many other factors, including how much rent you've agreed to pay. Also realize that for their own tax and borrow- ing reasons, many landlords are more willing to spend money providing tenant-requested improve- ments than they are cutting the rent by the same amount.

8. Improvements by Tenant

Nothing needs to be inserted. This section makes it clear you can improve or alter the space if you first get the landlord's written consent. If you know before you sign the lease that there are certain improvements you want to make, get the landlord's consent in the lease itself, listing the details in an Attachment.

SAMPLE:

Landlord consents to Tenant making the improvements and alterations of the items listed in Attachment _____ at Tenant's expense.

9. Tenant's Use of Premises

Describe your anticipated use of the space in suffi- ciently broad terms to cover all anticipated uses.

SAMPLES:

- Sale of office supplies; sale, leasing and servicing of office equipment; related business activities.
- Servicing and repair of electrical appliances and electronic equipment and related business activities.

10. Landlord's Representations

Nothing needs to be inserted here.

The landlord states that when your lease starts, the space will be properly zoned for your use and that the building will comply with all applicable laws and regulations. This last representation can be especially helpful if the government or an individual later claims that the building doesn't meet the requirements of the Americans with Disabilities Act—or a similar state law—and as a result extensive changes must be made.

The landlord also assures you that there are no known problems concerning toxic or hazardous substances.

11. Utilities and Services

Check the utilities and services that the landlord will furnish. You'll be responsible for any utilities that aren't itemized as the landlord's responsibility.

12. Maintenance and Repairs

Nothing need be filled in here. This section spells out the landlord's responsibilities and yours for maintenance and repairs.

can step into the shoes of the insured business (or be subrogated to that business's legal rights) and sue any person or business that caused the damage.

> **EXAMPLE:** Pericles Corporation is a tenant under a gross lease in a building owned by Town Development Associates. Pericles carries insurance on its furniture and equipment and Town Development carries insurance on the building. One evening, an employee of Pericles forgets to turn off the coffee maker before leaving. The machine overheats and a fire results, seriously damaging the building, as well as the furniture and equipment of Pericles. Pericles' insurance company pays for replacement of the damaged furniture and equipment, and Town Development's insurance company pays for repair of the building. Because the lease between Pericles and Town Development contains a "mutual waiver of subrogation" clause, the insurance company can't sue Pericles for the money it paid to repair the building—even though the fire was caused by the negligence of a Pericles employee.

13. Insurance

In subparagraph B, fill in the minimum dollar amounts of insurance that you'll be required to carry. Public liability insurance carried by most businesses covers payment to people who are injured on the premises or whose property is damaged there—usually as a result of negligence—but doesn't cover damage done to the building. (In a net lease, such as Form 6B or Form 6C, you'd be expected to pay for your landlord's insurance on the building as well.)

In subparagraph C, the landlord and tenant release each other from any liability to the other for certain losses covered by insurance. As explained in Chapter 11 of the *Legal Guide for Starting & Running a Small Business,* in the insurance law trade, this is called by the awful term "mutual waiver of subrogation." Without this waiver, if an insurance company pays an insured business for damage to property, it

Carry insurance on your business assets. The insurance language in the lease covers only the types of insurance that concern both you and the landlord. In addition, you'll want to make sure you have insurance on the furniture, equipment, inventory and other assets your business owns.

14. Taxes

Nothing needs to be filled in here. Note that even under a gross lease—where you're not responsible for insurance or taxes on the landlord's building—you'll be responsible for any personal property taxes your state or local government imposes on your furniture, fixtures and equipment.

15. Subletting and Assignment

Nothing needs to be filled in here. As discussed in the beginning of this chapter, landlords understandably want to retain some control over who and what kind of business will occupy the space if you decide to move out before the end of the lease term. That's fine, but you also want to know that if you need to leave early you can do so at little or no cost as long as you find a suitable new tenant. That's where the key words "not unreasonably withhold such consent" come in. See the beginning of this chapter for further details.

16. Damage to Premises

Nothing needs to be filled in here. This lease section protects you if the premises are damaged by a flood or fire, for example.

17. Notice of Default

This lease section gives you a chance to correct defaults; the landlord can't evict you until you've had the opportunity to take corrective action. Because in some states, giving a tenant three to five days to pay unpaid rent or cure other lease violations is common practice, your landlord may propose shortening the ten-day notice period.

18. Quiet Enjoyment

Nothing needs to be filled in here. The landlord assures you that you'll be able to peacefully occupy the space as long as you do what's required under the lease.

19. Eminent Domain

Nothing needs to be filled in here. Eminent domain is the procedure by which a government agency takes private property for a public purpose such as a road or school. Some leases use the word "condemnation" to describe this process.

20. Holding Over

Nothing needs to be filled in here. This covers the status of your tenancy if you continue to occupy the space after the lease ends.

21. Disputes

See Chapter 1, Section D, for more information about dispute resolution clauses. Note that the landlord

isn't required to participate in alternative methods of dispute resolution unless you've paid your rent to the landlord or placed it in escrow.

22. Additional Agreements

Fill in any other terms that you and the landlord have agreed to.

SAMPLES:

- Landlord will provide janitorial services three times a week.
- Landlord will add Tenant's name to the directory of building tenants.
- Landlord will rent no other space in the building to a retail food business.

If you prefer, you can document any additional conditions using Form 6J: Attachment to Lease. If you do add an attachment, refer to it by number in subparagraph A.

Standard Clauses

The remainder of the lease contains the standard clauses we discussed in Chapter 1, Section C. The only thing you'll need to fill in here is the name of the state whose law will apply to the contract in the paragraph called "Governing Law."

Signatures

Sign and date the lease. For more on signing contracts, see Chapter 1, Section B.

B. Form 6B: Net Lease for Entire Building

As discussed in the beginning of this chapter, in a net lease the tenant not only pays rent but also pays for some or all of the building's operating costs—property taxes, property insurance and maintenance. In the lingo of the real estate business, a lease that requires the tenant to pay for all of these costs is referred to as a "triple net" lease. Form 6B is a triple net lease that can be used when you're leasing an entire building, while Form 6C is for use when you're leasing just a portion of a building.

Consider getting help on the details of hybrid leases. As mentioned in the beginning of this chapter, in all lease negotiations, you and the landlord will jockey for position regarding who will bear the cost of any future increases in the cost of property taxes, insurance, maintenance, utilities and janitorial service. You obviously can negotiate with the landlord to modify Form 6B to change the allocation of any operating cost between you and the landlord. For example, you could have the tenant be responsible for maintenance but not for taxes and insurance, or you can negotiate to place a cap on the amount you're obligated to pay. If you make lots of changes, wording may get to be a bit of a challenge. So especially if you are new to the commercial real estate world, and especially if your lease is long and the rent is expensive, it makes sense to have a real estate or small business expert review your work and perhaps even do some or all of the negotiating for you.

Instructions for Form 6B: Net Lease for Entire Building

All the forms in this book are provided as tear-outs in Appendix B and on the accompanying forms CD-ROM. As you read the instructions for Form 6B, you may want to either tear out the form or open the form's file on the CD-ROM so you can follow along. Form 6B is in the file FORM6B.RTF on the CD-ROM. (For more information on using the forms CD-ROM, see Appendix A, "How to Use the CD-ROM.") If you don't use the forms CD-ROM, be sure to photocopy the agreement so you'll have a clean copy to use later.

1. Names
See the instructions for paragraph 1 of Form 6A.

2. Premises Being Leased
See the instructions for paragraph 2 of Form 6A.

3. Term of Lease
See the instructions for paragraph 3 of Form 6A.

4. Rent
See the instructions for paragraph 4 of Form 6A. Other portions of the lease make you responsible for expenses beyond the rent.

5. Option to Extend Lease
See the instructions for paragraph 5 of Form 6A.

6. Security Deposit
See the instructions for paragraph 6 of Form 6A.

7. Improvements by Landlord
See the instructions for paragraph 7 of Form 6A.

8. Improvements by Tenant
See the instructions for paragraph 8 of Form 6A.

9. Tenant's Use of Premises
See the instructions for paragraph 9 of Form 6A.

10. Landlord's Representations
See the instructions for paragraph 10 of Form 6A.

11. Utilities and Services
Nothing needs to be filled in here if you'll be paying for all utilities and services. If the landlord will be paying for some and you'll be paying for some, you'll need to customize the paragraph:

> **SAMPLE:**
> Landlord will pay for water. Tenant will pay for electricity and gas, including the electricity or gas needed for heating and air-conditioning.

12. Maintenance and Repairs
Nothing needs to be filled in here. You'll be paying for all maintenance and repairs.

13. Insurance
Fill in the amount of insurance you're required to carry on the building. See the instructions for paragraph 13 of Form 6A.

14. Taxes
Nothing needs to be filled in here. Note that you'll be responsible for both the real estate taxes and

your own personal property taxes—the taxes on your furniture and equipment—if your state or local government imposes a tax on such property.

15. Subletting and Assignment
See the instructions for paragraph 15 of Form 6A.

16. Notice of Default
See the instructions for paragraph 17 of Form 6A.

17. Quiet Enjoyment
See the instructions for paragraph 18 of Form 6A.

18. Holding Over
See the instructions for paragraph 20 of Form 6A.

19. Eminent Domain
See the instructions for paragraph 19 of Form 6A.

20. Disputes
See the instructions for paragraph 21 of Form 6A.

21. Additional Agreements
Fill in any other terms that you and the landlord have agreed to. For examples of language, see the instructions for paragraph 22 of Form 6A.

Standard Clauses
The remainder of the lease contains the standard clauses we discussed in Chapter 1, Section C. The only thing you'll need to fill in here is the name of the state whose law will apply to the contract in the paragraph called "Governing Law."

Signatures
Sign and date the lease. For more on signing contracts, see Chapter 1, Section B.

C. Form 6C: Net Lease for Part of Building

See the introductory material for Form 6B, which is almost identical to this form, except that 6B is designed for use in leasing an entire building. If

you use the lease discussed here, you're paying for only a portion of the building's operating expenses.

Instructions for Form 6C: Net Lease for Part of Building

All the forms in this book are provided as tear-outs in Appendix B and on the accompanying forms CD-ROM. As you read the instructions for Form 6C, you may want to either tear out the form or open the form's file on the CD-ROM so you can follow along. Form 6C is in the file FORM6C.RTF on the CD-ROM. (For more information on using the forms CD-ROM, see Appendix A, "How to Use the CD-ROM.") If you don't use the forms CD-ROM, be sure to photocopy the agreement so you'll have a clean copy to use later.

1. Names
See the instructions for paragraph 1 of Form 6A.

2. Premises Being Leased
See the instructions for paragraph 2 of Form 6A.

Think about how you get access if the building is closed. If you're renting space in a building where you enter through a door (lobby, entryway, elevator) also used by other tenants, make sure you'll have access to your space at all times you need it, even if the building is otherwise closed. (For example, if you like to come in at 6 a.m. or work until midnight, make sure you can do it.) If this might be a problem, ask that language be added to your lease specifying how you can get in when you need to, with specific reference to days and hours. Also, make sure you can control the lights, heating and cooling and any other essential systems when the building is normally closed. For example, if your office is on the eleventh floor, you'll want to be able to use the elevator.

3. Term of Lease
See the instructions for paragraph 3 of Form 6A.

4. Rent

See the instructions for paragraph 4 of Form 6A. Other portions of the lease make you responsible for expenses beyond the rent.

5. Option to Extend Lease

See the instructions for paragraph 5 of Form 6A.

6. Security Deposit

See the instructions for paragraph 6 of Form 6A.

7. Improvements by Landlord

See the instructions for paragraph 7 of Form 6A.

8. Improvements by Tenant

See the instructions for paragraph 8 of Form 6A.

9. Tenant's Use of Premises

See the instructions for paragraph 9 of Form 6A. If you're a retailer or food business sharing space in a building with other similar businesses, the landlord may propose limiting what you can sell so your activities won't directly compete with those of other tenants. For example, if you're leasing space for a bookstore in a building where other space is occupied by a sandwich shop, the landlord may insist on a clause saying you can't sell food or even coffee drinks. Or if you're leasing space for your art gallery in a shopping mall where other space is occupied by a jeweler, the landlord may want language prohibiting you from selling jewelry.

You may want protection from competitors or incompatible businesses. If you're a doctor or dentist renting space in a professional building, you understandably may want to protect your image by having the landlord agree to only rent retail space to compatible tenants such as a pharmacy, eyeglass store or home care equipment rental service. Or if you're renting space for a camera store that will sell and process film, you may want language in your lease to prohibit the landlord from allowing any other tenant (a drugstore, for example) from selling or processing film. If so, you'll need to bargain for it.

SAMPLE:

In all other leases or written rental agreements, covering space in the building at 456 University Avenue, Sarasota, Florida, Landlord will prohibit the tenant or any subtenant from selling or processing film.

10. Landlord's Representations

See the instructions for paragraph 10 of Form 6A.

11. Utilities and Services

In subparagraph A, check any utilities and services that are separately metered or billed for the space you're leasing.

Then, in subparagraph B, fill in the percentage you'll pay for utility and service charges that are not separately metered or billed, and check which charges those are. Usually the percentage is based on a ratio of how many square feet you're renting as compared to how many rentable square feet the building contains. Thus, if you're renting 5,000 square feet in a building that contains 50,000 square feet of rentable space, you'll likely be paying 10% of the utilities.

Next, fill in what day you will pay on.

Finally, fill in the frequency with which the landlord shows you the actual bills. Anywhere between two months and six months would seem reasonable.

Check out past bills and ask for a cap on your costs. Before you agree to pay for utilities, ask to see past bills for the building. It's also a good idea to ask for a reasonable cap on the amount you're obligated for. Otherwise, if a super-heavy utility user (for example, a business with a bunch of heavy-duty computer and network servers that run 24 hours a day) moves into the building and utility charges take a big jump, your bills will go way up.

12. Maintenance and Repair of Common Areas

Check the boxes for those parts of the common areas the landlord will maintain and repair.

Fill in the percentage of the costs you'll pay—probably the same percentage you used in paragraph 11—and the day you'll pay it.

13. Maintenance and Repair of Leased Premises

Check the boxes for those parts of the building the landlord will maintain and repair. (CD-ROM users can just delete the text they don't want to include.)

14. Insurance

In subparagraph A, fill in the minimum amounts of insurance you'll be required to carry.

In subparagraph B, fill in the percentage of the landlord's insurance costs you'll pay—probably the same percentage you used in paragraph 11.

15. Taxes

Fill in the percentage of the landlord's real estate taxes you'll pay—probably the same percentage you used in paragraph 11. Note that you'll also be responsible for your own personal property taxes—the taxes on your furniture, fixtures and equipment—if your state or local government imposes a tax on such property. Then, fill in the day of the month you'll make the payment.

⚠️ **A tax rise may be imminent.** Especially if you're renting space in a newly remodeled building, an upwards reassessment of property taxes may be imminent. Of course, many other factors can also trigger a new tax assessment. In short, it's always a good idea to check with the municipality to find out what to expect. And as with other open-ended obligations in a lease, it can make sense to bargain for a cap.

16. Subletting and Assignment

See the instructions for paragraph 15 of Form 6A.

17. Damage to Premises

See the instructions for paragraph 16 of Form 6A.

18. Notice of Default

See the instructions for paragraph 17 of Form 6A.

19. Quiet Enjoyment

See the instructions for paragraph 18 of Form 6A.

20. Eminent Domain

See the instructions for paragraph 19 of Form 6A.

21. Holding Over

See the instructions for paragraph 20 of Form 6A.

22. Disputes

See the discussion of dispute resolution clauses in Chapter 1, Section D, and the instructions for paragraph 21 of Form 6A.

23. Additional Agreements

Fill in any other terms that you and the landlord have agreed to. For examples of language, see the instructions for paragraph 22 of Form 6A.

Standard Clauses

The remainder of the lease contains the standard clauses we discussed in Chapter 1, Section C. The only thing you'll need to fill in here is the name of the state whose law will apply to the contract in the paragraph called "Governing Law."

Signatures

Sign and date the lease. For more on signing contracts, see Chapter 1, Section B.

D. Form 6D: Sublease

As explained in the beginning of this chapter, if you sublet your space, you become a landlord—or, more precisely, a "sublandlord"—as far as your subtenant is concerned. The subtenant will pay you whatever rent you charge and you, in turn, will remain responsible for paying your landlord the full rent called for by the original lease and honoring all the other terms of the lease.

If your lease doesn't mention subleasing, the law of your state normally gives you the legal right to sublet your space or assign the lease to another tenant, whether or not the landlord approves. But finding yourself in this situation is unusual. Most leases, like the ones in this book, say that a tenant can't sublet or assign without the written consent of the landlord. Using a lease of this type, you'll need to get the landlord's permission before a sublease is valid. Use Form 6E: Landlord's Consent to Sublease, to get the landlord's written consent.

If the landlord arbitrarily rejects your subtenant, you may be able to walk away from the lease. Suppose your lease requires the landlord's consent for you to sublet space or assign the lease, but also says that it won't be unreasonably withheld (or even if there's no such clause, courts in your state read in this requirement). You approach the landlord with a creditworthy subtenant who runs a reasonably quiet, nonpolluting business, but the landlord refuses to consent to your subleasing to that business. Chances are you're in a strong legal position to end the lease with no further obligation to pay rent. But since this is a tricky legal area and especially if a lot of money is at stake, we recommend you consult a local lawyer who specializes in commercial real estate law.

An assignment is often better than a sublease. If someone will be taking over all of your space for the remainder of the lease term, consider using Form 6F: Assignment of Lease, instead of a sublease. Under an assignment, the subtenant will pay the rent directly to the landlord—and if the subtenant is financially solid, the landlord may even agree to release you from any further obligation for unpaid rent or other responsibilities under the lease.

The instructions below for Form 6D assume that you're the sublandlord and are preparing the sublease form.

Instructions for Form 6D: Sublease

All the forms in this book are provided as tear-outs in Appendix B and on the accompanying forms CD-ROM. As you read the instructions for Form 6D, you may want to either tear out the form or open the form's file on the CD-ROM so you can follow along. Form 6D is in the file FORM6D.RTF on the CD-ROM. (For more information on using the forms CD-ROM, see Appendix A, "How to Use the CD-ROM.") If you don't use the forms CD-ROM, be sure to photocopy the agreement so you'll have a clean copy to use later.

1. Names

Insert the names of the sublandlord (you) and subtenant.

2. Property Subleased

Choose one of the two options. Check the first box if you're subleasing all of the space covered by your lease. Then fill in the location exactly as it appears in your lease. Check the second box if you're subleasing just part of the space covered by your lease. Then fill in the location and go on to describe the part of the space you're subleasing.

SAMPLES:
- 320 North Main Street, Ann Arbor, Michigan: the first floor.
- The portion of the building at 320 North Main Street, Ann Arbor, Michigan, that is outlined in blue ink on the drawing in Attachment #2.

If you're subletting part of your space to another business, you may wind up sharing some common areas. For example, you may own a vegetarian restaurant and decide to sublet some unneeded space to a business that sells vitamins and other dietary supplements, with the understanding that you'll share a common entry area and customer service counter. In such a situation, be sure to put precise language in the sublease defining what the common space is and how it will be shared.

3. Original Lease

Insert the name of your landlord and then your name.

Insert anything that will be different from the terms of the master lease.

SAMPLE:

In addition to paying rent, Subtenant will reimburse Sublandlord for one-half of the electric and water bills; subtenant will make such reimbursement within ten days after receiving a copy of the bills from Sublandlord. Subtenant will be entitled to use two of the parking spaces allotted to Sublandlord under the original lease.

It's okay to keep some information private. The subtenant needs to know most of the terms of the master lease to avoid inadvertently violating those terms. But there's no legal requirement that he or she know the details of your financial arrangements with your landlord. Although we generally think a policy of full disclosure is best in the long run, if you prefer to keep these details confidential, simply black out the financial terms on the copy of the original lease you attach to the sublease.

4. Term of Sublease

Fill in the dates the sublease starts and the date it ends.

5. Rent

Choose one of two options. Check the first box if the subtenant's rent will remain constant throughout the lease. Otherwise, check the second box and fill in the yearly rent amounts. If the original lease contains provisions for rent to go up based on cost-of-living increases or if you have to pay for increased taxes, it's usually appropriate for the subtenant to pay some or all of the increases. In such situations, you'll want to supplement the rent paragraph by adding language covering the subtenant's obligation to pay for increases.

Consider getting the rent early. It's often a good idea to have the subtenant pay you the rent a few days before you have to pay the landlord.

Otherwise, if the subtenant is a day or two late, you'll have to pay the landlord out of your own funds. For example, if you have to pay rent on the first day of each month, it makes sense to provide that the subtenant's rent will be due on the 25th day of the preceding month.

6. Option to Extend Sublease

An option gives the subtenant the choice of whether to stay in the space beyond the original term of the sublease. Before granting an option to the subtenant remember you can't give the subtenant any rights that you don't have, so make sure that your lease lasts as long as the option period or gives you an option to extend that is at least that long.

Insert the number of years or months that the lease will be extended if the subtenant exercises the option.

Then put in any changes in the terms that will apply during the extension period.

SAMPLE:

During the extension period, the rent will be $1,500.00 per month.

Finally, insert the subtenant's deadline for notifying you that he or she is exercising the option. If the option in the sublease will extend the sublease beyond the original term of the original lease, the deadline for exercising the option should obviously be earlier than the deadline to exercise the option in the original lease.

EXAMPLE: Al has a five-year original lease with an option to extend for another five years. After two years, Al subleases to Martha for the remaining three years of the lease with an option to extend the subtenancy for an additional five years. Obviously, Martha's deadline for notifying Al that she's extending the subtenancy must be earlier than Al's deadline for notifying his landlord. Al and Martha insert a date for renewing that sublease that's 60 days earlier than the date in Al's original lease for exercising his option.

It's often a poor idea to give a subtenant an option to extend the lease. If one of the reasons you're subleasing is that you're trying to get out of a lease obligation for good, it's usually a mistake to give the subtenant an option that will mean you in turn must notify the landlord that you're exercising your option to extend your lease. For example, suppose you want to sublease all or part of your space for the last two years of your lease because you're moving or closing your business. Even if you also have an option to renew for an additional two years, it would probably be a mistake to agree to a four-year sublease, since by doing so you double the time you're on the hook if the subtenant fails to pay rent or otherwise violates the lease.

7. Security Deposit

Insert the amount of any security deposit that you and the subtenant have agreed on. Make sure the amount is at least as much as what you have posted with the landlord.

8. Notices From Landlord

Nothing needs to be filled in here. This part of the sublease helps assure you that the lease won't get canceled or that you won't incur additional costs because the subtenant did something that violated the original lease.

9. Subletting and Assignment

Nothing needs to be filled in here. Both you and the landlord need to consent before the subtenant can sublet the space to someone else or assign the sublease.

10. Indemnification

Nothing needs to be filled in here. The subtenant promises to absorb any costs that result from the subtenant not meeting the terms of the sublease. Similarly, you and the landlord will be covered by the subtenant's insurance policies.

11. Condition of Premises

Nothing needs to be filled in here.

12. Landlord's Consent

Nothing needs to be filled in here. You can get the landlord's consent by using Form 6E: Landlord's Consent to Sublease.

13. Disputes

See the discussion of dispute resolution clauses in Chapter 1, Section D, and the instructions for paragraph 21 of Form 6A.

14. Additional Agreements

Fill in any other terms that you and the subtenant have agreed to.

Standard Clauses

The remainder of the sublease contains the standard clauses we discussed in Chapter 1, Section C. The only thing you'll need to fill in here is the name of the state whose law will apply to the contract in the paragraph called "Governing Law."

Signatures

Sign and date the lease. For more on signing contracts, see Chapter 1, Section B.

E. Form 6E: Landlord's Consent to Sublease

Leases usually require the landlord's written consent before a sublease is valid. This form accomplishes that.

Instructions for Form 6E: Landlord's Consent to Sublease

All the forms in this book are provided as tear-outs in Appendix B and on the accompanying forms CD-ROM. As you read the instructions for Form 6E, you may want to either tear out the form or open the form's file on the CD-ROM so you can follow along. Form 6E is in the file FORM6E.RTF on the CD-ROM. (For more information on using the forms CD-ROM, see Appendix A, "How to Use the CD-ROM.") If you don't use the forms CD-ROM, be sure to photocopy the agreement so you'll have a clean copy to use later.

1. Names

Insert the names of the landlord, tenant and subtenant.

2. Consent to Sublease

First, fill in the date the sublease between the sublandlord (the original tenant) and the subtenant (Form 6D) was signed. A copy of the sublease should be attached to this consent form.

Then, fill in a description of what is being subleased. If you're subleasing all the space covered by the original lease, simply use that description here. Otherwise, you'll need to create a new description.

 For examples of descriptions, see the instructions for paragraph 2 of Form 6A: Gross Lease.

3. Status of Original Lease

The language informs the tenant and subtenant that the original lease is in good standing. You don't need to add anything.

4. Notice of Default

Insert the number of days that you and the subtenant will have to cure any default. This clause makes sure that both you and the subtenant will get notice if the landlord thinks there's a default so you can have an opportunity to correct the problem.

Signatures

Date the contract. All parties need to sign it. For more on signatures, see Chapter 1, Section B.

F. Form 6F: Assignment of Lease

An assignment of a lease is often used where all of the leased space is being turned over to another business for the entire balance of the lease term, as would be appropriate if the original tenant goes out of business, sells the business or moves permanently. In an assignment, the original tenant (in legal jargon, the assignor) transfers the lease to a new tenant (the assignee). The new tenant usually pays the rent directly to the landlord, but the original tenant nevertheless remains responsible to the landlord for the rent and possibly other monetary obligations if the new tenant doesn't pay. However, with a financially strong new tenant, the landlord may be willing to release the original tenant from any further responsibility under the lease; you can use paragraph 9 of Form 6F: Assignment of Lease, to accomplish this.

Most leases require the landlord's written consent before an assignment of a lease is valid. (See the introduction to the instructions to Form 6D: Sublease.) In Form 6F: Assignment of Lease, the landlord actually signs the form so a separate consent isn't necessary.

Instructions for Form 6F: Assignment of Lease

All the forms in this book are provided as tear-outs in Appendix B and on the accompanying forms CD-

ROM. As you read the instructions for Form 6F, you may want to either tear out the form or open the form's file on the CD-ROM so you can follow along. Form 6F is in the file FORM6F.RTF on the CD-ROM. (For more information on using the forms CD-ROM, see Appendix A, "How to Use the CD-ROM.") If you don't use the forms CD-ROM, be sure to photocopy the agreement so you'll have a clean copy to use later.

1. Names

Insert the names of the original tenant, the new tenant (the person taking over the lease) and the landlord.

2. Assignment

Fill in the date of the lease between the landlord and the original tenant. Then, fill in the location of the space covered by the lease.

3. Effective Date

Fill in the date the assignment takes effect.

4. Acceptance

Nothing needs to be filled in here. The new tenant agrees to take over the lease and be bound by its terms.

5. Condition of Premises

Nothing needs to be filled in here. The new tenant knows the condition of the space and accepts it as is.

6. Landlord's Certification

In item A, fill in the date through which you've paid rent.

In item B, fill in the amount of any security deposit that the landlord is holding.

7. Reimbursement

As part of a lease assignment, the new tenant typically reimburses the original tenant for the security deposit that's been left with the landlord. Also, typically, the new tenant pays the original tenant for any rent and other items paid in advance. Check the applicable boxes.

EXAMPLE: On June 1, Rodrigo Portaformo & Associates paid rent for the entire month of June. The new tenant, Z-Pop Inc., is to take over the space on June 16. Z-Pop will reimburse Rodrigo for rent Rodrigo paid for the last half of June, so the second box is checked.

8. Landlord's Consent

This paragraph specifies that the landlord consents to the assignment. You don't need to fill in anything.

9. Release

Check the box if the landlord is willing to relieve you of any further responsibility to the landlord under the lease, once the assignment takes effect. You don't need to fill in anything.

Standard Clauses

The remainder of the assignment contains the standard clauses we discussed in Chapter 1, Section C. The only thing you'll need to fill in here is the name of the state whose law will apply to the contract in the paragraph called "Governing Law."

Signatures

Date the contract. All parties need to sign it. For more on signatures, see Chapter 1, Section B.

G. Form 6G: Notice of Exercise of Lease Option

Many leases give the tenant the option to extend the lease beyond its original term. Usually there's a deadline by which the tenant must notify the landlord in writing if the tenant chooses to exercise the option. You can use Form 6G for this purpose.

⚠️ **Options to renew often must be exercised far in advance.** Make sure you exercise an option to renew your lease in timely fashion. Also pay attention to whether the lease prescribes a certain means of delivery, such as certified mail.

Instructions for Form 6G: Notice of Exercise of Lease Option

All the forms in this book are provided as tear-outs in Appendix B and on the accompanying forms CD-ROM. As you read the instructions for Form 6G, you may want to either tear out the form or open the form's file on the CD-ROM so you can follow along. Form 6G is in the file FORM6G.RTF on the CD-ROM. (For more information on using the forms CD-ROM, see Appendix A, "How to Use the CD-ROM.") If you don't use the forms CD-ROM, be sure to photocopy the agreement so you'll have a clean copy to use later.

At the top of the form—in the first blank space—fill in the landlord's name.

1. Exercise of Lease Option

Put your name or the name of your business (depending on which the lease names as tenant) in the first blank. Then insert the date through which you're extending the lease.

Finally, insert the description of the premises—the same description that's in the original lease.

2. Notice to Landlord

Insert the date of the original lease.

Signatures

Date and sign the lease. For more on signatures, see Chapter 1, Section B.

H. Form 6H: Extension of Lease

Even if you've signed a lease that doesn't provide an option for the tenant to extend the lease, you and the landlord may nevertheless agree to a lease extension. As long as the lease terms will remain basically the same during the extension period, there's no need to prepare a whole new lease. You and the landlord can extend the lease by using Form 6H: Extension of Lease.

 It's sometimes best to do a completely new document. When modifying a lease which significantly changes the original, make sure that you don't end up with a confusing mess. In this situation, often it's easier to start over than to cut and paste, especially if you or your landlord have kept a copy of the original document on your computer hard drive or on a disk. In the revised document, specifically state that the revised document replaces the earlier one.

Instructions for Form 6H: Extension of Lease

All the forms in this book are provided as tear-outs in Appendix B and on the accompanying forms CD-ROM. As you read the instructions for Form 6H, you may want to either tear out the form or open the form's file on the CD-ROM so you can follow along. Form 6H is in the file FORM6H.RTF on the CD-ROM. (For more information on using the forms CD-ROM, see Appendix A, "How to Use the CD-ROM.") If you don't use the forms CD-ROM, be sure to photocopy the agreement so you'll have a clean copy to use later.

1. Names

Insert the names of the landlord and the tenant.

2. New Lease Term

First, insert the date the original lease was signed.

In the next set of blanks, fill in a description of the premises, which should be the same as the premises described in the original lease.

Then fill in the date through which the lease is extended.

3. Modifications to Lease

Insert any new terms and conditions that will apply during the extension period. If there are no modifications, insert the word "None." If the modifications are many, or complex, you're better off creating a new lease (using Form 6A, 6B or 6C) than using this extension.

SAMPLES:

- The rent will be $2,000.00 per month.
- By June 30, 20___, Landlord will install new carpeting of a type to be selected by Tenant, not to exceed $15 per square yard, including installation.
- Tenant will be entitled to the use of three additional parking spaces as shown on Attachment #2.

Signatures

Sign and date the lease. For more on signing contracts, see Chapter 1, Section B.

I. Form 6I: Amendment of Lease

Suppose while your lease is still in effect you and the landlord agree to make some changes. If there are more than a few, it's often best to redo the whole lease so that you don't get confused about what's in and what's out.

Keep the original lease on your computer. If you—or more likely your landlord—have kept the original lease on your computer hard drive or on a disk, it's a simple matter to make the changes and print out a new document, noting in the first sentence that the new document replaces the earlier one.

If the older version isn't available or the changes are minor, rather than redoing the entire lease, you can prepare and sign an Amendment of Lease. To do this, use Form 6I: Amendment of Lease. For more on amending contracts, see Chapter 1, Section E.

Instructions for Form 6I: Amendment of Lease

All the forms in this book are provided as tear-outs in Appendix B and on the accompanying forms CD-ROM. As you read the instructions for Form 6I, you may want to either tear out the form or open the form's file on the CD-ROM so you can follow along.

Form 6I is in the file FORM6I.RTF on the CD-ROM. (For more information on using the forms CD-ROM, see Appendix A, "How to Use the CD-ROM.") If you don't use the forms CD-ROM, be sure to photocopy the agreement so you'll have a clean copy to use later.

Amendment Number

At the top, fill in the number of the Amendment. If you have made no previous amendments, fill in "1"; number subsequent amendments successively.

1. Names

Fill in the names of the landlord and the tenant.

2. Terms Amended

Fill in the date of the original lease and the location of the premises.

Then, in plain English, put in the amended terms.

SAMPLES:

- By September 1, 20___, Landlord will reduce Tenant's space by moving the north wall of the space ten feet to the south. Beginning September 1, 20___, and for the balance of the lease term, the rent will be reduced to $1,500.00 per month.
- Effective immediately, Landlord will provide daily janitorial service to the leased premises. Also, effective immediately, Tenant will assume responsibility for maintaining the landscaping at the front of the building at Tenant's expense.

It's a good idea to attach a copy of all amendments to each copy of the original lease so that the lease terms are all in one place.

3. Effective Date

Fill in the date the amendment takes effect.

4. Other Terms of Lease

Nothing needs to be filled in here.

Signatures

Sign and date the lease. For more on signing contracts, see Chapter 1, Section B.

J. Form 6J: Attachment to Lease

If you use a preprinted lease form such as the ones in this book, you may encounter some situations that don't fit neatly into the main form. One simple way to deal with this problem is to create an attachment to the lease that legally is a part of it. Attachments are also discussed in Chapter 1, Section E.

Some examples of material that might go into an attachment:

- a lengthy and detailed legal description of property to be leased
- a drawing showing the exact location of the leased space within a building
- plans and specifications for improvements to be installed in the leased space by you or the landlord
- a list of new equipment that the landlord will provide within the leased space.

If you're producing your lease using the forms CD-ROM that accompanies this book, it should be easy to customize the lease to fit special circumstances.

Alternative method of handling attachments. When the material to be attached to the lease already exist as a document (for example, a sketch of the leased space or a list of improvements to be made), you can easily make it into an attachment by adding the following at the beginning of the document:

Attachment _____ to the lease dated _____
covering the premises at _____.

Fill in the appropriate number, date and location. If you and the landlord then initial the attachment, its contents will become a part of the lease.

Instructions for Form 6J: Attachment to Lease

All the forms in this book are provided as tear-outs in Appendix B and on the accompanying forms CD-ROM. As you read the instructions for Form 6J, you may want to either tear out the form or open the form's file on the CD-ROM so you can follow along. Form 6J is in the file FORM6J.RTF on the CD-ROM. (For more information on using the forms CD-ROM, see Appendix A, "How to Use the CD-ROM.") If you don't use the forms CD-ROM, be sure to photocopy the agreement so you'll have a clean copy to use later.

Attachment Number

If you're adding only one attachment, fill in the number "1." Where there's more than one attachment, number them consecutively (Attachment 1, Attachment 2, etc.). Remember to refer the attachment by number in the main body of the lease—for example, in the "Additional Agreements" paragraph at the end of Forms 6A, 6B and 6C.

1. Names

Insert the names of the landlord and the tenant.

2. Terms of Attachment

Insert the date of the lease and the location of the premises. Then insert the material that's being added to the lease.

SAMPLE:
Before the beginning of the lease period, Landlord will complete the following improvements to the leased premises at Landlord's expense …

Then list the specifics, including materials to be used.

Signatures

Sign and date the lease. For more on signing contracts, see Chapter 1, Section B. ■

Purchasing and Improving Real Estate

This chapter includes a variety of forms related to purchasing and renovating commercial real estate.

Form 7B: Contract to Purchase Building, is designed for use if you've found a building you want to buy and have negotiated the purchase terms with the present owner. But lots of deals to purchase aren't so simple. For example, perhaps you've located an attractive building and reached agreement with the owner on the price, but before you sign on the bottom line you want time to do some additional investigating, raise the down payment or simply to decide if you really want to buy it. In the meantime, you worry the building will be purchased by someone else. To tie up the building while you make a final decision, you need to negotiate with the owner—normally for a fee—for an option to buy the building at a set price for a stated period of time. Assuming you and the owner agree on such a deal, use Form 7C: Option to Purchase Building.

If, by contrast, you plan to build your own building, step one is obviously to buy land to put it on. Form 7D: Contract to Purchase Vacant Land, lets you start the process. And if you'd like to tie up the land while you mull over your decision whether to purchase it, you can use Form 7E: Option to Purchase Vacant Land, to buy yourself some time.

Buying or Leasing—Which Makes the Most Financial Sense?

In theory there can be financial advantages to owning your own building. Income tax laws, for example, encourage real estate ownership by allowing you to deduct depreciation, interest and taxes. And, assuming you pay a reasonable price and purchase a building in a desirable location, chances are you'll realize a decent profit when you eventually sell. And, of course, if you buy a building that's larger than you need, you may be able to rent out the remaining space for enough money to cover a good portion of your mortgage, taxes and other operational costs.

But buying a building isn't the best thing for every small business. Money is a scarce resource. You may have far better uses for it in developing your core business. If you operate a recreational fishing business, for example, it may make more sense for you to buy two more boats than a building. Or if you own a successful instant print shop, it may be better to open another well-equipped location rather than to place a bet on the future of the local real estate market by purchasing the building you currently occupy.

Remember, too, that at the best of times, real estate is a complicated business. It follows that since you likely know far more about your own field, it may be best to put your money where your smarts is.

No matter the type of property you want to buy or the details of the purchase contract you use, you may want to add material—such as a site plan, survey or lengthy legal description—to the contract. You can do this by using an attachment such as Form 7F: Attachment to Real Estate Purchase Contract.

Following the signing of a contract to purchase real estate, you and the seller may agree to change one or more of its terms. Maybe you want to move up the closing date or, if your inspection of the building unexpectedly reveals a substandard roof or foundation that could kill the deal (because of a contingency in the contract requiring a satisfactory inspection report from a contractor), the owner may be willing to save it by agreeing to make necessary repairs before the closing. Of course, there are dozens of other possible changes. The point is it's essential to put all significant changes in writing. To do this, use Form 7G: Amendment of Real Estate Purchase Contract.

Do a new contract if changes are extensive. Amending an existing contract usually works fine for minor changes. However, when a number of contract terms must be changed, it's far less confusing to do a new contract. This is especially easy to accomplish if you've kept the original contract on your computer or a disk. Simply correct the paragraphs that are being changed and then state in the first sentence of the revised contract that it replaces the earlier version.

It's also common for a real estate buyer to state in the purchase contract that the deal is contingent on a number of things happening. Two of the most common are the buyer being able to get adequate financing and the building being given a favorable inspection report from a professional inspector. Typically, the contract provides that all contingencies must be removed in writing before closing. You can use Form 7H: Removal of Contingency, to accomplish this task, either one by one as each contingency is satisfied or—if things are happening at the same time—all together.

To extend the time for removing a contingency, use Form 7I: Extension of Time to Remove Contingencies.

If you've obtained an option to purchase real estate and have decided to go ahead with the purchase, use Form 7J: Exercise of Option to Purchase Real Estate, to let the owner know that you're going to proceed.

You can use Form 7K: Renovation Contract, if you're going to hire a contractor to make major changes to an existing building.

A. Beware of Possible Environmental Problems

Before you buy real estate, you should research any possible environmental problems with the property. That's because if the real estate you're buying—or thinking of buying—is environmentally contaminated, you may wind up with big problems. For one thing, even though you didn't cause the contamination, you may get stuck with a huge bill for an environmental clean-up of the site. That's based on the federal Comprehensive Environmental Response Compensation and Liability Act (also called CERCLA or Superfund) and similar laws. Additionally, lending institutions will balk at lending you money to buy the property or fix it up if it's contaminated. And you may face lawsuits from neighboring property owners whose property is affected by contamination that originated on the site you're considering.

Contamination can be a particular problem if the property you're buying is—or was—home to a gas station, dry cleaner or manufacturing business. For example, there may be underground storage tanks that leak or the soil may be chemically contaminated. And many other businesses can also leave contamination in their wake. So before you make a binding commitment to buy real estate, you need to be sure that it's not contaminated or have a viable plan for cleaning it up.

The purchase contracts in this chapter allow you to make your purchase contingent on an environmental inspection. The option agreements automatically give you a chance to make whatever investigation you want before you're committed to buy.

If there's any chance at all that the property is contaminated, you need to get a Phase I Environmental Site Assessment (often simply called a Phase I) performed by an experienced consultant. This will let you know if there's a potential problem. If so, you'll need to dig even deeper by getting a Phase II, which definitely lets you know if there actually is contamination. That, in turn, can lead to further testing to find out the full extent of the problem—and the cost of cleaning up the site and preventing further contamination. Be aware that such in-depth testing can be very expensive and may be prohibitive for a small business to perform. If a Phase II assessment confirms that there's a problem, your best course may be to drop the deal.

There are two kinds of protective clauses you can include in your contract or option, if the seller is willing:

Warranties and Representations. See if the seller will warrant and represent that there is no environmental contamination on the site and that the site complies with all environmental laws and regulations.

Indemnification. See if the seller will indemnify you for clean-up costs and related expenses if an environmental condition comes to light that existed while the seller owned the property.

If you have a deep-pocket seller—or at least one who's likely to be solvent in the future—this can provide a way for you to recoup all or part of your losses if you later have to clean up the site.

Because environmental law is so complex and your legal exposure is potentially enormous, you should consult an experienced environmental lawyer if the Phase I assessment shows a possible problem. You may also want to get legal help before that point if environmental contamination is of special concern to you.

Legal Ownership: Whose Name Should Go on the Deed?

If your business is a sole proprietorship (you and the business are the same legal entity), the decision on ownership of real estate you purchase is easy: you'll almost always want to take title in your own name or jointly with your spouse. With other types of business entities, the decision on whose name you put on the deed as legal owner requires more extensive analysis. If your business is a partnership, corporation or LLC, one choice is for the business itself to own the real estate—in which case the name of the business would appear on the deed. But as an alternative, one or more of the business owners can personally own the real estate and lease it to the business, using much the same type of written lease you'd use with an outside tenant. This can be a useful arrangement if some of the business owners don't want the business to invest in real estate. And for a regular or C corporation (not an S corporation), some tax advisors see an advantage if the business owners personally own the real estate and lease it to the corporation, since this avoids the possibility of double taxation, which can occur if the corporation owns real estate.

EXAMPLE: Enterprise Corporation buys a building for $100,000. Two years later, Enterprise sells the building for $200,000. The corporation must pay tax on the $100,000 gain. Then, when the money is distributed to the shareholders, they must pay tax on the money they receive. By contrast, if the corporation's shareholders buy the building, keep the title in their own names and lease it to the corporation, there's only one tax to pay when they sell the building.

To help you decide whether legal title to real estate should be taken in the name of your business or in the name of one or more individuals who own the business, it's wise to consult a lawyer or CPA who is knowledgeable about taxes and business planning.

B. Form 7B: Contract to Purchase Building

Use this contract if you're buying an existing building. Note that "contingency clauses" let you get out of the contract if you can't get an adequate mortgage loan or if you receive an unsatisfactory inspection report from a contractor.

Negotiate the closing costs. In paragraphs 10, 11, 12 and 13, this contract allocates between you and the seller the various costs involved in making the deal happen. Although these allocations are, broadly speaking, reasonable, they're not the only way to do it; you and the seller can negotiate to rearrange who pays for what in any of half a hundred ways. For example, instead of using the formula for allocating real property taxes suggested in paragraph 12—which requires you to reimburse the seller for some of the taxes already paid—you can negotiate for language requiring you to pay only for real property taxes billed after the closing.

Indeed, all financial aspects of a purchase are negotiable. If, for example, the building or some essential equipment such as a furnace in it isn't in good repair, you'll need to decide if you should take it "as is"—negotiating, hopefully, for a lower price—or bargain for a deal requiring the seller to pay some or all of the money needed to fix it. And you can also negotiate regarding the allocation of the costs of inspections, land surveys and closing.

Instructions for Form 7B: Contract to Purchase Building

All the forms in this book are provided as tear-outs in Appendix B and on the accompanying forms CD-ROM. As you read the instructions for Form 7B, you may want to either tear out the form or open the form's file on the CD-ROM so you can follow along. Form 7B is in the file FORM7B.RTF on the CD-ROM. (For more information on using the forms CD-ROM,

see Appendix A, "How to Use the CD-ROM.") If you don't use the forms CD-ROM, be sure to photocopy the agreement so you'll have a clean copy to use later.

1. Names

Insert the names of the seller and purchaser.

2. Purchase of Real Estate

Insert the address of the property.

Then check one of the boxes concerning the legal description. Legal descriptions vary in length. They can be short ("Lot 50 of Georgetown Subdivision in the City of Detroit, Wayne County, Michigan") or can run on for several paragraphs or even pages. Unless the legal description is of the short variety, it's usually best to include it in an attachment to the contract. You can use Form 7F: Attachment to Real Estate Purchase Contract.

You can copy the legal description from the seller's deed or from the title insurance policy—the policy that was issued when the seller acquired the property. Be careful doing this, however. Check and double-check the legal description to make sure you've copied it correctly, because an incorrect legal description can cause problems later.

3. Purchase Price

Put the full purchase price in the first blank. Put the amount of your deposit in the second blank. In the third blank, fill in the name of the escrow company, title company or individual who will hold your deposit. Institutional escrow agents have forms for you and the seller to sign to define the escrow agent's responsibilities in acting as a neutral third party in handling the deposit.

Subtract the deposit from the full price and insert the balance in the last blank.

Keep the deposit as low as possible. A real estate broker or experienced lawyer can tell you what constitutes a typical deposit in your community, but in the final analysis, the amount is always negotiable. And if things go wrong, you'll be glad if you negotiated to keep it as low as possible.

That way, if you find yourself needing to cancel the purchase at some point for a reason that's not squarely allowed by the contract language, the amount that will be subject to forfeiture will be small.

4. Financing Contingency

Chances are you'll be borrowing part of the purchase price from a bank or other lender. The lender will expect you to pledge the real estate as security for payment of the loan. Legally, the security interest you give to the lender will be in the form of a mortgage or a deed of trust, depending on the practice in your state. By including a financing contingency in the contract, you're free to cancel the deal (and get your deposit back) if you can't get the financing you need. But the contract does obligate you to apply promptly for the financing and pursue the application in good faith.

It can pay to prequalify. Find out how much you can borrow from a bank or other lender before you sign a purchase contract. Most lenders are willing to look over your financial statement and give you at least a tentative loan commitment even before you find the right building. By knowing in advance how much you'll be able to borrow, you won't waste time trying to buy a building you can't afford.

Fill in the percent of the purchase price you'll need to borrow—60% or 70%, for example. When determining this amount, don't forget closing costs, the expense of moving and outlays that may be needed for repairs, renovation and decorating. Next, specify the number of days you'll have to apply for the loan.

Finally, insert a date by which you agree to remove the financing contingency. You should normally give yourself at least 30 to 45 days so the lender has time to process your application. Call a few lenders to see how long the mortgage process is currently taking.

Paragraph 18 of the contract tells what happens if you don't remove the mortgage contingency by the required date.

Seller financing lets you wheel and deal. When working out repayment terms, a seller may be more flexible than a bank or other commercial lender. Often, you can cut a deal in which you pay only interest or relatively small payments of principal and interest for a few years. You agree that at the end of that time, you'll pay off the land contract by getting financing elsewhere.

5. Inclusions

This paragraph makes it clear that you're not just buying the land but also the improvements (the building and outdoor pavement, for example) and fixtures (items such as the heating system or lighting fixtures which started out as personal property but became part of the building).

This paragraph also has a place to insert a list of any personal property that's specifically included in the purchase. (Personal property not listed and not attached to the building normally remains the property of the seller, unless specifically made part of the deal.) That might include, for example, shelving, display counters or machinery. The legal line between fixtures that go with the building and personal property that doesn't unless special provision is made isn't always clear; for example, depending on how it was secured in place and your state's law, a window-mounted air conditioner could fall into either category. If no additional personal property is to be included, insert "None."

When in doubt, list all property you intend to purchase. To be sure to get what you pay for, you don't need to read a legal treatise on fixtures. Instead, just list in your contract all items that you expect to acquire as part of the purchase, including those that a wily seller might feel inclined to remove. As long as an item is clearly made part of the deal, it makes no difference how or even whether it is attached to the building.

Financing a Real Estate Purchase

There are a number of ways to finance a real estate purchase:

1. **Pay Cash**

   If you have deep pockets, you can obviously pay for the property outright. This approach normally makes sense only if you don't need capital to build your business.

2. **Borrow the Purchase Money From a Commercial Lender**

   You can normally borrow much of the money needed to finance the purchase from a bank or other commercial lender. The lender will want you to have some money of your own in the deal—perhaps 30% or 40% of the purchase price. In addition, you'll need to secure the loan by giving the lender a mortgage or deed of trust on the building.

   If a mortgage is used as security for the loan, three basic documents are typically involved.

   - **Deed:** The seller signs a legal form entitled a deed transferring the legal ownership of the property to you.
   - **Promissory Note:** You agree in writing to make specified payments to the lender until the loan has been fully paid off.
   - **Mortgage:** In addition, you sign a legal form giving the lender the right to take the property and sell it to pay off the loan balance if you don't make your loan payments as promised. Sometimes the lender must go to court to enforce its right to sell the property.

     If the deed of trust procedure is used as security for the loan, you still need a deed and a promissory note, but instead of a mortgage, you need a legal form called a deed of trust.
   - **Deed of Trust:** In this legal form, you give the trustee (often a title company) the right to sell your property at the instruction of the lender, with no need of court approval, if you fail to make your payments on time.

3. **Pay the Seller Instead of a Bank**

   If the seller doesn't need all the money from the sale immediately, he or she may be willing to self-finance the deal. As with outside financing, the seller will deed the property to you, and you'll give the seller a down payment plus a promissory note and either a mortgage or deed of trust to secure payment of the balance.

   In many states, seller financing can also be accomplished by a land contract—an installment purchase agreement in which you promise to pay off the balance of the purchase price by making specified payments to the seller. If you don't keep up the payments, the seller can take back full ownership of the property through procedures called forfeiture or foreclosure.

   It's also possible to work out a combination of commercial and seller financing. You might, for example, borrow part of the purchase money from a bank, giving the lender a first mortgage or first deed of trust as security for the loan. Then, the seller might agree to accept a note for part of the balance, in return for your granting a second mortgage or second deed of trust. Using this procedure, you might buy a $200,000 building this way:

Down Payment From Savings	$ 20,000
Loan From Bank Secured by First Mortgage	100,000
Note to Seller Secured by Second Mortgage	80,000
Total Package	$ 200,000

6. Exclusions

The seller may want to exclude some items that would otherwise be included in the sale, such as a fancy light fixture, built-in trophy case or some cabinetry or machinery that's bolted to the building. If seller does not want to exclude any particular items, insert "None." (CD-ROM users can simply delete this paragraph and renumber all subsequent ones.)

7. Condition of Equipment

A warranty is a promise or guarantee that the seller makes. Here, the seller is promising that the equipment included in the sale will be in good working condition when you take over the building. This means if you move in and the air-conditioning isn't working, the seller must pay for repairing it. However, realize that if the air-conditioning is working when you move in but breaks down a week later, that's your problem—unless the seller has given you a longer-term warranty (which would be unusual in the purchase of a commercial building) or has hidden the fact that the air conditioner was on its last legs.

Insert the words "No Exceptions" if the seller is guaranteeing that all the equipment will be in good working condition. (CD-ROM users should just delete the words "except for:".) Insert a list of any equipment that the seller is not guaranteeing to be in good working condition—perhaps an old dishwasher in a restaurant or the heating system in an aging retail building—if the seller is guaranteeing just some of the equipment.

8. Physical Problems With Property

When you buy a building, you take it in "as-is" condition unless otherwise specified in the purchase contract. This means that since you can't hold the seller responsible for any problems you later discover, it's essential that you have a knowledgeable inspector carefully check out the place before you commit to close the deal. The big exception to this "buyer beware" rule is that if the seller knows of some hidden defect that you couldn't be expected to discover by having the building inspected, he or she has a legal duty to tell you (for example, the roof leaks when it rains heavily and the problem isn't apparent during the dry season when you're buying the building).

This paragraph gives the seller a chance to disclose in writing any hidden defects. Both you and the seller benefit from doing this. If the seller lists a hidden defect, you can take steps to learn about how serious it is and then perhaps negotiate a lower price or walk away from the deal. From the seller's perspective, if you're informed about all problems with the building, you can't complain later that the seller held back key information.

Insert the words "No exceptions" if the seller doesn't know of any hidden or hard-to-find physical problems with the building that wouldn't be apparent through an inspection. CD-ROM users should just delete the words "except for:".

If the seller lists problems but is willing to fix them before closing, you can insert the seller's commitment in paragraph 22, "Additional Agreements."

Make sure the building is completely inspected. A lot of money can ride on how thoroughly and competently the building you're interested in buying is inspected. This means you'll want to hire an experienced inspector with a reputation for thoroughness. If the building is old or large, consider having highly experienced experts make separate inspections of the electrical, plumbing and heating systems. Only if this has really been done well can you confidently propose to the seller a list of things that need fixing.

By checking the first box in paragraph 17 of this contract (discussed below), you make your purchase contingent on your being satisfied with what a thorough inspection of the building discloses.

Assuming you reserve the right to have one or more contractors inspect the premises (using the contingency portion of this form) and you uncover some problem the seller didn't tell you about, you can either cancel the deal or agree with the seller to amend the contract. The amended contract can address building conditions by (1) requiring the seller to make specified repairs, or (2) reducing the purchase price.

9. Cleaning of Premises

Nothing needs to be inserted here. This paragraph requires the seller to clean up the building before closing so you don't walk into a trash heap.

10. Special Assessments

Nothing needs to be inserted here. This paragraph specifies whether you or the seller pay for charges assessed for public improvements such as streets and sidewalks depending on when these charges are assessed.

11. Utility Charges

Nothing needs to be inserted here. This paragraph specifies whether you or the seller pay for other municipal charges which may not be classified as special assessments.

12. Real Estate Taxes

This paragraph allocates the real estate taxes between you and the seller. Nothing normally needs to be filled in or added here.

Allocating real estate taxes is called tax proration in legal jargon—and can appear confusing if you've never done it before. Although there are many local practices for how tax proration is accomplished, the formula in this contract is one of the simplest and fairest I've come across. Here's how it works. Suppose a real estate tax of $1,200 is due on July 1 and the seller pays it. You and the seller then close your purchase a month and a half later on August 15. Applying the language of the contract, the July 1 tax is treated as covering the year from July 1 through the following June 30. Since the seller has paid taxes for the period through the following June 30 and you'll be receiving the benefit of the payment, at closing you'd reimburse the seller for 10.5 months of the real estate tax ($1,050).

By treating each month as having 30 days, the task of computing the number of days you must pay for is simplified.

13. Other Prorations

This paragraph allocates other expenses associated with the property between you and the seller. Nothing normally needs to be filled in or added here.

14. Closing and Possession

Closing is real estate jargon for the date when you pay the money to the seller for the property and receive the deed in return. Insert the closing date here. Incidentally, requiring that you receive physical possession of the building at closing—as provided for in this paragraph—is normally far better for you than is agreeing that you'll get it later, as is sometimes provided. If the seller doesn't have to turn over possession until some future date, you will be inconvenienced if the seller is slow to move or pay rent for the holdover period.

15. Transfer of Title

By transferring title to you by a "warranty deed," the seller guarantees (warrants) that you have clear title (for example, that the seller really owns the building). If because of unpaid taxes or a contractor's lien this proves not to be true, you can sue the seller for damages. Generally, state and local transfer taxes are the seller's responsibility—a practice reflected in the language of this paragraph.

Nothing needs to be inserted here.

How Title Insurance Works

The title insurance process involves two distinct but related documents: a title insurance commitment and an owner's title insurance policy.

A title insurance commitment is normally issued to you a couple of weeks before closing by a title insurance company to let you know if there are any limitations on the insurance the title company is prepared to issue at closing. A commitment might say, in effect, "We'll guarantee clear title in your name if the seller gives you a warranty deed and pays off the existing mortgage at or before closing. Your title will, however, be subject to all building and use restrictions as well as easements." There might, for example, be a recorded easement giving the owner of the next-door property the right to drive over the rear ten feet of the property.

Because the commitment letter will be written in legal jargon, if there are significant conditions, strongly consider having an experienced local property lawyer review it for you. In addition, obtain or ask your lawyer to obtain copies of all significant legal documents—such as building and use restrictions and easement agreements—so that you can personally review them. Again, if these documents aren't clear to you, ask your lawyer to explain.

At the closing, the title company makes sure that all its requirements have been met for issuing the actual title insurance policy; typically, it will be a few weeks before the policy is prepared and mailed to you.

So far, we've been focusing on the owner's title insurance policy which the seller normally pays for and which insures that you own legal title to the building, subject to your lender's lien. You need this protection. Be careful not to confuse the owner's policy with a separate policy—one that insures that your bank or other lender has a valid first lien on or security interest in the building (in other words, that someone else doesn't already have a mortgage or lien). Although you'll be paying for it, this second policy is solely for your lender's protection.

In many parts of the country, the owner's title insurance policy will be issued with what the title company calls "standard exceptions." This means certain potential problems aren't covered by the title insurance. The two most important problems that are most typically not covered are boundary disputes and construction liens resulting from recent work on the building. Fortunately, it's almost always possible to have the title insurance company issue the title insurance policy without these standard exceptions, which means that you get broader coverage—and there's usually no extra cost involved for you or the seller. But to issue this broader coverage, the title insurance company will want two things:

- A land survey—which is easy to provide since your lender will probably order a physical survey of the land and its boundaries (in real estate jargon, a surveyor's "mortgage report") before making the loan.

- A written statement from the seller that there's been no recent work on the building or that, if there has been, it's been paid for—a guarantee a reasonable seller should be able to provide.

16. Title Insurance

A title insurance policy is like any other insurance policy: If you suffer a loss because you don't get clear title from the seller, the title insurance company is obligated to pay for your loss. This might occur if the seller conveys the property to you without clearing an existing mortgage or deed of trust or if there are other liens on the property or unpaid taxes.

Nothing needs to be filled in here.

17. Additional Contingencies

This paragraph is called "Additional Contingencies" because there is an earlier contingency in this contract—the financing contingency (paragraph 4).

Check the box for each contingency you want to include and fill in a date by which the contingency must be removed.

Here's some of the reasoning behind the various contingencies:

- **Contractor's Inspection.** An inspection by a contractor lets you find out what condition the building is in and whether you're likely to face any expensive repairs.
- **Architect's Inspection.** If you're thinking of doing any renovation or remodeling work, an architect's inspection can be very important. You want to be sure it's feasible to make the upgrades at a reasonable cost.
- **Environmental Inspection.** As we noted in Section A at the beginning of this chapter, an environmental inspection will let you know if there's any soil contamination or other environmental hazard that could involve you in a costly clean-up effort.
- **Building and Use Requirements.** These alert you to any restrictions on how you can use, remodel or add on to the building.
- **Survey.** A survey of the property will disclose any boundary problems such as a neighboring building or fence that occupies part of the property you're buying—and will also let you know if part of the building you're buying is on someone else's property.

- **Title Insurance Review.** This makes sure that you can cancel the deal if your lawyer isn't satisfied with the legal title.

18. Removal of Contingencies

Nothing needs to be filled in here. This paragraph tells what happens if a contingency isn't removed by the specified date.

19. Loss Before Closing

Nothing need to be filled in here. If the building burns down before closing, that's the seller's problem—not yours.

20. Default

Nothing needs to be filled in here. This paragraph tells what happens if you back out of the deal without a legally proper reason (such as not being able to remove the financing contingency because you don't qualify for a loan) and what happens if the seller refuses to proceed with the sale without a valid reason. Briefly, if you default, the seller can sue you for damages, which normally is the difference between the fair market value of the building (say, $300,000) and what you agreed to pay (say, $325,000). Or you and the seller can agree that if you default without a good reason, the seller can simply keep your deposit without having to show an actual monetary loss—a remedy known in legal jargon as agreeing to a "liquidated damages" clause.

If the seller defaults, you can enforce the contract by asking a judge to order the seller to deed the building to you (upon payment of the purchase price, of course). This is known in legal circles as specific performance. Or if you don't want to enforce the contract, you can sue for money damages—again, normally it's the difference between what you agreed to pay (say $290,000) and the fair market value of the building (say $300,000). Or you can skip the hassles and just get back your deposit.

21. Disputes

See the discussion of dispute resolution clauses in Chapter 1, Section D.

22. Additional Agreements

Insert any additional agreements that you and the seller have reached.

Standard Clauses

The remainder of the agreement contains the standard clauses we discussed in Chapter 1, Section C. The only thing you'll need to fill in here is the name of the state whose law will apply to the contract in the paragraph called "Governing Law."

Signatures

Sign and date the contract. For more on signing contracts, see Chapter 1, Section B.

Attachment

If you checked the second box in paragraph 2, include an attachment describing the property. You can use Form 7F: Attachment to Real Estate Purchase Contract to create an attachment.

C. Form 7C: Option to Purchase Building

This option contract gives you the right to take whatever amount of time you and the seller agree upon to decide whether you want to buy a building. You might use this contract if you're seriously looking at several buildings and aren't ready to make a firm offer on one. This option form also gives you a chance to investigate the condition of the building—and any other concerns you may have—before you commit yourself to proceeding with the purchase.

Because granting you an option to purchase prevents the seller from selling the building to someone else during the option period, the seller will undoubtedly ask you to pay a fee. Depending on how your contract is worded, if you don't proceed with the deal, the seller keeps the option fee. If you go ahead with the purchase, the fee will often, but not always, be applied to your down payment. Since at the time you sign the option you probably won't have had the building fully inspected or taken other steps to be sure you want to buy it, you'll be

wise to negotiate to keep the option fee as low as possible.

Instructions for Form 7C: Option to Purchase Building

All the forms in this book are provided as tear-outs in Appendix B and on the accompanying forms CD-ROM. As you read the instructions for Form 7C, you may want to either tear out the form or open the form's file on the CD-ROM so you can follow along. Form 7C is in the file FORM7C.RTF on the CD-ROM. (For more information on using the forms CD-ROM, see Appendix A, "How to Use the CD-ROM.") If you don't use the forms CD-ROM, be sure to photocopy the agreement so you'll have a clean copy to use later.

1. Names

Insert the names of the seller and purchaser.

2. Option to Purchase Building

Insert the amount you're paying up front to tie up the building while you make up your mind about the purchase.

Check the appropriate box. See the instructions for paragraph 2 of Form 7B for information about describing the property.

3. Exercise of Option

Insert the date by which you must exercise the option. Negotiate to give yourself enough time to make up your mind.

Check one or more boxes to indicate how you can deliver your written notice if you decide to exercise your option. If you check the second box, fill in the seller's address.

4. Purchase Price

Put the full purchase price in the first blank. Then check a box to indicate whether the option fee stated in paragraph 2 will or will not be applied toward the purchase price if you elect to go ahead and buy the building. It's customary to do this, but if the seller feels otherwise, this is a point you'll need to negotiate. One alternative is to agree that the option fee will be applied toward the purchase only if you exercise the option very promptly (say, within 30 days) but if it takes longer you get no (or only partial) credit for it.

5. Inclusions
See instructions for paragraph 5 of Form 7B.

6. Exclusions
See instructions for paragraph 6 of Form 7B.

7. Condition of Equipment
See instructions for paragraph 7 of Form 7B.

8. Access to Property
This paragraph allows the Purchaser to have experts come into the building and go on the surrounding land to make inspections or make a survey to determine the true boundaries. This will help you make an intelligent decision about whether or not to exercise your option to buy the building. Here's why you may want an inspection or survey:

- **Contractor's Inspection.** An inspection by a contractor lets you find out what condition the building is in and whether you're likely to face any expensive repairs.
- **Architect's Inspection.** If you're thinking of doing any renovation or remodeling work, you'll definitely want to have an architect inspect the building. You want to be sure it's feasible to make the upgrades at a reasonable cost.
- **Environmental Inspection.** As we discussed in more detail in Section A of this chapter, it's critical that you conduct an environmental inspection before you buy a building. An inspection will let you know if there's any soil contamination or other environmental hazard that could involve you in a costly clean-up effort.
- **Survey.** A survey of the property will disclose any boundary problems such as a neighboring building or fence that occupies part of the property you're buying—and will also let you know if part of the building you're buying is on someone else's property.

9. Physical Problems With Property
See instructions for paragraph 8 of Form 7B.

10. Cleaning of Premises
See instructions for paragraph 9 of Form 7B.

11. Special Assessments
Nothing needs to be filled in here. See instructions for paragraph 10 of Form 7B.

12. Utility Charges
Nothing needs to be filled in here. See instructions for paragraph 11 of Form 7B.

13. Real Estate Taxes
Nothing needs to be filled in here. See instructions for paragraph 12 of Form 7B.

14. Other Prorations
Nothing needs to be filled in here. See instructions for paragraph 13 of Form 7B.

15. Closing and Possession
See instructions for paragraph 14 of Form 7B.

16. Transfer of Title
Nothing needs to be inserted here. See instructions for paragraph 15 of Form 7B.

17. Title Insurance
See instructions for paragraph 16 of Form 7B for an explanation of title insurance.

Check the first box if your purchase will be contingent on your lawyer approving the title insurance commitment furnished by the seller.

Check the second box if your purchase will be contingent on your lawyer approving a survey of the property furnished by the seller.

If you check either or both boxes, insert the date by which the seller is to deliver to you the title insurance commitment, survey or both documents.

Then insert the numbers of days you have to remove the contingency after you receive the documents. Two weeks will usually give you and your lawyer ample time to look over a title insurance commitment or survey.

If you don't remove the contingency, you'll get back your option fee.

18. Loss Before Closing
Nothing needs to be filled in here. See instructions for paragraph 19 of Form 7B.

19. Default
Nothing needs to be filled in here. See instructions for paragraph 20 of Form 7B.

20. Disputes
See the discussion of dispute resolution clauses in Chapter 1, Section D.

21. Additional Agreements
Insert any additional agreements that you and the seller have reached.

Standard Clauses
The remainder of the contract contains the standard clauses we discussed in Chapter 1, Section C. The only thing you'll need to fill in here is the name of the state whose law will apply to the contract in the paragraph called "Governing Law."

Signatures
Sign and date the contract. For more on signing contracts, see Chapter 1, Section B.

Attachment
If you checked the second box in paragraph 2, include an attachment describing the property. You can use Form 7F: Attachment to Real Estate Purchase Contract, to create an attachment.

D. Form 7D: Contract to Purchase Vacant Land

You may want to buy vacant land for one of several reasons. Perhaps you want to build your own custom structure. Or maybe you're not ready to own a building yet but want to tie up an attractive piece of land to build on in the future, figuring you can always sell the land (ideally, at a profit) if you later determine you can't or don't want to build. Alternatively, you might want vacant land for a use connected with your business—parking or storing cars or equipment, for example, or as an outdoor sales area for garden supplies, pools or patio furniture, or for serving food if you're in the restaurant business.

Buying land is a bit easier than buying a building—mainly, because there's obviously no building to inspect. But you still have plenty of homework to accomplish before you can be comfortable with being contractually locked into a purchase. For example, as with the purchase of a building, you may need to borrow a big chunk of the purchase price, so you'll want to make sure any contract you sign contains a contingency clause that permits you to terminate the contract if you can't arrange adequate financing for your purchase.

Similarly, it's critical that you find out whether local zoning ordinances and building codes permit you to proceed with the type of use and construction you envision for the site. If not, you'll want to the contract to be contingent on the ability to get the land rezoned to permit your desired use or to get an appropriate zoning variance from a local appeals board before you're obligated to close on the deal. And you need to be sure that utility services are available—or, outside of urban areas where utilities may not be available, that the land can be served by an on-site well and septic system.

Another major concern these days is whether the land has ever been used as a dump site for toxic substances; if so, this can have major consequences later on as you may be required to pay a ton of money to clean up the land. To protect yourself, make the contract contingent on your receiving a satisfactory report from an environmental expert hired by you to inspect the site.

Get help from professionals. Land development is not a game for the inexperienced person. If you've never bought land before, it's important to seek the advice of engineers, architects, contractors and possibly a lawyer to make sure you'll be able to put the land to your intended use.

Instructions for Form 7D: Contract to Purchase Vacant Land

All the forms in this book are provided as tear-outs in Appendix B and on the accompanying forms CD-ROM. As you read the instructions for Form 7D, you may want to either tear out the form or open the form's file on the CD-ROM so you can follow along. Form 7D is in the file FORM7D.RTF on the CD-ROM. (For more information on using the forms CD-ROM, see Appendix A, "How to Use the CD-ROM.") If you don't use the forms CD-ROM, be sure to photocopy the agreement so you'll have a clean copy to use later.

1. Names

Insert the names of the seller and the purchaser.

2. Purchase of Real Estate

See the instructions for paragraph 2 of Form 7B.

3. Purchase Price

See the instructions for paragraph 3 of Form 7B.

4. Financing Contingency

See the instructions for paragraph 4 of Form 7B.

5. Special Assessments

See the instructions for paragraph 10 of Form 7B. Be aware that if streets, sidewalks, water and sewers need to be extended to the land to make it usable, getting this to happen is often far from automatic. Assuming it's possible at all, it may be prohibitively expensive. Check with the local authorities on what to expect.

6. Utility Charges

See the instructions for paragraph 11 of Form 7B. Again, it's wise to check with the local authorities on what these charges might be when you begin to develop the property.

7. Real Estate Taxes

Nothing needs to be filled in here. See the instructions for paragraph 12 of Form 7B.

8. Closing and Possession

See the instructions for paragraph 14 of Form 7B.

9. Transfer of Title

Nothing needs to be inserted here. See the instructions for paragraph 15 of Form 7B.

10. Title Insurance

Nothing needs to be filled in here. See the instructions for paragraph 16 of Form 7B.

11. Additional Contingencies

See the instructions for paragraph 17 of Form 7B. You want to make sure you have a chance to make all necessary investigations about your ability to develop the land as you would like to.

12. Removal of Contingencies

Nothing needs to be filled in here. See the instructions for paragraph 18 of Form 7B.

13. Default

Nothing needs to be filled in here. See the instructions for paragraph 20 of Form 7B.

14. Disputes

See the discussion of dispute resolution in Chapter 1, Section C.

15. Additional Agreements and Amendments

Insert any additional agreements that you and the seller have reached.

Signatures

Sign and date the contract. For more on signing contracts, see Chapter 1, Section B.

Attachment

If you checked the second box in paragraph 2, include an attachment describing the property. You can use Form 7F: Attachment to Real Estate Purchase Contract, to create an attachment.

E. Form 7E: Option to Purchase Vacant Land

This option contract allows you to tie up vacant land while you decide whether or not to buy it.

See the instructions for Form 7C: Option to Purchase Building, for an explanation of how an option-to-purchase agreement works.

If you use this form, you'll have a chance to investigate the condition of the land—and any other concerns you may have—before you exercise the option. Among other things, you'll want to be sure that the land is free from environmental contamination, that you can build the type of building you plan to build on it, that needed utility services are or can be available at an affordable price and that the type of building you plan will comply with local zoning ordinances. If you find problems with any of these items or if you can't arrange for needed financing, you can drop the deal entirely. By contrast, if everything checks out and you exercise this option, you commit yourself to proceeding with the purchase.

Instructions for Form 7E: Option to Purchase Vacant Land

All the forms in this book are provided as tear-outs in Appendix B and on the accompanying forms CD-ROM. As you read the instructions for Form 7E, you may want to either tear out the form or open the form's file on the CD-ROM so you can follow along. Form 7E is in the file FORM7E.RTF on the CD-ROM. (For more information on using the forms CD-ROM, see Appendix A, "How to Use the CD-ROM.") If you don't use the forms CD-ROM, be sure to photocopy the agreement so you'll have a clean copy to use later.

1. Names

Insert the names of the seller and the purchaser.

2. Option to Purchase Vacant Land

Insert the amount you're paying up front to tie up the property while you make up your mind about the purchase. Remember that an option fee is not like a deposit that you can get back if the contingencies aren't satisfactory. With an option fee, if you decide not to buy the property (exercise your option), the option agreement normally provides that the seller keeps the money.

See the instructions for paragraph 2 of Form 7B regarding the identification of the property.

3. Exercise of Option

Insert the date by which you must exercise the option. Check one or more boxes to indicate how you can deliver your written notice if you decide to exercise your option. If you check the second box, fill in the seller's address.

4. Purchase Price

See the instructions for paragraph 4 of Form 7C.

5. Access to Property

This paragraph allows the purchaser to have experts go on the land to make inspections or make a survey to determine the true boundaries. This will help you make an intelligent decision about whether or not to exercise your option to buy the property. Here's some of the reasoning behind making these inspections (or ordering a survey):

- **Contractor's Inspection.** An inspection by a contractor lets you find out about the cost of building on the land—and any possible construction problems.
- **Architect's Inspection.** If you're interested in constructing a building, an architect's inspection can help you decide if the land is a feasible site for the type of building you'd like to erect.
- **Environmental Inspection.** As we discussed in more detail in Section A of this chapter, it's critical that you conduct an environmental inspection of the property before you buy it. This will let you know if there's any soil contamination or other environmental hazard that could involve you in a costly clean-up effort.
- **Survey.** A survey of the property will disclose any boundary problems such as a neighboring building or fence that occupies part of the property you're buying—and will also let you know if you have enough room to build on the site.

6. Special Assessments

Check the appropriate box. See the instructions for paragraph 10 of Form 7B.

7. Utility Charges

Check the appropriate box. See the instructions for paragraph 11 of Form 7B.

8. Real Estate Taxes

Nothing needs to be filled in here.

9. Closing and Possession

See the instructions for paragraph 14 of Form 7B.

10. Transfer of Title

Nothing needs to be inserted here. See the instructions for paragraph 15 of Form 7B.

11. Title Insurance

See the instructions for paragraph 17 of Form 7C.

12. Default

Nothing needs to be filled in here. See the instructions for paragraph 20 of Form 7B.

13. Disputes

See the discussion of dispute resolution clauses in Chapter 1, Section D.

14. Additional Agreements

Insert any additional agreements that you and the seller have reached.

Standard Clauses

The remainder of the contract contains the standard clauses we discussed in Chapter 1, Section C. The only thing you'll need to fill in here is the name of the state whose law will apply to the contract in the paragraph called "Governing Law."

Signatures

Sign and date the contract. For more on signing contracts, see Chapter 1, Section B.

Attachment

If you checked the second box in paragraph 2, include an attachment describing the property. You can use Form 7F: Attachment to Real Estate Purchase Contract, to create an attachment.

F. Form 7F: Attachment to Real Estate Purchase Contract

Often when you prepare a real estate purchase contract, there are some terms, conditions and miscellaneous details that are so wordy they don't fit neatly into the main form. You can deal with this problem by creating an attachment to the contract (material tacked on the end of the contract that becomes a part of it).

Some items that might go into an attachment:

- The legal description of the property
- Plans and specifications for improvements to be made by the seller before the closing

SAMPLE:

Before closing, Seller will complete the following improvements to the property at Seller's expense: *[List the specifics, including detailed drawings and materials to be used.]*

- Agreements relating to seller's continuing use of premises

SAMPLE:

For 30 days following the closing, Seller will have the right to store the following equipment in the basement storage area at no charge: *[Insert list of equipment to be stored.]* While Seller's equipment is stored there, Purchaser will keep the access door to the basement locked, but will open it on request of Seller.

SAMPLE:

At closing, Seller and Purchaser will enter into the following one-year lease allowing Seller to continue to occupy the second-floor office space.
[Then attach the actual lease.]

Instructions for Form 7F: Attachment to Real Estate Purchase Contract

All the forms in this book are provided as tear-outs in Appendix B and on the accompanying forms CD-ROM. As you read the instructions for Form 7F, you may want to either tear out the form or open the form's file on the CD-ROM so you can follow along. Form 7F is in the file FORM7F.RTF on the CD-ROM. (For more information on using the forms CD-ROM, see Appendix A, "How to Use the CD-ROM.") If you don't use the forms CD-ROM, be sure to photocopy the agreement so you'll have a clean copy to use later.

For clarity, an attachment should include the name of the seller and the buyer, and a description of the property being sold. Where there's more than one attachment, number them consecutively and refer to them by number (Attachment 1, Attachment 2, etc.) in the main body of the contract. Attach them to the end of the contract.

In the first paragraph, insert the names of both parties (paragraph 1 of the contract) and the date the original contract was signed.

If you're attaching a legal description of the property (paragraph 2 of Forms 7B and 7C), after "described as" insert the same short description as you did in paragraph 2.

Use the space before the date and signature line to insert the full legal description or other details. Then date and sign the attachment.

G. Form 7G: Amendment of Real Estate Purchase Contract

Suppose, as is common, you and the seller agree to make changes in the terms of your real estate purchase contract before closing. There's no need to redo the entire contract, which might even risk opening up a wide range of issues best left alone. Instead, you can simply prepare and sign an amendment.

What can you put in an amendment? The possibilities are virtually unlimited. A price reduction might be appropriate, for example, if your contractor's inspection has disclosed several expensive problems with the building. In this situation, unless the seller is willing to pay a contractor directly to accomplish the needed work, the two of you might agree on a reduced purchase price as a condition of your removing the contingency requiring a satisfactory contractor's report.

SAMPLE:

Paragraph 3 is amended to reduce the purchase price from $500,000 to $450,000. Paragraph 17 is amended by removing the contingency requiring a satisfactory contractor's report.

Or you and the seller may agree to split the cost of replacing an item that your inspector found to be in questionable condition:

SAMPLE:

Paragraph 7 is amended by the addition of the following: Before closing, Seller will arrange to have the air conditioning unit replaced with a new one of the same brand and capacity. Seller and Purchaser will share equally the cost of the new unit and its installation. Paragraph 17 is amended by removing the contingency requiring a satisfactory contractor's report.

If the seller or a current tenant needs additional time to move out of the building, making the scheduled closing date impractical, you and the seller might agree to an amendment extending the time for closing.

SAMPLE:

Paragraph 14 is amended to move the time for closing and delivery of possession from May 15, 20____, to June 1, 20____.

A change like this might also be appropriate if you learn your lender can't put together the necessary paperwork by the original closing date.

Or suppose you've signed a contract to buy a building in a research park with the idea that you'll be doing some light manufacturing in addition to research and office usage. You then receive the covenants, conditions and restrictions for the building and learn that manufacturing is permitted only by permission of managers of the research park association. You and the seller may agree to amend

the contract to give you a chance to address this issue rather than have you simply cancel the deal and face a possible fight over whether you're entitled to get your deposit back.

SAMPLE:

The following clause is added to paragraph 17: Purchaser will apply promptly to the research park association for permission to use the building for light manufacturing. The closing will be moved from September 1, 20____, to October 1, 20____, to allow Purchaser enough time to accomplish this. The parties agree that if such permission is not granted by the new closing date, the contract will be canceled and Seller will return Purchaser's deposit.

Instructions for Form 7G: Amendment of Real Estate Purchase Contract

All the forms in this book are provided as tear-outs in Appendix B and on the accompanying forms CD-ROM. As you read the instructions for Form 7G, you may want to either tear out the form or open the form's file on the CD-ROM so you can follow along. Form 7G is in the file FORM7G.RTF on the CD-ROM. (For more information on using the forms CD-ROM, see Appendix A, "How to Use the CD-ROM.") If you don't use the forms CD-ROM, be sure to photocopy the agreement so you'll have a clean copy to use later.

After identifying the original contract by subject and date, your next step is to fill in the description of the property, which of course should be exactly the same as the property described in the original contract. Then insert any changes, carefully indicating which paragraphs of the contract are being amended. If there is more than one amendment, number them consecutively and attach a copy of each to the original contract.

Signatures

Both parties must sign and date the amendment. For more on signing contracts, see Chapter 1, Section B.

H. Form 7H: Removal of Contingency

As you surely know, real estate purchase contracts are almost always made contingent upon the buyer being able to do certain things such as arrange for financing or obtain satisfactory reports from contractors and others hired to inspect the property. (See, for example, paragraphs 4 and 17 of Form 7B: Contract to Purchase Building.) Typically, there's a deadline in the purchase contract by which the purchaser must remove a contingency.

Assuming that you're able to clear up whatever possible impediment you identified when you inserted a contingency in the original contract (for example, arranged financing or had the property satisfactorily inspected), you can use Form 7H: Removal of Contingency, to let the seller know that you're removing a contingency.

Instructions for Form 7H: Removal of Contingency

All the forms in this book are provided as tear-outs in Appendix B and on the accompanying forms CD-ROM. As you read the instructions for Form 7H, you may want to either tear out the form or open the form's file on the CD-ROM so you can follow along. Form 7H is in the file FORM7H.RTF on the CD-ROM. (For more information on using the forms CD-ROM, see Appendix A, "How to Use the CD-ROM.") If you don't use the forms CD-ROM, be sure to photocopy the agreement so you'll have a clean copy to use later.

Insert the seller's name and then your name (the purchaser).

Insert the date of the original contract and the location of the property.

Now check a box for each contingency you're removing and insert the paragraph number where the contingency is located in the original contract.

You, as purchaser, should sign and date the document.

💡 **You may want to remove contingencies one by one.** It's common for your purchase contract to have different deadlines for removing different contingencies. You may, for example, have only ten days to remove the contingency for a satisfactory contractor's inspection but 30 days to remove the contingency for arranging financing. In that situation, you'll have to give the seller more than one Removal of Contingency form. But even if the purchase contract has just one deadline that applies to all the contingencies, you may still want to remove the contingencies one by one as you're able to do so, since doing this reassures the seller that you're serious about going forward with the deal.

I. Form 7I: Extension of Time to Remove Contingencies

You may find that, despite your best efforts, you need more time before you can safely remove a contingency. The lender, for example, may be taking longer than expected to review your loan application or you may need to have an additional inspection made of the property. In that situation, the seller—especially if he or she is convinced you've been moving forward in good faith—is likely to agree to extend the time for you to remove one or more contingencies. You can use Form 7I: Extension of Time to Remove Contingencies, to document this agreement.

Instructions for Form 7I: Extension of Time to Remove Contingencies

All the forms in this book are provided as tear-outs in Appendix B and on the accompanying forms CD-ROM. As you read the instructions for Form 7I, you may want to either tear out the form or open the form's file on the CD-ROM so you can follow along. Form 7I is in the file FORM7I.RTF on the CD-ROM. (For more information on using the forms CD-ROM, see Appendix A, "How to Use the CD-ROM.") If you don't use the forms CD-ROM, be sure to photocopy the agreement so you'll have a clean copy to use later.

Insert the seller's name and then your name (as purchaser).

Insert the date of the original contract and the location of the property.

Now check a box for each contingency for which the removal date is being extended and fill in the new deadline date.

Both parties—seller and purchaser—need to sign this agreement.

J. Form 7J: Exercise of Option to Purchase Real Estate

This form is for use if you've signed an option contract, such as Form 7C: Option to Purchase Building, or Form 7E: Option to Purchase Vacant Land, and decide to exercise your option.

When you properly deliver this form to the seller using one of the methods called for in the option contract, you've got a firm deal—subject to a review of the title insurance commitment.

Instructions for Form 7J: Exercise of Option to Purchase Real Estate

All the forms in this book are provided as tear-outs in Appendix B and on the accompanying forms CD-ROM. As you read the instructions for Form 7J, you may want to either tear out the form or open the form's file on the CD-ROM so you can follow along. Form 7J is in the file FORM7J.RTF on the CD-ROM. (For more information on using the forms CD-ROM, see Appendix A, "How to Use the CD-ROM.") If you don't use the forms CD-ROM, be sure to photocopy the agreement so you'll have a clean copy to use later.

Insert the name of the seller.

Then insert your own name (as purchaser).

Fill in the description of the property you're purchasing and the date of the original agreement.

You, the purchaser, need to date and sign the document.

K. Form 7K: Renovation Contract

You can use this form if you own a building and are hiring a contractor to renovate it. This form can be used whether you have the cash to finance the renovation yourself or you're getting a renovation loan. It also contains language to help assure that the contractor is paying all subcontractors, laborers and suppliers so you don't wind up with construction or mechanic's liens on your property. Be aware that because techniques may differ on how to best protect yourself from liens, it's also wise to check with someone who's knowledgeable about how this is done in your state: an architect, a banker, a title insurance company or a real estate lawyer, for example.

This contract is appropriate for a relatively small-scale renovation job. On a larger project or when working with a major contractor, you'll almost certainly be required to start with a contract prepared by the contractor and which is likely to contain numerous paragraphs intended to protect the contractor from a wide range of possible disasters. In that situation, you'll almost always want to add language to protect your own interests, using this form as a source of ideas and wording.

Instructions for Form 7K: Renovation Contract

All the forms in this book are provided as tear-outs in Appendix B and on the accompanying forms CD-ROM. As you read the instructions for Form 7K, you may want to either tear out the form or open the form's file on the CD-ROM so you can follow along. Form 7K is in the file FORM7K.RTF on the CD-ROM. (For more information on using the forms CD-ROM, see Appendix A, "How to Use the CD-ROM.") If you don't use the forms CD-ROM, be sure to photocopy the agreement so you'll have a clean copy to use later.

1. Names
Insert the names of the owner (you) and the contractor.

2. Scope and Location
Insert the address of the building that will be renovated.

3. Plans, Specifications and Warranty
Insert the date of the plans and specifications and include them as an attachment. See Chapter 1, Section E, on adding attachments to your documents.

Also make sure you get a commitment that the contractor will fix any problems in the renovation work after it's done. This commitment is called a warranty and should be part of the contract. Understandably, no contractor will agree to fix all problems forever. Typically, the contractor will agree to remedy defects in materials and workmanship that appear during the first 12 months after the job is done. But if the contractor's normal warranty contains too many loopholes to adequately protect you, you'll want to negotiate a more customer-friendly clause. Include the warranty as a separate attachment, as well. (See Chapter 1, Section E, on adding attachments.)

The value of the contractor's warranty will depend both on the contractor's financial strength and reputation for promptly attending to warranty problems. Since obviously it can be frustrating to deal with a contractor who has a nonchalant attitude about doing quality work and standing behind it, it's extremely wise to take the time to talk to at least a few prior customers before signing on the bottom line.

4. Price
Insert the price for the job.

5. Financing Contingency
This paragraph is optional. If you'll need funds from a loan to finance the renovation, check the box. Then insert the amount you'll need to borrow and your deadline for removing this contingency. CD-ROM users who don't want to include this optional paragraph should delete it, and renumber the subsequent paragraphs.

6. Payment Terms
Check one of the two boxes. If you'll be applying for a loan for the renovation, check the first box. If you already have the necessary cash, check the second box. Whichever box you check, fill in the amount of the down payment.

Typically, you'll pay the contractor periodically as different stages of the renovation are completed. This form assumes that you'll include a payment schedule as an additional attachment—Attachment 3—to the contract that details how much you'll pay the contractor at each stage of the renovation. See Chapter 1, Section E, on adding attachments.

One way to make sure that each renovation stage meets your reasonable requirements is to hire a construction supervisor, such as an architect, whose job it is to inspect and approve the work before you pay the contractor. If you do this, you'll want to add some appropriate language to paragraph 6.

SAMPLE:

Contractor's right to payment will be subject to the approval of Owner's construction supervisor, Marilyn Baker, who will determine if Contractor is in substantial compliance with the terms of the contract or whether grounds exist (as listed above) for the withholding of a reasonable part of any payment. Marilyn Baker will also determine the amount, if any, to be withheld.

An additional way to deal with disputes that prove impossible to negotiate among the parties over whether the contractor has satisfactorily met the contract requirements for payment at any stage of the work is to provide for mediation—followed, perhaps, by arbitration if necessary. The key is to have any dispute resolved as promptly as possible so the job can go ahead. On a smaller job, formal mediation or arbitration through a dispute resolution agency such as the American Arbitration Association may be too costly and time-consuming. That's why we advise that you and the contractor will normally do better to agree on an experienced architect or builder in advance and use your contract to empower him or her to mediate any disagreements.

SAMPLE:

If there is a dispute over whether Contractor has satisfactorily completed the work necessary to qualify for payment at any of the "construction stages" of this contract as set out in Attachment _____, or has met all other requirements of paragraph 6, the parties agree to submit the dispute to James Martin of the firm of Martin & Klein of Davenport, Iowa, who will serve as mediator. If through good faith mediation the dispute is not resolved within seven days, it will be submitted to Anne Lee of Davenport, Iowa, for arbitration. Owner and Contractor will each pay one-half of the mediator's and arbitrator's fees.

7. Commencement of Renovation

Check the box that fits when you've agreed that the contractor will apply for the permits needed to begin the renovation.

8. Completion of Renovation

Insert the agreed date of completion. Then insert a second date which is the date by which the contractor must wrap up the job, regardless of any reasons for delay.

9. Change Orders

Nothing needs to be filled in here. To avoid arguments over whether changes in the work were authorized, you and the contractor should agree in writing to any changes.

10. Toxic Materials

Nothing needs to be filled in here. Sometimes a renovation will reveal the presence of toxic materials such as asbestos or lead-based paint, or toxic conditions such as radon gas, that no one knew were there. This paragraph defines the responsibility of you and the contractor if such materials should surface. First the contractor has to let you know what's been found and handle it safely. Then you have to arrange for proper containment, removal or mitigation of the toxic materials or toxic conditions at your expense. For example, if lead-based paint is discovered, you may authorize proper steps to cover it. If radon is found, you may elect to have it dealt with by better ventilation of the building's basement.

 Add more detail if you know or suspect that toxics are present. Most buildings of a certain age will have lead-based paint in them somewhere and most contractors are probably prepared to deal with it safely. Asbestos, depending on where it is and what form it takes, may be more of a problem and require more specialized licensing and training on the part of the contractor. Where you know or suspect that asbestos or another toxic material is present, add specific language to the contract dealing directly with how the problem will be handled during the renovation.

11. Insurance

This paragraph assumes that there's already insurance in place covering damage to the building you occupy and its contents, and that you're carrying ample insurance in case someone is injured on the premises.

Nothing needs to be inserted.

An insurance pro can guide you. An insurance agent or broker who has experience in the construction field can help you determine if your own insurance plus the coverage the contract requires the contractor to carry is adequate for the renovation work. Reviewing this contract language with an insurance pro is especially appropriate on bigger jobs or those where toxic materials are or may be present.

12. Indemnification

Nothing needs to be filled in here.

13. Inspections

Nothing needs to be filled in here

14. Final Payment

Nothing needs to be filled in here.

15. Standards of Performance

Insert the number of the plans and specification attachment (the first one referred to in paragraph 3—most likely, Attachment 1). At the end of this paragraph, fill in the name of your community.

16. Contractor's Default

Nothing needs to be filled in here.

17. Owner's Default

Insert the name of your state.

18. Disputes

See the discussion of dispute resolution clauses in Chapter 1, Section D.

19. Additional Agreements

Insert any additional agreements that you and the seller have reached.

Standard Clauses

The remainder of the contract contains the standard clauses we discussed in Chapter 1, Section C. The only thing you'll need to fill in here is the name of the state whose law will apply to the contract in the paragraph called "Governing Law."

Signatures

Both parties need to sign. See Chapter 1, Section B, for instructions on signing contracts.

Attachments

You should add the three attachments described in the instructions for paragraph 3 (Attachments 1 and 2) and paragraph 6 (Attachment 3), above. ∎

8

Buying, Selling, Manufacturing

I f your business sells goods at retail and customers pay you in full at the time of sale, you'll rarely need to worry about purchase contracts. When a sale is completed on the spot, there are relatively few loose ends. On the other hand, if your business buys or sells goods for later delivery, you'll likely want to record the deal with Form 8A: Sales Contract —Lump Sum Payment, or Form 8B: Sales Contract— Installment Payments.

For more information on laws affecting sales transactions, see the *Legal Guide for Starting and Running a Small Business*, by Fred S. Steingold (Nolo). Chapter 17 covers the legal requirements for dealing with customers. Chapter 18 deals with the legal issues involved with receiving cash, checks and credit cards. And finally, Chapter 19 provides a more in-depth discussion on the issues of extending credit and getting paid.

Form 8C: Bill of Sale is designed primarily for use by a seller to document the transfer of ownership of goods to a buyer. It may be used be in conjunction with a sales contract such as Form 8A or Form 8B. In a typical sale, however, delivery to the buyer together with a receipt signed by the buyer is sufficient legal evidence that ownership has been transferred. In the real world of starting or running a small business, you'd be most likely to use a bill of sale in the following situations:

- **Purchase of a Business.** To document the transfer of ownership of inventory, furniture and equipment to someone who's buying all the assets of a business.
- **Purchase of a Building.** To document the transfer of ownership of furniture and equipment presently in a building to someone who's buying that building.
- **Transfers to or From Business Owners.** To document the transfer of ownership from shareholders, for example, who are transferring tangible property they own (computers, furniture, and so on) to their corporation, or the transfer of ownership of property from a partnership to individual partners upon breakup of the partnership.
- **Sale of Expensive Items.** To document the transfer of ownership of costly and possibly unique equipment (a customized alarm system, a packaging device or a work of art, for example) which, unlike a car, truck, boat or plane, isn't registered—especially when the buyer anticipates that ownership may need to be proven at a later time.

When the purchase price is going to be paid over time and the sale involves valuable items, the seller will want the right to take back the goods or equipment if the buyer doesn't make payments. The seller does this by retaining an ownership interest (in legal jargon, a security interest) in the property. This can be accomplished using Form 8D: Security Agreement, in which the buyer acknowledges the right of the seller to repossess if timely payments aren't made.

If your goods will be custom-manufactured, both the manufacturer and the customer have a real need to prepare and sign a written contract detailing the terms of the transaction, such as Form 8E: Contract for Manufacture of Goods. Doing this will help avoid later disputes about whether the exact specifications of the goods and the payment terms have been met.

To record terms and details, you'll also want to prepare a written contract if you're:

- renting equipment to a customer (Form 8F: Equipment Rental Contract)
- storing items for someone (Form 8G: Storage Contract), or
- accepting items on consignment (Form 8H: Consignment Contract).

A. Form 8A: Sales Contract (Lump Sum Payment)

This form assumes that the buyer will make a down payment when the contract is signed and pay the balance due in one lump sum—most likely when the items are turned over to the seller. For example, you're planning to open a restaurant and have agreed to buy seven tables and 28 chairs from a restaurant across town that is closing in a month. To avoid the possibility of confusion about what you bought, when you can expect delivery and when you'll pay for the tables and chairs, you need a clear written agreement setting forth all key terms of your deal.

Or perhaps you're selling your present computer system to another business to make room for your new improved set-up which is scheduled to arrive soon. In addition to recording the basic facts of the transaction such as what you're selling, the purchase price and the deposit amount, you may want to tie the delivery date of your existing system to the arrival of your new one. You might also use this form to spell out the extent of your obligation to install the old system at the buyer's business place.

Instructions for Form 8A: Sales Contract (Lump Sum Payment)

All the forms in this book are provided as tear-outs in Appendix B and on the accompanying forms CD-ROM. As you read the instructions for Form 8A, you may want to either tear out the form or open the form's file on the CD-ROM so you can follow along. Form 8A is in the file FORM8A.RTF on the CD-ROM. (For more information on using the forms CD-ROM, see Appendix A, "How to Use the CD-ROM.") If you don't use the forms CD-ROM, be sure to photocopy the agreement so you'll have a clean copy to use later.

1. Names
Insert the names of the seller and the buyer. See Chapter 1, Section A, for a discussion of how to identify the parties in legal forms.

2. Property Being Sold
Describe the items you're buying or selling. Be as specific as is necessary to clearly identify the items, using a serial number if there is one.

SAMPLES:
- The ten-year-old, 16-foot-long Star Town refrigerated display case (Serial #1875) presently used at Sunflower Bakery.
- Canon color copier, serial #1234, together with stand and ten reams of 20-pound laser-grade bond paper.
- 2,000 men's 100% cotton T-Shirts manufactured by Fruit of the Loom in assorted sizes and colors.

3. Condition of Property
If the property being sold is new, check the first box.

If the property being sold is used, check the second box. Then check one of the two remaining boxes to indicate if the buyer will accept the property in "as-is" condition or the seller will be modifying the property before delivery, in which case the details should be inserted.

4. Disclaimer of Warranties
Manufacturers and sellers sometimes promise buyers that the goods they're about to use will last for a certain period of time or perform a specific function. For example, you may sell someone new chairs for their restaurant, and tell them that the chairs will last for ten years. These explicit promises are called "express warranties." They're a guarantee that the buyer may rely upon—and if the goods don't measure up, the buyer will have grounds to sue.

Sometimes, warranties are also "implied," meaning that these warranties automatically apply to the goods you're selling, whether you promise anything to the buyer or not. One of these warranties is the "implied warranty of merchantability"—a guarantee that the goods are fit for the ordinary purposes for which they're generally used. Another is the "implied warranty of fitness for a particular purpose"; here, if a seller has reason to know that the buyer has a particular purpose in mind for the goods, the seller guarantees that the goods are fit for that purpose. Since implied warranties are created by law (rather than what you say), they are much more difficult to deny than express warranties.

The disclaimer in this section attempts to disclaim or deny any express warranties you might have made to the buyer, as well as any implied warranties. If you or the buyer are not comfortable including it, simply delete this paragraph. If you do include it, you should be aware that although a disclaimer may help you if a buyer later sues you for breach of warranty, you could still be held liable. That's because such disclaimers are not popular with judges. Of course, the best policy is simply to be honest with buyer about the product you're selling, and allow them to choose whether or not they're comfortable buying it.

This is just the tip of the warranty iceberg. Chapter 17 of the *Legal Guide to Starting & Running a Small Business,* by Fred S. Steingold (Nolo) contains an in-depth discussion of warranties, disclaimers and tips on dealing with consumers.

Full disclosure of known defects can head off problems. Even when used property is sold "as is"—especially when the property is a used vehicle—it's a good idea for the seller to disclose in writing to the buyer any known defects or problems with the property that the buyer wouldn't likely discover on his own. The seller can insert these disclosures into this contract or put them into an attachment. Disclosures reduce the possibility that a buyer can later successfully argue that there was fraud or misrepresentation in the sale.

5. Purchase Price

Insert the price.

6. Down Payment

If the buyer is making a down payment, check the first box and insert the amount. Otherwise, check the second box. If the buyer is using a credit card for the down payment or any part of the purchase price, the seller will need to obtain the buyer's credit card number and the card's expiration date, and otherwise comply with the processing bank's rules.

7. Time of Payment

Check the first box if the balance of the purchase price will be due on delivery of the goods or equipment.

Check the second box if the balance of the purchase price will be due in one lump sum at some time other than delivery and insert the agreed date.

8. Method of Payment

Check the box that indicates the method of payment. If by credit card, insert the specific credit card and issuer—such as Citibank Visa, Wells Fargo Master-Card or American Express.

9. Delivery

Fill in the date and location of delivery.

10. Ownership

Nothing needs to be inserted here.

11. Transfer of Ownership

For most types of property, check the first box indicating that the seller will give the buyer a separate bill of sale. A bill of sale allows the buyer to easily prove—if challenged in a lawsuit, for example—that legal ownership of the property has been transferred. To accomplish this, use Form 8C.

If You're the Buyer, It's Wise to Do a Lien Check

It's possible that the seller previously gave someone else a lien on the property you're buying—probably because the seller didn't fully pay for it in the first place or used it as collateral for a loan. If this is true, the third party with the lien has a legal ownership interest in the property unless the seller pays off what's owed. The lienholder could repossess the property from you because selling property that's subject to a lien usually triggers the lienholder's right to seize the property. If that happened, you could sue the seller for incorrectly asserting that there were no liens on the property, but that could be both inconvenient and expensive—and might yield you nothing if the seller had already spent your money.

To avoid this possibility, you'll want to see if any liens have been filed against a particular item of property.

For a vehicle, boat or plane, the lien will usually be on file with the state agency (often the Department of Motor Vehicles) that handles registrations and transfers. When you locate the proper office, ask how you can look at or order a copy of the lien record for the item you're buying.

For other personal property, the lien will usually take the form of a Uniform Commercial Code Financing Statement, or UCC-1, filed with the proper state or county office or both. Less frequently (but equally important to be aware of), personal property may be subject to something called a judgment lien. This is a lien imposed by the state against someone's property when he or she loses a lawsuit, so that this property can be taken to pay the judgment. To learn whether property is subject to these types of liens, start by contacting your Secretary of State's office for information about where UCC and other liens are recorded. Then inquire specifically about whether there's a lien on the property you're buying. Lien checks usually cost a few dollars, but it's obviously money well spent to be sure no one else has a claim on the property you're buying.

If you do run a UCC financing statement or a lien check, make sure to do it in any state in which the seller or the property was ever located. In addition, make sure to check every possible name the seller might have used (including a fictitous business name)—not searching under the right name means you could miss a lien.

⚠️ **To transfer cars, trucks, boats and planes, official forms are needed.** As you probably know, a garden-variety bill of sale won't work for the few types of property such as vehicles, boats and planes which are registered with a state government. For these, a change of ownership (transfer of title) must be documented on a state transfer of title form. If the sale involves that type of property, check the second box instead of the first one and fill in the name of the state. The secretary of state's office or bureau of vehicle registration can tell you if the type of property being transferred requires a state transfer of title form.

12. Other Terms and Conditions

Fill in any other terms you've agreed to.

SAMPLES:

- Buyer will arrange for transporting the 16-foot Star Town refrigerated display case (Serial # 1875) from the Sunflower Bakery to Buyer's place of business and will pay for that transportation. Seller warrants that the display case will be in good working order when Buyer's transportation agent comes to get it.

- If the Canon copier (Serial #96810) needs repair within 30 days of delivery to Buyer, Seller will pay the repair cost. During the next 60 days after the initial 30-day period, Seller and Buyer will share any needed repair costs 50/50. After 90 days from delivery, Buyer is 100% responsible for any repair costs.

Standard Clauses

The remainder of the contract contains the standard clauses we discussed in Chapter 1, Section C. The only thing you'll need to fill in here is the name of the state whose law will apply to the contract in the paragraph called "Governing Law."

Signatures

See Chapter 1, Section B, for instructions on signing contracts.

B. Form 8B: Sales Contract (Installment Payments)

As with Form 8A: Sales Contract—Lump Sum Payment, this form is designed for situations where you agree to buy or sell goods or equipment to be delivered in the future. But instead of requiring the entire purchase price to be paid on delivery, Form 8B: Sales Contract (Installment Payments), provides for the buyer to pay for the items over a period of months or years.

Instructions for Form 8B: Sales Contract (Installment Payments)

All the forms in this book are provided as tear-outs in Appendix B and on the accompanying forms CD-ROM. As you read the instructions for Form 8B, you may want to either tear out the form or open the form's file on the CD-ROM so you can follow along. Form 8B is in the file FORM8B.RTF on the CD-ROM. (For more information on using the forms CD-ROM, see Appendix A, "How to Use the CD-ROM.") If you don't use the forms CD-ROM, be sure to photocopy the agreement so you'll have a clean copy to use later.

1. Names

Insert the names of the seller and the buyer. (See Chapter 1, Section A, for a discussion of how to identify the parties in legal forms.)

2. Property Being Sold

See instructions for paragraph 2 of Form 8A.

3. Condition of Property

See instructions for paragraph 3 of Form 8A.

4. Disclaimer of Warranties

See the instructions for paragraph 4 of Form 8A.

5. Purchase Price

Insert the price.

6. Down Payment

See the instructions for paragraph 6 of Form 8A.

7. Time of Payment

Specify how the balance of the purchase price will be paid.

SAMPLES:

- In two installments of $3,000 each. The first will be due on July 1, 20___; the second will be due on September 1, 20___. Payments will be made by cashier's check.
- In 36 monthly installments of $300 each to be paid on the first day of each month beginning July ___, 20___.

Think twice before charging interest. To keep matters simple, the seller and buyer may want to agree to a higher purchase price instead of trying to cope with the details of interest, finance charges and late fees—all of which are regulated by often complex laws that can vary widely from state to state. If, however, you're a seller and prefer to charge interest on the balance owed, then (especially when the buyer is a consumer—not a business) you'll need to familiarize yourself with the laws in your state covering installment purchases. Your state chamber of commerce or a trade association serving your industry is a good starting point for getting this information.

8. Delivery

Fill in the date and location of delivery.

9. Ownership

Nothing needs to be inserted here. See the instructions for paragraph 10 of Form 8A.

10. Transfer of Ownership

See the instructions for paragraph 11 of Form 8A.

11. Security Interest

Often, a seller of expensive goods or equipment will want to retain a security or ownership interest in the property being sold—a kind of lien giving the seller the right to take back property if the buyer doesn't make installment payments as promised. If the seller won't be retaining a security interest in the property, check the first box. Otherwise, check the second box and complete Form 8D: Security Agreement.

12. Other Terms and Conditions

Fill in any other terms you've agreed to. See the instructions for paragraph 12 of Form 8A.

Standard Clauses

The remainder of the contract contains the standard clauses we discussed in Chapter 1, Section C. The only thing you'll need to fill in here is the name of the state whose law will apply to the contract in the paragraph called "Governing Law."

Signatures

See Chapter 1, Section B, for instructions on signing contracts.

C. Form 8C: Bill of Sale

When real estate is sold, the seller transfers legal ownership or title to the buyer by deed. To formally document the transfer of ownership of goods or equipment, a bill of sale such as Form 8C may be used. See the introduction to this chapter for a discussion of the situations in which it's particularly appropriate to formally document a transfer of ownership through a bill of sale. For a few types of personal property, such as vehicles, boats and planes, which are typically registered with an agency of state government, a bill of sale won't be adequate to transfer legal title. You'll need to use the official transfer of title forms provided by the state agency.

Instructions for Form 8C: Bill of Sale

All the forms in this book are provided as tear-outs in Appendix B and on the accompanying forms CD-ROM. As you read the instructions for Form 8C, you may want to either tear out the form or open the form's file on the CD-ROM so you can follow along. Form 8C is in the file FORM8C.RTF on the CD-ROM. (For more information on using the forms CD-ROM, see Appendix A, "How to Use the CD-ROM.") If you don't use the forms CD-ROM, be sure to photocopy the agreement so you'll have a clean copy to use later.

1. Names

Insert the names of the seller and the buyer. See Chapter 1, Section A, for a discussion of how to identify the parties in legal forms.

2. Transfer of Ownership

Describe the property being sold. You can normally use the same description you've used in paragraph 2 of the sales contract.

3. Condition of Property

Check the first box if the property is new.

Check the second box if the property is used.

4. Warranty of Ownership

Nothing needs to be inserted here. See the sidebar in the instructions for paragraph 11 of Form 8A describing how a buyer can check for any liens on the property being purchased.

Signatures

Only the seller needs to sign. See Chapter 1, Section B, for instructions on signing contracts.

D. Form 8D: Security Agreement

Form 8D can be used to provide the seller with a security—or ownership—interest in property being sold. It would typically be used in conjunction with Form 8B: Sales Contract (Installment Payments) to give the seller the legal right to take back the property if the buyer doesn't make payments when they come due.

See a lawyer before seizing property. Suppose you're the seller and the buyer hasn't kept up payments on the property you've sold. Recovering the property covered by the security agreement can be as simple as walking into the building where the property is located and taking it. But state law may require that you notify the buyer before you take back the property and will probably prohibit you from forcing your way onto the buyer's private business space or house if the buyer tells you to keep out.

In short, if you make a mistake in seizing property, you may have to answer to civil charges of trespass or wrongful entry or criminal charges of breaking and entering or theft—and if someone resists your taking the property, even assault. So before you bravely try to exercise your rights under a security agreement, get advice from an experienced business lawyer. Specifically, ask what kind of notice, if any, you need to give before seizing the property, and whether it's lawful to simply take the property if you can get to it by peaceful means or if you'll need to obtain a court order.

Instructions for Form 8D: Security Agreement

All the forms in this book are provided as tear-outs in Appendix B and on the accompanying forms CD-ROM. As you read the instructions for Form 8D, you may want to either tear out the form or open the form's file on the CD-ROM so you can follow along. Form 8D is in the file FORM8D.RTF on the CD-ROM. (For more information on using the forms CD-ROM, see Appendix A, "How to Use the CD-ROM.") If you don't use the forms CD-ROM, be sure to photocopy the agreement so you'll have a clean copy to use later.

1. Names

Insert the names of the seller and the buyer. See Chapter 1, Section A, for a discussion of how to identify the parties in legal forms.

2. Grant of Security Interest

Describe the property—use the same description you used in the sales contract. Add an attachment if the description is lengthy.

3. Installment Payments

List the amounts of the installment payments and when they're due.

4. Financing Statement

Nothing needs to be inserted here. When a Uniform Commercial Code (UCC) financing statement is completed and filed with the correct county or state office, there's a public record of the seller's lien on the property. If the buyer sells the property to someone else, the original owner still has ownership rights until the balance owed is paid. See the instructions for paragraph 4 of Form 4G for more information on financing statements

Get a UCC financing statement—and file it promptly. Although many states now accept the "national" financing state form, you'll still need to check with your Secretary of State to determine if it's acceptable for filing in your state. Fortunately, most state government agencies are now on the Internet. For links to these state agency websites, go to http://www.piperinfo.com, which contains links to government websites in all 50 states and the District of Columbia. And if you're the seller, it's essential that you file the financing statement with the appropriate governmental office as soon as possible. Otherwise, without your knowing it, someone else may beat you to the punch and file a financing statement signed by the same buyer and covering the same property. If that happens, the first filer will have first dibs on the secured property—probably leaving nothing for you to seize if the buyer fails to pay you.

5. Use and Care of the Secured Property

This paragraph spells out the buyer's duty to safeguard the property so that the seller has something of value to take back if the buyer defaults.

Insert the location where the buyer will keep the secured property.

6. Default of Buyer

Nothing needs to be inserted here. This paragraph says the buyer is in default if he or she doesn't make required payments or doesn't promptly correct any violations of the requirements listed in the preceding paragraph.

7. Rights of Seller

Insert the name of your state.

8. Notice to Buyer

Insert the address where the seller can send notice to the buyer.

In most states, the Uniform Commercial Code requires the seller to notify the buyer in writing before the secured property is sold or otherwise disposed of. This gives the buyer the chance to get back the secured property by paying off the debt in full before the property is turned over to someone else.

Standard Clauses

The remainder of the agreement contains the standard clauses we discussed in Chapter 1, Section C.

The only thing you'll need to fill in here is the name of the state whose law will apply to the contract in the paragraph called "Governing Law."

Signatures

Both parties must sign. See Chapter 1, Section B, for instructions on signing contracts.

E. Form 8E: Contract for Manufacture of Goods

Sometimes, the goods the buyer wants to purchase don't exist yet or, if they do exist, must be modified or "customized" to meet the buyer's specifications. Use Form 8E: Contract for Manufacture of Goods, when a seller agrees to make or customize goods for a buyer.

Instructions for Form 8E: Contract for Manufacture of Goods

All the forms in this book are provided as tear-outs in Appendix B and on the accompanying forms CD-ROM. As you read the instructions for Form 8E, you may want to either tear out the form or open the form's file on the CD-ROM so you can follow along. Form 8E is in the file FORM8E.RTF on the CD-ROM. (For more information on using the forms CD-ROM, see Appendix A, "How to Use the CD-ROM.") If you don't use the forms CD-ROM, be sure to photocopy the agreement so you'll have a clean copy to use later.

1. Names

Insert the names of the seller and the buyer. See Chapter 1, Section A, for a discussion of how to identify the parties in legal forms.

2. Property Description

Check the boxes that indicate whether the property will be manufactured or merely customized.

Then describe the property.

SAMPLES:

- Four modular computer workstations as shown on the attached plans and specifications.
- A portable exhibit unit for use at trade shows based on Model 600 shown in Seller's current catalog, but modified according to Attachment 1.
- Five hundred computer circuit boards, built in accordance with the attached specifications.
- One thousand red and blue baseball hats (catalog #27) printed with Buyer's name and logo on the front as shown in the drawing set out in Attachment 1.

Take the time to make specifications as precise as possible. To avoid disputes over exactly what is being ordered, describe the goods carefully. One of the best ways to do this is to include a contract attachment with detailed plans, drawings, parts lists or whatever else it takes to define exactly what the contract covers.

3. Purchase Price

Insert the purchase price.

4. Down Payment

If the buyer will make a down payment, check the first box and insert the amount. Otherwise, check the second box.

5. Time of Payment

Check the first box if the purchase price (less any down payment) is due upon delivery.

Check the second box if the purchase price will be due at a time other than that of delivery, and describe when it is due.

Check the third box if payment will be due in installments; then prepare an attachment containing the payment schedule. See Chapter 1, Section E, on adding attachments.

6. Method of Payment

See the instructions for paragraph 8 of Form 8A.

7. Delivery

Fill in the date of delivery. Then check where the manufactured or customized items will be delivered.

8. Disclaimer of Warranties

See the instructions for paragraph 4 of Form 8A.

9. Bill of Sale

Nothing needs to be inserted here. A bill of sale allows the buyer to easily prove—if challenged in a lawsuit, for example—that legal ownership of the property has been transferred. To accomplish this, use Form 8C: Bill of Sale.

10. Security Interest

See the instructions for paragraph 11 of Form 8B.

11. Other Terms and Conditions

Fill in any other terms you've agreed to.

SAMPLE:

Seller will be responsible for transporting the workstations to Buyer's place of business and installing them there.

Standard Clauses

The remainder of the contract contains the standard clauses we discussed in Chapter 1, Section C. The only thing you'll need to fill in here is the name of the state whose law will apply to the contract in the paragraph called "Governing Law."

Signatures

Both parties need to sign. See Chapter 1, Section B, for instructions on signing contracts.

Attachments

Be sure to add any attachments that are needed (for example, see instructions for paragraphs 2 and 5, above).

See Chapter 1, Section E, on adding attachments. Form 7F: Attachment to Real Estate Purchase Contract, can also be modified for these purposes.

F. Form 8F: Equipment Rental Contract

This contract can be used if you rent, rather than sell, equipment to customers.

Instructions for Form 8F: Equipment Rental Contract

All the forms in this book are provided as tear-outs in Appendix B and on the accompanying forms CD-ROM. As you read the instructions for Form 8F, you may want to either tear out the form or open the form's file on the CD-ROM so you can follow along. Form 8F is in the file FORM8F.RTF on the CD-ROM. (For more information on using the forms CD-ROM, see Appendix A, "How to Use the CD-ROM.") If you don't use the forms CD-ROM, be sure to photocopy the agreement so you'll have a clean copy to use later.

1. Names

Insert the names of the owner (you) and the renter. (See Chapter 1, Section A, on identifying the parties to a contract.)

2. Equipment Being Rented

Describe the equipment being rented, being as specific as necessary.

> **SAMPLES:**
> - The following two portable space heaters:
>   SunRay Model R—Serial No. 1234
>   SunRay Model R—Serial No. 1235
> - One 16-foot heavy-duty Reliance Electric extension cord.

3. Duration of Rental Period

Insert the times and dates the rental period will begin and end.

> **SAMPLE:**
> The rental will begin at 5:00 p.m. on December 1, 2000, and will end at 5:00 p.m. on January 31, 2001.

4. Rental Amount

Specify the rental rate. Then check the period covered by the rate—daily, weekly or monthly.

5. Payment

Indicate the amount the renter agrees to pay up front for the stated rental period.

If the owner requires a security deposit, check this box and enter the amount of the deposit. (CD-ROM users can just delete the optional language if they don't wish to include it.) The owner may want the deposit to cover at least the full value of the equipment.

Benefit from the experience of others. If equipment rental is a major part of your business, contact an industry trade association for workable ideas on how to minimize your losses stemming from lost or damaged items. Also, focus on how to cope with the predictable problem that some property will be returned late. Many rental businesses, for example, require a cash deposit to cover rental and security deposit charges or have the customer put this amount on a credit card. If a renter uses a credit card, when he or she returns the equipment in good condition and pays or charges the rent amount owed, the rental shop rips up the unused charge slip containing the deposit amount. Generally, the security deposit should be large enough to cover the full value of the rented items as specified in paragraph 8.

6. Delivery

Specify the delivery date—probably the date the rental begins. Then check the box that indicates where delivery will be made.

7. Late Return

Fill in a daily amount for the renter to pay if the returned equipment comes back late. To encourage timely return of rented items, the owner should consider charging a higher rent for the property after the agreed rental period ends.

8. Damage or Loss

Describe any defects in the equipment.

> **SAMPLES:**
> - There is a dent on the top of the air conditioning unit.
> - The power washer is missing a side panel.
> - The quarter-inch drill bit is missing from the drill bit collection.

Then fill in the total current value of the rented property. This figure will help establish what's owed if the property is lost or damaged. To minimize the possibility of future court hassles, don't overstate how much the property is worth. A used lawn mower, for example, will obviously have a value that's lower than a brand-new one.

9. Use of Equipment

This clause is optional. If you rent equipment that could be dangerous if used improperly, such as jet-skis or lawnmowers, you may want to consider including this clause to protect your business from liability if someone is injured (through no fault of yours) while using your equipment. However, while including this clause certainly can't hurt you, many judges don't like clauses that attempt to disclaim liability, and it might not be enforceable in all courts. So, even if you decide to include this clause, you should always take reasonable safety precautions. This includes properly maintaining the equipment to ensure it's in safe condition and providing renters with instructions and warnings regarding equipment use. And for further protection, be sure to maintain adequate liability insurance.

 Obtaining the right insurance is essential if you want to protect your business. If you want to know more about buying insurance for your small business, Chapter 12 of the *Legal Guide for Starting & Running a Small Business*, by Fred S. Steingold (Nolo), contains invaluable information about researching, buying and negotiating a business insurance policy.

Standard Clauses

The remainder of the contract contains the standard clauses we discussed in Chapter 1, Section C. The only thing you'll need to fill in here is the name of the state whose law will apply to the contract in the paragraph called "Governing Law."

Signatures

See Chapter 1, Section B, for instructions on signing contracts.

G. Form 8G: Storage Contract

Use Form 8G: Storage Contract when a business will take temporary possession of and store goods or equipment owned by an individual or another business. This contract isn't designed for use when a customer is renting a storage locker or closed storage area to which only the customer has access. In that situation, the storage company will almost surely have a predrafted contract all customers must sign.

Bailing Out of Archaic Language

You may come across a storage contract that uses the archaic legal terms bailment, bailor or bailee. This jargon reflects the fact that historically and technically, storage contracts are part of something called bailment law.

A bailment was created whenever one person turned over tangible personal property (goods and equipment) to another person for safekeeping. The person who turned over the property was called a bailor; the person who received the property was called a bailee. Over the centuries, judges have created a web of rules covering the bailment relationship—including fine distinctions between whether the bailee is just doing the bailor a favor by accepting the goods (a gratuitous bailment) or is getting paid (a bailment for hire).

Today there's no legal reason to use these old-fashioned terms, which have been dropped from the law in many states. A storage contract written in plain English which spells out the responsibilities of each person is perfectly legal. If there's a dispute that winds up in court, the judge will be guided by your contract language—not by the centuries-old rules concerning bailment.

Instructions for Form 8G: Storage Contract

All the forms in this book are provided as tear-outs in Appendix B and on the accompanying forms CD-ROM. As you read the instructions for Form 8G, you may want to either tear out the form or open the form's file on the CD-ROM so you can follow along. Form 8G is in the file FORM8G.RTF on the CD-ROM. (For more information on using the forms CD-ROM, see Appendix A, "How to Use the CD-ROM.") If you don't use the forms CD-ROM, be sure to photocopy the agreement so you'll have a clean copy to use later.

1. Names
Insert the names of the customer who owns the property being stored and the storer—the person or business that will hold on to the property.

2. Property Being Stored
Describe what's being stored.

> **SAMPLES:**
> - Three Andover halogen desk lamps and a Dell computer system, serial #1234, in good condition.
> - One four-foot by six-foot teak office desk (Scandi brand) with a large scratch across the writing surface.

3. Storage Period
Identify the storage period beginning and ending dates.

4. Storage Fees
Specify the amount the customer is paying for storage.

5. Additional Fees
Insert the charge that will be due if the customer leaves the property in storage after the storage period ends and check whether it will be weekly or monthly.

6. Refunds
Nothing needs to be inserted here. But note that the customer won't be entitled to a refund for removing the property early.

7. End of Storage
Insert the number of days notice the customer must receive before the storer ends the storage contract.

If the storer ends the storage contract and sells the stored property, he or she must do so in a commercially reasonable manner. What's reasonable for different types of property may vary (you would probably sell a horse differently than a tractor, for example), but generally the storer should advertise the property for sale in an appropriate place or sell it at public auction.

8. Storage Location
Fill in the location where the property will be stored.

9. Value of Property
Because it's possible that the stored property will get lost or damaged as a result of the storer's actions or negligence, it's wise for the customer and storer to agree in advance on its replacement value. This clause gives you the option of not doing so, however, by leaving the box unchecked. (CD-ROM users who don't want to include this option should delete it and renumber the paragraphs that follow.)

A storer should take precautions. If you're a storer and accept used goods or equipment for storage, you'll want to insert a dollar amount for replacement should the goods be damaged or destroyed that reflects the age and actual condition of the items being stored. You wouldn't want to pay for new goods if the item lost was several years old. Also, if storing goods is a routine part of your business, check with an insurance broker or agent to see what coverage is available to pay for damage and losses.

A customer should maintain insurance. If you're a customer leaving goods or equipment with a storage company, you can be reasonably confident that the company carries insurance on stored items. But if storage is just a sideline for the storer and especially if you're leaving extremely valuable items for storage, you'll want to make sure you have insurance of your own to cover damage or loss by fire, flood, theft and other causes that are normally beyond the control of the storer.

10. Condition of Property

List any defects in the property.

11. Reasonable Care

Nothing needs to be inserted here. In general, a storer is legally obligated to use reasonable care in looking after stored property. This wording reflects that general principle of law. As noted above, the customer is responsible for loss or damage to the stored property caused by events beyond the storer's control—so the customer should maintain adequate insurance coverage.

12. Other Terms and Conditions

Fill in any other terms.

> **SAMPLE:**
> Storer will keep the property in a cool and dry place at all times.

Standard Clauses

The remainder of the contract contains the standard clauses we discussed in Chapter 1, Section C. The only thing you'll need to fill in here is the name of the state whose law will apply to the contract in the paragraph called "Governing Law."

Signatures

See Chapter 1, Section B, for instructions on signing contracts.

H. Form 8H: Consignment Contract

In a consignment agreement, the owner of goods (in legal jargon, the consignor) puts the goods in the hands of a consignee (another person or business—usually a retailer) who then attempts to sell them. If the goods are sold, the consignee receives a fee, which is usually a percentage of the purchase price, with the rest of the money being sent to its

owner—the consignor. A sculptor (the consignor), for example, might place his or her work for sale at an art gallery (as consignee) with the understanding that if the artwork sells, the gallery keeps 50% of the sale price. Or a homeowner as consignor might leave old furniture with a resale shop as consignee, which would keep one-third of the proceeds if the item sells. Typically, the consignor or owner of the goods remains the owner until the consignee sells the goods.

Use Form 8H: Consignment Contract if you're leaving or accepting goods on consignment.

Instructions for Form 8H: Consignment Contract

All the forms in this book are provided as tear-outs in Appendix B and on the accompanying forms CD-ROM. As you read the instructions for Form 8H, you may want to either tear out the form or open the form's file on the CD-ROM so you can follow along. Form 8H is in the file FORM8H.RTF on the CD-ROM. (For more information on using the forms CD-ROM, see Appendix A, "How to Use the CD-ROM.") If you don't use the forms CD-ROM, be sure to photocopy the agreement so you'll have a clean copy to use later.

1. Names

Insert the names of the owner of the goods and the consignee (the business that will market the goods to the public).

2. Property Consigned

Check the appropriate box to indicate whether the goods have been delivered or will be delivered to the consignee. Then list the goods and the prices at which they'll be offered for sale.

3. Efforts to Sell

Nothing needs to be inserted here. The consignee can attempt to sell the goods for more than the listed price (in which case the commission would be higher since it's based on the sale price). The consignee cannot sell the goods for less than the listed price unless the owner consents.

4. Proceeds of Sale

Insert the percentage of the sale price that the consignee will receive if the goods are sold.

5. Ownership Before Sale

Nothing needs to be inserted here. This sentence recognizes that the owner isn't giving up ownership of the goods.

6. Risk of Loss

Nothing needs to be inserted here. The owner wants to be protected if the goods are lost or stolen while in the consignee's possession. If you're leaving goods on consignment and are concerned about the consignee's ability to pay you if the goods are lost or stolen, ask to see a copy of the consignee's insurance policy. When very valuable items are being consigned, it's often appropriate to ask to be named as a co-insured so that you can receive a share of the insurance proceeds if a loss occurs.

If you're a consignee, check your insurance coverage. Before you accept the risk of loss or theft, make sure your business insurance policy covers you for loss of "personal property of others" left in your possession—and that the amount of coverage is adequate. Getting full reimbursement for the selling price of consigned goods may require an added endorsement (supplement) to your insurance policy. Check with your insurance agent or broker.

7. Termination of Consignment

Check the box indicating where the goods will be returned to the owner if either party ends the consignment agreement.

8. Other Terms and Conditions

Insert any other agreed-upon terms.

> **SAMPLE:**
> Consignee in its discretion may reduce the sale price of an item by 10% to facilitate a sale. Consignee's commission will be computed based on the actual sale price.

Standard Clauses

The remainder of the contract contains the standard clauses we discussed in Chapter 1, Section C. The only thing you'll need to fill in here is the name of the state whose law will apply to the contract in the paragraph called "Governing Law."

Signatures

See Chapter 1, Section B, for instructions on signing contracts. ■

9

Hiring Employees and Independent Contractors

Hiring, managing and firing employees can expose you to a number of legal pitfalls. If something goes amiss, you may become involved in nasty lawsuits by rejected job applicants or fired employees—and even enforcement actions by federal and state agencies. Unfortunately, hiring independent contractors rather than employees doesn't necessarily improve things, since here too, if you manage carelessly, you can face a plethora of worker-related legal problems. The IRS, for example, may severely penalize you if you improperly classify an employee as an independent contractor.

To fully understand how best to use the forms in this chapter and to reduce the likelihood of costly legal entanglements, become familiar with the basic legal principles involved in hiring both employees and independent contractors. The books recommended below offer the guidance you need.

Chapter 15 of the *Legal Guide for Starting & Running a Small Business*, by Fred S. Steingold (Nolo), contains a thorough survey of the legal principles that govern the hiring of workers and considerable useful advice on how to stay out of hot water.

For even greater depth on the legal side of hiring, managing and firing workers, see *The Employer's Legal Handbook*, by Fred S. Steingold (Nolo).

Hiring Independent Contractors: The Employer's Legal Guide, by Stephen Fishman (Nolo), will help you decide if you can hire a worker as an independent contractor without violating IRS regulations. Then, if you decide it's legally safe to proceed, you can use the forms CD-ROM that comes with the book to document the terms of the independent contractor relationship.

Working for Yourself: Law & Taxes for Independent Contractors, Freelancers and Consultants, by Stephen Fishman (Nolo), contains a wealth of information and forms for independent contractors who run their own business.

One peril you face in the hiring process is that your job application form may violate laws that protect applicants from discrimination—for example,

because of age, gender, race, ethnicity or disability. Another legal pitfall is that you might invade the applicant's privacy by seeking information about personal matters unrelated to the applicant's job qualifications—for example, inquiring about the applicant's marital history or political beliefs. Form 9A: Employment Application, helps you focus on legitimate information you are legally entitled to solicit from the applicant while helping you avoid getting into the many sensitive areas that can land you in legal hot water.

Of course, it pays to follow up on information the applicant gives you to be sure it's accurate and hasn't been shaded to paint an overly favorable picture. Specifically, you'll probably want to check with the applicant's prior employers and, if academic credentials are important to you, with the schools the applicant lists. If the job would give the employee access to cash or your business bank accounts, you'll surely want to get a credit report to make sure the applicant isn't in an overstretched financial situation. To avoid claims that you've invaded the applicant's privacy by seeking information without express permission, have him or her sign Form 9B: Authorization to Release Information. When you present this to prior employers, schools or credit reporting agencies, chances of gaining their cooperation will go way up.

An employer and an employee can differ in recalling the terms of employment that were offered at the beginning of the employment relationship. Putting the terms in writing by using Form 9C: Offer of Employment, can head off potential misunderstandings about the scope and length of employment, especially as to whether a job was guaranteed for any time period.

In some types of work, there's the possibility that a employee can harm your business in at least two important ways: The employee may misuse confidential information while working for you or may later begin a business that competes with yours using information gained while working for you. Whether worrying about this is reasonable will depend on a number of factors, including the type of business you're in and the level of skill and trust the employee's work will entail. If you're concerned about a key employee being able to harm your business in the future, you can get a measure of legal protection by having the employee sign Form 9D: Confidentiality Agreement, and Form 9E: Covenant Not to Compete.

The vast majority of employees don't have written contracts. They simply work at will, meaning you can fire them at any time for any reason or no reason at all as long as you don't violate antidiscrimination or other employee protection laws. Of course, an at-will employee is also free to quit at any time. But a key employee, especially a senior manager, may request the security of a written contract or you may want to obtain a long-term commitment from a highly valued employee. In such cases, you can use Form 9F: Contract With Employee.

It's more typical to have a written contract when a worker is an independent contractor—especially if, as is common, you're concerned that the IRS may attempt to reclassify the worker as an employee. Form 9G: Contract With Independent Contractor can be used for this purpose.

Additional Paperwork Requirements

In addition to the forms in this chapter, you may need to—or want to—prepare or obtain other documents when you hire an employee.

INS Form I-9. This form, required by the U.S. Immigration and Naturalization Service, is intended to help exclude undocumented workers from the workforce. The employee completes Section 1 of the form; you complete Section 2. For full details, see the free publication, Handbook for Employers: Instructions for Completing Form I-9, available from the INS. To obtain a copy, call the nearest regional office of the INS, which you'll find listed under the United States Government heading in any metropolitan phone book or go the http://www.ins.usdoj.gov.

IRS Form W-4. Each employee must complete this form so you can determine the level of tax to withhold from every paycheck. A form W-4 is included on the forms CD-ROM in the file FW4.PDF.

Employee Benefit Sign-up. If your business has established employee benefit programs such as health insurance or a 401(k) plan, you'll need a sign-up procedure so employees can name their dependents and select options.

IRS Form SS-4—New Employers Only. The IRS requires an Employer Identification Number for all employers except sole proprietorships (single-owner, unincorporated businesses), which have the option of using the owner's Social Security number. To apply for a number, use IRS Form SS-4. A Form SS-4 is included on the forms CD-ROM in the file FSS4.PDF.

Employee Handbook. Although not required, it can be an excellent idea to have a handbook describing your business's employee policies and making it clear that employment is at will unless an employee has signed a written employment contract. Make sure every potential employee is given a summary of your policies at the interview stage and a complete copy as part of your job offer.

For more information on these additional forms, see *The Employer's Legal Handbook*, by Fred S. Steingold (Nolo).

A. Form 9A: Employment Application

You can reduce the legal risks of hiring employees well before you ask an applicant to fill out an employment application. Start by writing a job description for each position. In listing job duties, stick to absolute essentials. That way, chances will go way down that you'll violate antidiscrimination laws or the Americans with Disabilities Act (ADA), which prohibits you from excluding an applicant who's able to perform the core of the job but whose disability might make it impossible to perform a marginal duty.

> **EXAMPLE:** Moonbeam Manufacturing Company needs a file clerk to file and retrieve various sales documents. Other employees usually answer the phone. Since answering the phone isn't an essential file clerk job duty, Moonbeam should not list it as a requirement in the job description. If Moonbeam did list it, it could needlessly discourage an applicant whose hearing is impaired and has trouble with phone calls.

Also, in writing a job description, be realistic in listing the education and experience requirements. If, for example, you require a college degree for a job that can easily be done by someone with a high school education, you may exclude a disproportionate number of applicants in your area who are members of minority groups protected by antidiscrimination laws.

When you begin advertising for applicants, avoid any nuances that can be interpreted as evidence that you discriminate on the basis of sex, age, marital status or any other illegal category. For example, use "salesperson" instead of "salesman," "energetic" instead of "young" and "two-person job" instead of "married couple."

In the job application and during interviews, tightly focus on the applicant's skills and experience. Don't ask questions such as what year a potential employee graduated from high school or college;

that may be used as evidence of discrimination based on the applicant's age. Similarly, it's a mistake to ask if a person is married (possible evidence of marital status discrimination) or what language is spoken in the home (possible evidence of national origin discrimination) or whether the person has a health problem (possible evidence of health status discrimination).

 For thorough information on the legal limitations on what you can inquire into and how to ask questions that will provide the information you need without landing you in legal trouble, see Chapter 1 of *The Employer's Legal Handbook*, by Fred S. Steingold (Nolo).

Form 9A: Employment Application, is designed to avoid questions that may be viewed as discriminatory or that may unnecessarily invade the applicant's privacy. It focuses on the applicant's education and job experiences, but also gives the applicant a chance to state any other training, skills or achievements that may be important.

It may be appropriate to ask an applicant about prior felony convictions. If the job you're offering requires handling cash, entering people's homes or working with children, minors or vulnerable adults, you may want to add a question or two to your application form inquiring about felony convictions. But proceed cautiously, even if the job meets these criteria. In some states, you can't reject an applicant who's been convicted unless the conviction is substantially related to a particular job or disqualifies the applicant from getting a required bond.

Instructions to Form 9A: Employment Application

All the forms in this book are provided as tear-outs in Appendix B and on the accompanying forms CD-ROM. As you read the instructions for Form 9A, you may want to either tear out the form or open the form's file on the CD-ROM so you can follow along. Form 9A is in the file FORM9A.RTF on the CD-ROM. (For more information on using the forms CD-ROM, see Appendix A, "How to Use the CD-ROM.") If you don't use the forms CD-ROM, be sure to photocopy the agreement so you'll have a clean copy to use later.

At the beginning of the last paragraph of the form, following the word "To," insert the name of your business. Otherwise, the form is self-explanatory.

B. Form 9B: Authorization to Release Information

After taking an employment application from a potential employee and interviewing him or her, you'll almost surely want to dig a bit deeper into the person's background by contacting former places of employment and verifying academic credentials. Occasionally, researching an applicant's credit history may also be useful.

Legally, much of this information is confidential; it can't be released to you without the applicant's consent. You can smooth out the process by asking the applicant to sign Form 9B: Authorization to Release Information. This will let the former employer and school recordkeeper know that they're on safe legal ground because the applicant has authorized them to release the information to you. Also, it will eliminate any invasion of privacy claim the applicant might otherwise try to assert against you for obtaining confidential information without permission.

 Be prepared for special forms that schools and colleges may prefer. Schools and colleges, fearful of legal problems, may insist on the use of their release forms and may not accept a form such as the one included here. You can speed up the process by calling to see if they require you to use their own release and, if so, asking that one be faxed or mailed to you.

 Chapter 15 of the *Legal Guide for Starting & Running a Small Business*, by Fred S. Steingold (Nolo), covers the legal basics of how to investigate job applicants before hiring them. For more information—including legal guidelines for pre-employment testing and criminal checks—see *The Employer's Legal Handbook*, by Fred S. Steingold (Nolo).

Instructions to Form 9B: Authorization to Release Information

All the forms in this book are provided as tear-outs in Appendix B and on the accompanying forms CD-ROM. As you read the instructions for Form 9B, you may want to either tear out the form or open the form's file on the CD-ROM so you can follow along. Form 9B is in the file FORM9B.RTF on the CD-ROM. (For more information on using the forms CD-ROM, see Appendix A, "How to Use the CD-ROM.") If you don't use the forms CD-ROM, be sure to photocopy the agreement so you'll have a clean copy to use later.

Insert the name of your business in each of the first three blank lines. The applicant will fill in the rest.

C. Form 9C: Offer of Employment

By using Form 9C: Offer of Employment to put a job offer in writing—and having the new employee sign it—you decrease the possibility of disputes over exactly what you promised the employee and what the employee agreed to do in return. You can use this form, with appropriate modifications, whenever you hire employees to whom you will not offer a written contract granting job security. Since very few if any employees will qualify to have written contracts, this means Form 9C should be used in most situations.

Instructions to Form 9C: Offer of Employment

All the forms in this book are provided as tear-outs in Appendix B and on the accompanying forms CD-ROM. As you read the instructions for Form 9C, you may want to either tear out the form or open the form's file on the CD-ROM so you can follow along. Form 9C is in the file FORM9C. RFT on the CD-ROM. (For more information on using the forms CD-ROM, see Appendix A, "How to Use the CD-ROM.") If you don't use the forms CD-ROM, be sure to photocopy the agreement so you'll have a clean copy to use later.

Letterhead

It's usually both customary and a good idea to put the offer on your business letterhead.

First Paragraph

Fill in the title of the position, the starting date, the starting compensation and how frequently it will be paid—for example, weekly, every two weeks, twice a month or monthly.

Second Paragraph

Nothing needs to be inserted here. This paragraph assumes that your business has an employee handbook that describes your employment policies and the benefits you offer.

See Chapter 2 of *The Employer's Legal Handbook*, by Fred S. Steingold (Nolo), for more information on employee handbooks.

If you don't have an employee handbook, you'll have to omit or modify this paragraph. But a word to the wise. At the very least, you should put together an informational sheet or a small brochure describing your normal work schedule, days your business is closed and any benefits you offer to employees including such things as paid vacation and sick days, health insurance and so on. This is also a good place to include your basic policies in areas such as nondiscrimination, smoking and so on.

Third Paragraph

This paragraph clearly states that you're making no commitments to the employee beyond those stated in the employee handbook, now or in the future, unless they're in writing and signed by both of you. Nothing needs to be inserted here.

Fourth Paragraph

Nothing needs to be inserted here. This paragraph says you're establishing an at-will relationship with the employee. You reserve the right to fire the employee for any reason or no reason at all and the employee is always free to quit.

Treat Employees Fairly

Even though you and the employee have agreed to an at-will relationship—meaning that you can fire the employee at any time—it makes excellent practical and legal sense to be scrupulously fair in dealing with the employee. Arbitrary actions—no matter what's stated in the offer of employment—can and do result in lawsuits.

Before firing a worker, be sure you have a valid, documented reason—for example, you're reducing the size of the workforce or the employee isn't getting the job done or is chronically late to work. The simple truth is this: if a fired employee you obviously treated badly sues you claiming an unfair discharge, jurors hearing your case may not be impressed with your argument that you had the legal right to fire the person without a good reason. Or put another way, if you come off as being arrogant and unfair—which is likely if you can't document a good reason to fire the person—a jury may find a way to make you pay through the nose.

For tips and information on firing employees fairly, see *Firing Without Fear*, by Barbara Kate Repa (Nolo).

Fifth Paragraph

Nothing needs to be inserted here. To allow you to easily establish that the employee agreed to its terms, ask him or her to sign a copy of the letter.

Signature

Presumably, the letter will be on your business letterhead. You sign, giving your title, for example:

Type of Business	Title
Sole Proprietorship	Owner
Partnership	Partner
Corporation	President or Chief Executive Officer
Limited Liability Company	Member/Manager

See also Chapter 1, Section B, on signing the forms in this book. The new employee should receive an original and copy of the offer of employment—both signed by you. He or she should sign either the original or the copy and return it to you so you can place it in that person's employment file.

D. Form 9D: Confidentiality Agreement

While fortunately it's not a widespread practice, employees sometimes use confidential business information for their personal advantage and may even disclose it to competitors. To capture in writing the employee's commitment not to benefit personally from confidential information or improperly disclose it to others, use Form 9D: Confidentiality Agreement. If, despite signing the form, the employee misuses your sensitive information, you'll have a strong legal leg up if you file a lawsuit in an effort to stop or enjoin further improper conduct.

You don't need to use this form with every new employee since workers in most jobs aren't exposed to much truly confidential information. But where you do perceive a possible threat, make sure you get the person's signature on this form at the time of employment; later on, the employee may not have much incentive to sign.

Instructions to Form 9D: Confidentiality Agreement

All the forms in this book are provided as tear-outs in Appendix B and on the accompanying forms CD-ROM. As you read the instructions for Form 9D, you may want to either tear out the form or open the form's file on the CD-ROM so you can follow along. Form 9D is in the file FORM9D.RTF on the CD-ROM. (For more information on using the forms CD-ROM, see Appendix A, "How to Use the CD-ROM.") If you don't use the forms CD-ROM, be sure to photocopy the agreement so you'll have a clean copy to use later.

1. Agreement Not to Disclose Confidential Information

Fill in the name of your employee. This paragraph prevents your employee from disclosing your confidential information to third parties except when the employee is required to do so as part of their employment or when required to do so by law.

2. Return of Confidential Information

You definitely don't want a former employee to keep any documents, computer disks or other materials containing your confidential information. Here, the employee must return any copies of your confidential information or materials which may contain confidential information when he or she leaves your company.

3. Right to an Injunction

If you need to go to court for any reason to enforce this agreement, this paragraph will help you show a judge that you are entitled to an injunction (a court order stopping the employee from violating the agreement), instead of simply receiving money damages.

4. Reasonableness

Here, your employee is acknowledging that the restrictions you've placed on the employee's ability to disclose your confidential information are reasonable. This helps prevent the employee from later claiming that the restrictions aren't really necessary to protect your business.

5. Survivability

This paragraph means that the employee has to keep your confidential information a secret even after he or she is no longer employed by your company.

Standard Clauses

The remainder of the agreement contains the standard clauses we discussed in Chapter 1, Section C. The only thing you'll need to fill in here is the name of the state whose law will apply to the contract in the paragraph called "Governing Law."

⚠ Take additional steps to maintain secrecy. Merely listing a type of information in a confidentiality agreement is usually insufficient to give it confidential status in the eyes of the law. A court probably won't conclude that information is really confidential unless you actually limit access to it. In short, if you start handing out a secret recipe to favored customers or make no effort to restrict access to your customer list, this sort of agreement is unlikely to be enforced if the employee later begins to make use of the information.

E. Form 9E: Covenant Not to Compete

Occasionally, employees quit and go into business in competition with a former employer or take a job with a competitor. To capture in writing the employee's commitment not to unfairly learn from you and then become a rival in the marketplace, use Form 9E: Covenant Not to Compete. Then, if the employee violates the covenant, you'll have a decent shot at getting a court to enjoin, or stop, further improper conduct.

Use this form selectively. Few employees have the practical ability to set up a competing shop or

work for a competitor and lure away a significant number of your customers. You should know that courts are not fond of employee noncompete agreements because they prevent people from earning a living. If a court thinks a noncompete agreement is unfair to a former employee, it probably won't enforce it. But where you sincerely believe the employee may pose a potential threat, make sure you get the person's signature on this form at the time of employment when there's an incentive to sign.

⚠ California won't enforce employee noncompete covenants. California Bus. & Prof. Code §§16600-16602 invalidates any contract that restrains anyone from engaging in a lawful profession, trade or business. This means that a typical noncompete covenant signed by an employee can't be enforced in California. About the most a California court will enforce is an agreement such as Form 9D: Confidentiality Agreement, with perhaps the additional promise that the employee won't solicit the employer's customers.

Elsewhere, although a California-type statute may not be in effect, many courts are reluctant to enforce covenants not to compete—particularly those that not only prohibit an employee from starting a competing business, but also bar the employee from working for a competitor. And even where courts are more willing to enforce these covenants, the judges need to be convinced that the limitations are basically fair. If a former employee someday challenges the validity of the noncompete covenant, one of the main legal theories advanced is sure to be that it's unreasonably restrictive as to duration, geographical scope or subject matter. Especially with a lower-echelon employee, a court may modify or even invalidate the noncompete agreement if it's perceived as unfairly limiting the employee's right to earn a living. To help ensure this doesn't happen, be conservative in restricting an employee from operating a competing business. In short, only ask an employee for a noncompetition covenant that's absolutely necessary to protect your business interests in the immediate future.

> **EXAMPLE 1:** The Tax Shop, a storefront business specializing in preparing tax returns, has its key employees agree in writing that for 18 months after leaving their jobs, they won't open a competing tax preparation business within three miles of The Tax Shop's office. The restriction appears reasonable and will likely withstand a legal challenge by an employee.

> **EXAMPLE 2:** Solution 1040, another tax preparation service, requires its employees to agree that for five years after leaving their jobs, they won't work anywhere in the state at a job that involves doing tax returns. The restriction appears to be overly broad and almost surely wouldn't be enforced by a court.

Instructions for Form 9E: Covenant Not to Compete

All the forms in this book are provided as tear-outs in Appendix B and on the accompanying forms CD-ROM. As you read the instructions for Form 9E, you may want to either tear out the form or open the form's file on the CD-ROM so you can follow along. Form 9E is in the file FORM9E.RTF on the CD-ROM. (For more information on using the forms CD-ROM, see Appendix A, "How to Use the CD-ROM.") If you don't use the forms CD-ROM, be sure to photocopy the agreement so you'll have a clean copy to use later.

1. Agreement Not to Compete

Fill in your employee's name. Next, insert the number of months or years after leaving your employment that the employee is not permitted to compete with your business. Here, the key is to be realistic—don't insert an unreasonable amount of time simply to punish your employee for leaving. Instead, think about how much time you'll really

need, such as the time it will take you to train a new employee, or how long the employee's skills and knowledge could potentially harm your business. Since many courts don't like employee noncompete covenants, keep the duration as short as you can—six months to a year should be plenty of time. If you ask for anything longer than this, you're not going to get a lot of sympathy from a judge if you take your agreement to court, and you risk a judge refusing to enforce your agreement at all.

2. Right to an Injunction

See the instructions for paragraph 3 of Form 9D.

3. Reasonable Restrictions

See the instructions for paragraph 4 of Form 9D.

4. Survivability

See the instructions for paragraph 5 of Form 9D.

Standard Clauses

The remainder of the agreement contains the standard clauses we discussed in Chapter 1, Section C. The only thing you'll need to fill in here is the name of the state whose law will apply to the contract in the paragraph called "Governing Law."

After the employee signs, put the form in the employee's file.

Cyberbusiness May Make Geographical Limits Ineffective

The idea for noncompete covenants developed in an era when a business was at a fixed location and customers came there because the location was convenient. If you owned a wine shop and developed a loyal clientele, you might feel relatively secure if a former employee couldn't set up a competing shop within three miles of your place.

Obviously, a lot of businesses don't fit that model today—especially the increasing number of businesses that handle transactions over the Internet or by email, fax or phone. Geography doesn't mean a thing. If your business does taxes online, for example, a former employee can cut into your income by operating a similar online service a thousand miles away. Probably the best you can do is have the employee agree not to engage in an online tax service for six months after leaving employment at your place. How courts will deal with restrictions on cyber competition is still an open question.

F. Form 9F: Contract With Employee

Written contracts of employment that guarantee employment for a set period are rare. As mentioned in the discussion of the offer of employment (Form 9C), most employees work at will—meaning they have no contract and their job can be ended at any time for any reason or no reason at all. Of course, an employer who fires people must not violate anti-discrimination laws (for example, get rid of employees over age 50 to make room for younger workers) or run afoul of public policy (for example, fire employees because they file legitimate workers' compensation claims).

Although a written contract limits an employer's flexibility, there are exceptional situations where one is either desirable or a virtual necessity. For example, suppose you've been trying to hire a highly experienced person to be the general manager of your business and the person you've set your sights on already has a good job in another city. The employee you wish to hire may understandably be reluctant to leave his or her job and move unless you can offer a measure of job security. In this situation, a written employment contract for two, three or even five years may be in order.

If you do decide to sign a written contract with an employee, consider using Form 9F. If you use this form or any other employment contract, do not use either Form 9C, Form 9D or Form 9E—all three of which are designed for noncontractual employees.

⚠ **Courts sometimes find and enforce unwritten employment contracts.** While most employees without written contracts truly do work at will (that is, can be fired for any reason that's not illegal—or for no reason at all), courts have sometimes found and enforced an implied employment contract based on oral statements an employer made in a pre-employment interview or in the language of a letter or employee handbook. For example, an employer, enthusiastic about an applicant, may offer a job and say, "As long as you meet your deadlines for the projects we give you, you'll be a part of our team." Oops! A court may later rule that those words added up to an implied contract—a promise that the employee wouldn't be fired without good cause.

The best way to avoid the possibility of creating an implied contract you didn't intend is to make it clear in all written documents you give a new employee—including your employee handbook—that employment is at will and to also clearly state that your company never makes oral employment commitments.

📖 For more information on the types of situations in which courts may find that an employer has entered into a non-written contract with an employee, see *The Employer's Legal Handbook*, by Fred S. Steingold (Nolo).

Instructions for Form 9F: Contract With Employee

All the forms in this book are provided as tear-outs in Appendix B and on the accompanying forms CD-ROM. As you read the instructions for Form 9F, you may want to either tear out the form or open the form's file on the CD-ROM so you can follow along. Form 9F is in the file FORM9F.RTF on the CD-ROM. (For more information on using the forms CD-ROM, see Appendix A, "How to Use the CD-ROM.") If you don't use the forms CD-ROM, be sure to photocopy the agreement so you'll have a clean copy to use later.

1. Names

Fill in the name of the employer and the employee.

2. Job Duties

Fill in the title of the job and list the job duties.

3. Duration of Employment

Fill in the dates the employment will begin and end.

4. Compensation

Fill in the compensation the employee will receive.

5. Other Benefits

List all of the nonsalary benefits you've agreed to provide to the employee, such as medical coverage, paid vacation time, use of a car and so on. However, you may want to simply reference the benefits set forth in the employee handbook instead. Here's some sample language you can use to accomplish this:

> SAMPLE:
>
> Employer will provide Employee with the same benefits Employer provides to its other employees, as set out from time to time in the employee handbook.

6. Employer's Policies

You need not insert anything here. This paragraph makes it clear that the employee is bound by the contents of the employee handbook in addition to the terms of the contract.

 Written employment policies can head off disputes. As noted, most companies with more than 25 employees put their employment policies into an employee handbook, which is given to each new employee. There are good practical and legal reasons for even a smaller business to do so as well. Once you give an employee a well-drafted handbook, there can be no dispute over what days off are paid for or how vacation pay is handled.

In addition, having fair and uniform policies published in a handbook backed up by regular and objective employee evaluations can help if you're ever sued for wrongful discharge. For a very small business or as a stop-gap measure, you can summarize your policies in a brief handout.

 For more on employee handbooks including an in-depth discussion of what they should contain, see Chapter 2 of *The Employer's Legal Handbook*, by Fred S. Steingold (Nolo).

7. Termination

Nothing needs to be inserted here.

Because a contract is involved, this paragraph makes it clear that you're not free to fire the employee during the term of the contract unless you have good cause. In short, you can fire the employee only if he or she doesn't satisfactorily perform the job duties or violates your policies.

 Fire only as a last resort. Even though an employment contract gives you the right to fire the employee for good cause, that's usually not wise unless the employee has done something truly bad such as stealing or attacking a customer. The fact that you don't like a senior employee's work as much as you imagined you would—or you disagree with how he or she is doing the job—is not a good cause to end a contractual relationship. Even if an employee who has a contract is doing an obviously terrible job—for example, only shows up for work three days a week and does almost nothing—your first step should normally be to give the person notice of the problem and a chance to correct the offending behavior. And, of course, you should document the employee's misconduct and put your written warning in his or her personnel file. Then if you do fire the employee for breach of contract and end up embroiled in a lawsuit as a result, you'll be able to prove that you had continuing and serious problems with the employee, which were repeatedly brought to the employee's attention.

For great information, insights and advice safely firing employees, see *Firing Without Fear*, by Barbara Kate Repa (Nolo).

8. Agreement Not to Disclose Confidential Information

See the instructions for paragraph 1 of Form 9D.

9. Return of Confidential Information

See the instructions for paragraph 2 of Form 9D.

10. Agreement Not to Compete

See the instructions for paragraph 1 of Form 9E.

11. Right to an Injunction

See the instructions for paragraph 3 of Form 9D.

Standard Clauses

The remainder of the agreement contains the standard clauses we discussed in Chapter 1, Section C. The only thing you'll need to fill in here is the name of the state whose law will apply to the contract in the paragraph called "Governing Law."

Signatures

Both you and your employee need to sign. See Chapter 1, Section B, for instructions on signing contracts.

G. Form 9G: Contract With Independent Contractor

Independent contractors are people who contract to work for others without having the legal status of an employee. The IRS strongly prefers that workers be treated as employees and not as independent contractors. If you classify someone as an independent contractor and the person should be treated as an employee, you face IRS penalties. To withstand an IRS challenge to independent contractor classification, you must show that the worker will control both the outcome of the project and how the job gets done. It also helps if you can show that the worker has at least some control over how he or she charges for the job.

If you engage a worker who qualifies under the law as an independent contractor, you don't have to pay the employer's share of the worker's Social Security and Medicare taxes, nor do you have to withhold the worker's share of those taxes or the worker's income taxes or forward those taxes to the IRS. However, you must inform the IRS if you've paid an independent contractor $600 or more in one year. But the independent contractor is responsible for reporting and paying all Social Security, Medicare and income taxes on his or her earnings.

In addition to the reduced bookkeeping and financial obligations you have when you hire an independent contractor instead of an employee, you're not bound by many of the federal and state laws that normally govern the employer-employee relationship.

It's sometimes difficult to know whether the IRS will agree that you've correctly classified a worker as an independent contractor. The easy cases involve workers who clearly are in business for themselves, demonstrated by such characteristics as:

- The worker is available to perform services for many businesses.
- The worker has a fixed base of operations—a commercial or office location perhaps, or a room at home—and ongoing business expenses.

- The worker lists the business in the phone book and may also drum up business through newspaper ads, radio commercials and circulars.
- The worker undertakes a job based on the results the client wants, but remains free to decide how to get the job done.
- Depending on how the business goes, the worker may earn a large profit, a small profit or none at all—perhaps even suffering a loss.

By contrast, people who work under your close supervision for fixed wages are almost certainly employees rather than independent contractors. Unfortunately, some workers fall into an ambiguous area where the distinction between an employee and an independent contractor gets fuzzy. To be super-safe and free of the risk of misclassification, you can either treat such a worker as an employee or have the worker incorporate (as explained below).

Otherwise, in the case of workers whose status is ambiguous, you may wish to get advice from a tax expert before classifying someone as an independent contractor. If you do decide to treat the worker as an independent contractor, having a written contract such as Form 9G helps you establish that the classification is proper.

IRS penalties for misclassifying a worker can be severe. The harshest penalties, of course, apply to businesses that intentionally misclassify someone by treating the worker as an independent contractor when he or she clearly is an employee. But you can be penalized even if you misclassify someone in good faith. Here, the amount of the assessment will turn on whether or not you filed IRS Form 1099-MISC reporting the payments you made to the worker. The following rules apply to an unintentional misclassification:

- **1099 Filed.** You'll have to pay 20% of the Social Security and Medicare taxes you should have withheld from the worker's pay PLUS 0.29% of the worker's wages PLUS 100% of the Social Security and Medicare taxes you should have paid on the worker's wages PLUS a penalty of 1.5% of the wages paid

PLUS all federal unemployment taxes (FUTA) you should have paid. These amounts can really add up. And running your business as a corporation or LLC may not protect you from personal liability for these penalties. If you're an officer of the business or have authority to make payroll decisions, you may have to pay the penalties yourself.

- **1099 Not Filed.** Here, some of the amounts listed above may be doubled!

So be sure to use the utmost care in treating someone as an independent contractor—and be sure to report your payments on Form 1099-MISC.

 A contract by itself can't create an independent contractor relationship. A contract is useful to document the financial arrangements to which you and the worker agree and who has control over how the work is to be done. But a contract, by itself, can't magically convert someone who's an employee, as defined by IRS rules, into an independent contractor.

 Chapter 15 of the *Legal Guide for Starting & Running a Small Business*, by Fred S. Steingold (Nolo), explains the differences between employees and independent contractors and how you can avoid legal problems and penalties when you classify workers.

For more on the legal and practical facets of engaging independent contractors and for a large variety of legal forms, see *Hiring Independent Contractors*, by Stephen Fishman (Nolo).

If you are an independent contractor who is hired by others, see *Working for Yourself: Law & Taxes for Independent Contractors, Freelancers and Consultants*, by Stephen Fishman (Nolo).

 It's safest to deal with corporations. Sometimes it's unclear whether you can safely treat a worker as an independent contractor. Although, as noted, a written contract can be very helpful in establishing independent contractor status, even with such a contract, there's no guarantee that the IRS or other government agency will agree with your classification of the worker. To achieve a higher degree of assurance that you won't have IRS problems, consider asking the worker to incorporate. Then enter into a contract with the corporation—not the individual. The IRS will almost always accept the fact that an incorporated worker isn't your employee but instead is an employee of his or her own corporation. Incidentally, it's legal in every state to form a one-person corporation.

Instructions for Form 9G: Contract With Independent Contractor

All the forms in this book are provided as tear-outs in Appendix B and on the accompanying forms CD-ROM. As you read the instructions for Form 9G, you may want to either tear out the form or open the form's file on the CD-ROM so you can follow along. Form 9G is in the file FORM9G.RTF on the CD-ROM. (For more information on using the forms CD-ROM, see Appendix A, "How to Use the CD-ROM.") If you don't use the forms CD-ROM, be sure to photocopy the agreement so you'll have a clean copy to use later.

1. Names
Insert your name (the client) and the name of the independent contractor who will be performing services for you.

2. Services to Be Performed
Describe the services that the independent contractor will be performing for you. Concentrate on the results the independent contractor is expected to achieve—not on how he or she is to achieve those results. You want to avoid creating the impression that you have the right to control how the work is performed.

3. Time for Performance
If there's a cut-off date for the completion of the services, check the first box and include the dead-line. If services will be performed at various times, check the second box and insert the schedule.

4. Payment
Insert the payment arrangements. The two main methods are the fixed fee and payment by unit of time.

SAMPLE OF FIXED FEE:
Client will pay Contractor $400 for Phase I of the job and $600 for Phase II of the job.

SAMPLE OF PAYMENT BY UNIT OF TIME:
Client will pay Contractor $15.00 an hour.

In case of an IRS audit, the first method—payment of a fixed fee—can add weight to your position that you've correctly classified the worker as an independent contractor. If you use the second method, consider putting a cap on the independent contractor's total compensation. The independent contractor then bears much of the risk of correctly estimating how much time it will take to do the job and how profitable the job will be.

5. State and Federal Taxes
Stating in writing that you will not pay state or federal withholding for the contractor is one way of making it clear the contractor is not an employee. Also, since the penalties for misclassifying a worker can be so severe, you want the contractor to take seriously his or her responsibility to pay taxes. Here, the contractor is agreeing that he or she will pay any applicable taxes. If the contractor doesn't pay these taxes (which sometimes happens), and a government agency decides to reclassify the worker and comes after your business for payment, the contractor has agreed to reimburse you for any amounts you're required to pay on their behalf. However, if a contractor balks at signing something that says this, consider taking it out. In the end, it's really your responsibility, as an employer, to make sure you correctly classify workers.

6. Fringe Benefits

You'll reduce your chances of having a contractor reclassified as an employee if you make it clear that the worker is not entitled to receive the same benefits as a regular employee.

7. Invoices

Nothing needs to be inserted here. Requiring the independent contractor to submit invoices for services performed can help to differentiate the worker from an employee, since employees don't submit invoices.

8. Independent Contractor Status

Nothing needs to be inserted here. Giving the independent contractor the right to control the work is—assuming, of course, it's true—very strong evidence that he or she isn't an employee.

9. Other Clients

Nothing needs to be inserted here. Making it clear that the independent contractor has the right to work for others helps to establish independent contractor rather than employee status. Of course, if the independent contractor rarely or never ever does this, the IRS may ignore this provision.

10. Assistants

Nothing needs to be inserted here. Requiring the independent contractor to pay for the work of assistants is one more indication that he or she isn't an employee.

11. Equipment and Supplies

If the independent contractor will be providing all the necessary equipment, tools and supplies to do the work, write the words "no exceptions" in the space provided in the first paragraph. (CD-ROM users can just delete the subparagraph.) Otherwise, write in the equipment, tools and supplies that you will provide.

If the independent contractor will be responsible for all expenses, write the words "no exceptions" in the space provided in the second paragraph. (CD-ROM users can just delete the subparagraph.) Otherwise, write in the expenses for which you'll be responsible.

 A worker's investment in tools and supplies helps show independence.
Requiring the worker you're contracting with to provide all or most equipment, tools and supplies and to pay all or most expenses can help establish the existence of a true independent contractor relationship. It's more evidence that the worker has a financial investment in the project that a typical employee wouldn't have.

12. Disputes

See the discussion of dispute resolution clauses in Chapter 1, Section D.

Standard Clauses

The remainder of the agreement contains the standard clauses we discussed in Chapter 1, Section C. The only thing you'll need to fill in here is the name of the state whose law will apply to the contract in the paragraph called "Governing Law."

Signatures

Both contractor and client need to sign. Remember, the contractor needs to use the correct signature form for its type of business—sole proprietorship, partnership, corporation, etc. See Chapter 1, Section B, for instructions on signing contracts. ■

How to Use the CD-ROM

The tear-out forms in Appendix B are included on a CD-ROM in the back of the book. This CD-ROM, which can be used with Windows computers, installs files that can be opened, printed and edited using a word processor or other software. It is NOT a stand-alone software program. Please read this Appendix and the README.TXT file included on the CD-ROM for instructions on using the forms CD.

Note to Mac users: This CD-ROM and its files should also work on Macintosh computers. Please note, however, that Nolo cannot provide technical support for non-Windows users.

How to View the README File

If you do not know how to view the file README.TXT, insert the forms CD into your computer's CD-ROM drive and follow these instructions:

- Windows 95, 98, 2000 and ME: (1) On your PC's desktop, double-click the My Computer icon; (2) double-click the icon for the CD-ROM drive into which the forms CD was inserted; (3) double-click the file README.TXT.
- Macintosh: (1) On your Mac desktop, double-click the icon for the CD-ROM that you inserted; (2) double-click on the file README.TXT.

While the README file is open, print it out by using the Print command in the File menu.

Two different kinds of forms are contained on the CD-ROM:

- Word processing (RTF) forms that you can open, complete, print and save with your word processing program (see Section B, below), and
- Government (PDF) forms that can be viewed only with Adobe Acrobat Reader 4.0 or higher. You can install Acrobat Reader from the forms CD (see Section C below). Some of these forms have fill-in text fields, and can be

completed using your computer. You will not, however, be able to save the completed forms with the filled-in data. PDF forms without fill-in text fields must be printed out and filled in by hand or with a typewriter.

See Appendix B for a list of forms, their file names and file formats.

A. Installing the Form Files Onto Your Computer

Before you can do anything with the files on the CD-ROM, you need to install them onto your hard disk. In accordance with U.S. copyright laws, remember that copies of the CD-ROM and its files are for your personal use only.

Insert the forms CD and do the following:

1. Windows 95, 98, 2000 and ME Users

Follow the instructions that appear on the screen. (If nothing happens when you insert the forms CD-ROM, then (1) double-click the My Computer icon; (2) double-click the icon for the CD-ROM drive into which the forms CD was inserted; and (3) double click the file SETUP.HLP.)

By default, all the files are installed to the \Small Business Legal Forms folder in the \Program Files folder of your computer. A folder called "Small Business Legal Forms" is added to the "Programs" folder of the Start menu.

2. Macintosh Users

Step 1: If the "Small Business Forms CD" window is not open, open it by double-clicking the "Small Business Forms CD" icon.

Step 2: Select the "Small Business Legal Forms" folder icon.

Step 3: Drag and drop the folder icon onto the icon of your hard disk.

B. Using the Word Processing Files to Create Documents

This section concerns the files for forms that can be opened and edited with your word processing program.

All word processing forms come in rich text format (these files have the extension ".RTF").

For example, the form for the Checklist for Starting a Sole Proprietorship discussed in Chapter 2 is on the file FORM2A.RTF. All forms, their file names and file formats are listed in Appendix B.

RTF files can be read by most recent word processing programs including all versions of MS Word for Windows and Macintosh, WordPad for Windows, and recent versions of WordPerfect for Windows and Macintosh.

To use a form from the CD to create your documents you must: (1) open a file in your word processor or text editor; (2) edit the form by filling in the required information; (3) print it out; (4) rename and save your revised file.

The following are general instructions on how to do this. However, each word processor uses different commands to open, format, save and print documents. Please read your word processor's manual for specific instructions on performing these tasks.

DO NOT CALL NOLO'S TECHNICAL SUPPORT IF YOU HAVE QUESTIONS ON HOW TO USE YOUR WORD PROCESSOR.

Step 1: Opening a File

There are three ways to open the word processing files included on the CD-ROM after you have installed them onto your computer.

- Windows users can open a file by selecting its "shortcut" as follows: (1) Click the Windows "Start" button; (2) open the "Programs" folder; (3) open the "Small Business Legal Forms" subfolder; (4) open the "RTF" subfolder; (5) open the appropriate Chapter folder, if applicable; and (6) click on the shortcut to the form you want to work with.

- Both Windows and Macintosh users can open a file directly by double-clicking on it. Use My Computer or Windows Explorer (Windows 95, 98, 2000 or ME) or the Finder (Macintosh) to go to the folder you installed or copied the CD's files to. Then, double-click on the specific file you want to open.

- You can also open a file from within your word processor. To do this, you must first start your word processor. Then, go to the File menu and choose the Open command. This opens a dialog box where you will tell the program (1) the type of file you want to open (*.RTF); and (2) the location and name of the file (you will need to navigate through the directory tree to get to the folder on your hard disk where the CD's files have been installed). If these directions are unclear you will need to look through the manual for your word processing program—Nolo's technical support department will NOT be able to help you with the use of your word processing program.

Where Are the Files Installed?

Windows Users

RTF files are installed by default to a folder named \Small Business Legal Forms\RTF in the \Program Files folder of your computer.

Macintosh Users

RTF files are located in the "RTF" folder within the "Small Business Legal Forms" folder.

Step 2: Editing Your Document

These instructions are for Word for Windows 95, 97 or 2000 users. If you are using WordPad or another Windows word processing program, please refer to the sidebar "Editing Tips for Other Word Processors," below. These instructions should work fine in the most recent versions of Word for Macintosh. (If you experience difficulties editing documents on a Mac, please follow the instructions in the sidebar "Editing Tips for Other Word Processors," below.)

The RTF files installed from the CD-ROM are Microsoft Word "template" files. If you have never used templates before, here are some helpful tips:

- To move from field to field, and enter the required information, use the Tab key. Editable fields, where you enter required information, have gray backgrounds.

- To select an option, put an "x" in the appropriate check box by tabbing to the check box and pressing the X key.

- To copy, cut, paste or otherwise edit text that is not in an editable field, you must first "unprotect" the form by choosing Tools > Unprotect Document from Word's menu bar. You will need to unprotect the form if you want to:
  - add, copy or cut extra signature lines
  - add, copy or cut extra lines for table or lists
  - delete optional or alternative clauses that you don't want to include in your document (however, you can simply use the check boxes to indicate the optional or alternative clauses you want)
  - edit any text outside the gray, editable fields.

- There's no need to delete instructional text that is red and has a dotted underline. Such instructional text is "hidden" and will not appear on the form when you print it. If you do not see any red instructional text in your document, go to Tools > Options and then click the View tab. Under Nonprinting characters, select the All check box.

Editing Tips for Other Word Processors

If you use a word processing program other than Word for Windows 95, 97 or 2000, the instructions in Step 2, above, do not apply to you. You will need to fill in the appropriate information according to the instructions and samples in the book as follows:

Underlines indicate where you need to enter information, and are often followed by red instructional text. *Be sure to delete the underlines and instructions from your edited document.*

Some of the forms have check boxes before text. The check boxes indicate:

- Optional text, where you choose whether to include or exclude the given text.
- Alternative text, where you select one alternative to include and exclude the other alternatives.

If you are using the tear-out forms in Appendix B, you simply mark the appropriate box to make your choice.

If you are using the forms CD, however, we recommend that instead of marking the check boxes, you do the following:

Optional text
If you **don't want** to include optional text, just delete it from your document.

If you **do want** to include optional text, just leave it in your document.

In either case, delete the check box itself as well as any red instructional text.

Alternative text
First delete all the alternatives that you do not want to include.

Then delete the remaining check boxes, as well as any red instructional text.

If you do not know how to use your word processor to edit an RTF file, you will need to look through the manual for your word processing program.

Step 3: Printing Out the Document

Use your word processor's or text editor's "Print" command to print out your document. If you do not know how to use your word processor to print a document, you will need to look through the manual for your word processing program—Nolo's technical support department will NOT be able to help you with the use of your word processing program.

Step 4: Saving Your Document

After filling in the form, use the "Save As" command to save and rename the file. Because all the files are "read-only" you will not be able to use the "Save" command. This is for your protection. IF YOU SAVE THE FILE WITHOUT RENAMING IT, THE UNDER-LINES THAT INDICATE WHERE YOU NEED TO ENTER YOUR INFORMATION WILL BE LOST AND YOU WILL NOT BE ABLE TO CREATE A NEW DOCUMENT WITH THIS FILE WITHOUT RECOPY-ING THE ORIGINAL FILE FROM THE CD-ROM.

If you do not know how to use your word processor to save a document, you will need to look through the manual for your word processing program—Nolo's technical support department will NOT be able to help you with the use of your word processing program.

C. Using Adobe Acrobat (PDF) Form Files

Electronic copies of useful forms from government agencies are included on the CD-ROM in Adobe Acrobat PDF format. You must have the Adobe Acrobat Reader 4.0 or higher installed on your computer (see below) to use these forms. All forms, their file names and file formats are listed in Appendix B. These form files were not created by Nolo.

Some of these forms have fill-in text fields. To create your document using these files, you must: (1) open a file; (2) fill-in the text fields using either your mouse or the tab key on your keyboard to navigate from field to field; and (3) print it out;

NOTE: While you can print out your completed form, you will NOT be able to save your completed form to disk.

Forms without fill-in text fields cannot be filled out using your computer. To create your document using these files, you must: (1) open the file; (2) print it out; and (3) complete it by hand or type-writer.

Installing Acrobat Reader

To install the Adobe Acrobat Reader, insert the CD into your computer's CD-ROM drive and follow these instructions:

- Windows 95, 98, 2000 and ME: Follow the instructions that appear on screen. (If nothing happens when you insert the forms CD-ROM, then (1) double-click the My Computer icon; (2) double-click the icon for the CD-ROM drive into which the forms CD was inserted; and (3) double click the file SETUP.HLP)
- Macintosh: (1) If the "Small Business Forms CD" window is not open, open it by double-clicking the "Small Business Forms CD" icon; and (2) double-click on the "Reader Installer" icon.

If you do not know how to use Adobe Acrobat to view and print the files, you will need to consult the online documentation that comes with the Acrobat Reader program.

Do NOT call Nolo technical support if you have questions on how to use Acrobat Reader.

Step 1: Opening PDF Files

PDF files, like the word processing files, can be opened one of three ways.

- Windows users can open a file by selecting its "shortcut" as follows: (1) Click the Windows "Start" button; (2) open the "Programs" folder; (3) open the "Small Business Legal Forms" subfolder; (4) open the "PDF" folder; and (5) click on the shortcut to the form you want to work with.

- Both Windows and Macintosh users can open a file directly by double-clicking on it. Use My Computer or Windows Explorer (Windows 95, 98, 2000 or ME) or the Finder (Macintosh) to go to the folder you created and copied the CD's files to. Then, double-click on the specific file you want to open.

- You can also open a PDF file from within Acrobat Reader. To do this, you must first start Reader. Then, go to the File menu and choose the Open command. This opens a dialog box where you will tell the program the location and name of the file (you will need to navigate through the directory tree to get to the folder on your hard disk where the CD's files have been installed). If these directions are unclear you will need to look through the manual for your word processing program—Nolo's technical support department will NOT be able to help you with the use of your word processing program.

Step 2: Filling In PDF Files

Use your mouse or the Tab key on your keyboard to navigate from field to field within these forms. Be sure to have all the information you will need to complete a form on hand, because you will not be able to save a copy of the filled-in form to disk. You can, however, print out a completed version.

NOTE: This step is only applicable to forms that have been created with fill-in text fields. Forms without fill-in fields must be completed by hand or typewriter after you have printed them out.

Where Are the PDF Files Installed?

Windows Users
PDF files are installed by default to a folder named \Small Business Legal Forms\PDF in the \Program Files folder of your computer.

Macintosh Users
PDF files are located in the "PDF" folder within the "Small Business Legal Forms" folder.

Step 3: Printing PDF Files

Choose Print from the Acrobat Reader File menu. This will open the Print dialog box. In the "Print Range" section of the Print dialog box, select the appropriate print range, then click OK. ∎

Tear-Out Forms

Form Name	Instructions in Ch. Sec.	File Name
Attachment to Contract	1E	ATTACH.RTF
Amendment of Contract	1E	AMEND.RTF
Checklist for Starting a Sole Proprietorship	2A	FORM2A.RTF
IRS Form SS-4: Application for Employer Identification Number	2A	FSS4.PDF*
IRS Form W-4: Employee's Withholding Allowance Certificate	2A	FW4.PDF
INS Form I-9: Employment Eligibility Verification	2A	I-9.PDF
Partnership Agreement	2B	FORM2B.RTF
Pre-Incorporation Agreement	2C	FORM2C.RTF
Corporate Bylaws	2D	FORM2D.RTF
Stock Agreement	2E	FORM2E.RTF
LLC Operating Agreement for Single-Member LLC	2F	FORM2F.RTF
Notice of Shareholders' Meeting	3A	FORM3A.RTF
Notice of Directors' Meeting	3B	FORM3B.RTF
Shareholder Proxy	3C	FORM3C.RTF
Minutes of Shareholders' Meeting	3D	FORM3D.RTF
Minutes of Directors' Meeting	3E	FORM3E.RTF
Minutes of Telephone Conference Directors' Meeting	3F	FORM3F.RTF
Consent of Shareholders	3G	FORM3G.RTF

* This file is in Adobe Acrobat PDF Format with fill-in text fields.

Form Name	Instructions in Ch. Sec.	File Name
Contract to Purchase Vacant Land	7D	FORM7D.RTF
Option to Purchase Vacant Land	7E	FORM7E.RTF
Attachment to Real Estate Purchase Contract	7F	FORM7F.RTF
Amendment of Real Estate Purchase Contract	7G	FORM7G.RTF
Removal of Contingency	7H	FORM7H.RTF
Extension of Time to Remove Contingencies	7I	FORM7I.RTF
Exercise of Option to Purchase Real Estate	7J	FORM7J.RTF
Renovation Contract	7K	FORM7K.RTF
Sales Contract (Lump Sum Payment)	8A	FORM8A.RTF
Sales Contract (Installment Payments)	8B	FORM8B.RTF
Bill of Sale	8C	FORM8C.RTF
Security Agreement	8D	FORM8D.RTF
Contract for Manufacture of Goods	8E	FORM8E.RTF
Equipment Rental Contract	8F	FORM8F.RTF
Storage Contract	8G	FORM8G.RTF
Consignment Contract	8H	FORM8H.RTF
Employment Application	9A	FORM9A.RTF
Authorization to Release Information	9B	FORM9B.RTF
Offer of Employment	9C	FORM9C.RTF
Confidentiality Agreement	9D	FORM9D.RTF
Covenant Not to Compete	9E	FORM9E.RTF
Contract With Employee	9F	FORM9F.RTF
Contract With Independent Contractor	9G	FORM9G.RTF

Attachment to Contract

Attachment Number _____

1. Names

This attachment is made by _____

and _____ .

2. Terms of Attachment

We agree to the following Attachment to the _____

_____ dated _____ concerning

_____

_____

_____

_____

_____

_____

_____

_____

_____

_____

_____

Dated: _____

Name of Business: _____

a _____

By: _____

Printed Name and Title: _____

Address: _____

_____

Dated: _____

Name of Business: _____

a _____

By: _____

Printed Name and Title: _____

Address: _____

_____

Amendment of Contract

Amendment Number _____

_____ and

_____

agree to the following amendment of the _____

dated _____ concerning:

_____

_____

_____

_____

_____

_____

_____

_____

In all other respects, the terms of the original contract and any earlier amendments will remain in effect. If there is a conflict between this amendment and the original contract or any earlier amendment, the terms of this amendment will prevail.

Dated: _____

Name of Business: _____

a _____

By: _____

Printed Name and Title: _____

Address: _____

_____

Dated: _____

Name of Business: _____

a _____

By: _____

Printed Name and Title: _____

Address: _____

Form 2A: Checklist for Starting a Sole Proprietorship

Business Name

☐ Check on availability of name.

☐ File an assumed name or fictitious name certificate, if required, with local or state fictitious name office.

☐ Publish a notice of assumed name or fictitious name in a local newspaper, if required.

☐ Consider registering your trademark or service mark at the federal or state level if you will do business regionally or nationally and will use your business name to identify a product or service.

Licenses and Permits

☐ Get federal license, if required.

☐ Get state license, if required.

☐ Get local license, if required.

Insurance

☐ Normally, get liability insurance (for injury to other people and damage to their property).

☐ Make sure there's adequate coverage for your vehicles and those of your employees when used for business purposes.

☐ Normally, get property and theft insurance (covering damage to your business space and your tangible business assets).

☐ Get product liability insurance, if appropriate.

☐ Ask your insurance broker or agent about other recommended coverage.

Taxes

☐ Get IRS Publication 334, Tax Guide for Small Business.

☐ Get IRS Publication 583, Taxpayers Starting a Business.

☐ Check with state and local tax authorities regarding business taxes and any required registration.

☐ Consider getting QuickBooks (Intuit) or similar small business accounting software.

☐ Consider hiring a part-time bookkeeper and consulting an accountant about setting up a simple accounting system.

Home-Based Business

☐ Make sure your homeowners' insurance covers liability for business-related injuries to other people and damage to their property—especially if people will be coming to your house on business.

☐ Make sure your homeowners' insurance covers damage to and theft of your business assets.

☐ Check to be sure your business usage complies with:

☐ local zoning ordinances

☐ your lease

☐ covenants, conditions and restrictions affecting your property.

☐ Get IRS Publication 587, Business Use of Your Home.

Hiring People

☐ Obtain an Employer Identification Number from the IRS (Form SS-4).

☐ Get workers' compensation insurance.

☐ Register with the state government for payment of unemployment compensation taxes.

☐ Get a supply of IRS Form W-4 (employee withholding).

☐ Get a supply of INS Form I-9 (employment eligibility verification).

☐ Know the guidelines for hiring independent contractors.

Form W-4 (2001)

Purpose. Complete Form W-4 so your employer can withhold the correct Federal income tax from your pay. Because your tax situation may change, you may want to refigure your withholding each year.

Exemption from withholding. If you are exempt, complete only lines 1, 2, 3, 4, and 7, and sign the form to validate it. Your exemption for 2001 expires February 18, 2002.

Note: *You cannot claim exemption from withholding if (1) your income exceeds $750 and includes more than $250 of unearned income (e.g., interest and dividends) and (2) another person can claim you as a dependent on their tax return.*

Basic instructions. If you are not exempt, complete the **Personal Allowances Worksheet** below. The worksheets on page 2 adjust your withholding allowances based on itemized deductions, certain credits, adjustments to

income, or two-earner/two-job situations. Complete all worksheets that apply. They will help you figure the number of withholding allowances you are entitled to claim. **However, you may claim fewer (or zero) allowances.**

Head of household. Generally, you may claim head of household filing status on your tax return only if you are unmarried and pay more than 50% of the costs of keeping up a home for yourself and your dependent(s) or other qualifying individuals. See line **E** below.

Tax credits. You can take projected tax credits into account in figuring your allowable number of withholding allowances. Credits for child or dependent care expenses and the child tax credit may be claimed using the **Personal Allowances Worksheet** below. See **Pub. 919,** How Do I Adjust My Tax Withholding? for information on converting your other credits into withholding allowances.

Nonwage income. If you have a large amount of nonwage income, such as interest or dividends,

consider making estimated tax payments using **Form 1040-ES,** Estimated Tax for Individuals. Otherwise, you may owe additional tax.

Two earners/two jobs. If you have a working spouse or more than one job, figure the total number of allowances you are entitled to claim on all jobs using worksheets from only one Form W-4. Your withholding usually will be most accurate when all allowances are claimed on the Form W-4 for the highest paying job and zero allowances are claimed on the others.

Check your withholding. After your Form W-4 takes effect, use Pub. 919 to see how the dollar amount you are having withheld compares with your projected total tax for 2001. Get Pub. 919 especially if you used the **Two-Earner/Two-Job Worksheet** on page 2 and your earnings exceed $150,000 (Single) or $200,000 (Married).

Recent name change? If your name on line 1 differs from that shown on your social security card, call 1-800-772-1213 for a new social security card.

Personal Allowances Worksheet (Keep for your records.)

A Enter "1" for **yourself** if no one else can claim you as a dependent . . . . **A** _____

B Enter "1" if:
- You are single and have only one job; or
- You are married, have only one job, and your spouse does not work; or
- Your wages from a second job or your spouse's wages (or the total of both) are $1,000 or less.

. . **B** _____

C Enter "1" for your **spouse.** But, you may choose to enter -0- if you are married and have either a working spouse or more than one job. (Entering -0- may help you avoid having too little tax withheld.) . . . . **C** _____

D Enter number of **dependents** (other than your spouse or yourself) you will claim on your tax return . . . . **D** _____

E Enter "1" if you will file as **head of household** on your tax return (see conditions under **Head of household** above) . **E** _____

F Enter "1" if you have at least $1,500 of **child or dependent care expenses** for which you plan to claim a credit . . **F** _____

   (**Note:** *Do not include child support payments. See **Pub. 503,** Child and Dependent Care Expenses, for details.*)

G **Child Tax Credit** (including additional child tax credit):
- If your total income will be between $18,000 and $50,000 ($23,000 and $63,000 if married), enter "1" for each eligible child.
- If your total income will be between $50,000 and $80,000 ($63,000 and $115,000 if married), enter "1" if you have two eligible children, enter "2" if you have three or four eligible children, or enter "3" if you have five or more eligible children. **G** _____

H Add lines A through G and enter total here. (**Note:** *This may be different from the number of exemptions you claim on your tax return.*) ▶ **H** _____

For accuracy, complete all worksheets that apply.
- If you plan to **itemize or claim adjustments to income** and want to reduce your withholding, see the **Deductions and Adjustments Worksheet** on page 2.
- If you are **single,** have **more than one job** and your combined earnings from all jobs exceed $35,000, **or** if you are **married** and have a **working spouse or more than one job** and the combined earnings from all jobs exceed $60,000, see the **Two-Earner/Two-Job Worksheet** on page 2 to avoid having too little tax withheld.
- If **neither** of the above situations applies, **stop here** and enter the number from line H on line 5 of Form W-4 below.

- - - - - - - - - - - - - - - - - **Cut here and give Form W-4 to your employer. Keep the top part for your records.** - - - - - - - - - - - - - - - -

Form **W-4**
Department of the Treasury
Internal Revenue Service

Employee's Withholding Allowance Certificate

▶ **For Privacy Act and Paperwork Reduction Act Notice, see page 2.**

OMB No. 1545-0010

2001

1 Type or print your first name and middle initial	Last name		2 Your social security number

Home address (number and street or rural route)	3 ☐ Single ☐ Married ☐ Married, but withhold at higher Single rate.

Note: *If married, but legally separated, or spouse is a nonresident alien, check the Single box.*

City or town, state, and ZIP code	4 If your last name differs from that on your social security card, check here. You must call 1-800-772-1213 for a new card. ▶ ☐

5 Total number of allowances you are claiming (from line **H** above **or** from the applicable worksheet on page 2) **5** _____

6 Additional amount, if any, you want withheld from each paycheck . . . . **6** $ _____

7 I claim exemption from withholding for 2001, and I certify that I meet **both** of the following conditions for exemption:
- Last year I had a right to a refund of **all** Federal income tax withheld because I had **no** tax liability **and**
- This year I expect a refund of **all** Federal income tax withheld because I expect to have **no** tax liability.

If you meet both conditions, write "Exempt" here . . . . ▶ **7** _____

Under penalties of perjury, I certify that I am entitled to the number of withholding allowances claimed on this certificate, or I am entitled to claim exempt status.

Employee's signature
(Form is not valid unless you sign it.) ▶ _____ Date ▶ _____

8 Employer's name and address (Employer: Complete lines 8 and 10 only if sending to the IRS.)	9 Office code (optional)	10 Employer identification number

Cat. No. 10220Q

Deductions and Adjustments Worksheet

Note: *Use this worksheet only if you plan to itemize deductions, claim certain credits, or claim adjustments to income on your 2001 tax return.*

1	Enter an estimate of your 2001 itemized deductions. These include qualifying home mortgage interest, charitable contributions, state and local taxes, medical expenses in excess of 7.5% of your income, and miscellaneous deductions. (For 2001, you may have to reduce your itemized deductions if your income is over $132,950 ($66,475 if married filing separately). See **Worksheet 3** in Pub. 919 for details.) . . .	**1** $ _____
2	Enter: { $7,600 if married filing jointly or qualifying widow(er) $6,650 if head of household $4,550 if single $3,800 if married filing separately }	**2** $ _____
3	**Subtract** line 2 from line 1. If line 2 is greater than line 1, enter -0-	**3** $ _____
4	Enter an estimate of your 2001 adjustments to income, including alimony, deductible IRA contributions, and student loan interest	**4** $ _____
5	**Add** lines 3 and 4 and enter the total (Include any amount for credits from **Worksheet 7** in Pub. 919.) .	**5** $ _____
6	Enter an estimate of your 2001 nonwage income (such as dividends or interest)	**6** $ _____
7	**Subtract** line 6 from line 5. Enter the result, but not less than -0-	**7** $ _____
8	**Divide** the amount on line 7 by $3,000 and enter the result here. Drop any fraction	**8** _____
9	Enter the number from the **Personal Allowances Worksheet,** line H, page 1	**9** _____
10	**Add** lines 8 and 9 and enter the total here. If you plan to use the **Two-Earner/Two-Job Worksheet,** also enter this total on line 1 below. Otherwise, **stop here** and enter this total on Form W-4, line 5, page 1 .	**10** _____

Two-Earner/Two-Job Worksheet

Note: *Use this worksheet only if the instructions under line H on page 1 direct you here.*

1	Enter the number from line H, page 1 (or from line 10 above if you used the **Deductions and Adjustments Worksheet**)	**1** _____
2	Find the number in **Table 1** below that applies to the **lowest** paying job and enter it here	**2** _____
3	If line 1 is **more than or equal to** line 2, subtract line 2 from line 1. Enter the result here (if zero, enter -0-) and on Form W-4, line 5, page 1. **Do not** use the rest of this worksheet	**3** _____

Note: *If line 1 is **less than** line 2, enter -0- on Form W-4, line 5, page 1. Complete lines 4–9 below to calculate the additional withholding amount necessary to avoid a year end tax bill.*

4	Enter the number from line 2 of this worksheet	**4** _____	
5	Enter the number from line 1 of this worksheet	**5** _____	
6	**Subtract** line 5 from line 4		**6** _____
7	Find the amount in **Table 2** below that applies to the **highest** paying job and enter it here		**7** $ _____
8	**Multiply** line 7 by line 6 and enter the result here. This is the additional annual withholding needed . .		**8** $ _____
9	Divide line 8 by the number of pay periods remaining in 2001. For example, divide by 26 if you are paid every two weeks and you complete this form in December 2000. Enter the result here and on Form W-4, line 6, page 1. This is the additional amount to be withheld from each paycheck		**9** $ _____

Table 1: Two-Earner/Two-Job Worksheet

Married Filing Jointly				All Others			
If wages from **LOWEST** paying job are—	Enter on line 2 above	If wages from **LOWEST** paying job are—	Enter on line 2 above	If wages from **LOWEST** paying job are—	Enter on line 2 above	If wages from **LOWEST** paying job are—	Enter on line 2 above
$0 - $4,000	0	42,001 - 47,000	8	$0 - $6,000	0	65,001 - 80,000	8
4,001 - 8,000	1	47,001 - 55,000	9	6,001 - 12,000	1	80,001 - 105,000	9
8,001 - 14,000	2	55,001 - 65,000	10	12,001 - 17,000	2	105,001 and over	10
14,001 - 19,000	3	65,001 - 70,000	11	17,001 - 22,000	3		
19,001 - 25,000	4	70,001 - 90,000	12	22,001 - 28,000	4		
25,001 - 32,000	5	90,001 - 105,000	13	28,001 - 40,000	5		
32,001 - 38,000	6	105,001 - 115,000	14	40,001 - 50,000	6		
38,001 - 42,000	7	115,001 and over	15	50,001 - 65,000	7		

Table 2: Two-Earner/Two-Job Worksheet

Married Filing Jointly		All Others	
If wages from **HIGHEST** paying job are—	Enter on line 7 above	If wages from **HIGHEST** paying job are—	Enter on line 7 above
$0 - $50,000	$440	$0 - $30,000	$440
50,001 - 100,000	800	30,001 - 60,000	800
100,001 - 130,000	900	60,001 - 120,000	900
130,001 - 250,000	1,000	120,001 - 270,000	1,000
250,001 and over	1,100	270,001 and over	1,100

Form **SS-4**

(Rev. April 2000)

Department of the Treasury
Internal Revenue Service

Application for Employer Identification Number

(For use by employers, corporations, partnerships, trusts, estates, churches, government agencies, certain individuals, and others. See instructions.)

▶ Keep a copy for your records.

EIN

OMB No. 1545-0003

Please type or print clearly.

1 Name of applicant (legal name) (see instructions)

2 Trade name of business (if different from name on line 1)

3 Executor, trustee, "care of" name

4a Mailing address (street address) (room, apt., or suite no.)

5a Business address (if different from address on lines 4a and 4b)

4b City, state, and ZIP code

5b City, state, and ZIP code

6 County and state where principal business is located

7 Name of principal officer, general partner, grantor, owner, or trustor—SSN or ITIN may be required (see instructions) ▶

8a Type of entity (Check only one box.) (see instructions)

Caution: If applicant is a limited liability company, see the instructions for line 8a.

- ☐ Sole proprietor (SSN) _____
- ☐ Partnership
- ☐ REMIC
- ☐ State/local government
- ☐ Church or church-controlled organization
- ☐ Other nonprofit organization (specify) ▶ _____
- ☐ Other (specify) ▶

- ☐ Personal service corp.
- ☐ National Guard
- ☐ Farmers' cooperative

- ☐ Estate (SSN of decedent) _____
- ☐ Plan administrator (SSN) _____
- ☐ Other corporation (specify) ▶ _____
- ☐ Trust
- ☐ Federal government/military

(enter GEN if applicable) _____

8b If a corporation, name the state or foreign country (if applicable) where incorporated

State	Foreign country

9 Reason for applying (Check only one box.) (see instructions)
- ☐ Started new business (specify type) ▶ _____
- ☐ Hired employees (Check the box and see line 12.)
- ☐ Created a pension plan (specify type) ▶
- ☐ Banking purpose (specify purpose) ▶ _____
- ☐ Changed type of organization (specify new type) ▶ _____
- ☐ Purchased going business
- ☐ Created a trust (specify type) ▶ _____
- ☐ Other (specify) ▶

10 Date business started or acquired (month, day, year) (see instructions)

11 Closing month of accounting year (see instructions)

12 First date wages or annuities were paid or will be paid (month, day, year). **Note:** *If applicant is a withholding agent, enter date income will first be paid to nonresident alien. (month, day, year)* . . . . ▶

13 Highest number of employees expected in the next 12 months. **Note:** *If the applicant does not expect to have any employees during the period, enter -0-. (see instructions)* . . . . ▶

Nonagricultural	Agricultural	Household

14 Principal activity (see instructions) ▶

15 Is the principal business activity manufacturing? . . . . ☐ Yes ☐ No
If "Yes," principal product and raw material used ▶

16 To whom are most of the products or services sold? Please check one box. ☐ Business (wholesale)
☐ Public (retail) ☐ Other (specify) ▶   ☐ N/A

17a Has the applicant ever applied for an employer identification number for this or any other business? . . . . ☐ Yes ☐ No
Note: *If "Yes," please complete lines 17b and 17c.*

17b If you checked "Yes" on line 17a, give applicant's legal name and trade name shown on prior application, if different from line 1 or 2 above.
Legal name ▶   Trade name ▶

17c Approximate date when and city and state where the application was filed. Enter previous employer identification number if known.

Approximate date when filed (mo., day, year)	City and state where filed	Previous EIN

Under penalties of perjury, I declare that I have examined this application, and to the best of my knowledge and belief, it is true, correct, and complete.

Business telephone number (include area code)
(   )

Fax telephone number (include area code)
(   )

Name and title (Please type or print clearly.) ▶

Signature ▶   Date ▶

Note: *Do not write below this line. For official use only.*

Please leave blank ▶	Geo.	Ind.	Class	Size	Reason for applying

For Privacy Act and Paperwork Reduction Act Notice, see page 4.   Cat. No. 16055N   Form **SS-4** (Rev. 4-2000)

General Instructions

Section references are to the Internal Revenue Code unless otherwise noted.

Purpose of Form

Use Form SS-4 to apply for an employer identification number (EIN). An EIN is a nine-digit number (for example, 12-3456789) assigned to sole proprietors, corporations, partnerships, estates, trusts, and other entities for tax filing and reporting purposes. The information you provide on this form will establish your business tax account.

Caution: *An EIN is for use in connection with your business activities only. Do not use your EIN in place of your social security number (SSN).*

Who Must File

You must file this form if you have not been assigned an EIN before and:

● You pay wages to one or more employees including household employees.

● You are required to have an EIN to use on any return, statement, or other document, even if you are not an employer.

● You are a withholding agent required to withhold taxes on income, other than wages, paid to a nonresident alien (individual, corporation, partnership, etc.). A withholding agent may be an agent, broker, fiduciary, manager, tenant, or spouse, and is required to file **Form 1042,** Annual Withholding Tax Return for U.S. Source Income of Foreign Persons.

● You file **Schedule C,** Profit or Loss From Business, **Schedule C-EZ,** Net Profit From Business, or **Schedule F,** Profit or Loss From Farming, of **Form 1040,** U.S. Individual Income Tax Return, **and** have a Keogh plan or are required to file excise, employment, or alcohol, tobacco, or firearms returns.

The following must use EINs even if they do not have any employees:

● State and local agencies who serve as tax reporting agents for public assistance recipients, under Rev. Proc. 80-4, 1980-1 C.B. 581, should obtain a separate EIN for this reporting. See **Household employer** on page 3.

● Trusts, except the following:

1. Certain grantor-owned trusts. (See the **Instructions for Form 1041,** U.S. Income Tax Return for Estates and Trusts.)

2. Individual retirement arrangement (IRA) trusts, unless the trust has to file **Form 990-T,** Exempt Organization Business Income Tax Return. (See the **Instructions for Form 990-T.)**

● Estates

● Partnerships

● REMICs (real estate mortgage investment conduits) (See the **Instructions for Form 1066,** U.S. Real Estate Mortgage Investment Conduit (REMIC) Income Tax Return.)

● Corporations

● Nonprofit organizations (churches, clubs, etc.)

● Farmers' cooperatives

● Plan administrators (A plan administrator is the person or group of persons specified as the administrator by the instrument under which the plan is operated.)

When To Apply for a New EIN

New Business. If you become the new owner of an existing business, **do not** use the EIN of the former owner. **If you already have an EIN, use that number.** If you do not have an EIN, apply for one on this form. If you become the "owner" of a corporation by acquiring its stock, use the corporation's EIN.

Changes in Organization or Ownership. If you already have an EIN, you may need to get a new one if either the organization or ownership of your business changes. If you incorporate a sole proprietorship or form a partnership, you must get a new EIN. However, **do not** apply for a new EIN if:

● You change only the name of your business,

● You elected on **Form 8832,** Entity Classification Election, to change the way the entity is taxed, or

● A partnership terminates because at least 50% of the total interests in partnership capital and profits were sold or exchanged within a 12-month period. (See Regulations section 301.6109-1(d)(2)(iii).) The EIN for the terminated partnership should continue to be used.

Note: *If you are electing to be an "S corporation," be sure you file* **Form 2553,** *Election by a Small Business Corporation.*

File Only One Form SS-4. File only one Form SS-4, regardless of the number of businesses operated or trade names under which a business operates. However, each corporation in an affiliated group must file a separate application.

EIN Applied for, But Not Received. If you do not have an EIN by the time a return is due, write "Applied for" and the date you applied in the space shown for the number. **Do not** show your social security number (SSN) as an EIN on returns.

If you do not have an EIN by the time a tax deposit is due, send your payment to the Internal Revenue Service Center for your filing area. (See **Where To Apply** below.) Make your check or money order payable to "United States Treasury" and show your name (as shown on Form SS-4), address, type of tax, period covered, and date you applied for an EIN. Send an explanation with the deposit.

For more information about EINs, see **Pub. 583,** Starting a Business and Keeping Records, and **Pub. 1635,** Understanding Your EIN.

How To Apply

You can apply for an EIN either by mail or by telephone. You can get an EIN immediately by calling the Tele-TIN number for the service center for your state, or you can send the completed Form SS-4 directly to the service center to receive your EIN by mail.

Application by Tele-TIN. Under the Tele-TIN program, you can receive your EIN by telephone and use it immediately to file a return or make a payment. To receive an EIN by telephone, complete Form SS-4, then call the Tele-TIN number listed for your state under **Where To Apply.** The person making the call must be authorized to sign the form. (See **Signature** on page 4.)

An IRS representative will use the information from the Form SS-4 to establish your account and assign you an EIN. Write the number you are given on the upper right corner of the form and sign and date it.

Mail or fax (facsimile) the signed Form SS-4 within 24 hours to the Tele-TIN Unit at the service center address for your state. The IRS representative will give you the fax number. The fax numbers are also listed in Pub. 1635.

Taxpayer representatives can receive their client's EIN by telephone if they first send a fax of a completed **Form 2848,** Power of Attorney and Declaration of Representative, or **Form 8821,** Tax Information Authorization, to the Tele-TIN unit. The Form 2848 or Form 8821 will be used solely to release the EIN to the representative authorized on the form.

Application by Mail. Complete Form SS-4 at least 4 to 5 weeks before you will need an EIN. Sign and date the application and mail it to the service center address for your state. You will receive your EIN in the mail in approximately 4 weeks.

Where To Apply

The Tele-TIN numbers listed below will involve a long-distance charge to callers outside of the local calling area and can be used to apply for an EIN. **The numbers may change without notice.** Call 1-800-829-1040 to verify a number or to ask about the status of an application by mail.

If your principal business, office or agency, or legal residence in the case of an individual, is located in: ▼	Call the Tele-TIN number shown or file with the Internal Revenue Service Center at: ▼
Florida, Georgia, South Carolina	Attn: Entity Control Atlanta, GA 39901 770-455-2360
New Jersey, New York (New York City and counties of Nassau, Rockland, Suffolk, and Westchester)	Attn: Entity Control Holtsville, NY 00501 516-447-4955
New York (all other counties), Connecticut, Maine, Massachusetts, New Hampshire, Rhode Island, Vermont	Attn: Entity Control Andover, MA 05501 978-474-9717
Illinois, Iowa, Minnesota, Missouri, Wisconsin	Attn: Entity Control Stop 6800 2306 E. Bannister Rd. Kansas City, MO 64999 816-926-5999
Delaware, District of Columbia, Maryland, Pennsylvania, Virginia	Attn: Entity Control Philadelphia, PA 19255 215-516-6999
Indiana, Kentucky, Michigan, Ohio, West Virginia	Attn: Entity Control Cincinnati, OH 45999 859-292-5467

Kansas, New Mexico, Oklahoma, Texas	Attn: Entity Control Austin, TX 73301 512-460-7843
Alaska, Arizona, California (counties of Alpine, Amador, Butte, Calaveras, Colusa, Contra Costa, Del Norte, El Dorado, Glenn, Humboldt, Lake, Lassen, Marin, Mendocino, Modoc, Napa, Nevada, Placer, Plumas, Sacramento, San Joaquin, Shasta, Sierra, Siskiyou, Solano, Sonoma, Sutter, Tehama, Trinity, Yolo, and Yuba), Colorado, Idaho, Montana, Nebraska, Nevada, North Dakota, Oregon, South Dakota, Utah, Washington, Wyoming	Attn: Entity Control Mail Stop 6271 P.O. Box 9941 Ogden, UT 84201 801-620-7645
California (all other counties), Hawaii	Attn: Entity Control Fresno, CA 93888 559-452-4010
Alabama, Arkansas, Louisiana, Mississippi, North Carolina, Tennessee	Attn: Entity Control Memphis, TN 37501 901-546-3920
If you have no legal residence, principal place of business, or principal office or agency in any state	Attn: Entity Control Philadelphia, PA 19255 215-516-6999

Specific Instructions

The instructions that follow are for those items that are not self-explanatory. Enter N/A (nonapplicable) on the lines that do not apply.

Line 1. Enter the legal name of the entity applying for the EIN exactly as it appears on the social security card, charter, or other applicable legal document.

Individuals. Enter your first name, middle initial, and last name. If you are a sole proprietor, enter your individual name, not your business name. Enter your business name on line 2. Do not use abbreviations or nicknames on line 1.

Trusts. Enter the name of the trust.

Estate of a decedent. Enter the name of the estate.

Partnerships. Enter the legal name of the partnership as it appears in the partnership agreement. **Do not** list the names of the partners on line 1. See the specific instructions for line 7.

Corporations. Enter the corporate name as it appears in the corporation charter or other legal document creating it.

Plan administrators. Enter the name of the plan administrator. A plan administrator who already has an EIN should use that number.

Line 2. Enter the trade name of the business if different from the legal name. The trade name is the "doing business as" name.

Note: *Use the full legal name on line 1 on all tax returns filed for the entity. However, if you enter a trade name on line 2 and choose to use the trade name instead of the legal name, enter the trade name on all returns you file. To prevent processing delays and errors, **always** use either the legal name only or the trade name only on all tax returns.*

Line 3. Trusts enter the name of the trustee. Estates enter the name of the executor, administrator, or other fiduciary. If the entity applying has a designated person to receive tax information, enter that person's name as the "care of" person. Print or type the first name, middle initial, and last name.

Line 7. Enter the first name, middle initial, last name, and SSN of a principal officer if the business is a corporation; of a general partner if a partnership; of the owner of a single member entity that is disregarded as an entity separate from its owner; or of a grantor, owner, or trustor if a trust. If the person in question is an alien individual with a previously assigned individual taxpayer identification number (ITIN), enter the ITIN in the space provided, instead of an SSN. You are not required to enter an SSN or ITIN if the reason you are applying for an EIN is to make an entity classification election (see Regulations section 301.7701-1 through 301.7701-3), and you are a nonresident alien with no effectively connected income from sources within the United States.

Line 8a. Check the box that best describes the type of entity applying for the EIN. If you are an alien individual with an ITIN previously assigned to you, enter the ITIN in place of a requested SSN.

Caution: *This is not an election for a tax classification of an entity. See "Limited liability company (LLC)" below.*

If not specifically mentioned, check the "Other" box, enter the type of entity and the type of return that will be filed (for example, common trust fund, Form 1065). Do not enter N/A. If you are an alien individual applying for an EIN, see the **Line 7** instructions above.

Sole proprietor. Check this box if you file Schedule C, C-EZ, or F (Form 1040) and have a qualified plan, or are required to file excise, employment, or alcohol, tobacco, or firearms returns, or are a payer of gambling winnings. Enter your SSN (or ITIN) in the space provided. If you are a nonresident alien with are a nonresident alien with no effectively

connected income from sources within the United States, you do not need to enter an SSN or ITIN.

REMIC. Check this box if the entity has elected to be treated as a real estate mortgage investment conduit (REMIC). See the Instructions for Form 1066 for more information.

Other nonprofit organization. Check this box if the nonprofit organization is other than a church or church-controlled organization and specify the type of nonprofit organization (for example, an educational organization).

If the organization also seeks tax-exempt status, you must file either **Package 1023,** Application for Recognition of Exemption, or **Package 1024,** Application for Recognition of Exemption Under Section 501(a). Get **Pub. 557,** Tax Exempt Status for Your Organization, for more information.

Group exemption number (GEN). If the organization is covered by a group exemption letter, enter the four-digit GEN. (Do not confuse the GEN with the nine-digit EIN.) If you do not know the GEN, contact the parent organization. Get Pub. 557 for more information about group exemption numbers.

Withholding agent. If you are a withholding agent required to file Form 1042, check the "Other" box and enter "Withholding agent."

Personal service corporation. Check this box if the entity is a personal service corporation. An entity is a personal service corporation for a tax year only if:

● The principal activity of the entity during the testing period (prior tax year) for the tax year is the performance of personal services substantially by employee-owners, and

● The employee-owners own at least 10% of the fair market value of the outstanding stock in the entity on the last day of the testing period.

Personal services include performance of services in such fields as health, law, accounting, or consulting. For more information about personal service corporations, see the **Instructions for Forms 1120 and 1120-A,** and **Pub. 542,** Corporations.

Limited liability company (LLC). See the definition of limited liability company in the **Instructions for Form 1065,** U.S. Partnership Return of Income. An LLC with two or more members can be a partnership or an association taxable as a corporation. An LLC with a single owner can be an association taxable as a corporation or an entity disregarded as an entity separate from its owner. See Form 8832 for more details.

Note: *A domestic LLC with at least two members that does not file Form 8832 is classified as a partnership for Federal income tax purposes.*

● If the entity is classified as a partnership for Federal income tax purposes, check the "partnership" box.

● If the entity is classified as a corporation for Federal income tax purposes, check the "Other corporation" box and write "limited liability co." in the space provided.

● If the entity is disregarded as an entity separate from its owner, check the "Other" box and write in "disregarded entity" in the space provided.

Plan administrator. If the plan administrator is an individual, enter the plan administrator's SSN in the space provided.

Other corporation. This box is for any corporation other than a personal service corporation. If you check this box, enter the type of corporation (such as insurance company) in the space provided.

Household employer. If you are an individual, check the "Other" box and enter "Household employer" and your SSN. If you are a state or local agency serving as a tax reporting agent for public assistance recipients who become household employers, check the "Other" box and enter "Household employer agent." If you are a trust that qualifies as a household employer, you do not need a separate EIN for reporting tax information relating to household employees; use the EIN of the trust.

QSub. For a qualified subchapter S subsidiary (QSub) check the "Other" box and specify "QSub."

Line 9. Check only **one** box. Do not enter N/A.

Started new business. Check this box if you are starting a new business that requires an EIN. If you check this box, enter the type of business being started. **Do not** apply if you already have an EIN and are only adding another place of business.

Hired employees. Check this box if the existing business is requesting an EIN because it has hired or is hiring employees and is therefore required to file employment tax returns. **Do not** apply if you already have an EIN and are only hiring employees. For information on the applicable employment taxes for family members, see **Circular E,** Employer's Tax Guide (Publication 15).

Created a pension plan. Check this box if you have created a pension plan and need an EIN for reporting purposes. Also, enter the type of plan.

Note: *Check this box if you are applying for a trust EIN when a new pension plan is established.*

Banking purpose. Check this box if you are requesting an EIN for banking purposes only, and enter the banking purpose (for example, a bowling league for depositing dues or an investment club for dividend and interest reporting).

Changed type of organization. Check this box if the business is changing its type of organization, for example, if the business was a sole proprietorship and has been incorporated or has become a partnership. If you check this box, specify in the space provided the type of change made, for example, "from sole proprietorship to partnership."

Purchased going business. Check this box if you purchased an existing business. **Do not** use the former owner's EIN. **Do not** apply for a new EIN if you already have one. Use your own EIN.

Created a trust. Check this box if you created a trust, and enter the type of trust created. For example, indicate if the trust is a nonexempt charitable trust or a split-interest trust.

Note: *Do not check this box if you are applying for a trust EIN when a new pension plan is established. Check "Created a pension plan."*

Exception. Do **not** file this form for certain grantor-type trusts. The trustee does not need an EIN for the trust if the trustee furnishes the name and TIN of the grantor/owner and the address of the trust to all payors. See the Instructions for Form 1041 for more information.

Other (specify). Check this box if you are requesting an EIN for any other reason, and enter the reason.

Line 10. If you are starting a new business, enter the starting date of the business. If the business you acquired is already operating, enter the date you acquired the business. Trusts should enter the date the trust was legally created. Estates should enter the date of death of the decedent whose name appears on line 1 or the date when the estate was legally funded.

Line 11. Enter the last month of your accounting year or tax year. An accounting or tax year is usually 12 consecutive months, either a calendar year or a fiscal year (including a period of 52 or 53 weeks). A calendar year is 12 consecutive months ending on December 31. A fiscal year is either 12 consecutive months ending on the last day of any month other than December or a 52-53 week year. For more information on accounting periods, see **Pub. 538,** Accounting Periods and Methods.

Individuals. Your tax year generally will be a calendar year.

Partnerships. Partnerships generally must adopt one of the following tax years:
● The tax year of the majority of its partners,
● The tax year common to all of its principal partners,
● The tax year that results in the least aggregate deferral of income, or
● In certain cases, some other tax year.
See the Instructions for Form 1065 for more information.

REMIC. REMICs must have a calendar year as their tax year.

Personal service corporations. A personal service corporation generally must adopt a calendar year unless:
● It can establish a business purpose for having a different tax year, or
● It elects under section 444 to have a tax year other than a calendar year.

Trusts. Generally, a trust must adopt a calendar year except for the following:
● Tax-exempt trusts,
● Charitable trusts, and
● Grantor-owned trusts.

Line 12. If the business has or will have employees, enter the date on which the business began or will begin to pay wages. If the business does not plan to have employees, enter N/A.

Withholding agent. Enter the date you began or will begin to pay income to a nonresident alien. This also applies to individuals who are required to file Form 1042 to report alimony paid to a nonresident alien.

Line 13. For a definition of agricultural labor (farmwork), see **Circular A,** Agricultural Employer's Tax Guide (Publication 51).

Line 14. Generally, enter the exact type of business being operated (for example, advertising agency, farm, food or beverage establishment, labor union, real estate agency, steam laundry, rental of coin-operated vending machine, or investment club). Also state if the business will involve the sale or distribution of alcoholic beverages.

Governmental. Enter the type of organization (state, county, school district, municipality, etc.).

Nonprofit organization (other than governmental). Enter whether organized for religious, educational, or humane purposes, and the principal activity (for example, religious organization—hospital, charitable).

Mining and quarrying. Specify the process and the principal product (for example, mining bituminous coal, contract drilling for oil, or quarrying dimension stone).

Contract construction. Specify whether general contracting or special trade contracting. Also, show the type of work normally performed (for example, general contractor for residential buildings or electrical subcontractor).

Food or beverage establishments. Specify the type of establishment and state whether you employ workers who receive tips (for example, lounge—yes).

Trade. Specify the type of sales and the principal line of goods sold (for example, wholesale dairy products, manufacturer's representative for mining machinery, or retail hardware).

Manufacturing. Specify the type of establishment operated (for example, sawmill or vegetable cannery).

Signature. The application must be signed by (a) the individual, if the applicant is an individual, (b) the president, vice president, or other principal officer, if the applicant is a corporation, (c) a responsible and duly authorized member or officer having knowledge of its affairs, if the applicant is a partnership or other unincorporated organization, or (d) the fiduciary, if the applicant is a trust or an estate.

How To Get Forms and Publications

Phone. You can order forms, instructions, and publications by phone 24 hours a day, 7 days a week. Just call 1-800-TAX-FORM (1-800-829-3676). You should receive your order or notification of its status within 10 workdays.

Personal computer. With your personal computer and modem, you can get the forms and information you need using IRS's Internet Web Site at **www.irs.gov** or File Transfer Protocol at **ftp.irs.gov.**

CD-ROM. For small businesses, return preparers, or others who may frequently need tax forms or publications, a CD-ROM containing over 2,000 tax products (including many prior year forms) can be purchased from the National Technical Information Service (NTIS).

To order **Pub. 1796,** Federal Tax Products on CD-ROM, call **1-877-CDFORMS** (1-877-233-6767) toll free or connect to **www.irs.gov/cdorders**

Privacy Act and Paperwork Reduction Act Notice. We ask for the information on this form to carry out the Internal Revenue laws of the United States. We need it to comply with section 6109 and the regulations thereunder which generally require the inclusion of an employer identification number (EIN) on certain returns, statements, or other documents filed with the Internal Revenue Service. Information on this form may be used to determine which Federal tax returns you are required to file and to provide you with related forms and publications. We disclose this form to the Social Security Administration for their use in determining compliance with applicable laws. We will be unable to issue an EIN to you unless you provide all of the requested information which applies to your entity.

You are not required to provide the information requested on a form that is subject to the Paperwork Reduction Act unless the form displays a valid OMB control number. Books or records relating to a form or its instructions must be retained as long as their contents may become material in the administration of any Internal Revenue law. Generally, tax returns/return information are confidential, as required by section 6103.

The time needed to complete and file this form will vary depending on individual circumstances. The estimated average time is:

Recordkeeping	7 min.
Learning about the law or the form	22 min.
Preparing the form	46 min.
Copying, assembling, and sending the form to the IRS . .	20 min.

If you have comments concerning the accuracy of these time estimates or suggestions for making this form simpler, we would be happy to hear from you. You can write to the Tax Forms Committee, Western Area Distribution Center, Rancho Cordova, CA 95743-0001. **Do not** send the form to this address. Instead, see **Where To Apply** on page 2.

U.S. Department of Justice
Immigration and Naturalization Service

OMB No. 1115-0136

Employment Eligibility Verification

INSTRUCTIONS
PLEASE READ ALL INSTRUCTIONS CAREFULLY BEFORE COMPLETING THIS FORM.

Anti-Discrimination Notice. It is illegal to discriminate against any individual (other than an alien not authorized to work in the U.S.) in hiring, discharging, or recruiting or referring for a fee because of that individual's national origin or citizenship status. It is illegal to discriminate against work eligible individuals. Employers **CANNOT** specify which document(s) they will accept from an employee. The refusal to hire an individual because of a future expiration date may also constitute illegal discrimination.

Section 1 - Employee. All employees, citizens and noncitizens, hired after November 6, 1986, must complete Section 1 of this form at the time of hire, which is the actual beginning of employment. **The employer is responsible for ensuring that Section 1 is timely and properly completed.**

Preparer/Translator Certification. The Preparer/Translator Certification must be completed if Section 1 is prepared by a person other than the employee. A preparer/translator may be used only when the employee is unable to complete Section 1 on his/her own. However, the employee must still sign Section 1.

Section 2 - Employer. For the purpose of completing this form, the term "employer" includes those recruiters and referrers for a fee who are agricultural associations, agricultural employers or farm labor contractors.

Employers must complete Section 2 by examining evidence of identity and employment eligibility within three (3) business days of the date employment begins. If employees are authorized to work, but are unable to present the required document(s) within three business days, they must present a receipt for the application of the document(s) within three business days and the actual document(s) within ninety (90) days. However, if employers hire individuals for a duration of less than three business days, Section 2 must be completed at the time employment begins. **Employers must record: 1) document title; 2) issuing authority; 3) document number, 4) expiration date, if any; and 5) the date employment begins.** Employers must sign and date the certification. Employees must present original documents. Employers may, but are not required to, photocopy the document(s) presented. These photocopies may only be used for the verification process and must be retained with the I-9. **However, employers are still responsible for completing the I-9.**

Section 3 - Updating and Reverification. Employers must complete Section 3 when updating and/or reverifying the I-9. Employers must reverify employment eligibility of their employees on or before the expiration date recorded in Section 1. Employers **CANNOT** specify which document(s) they will accept from an employee.

- If an employee's name has changed at the time this form is being updated/ reverified, complete Block A.

- If an employee is rehired within three (3) years of the date this form was originally completed and the employee is still eligible to be employed on the same basis as previously indicated on this form (updating), complete Block B and the signature block.

- If an employee is rehired within three (3) years of the date this form was originally completed and the employee's work authorization has expired **or** if a current employee's work authorization is about to expire (reverification), complete Block B and:
  - examine any document that reflects that the employee is authorized to work in the U.S. (see List A **or** C),
  - record the document title, document number and expiration date (if any) in Block C, and complete the signature block.

Photocopying and Retaining Form I-9. A blank I-9 may be reproduced, provided both sides are copied. The Instructions must be available to all employees completing this form. Employers must retain completed I-9s for three (3) years after the date of hire or one (1) year after the date employment ends, whichever is later.

For more detailed information, you may refer to the INS Handbook for Employers, (Form M-274). You may obtain the handbook at your local INS office.

Privacy Act Notice. The authority for collecting this information is the Immigration Reform and Control Act of 1986, Pub. L. 99-603 (8 USC 1324a).

This information is for employers to verify the eligibility of individuals for employment to preclude the unlawful hiring, or recruiting or referring for a fee, of aliens who are not authorized to work in the United States.

This information will be used by employers as a record of their basis for determining eligibility of an employee to work in the United States. The form will be kept by the employer and made available for inspection by officials of the U.S. Immigration and Naturalization Service, the Department of Labor and the Office of Special Counsel for Immigration Related Unfair Employment Practices.

Submission of the information required in this form is voluntary. However, an individual may not begin employment unless this form is completed, since employers are subject to civil or criminal penalties if they do not comply with the Immigration Reform and Control Act of 1986.

Reporting Burden. We try to create forms and instructions that are accurate, can be easily understood and which impose the least possible burden on you to provide us with information. Often this is difficult because some immigration laws are very complex. Accordingly, the reporting burden for this collection of information is computed as follows: **1)** learning about this form, 5 minutes; **2)** completing the form, 5 minutes; and **3)** assembling and filing (recordkeeping) the form, 5 minutes, for an average of 15 minutes per response. If you have comments regarding the accuracy of this burden estimate, or suggestions for making this form simpler, you can write to the Immigration and Naturalization Service, HQPDI, 425 I Street, N.W., Room 4307r, Washington, DC 20536. OMB No. 1115-0136.

EMPLOYERS MUST RETAIN COMPLETED FORM I-9
PLEASE DO NOT MAIL COMPLETED FORM I-9 TO INS

Form I-9 (Rev. 11-21-91)N

Employment Eligibility Verification

Please read instructions carefully before completing this form. The instructions must be available during completion of this form. ANTI-DISCRIMINATION NOTICE: It is illegal to discriminate against work eligible individuals. Employers CANNOT specify which document(s) they will accept from an employee. The refusal to hire an individual because of a future expiration date may also constitute illegal discrimination.

Section 1. Employee Information and Verification. To be completed and signed by employee at the time employment begins.

Print Name: Last	First	Middle Initial	Maiden Name

Address (Street Name and Number) | Apt. # | Date of Birth (month/day/year)

City | State | Zip Code | Social Security #

I am aware that federal law provides for imprisonment and/or fines for false statements or use of false documents in connection with the completion of this form.

I attest, under penalty of perjury, that I am (check one of the following):
- ☐ A citizen or national of the United States
- ☐ A Lawful Permanent Resident (Alien # A_____)
- ☐ An alien authorized to work until ___/___/___
  (Alien # or Admission #) _____

Employee's Signature | Date (month/day/year)

Preparer and/or Translator Certification. (To be completed and signed if Section 1 is prepared by a person other than the employee.) I attest, under penalty of perjury, that I have assisted in the completion of this form and that to the best of my knowledge the information is true and correct.

Preparer's/Translator's Signature | Print Name

Address (Street Name and Number, City, State, Zip Code) | Date (month/day/year)

Section 2. Employer Review and Verification. To be completed and signed by employer. Examine one document from List A OR examine one document from List B and one from List C, as listed on the reverse of this form, and record the title, number and expiration date, if any, of the document(s)

List A	OR	List B	AND	List C

Document title: _____

Issuing authority: _____

Document #: _____

Expiration Date (if any): ___/___/___

Document #: _____

Expiration Date (if any): ___/___/___

CERTIFICATION - I attest, under penalty of perjury, that I have examined the document(s) presented by the above-named employee, that the above-listed document(s) appear to be genuine and to relate to the employee named, that the employee began employment on (month/day/year) ___/___/___ and that to the best of my knowledge the employee is eligible to work in the United States. (State employment agencies may omit the date the employee began employment.)

Signature of Employer or Authorized Representative | Print Name | Title

Business or Organization Name | Address (Street Name and Number, City, State, Zip Code) | Date (month/day/year)

Section 3. Updating and Reverification. To be completed and signed by employer.

A. New Name (if applicable) | B. Date of rehire (month/day/year) (if applicable)

C. If employee's previous grant of work authorization has expired, provide the information below for the document that establishes current employment eligibility.

Document Title: _____ Document #: _____ Expiration Date (if any): ___/___/___

I attest, under penalty of perjury, that to the best of my knowledge, this employee is eligible to work in the United States, and if the employee presented document(s), the document(s) I have examined appear to be genuine and to relate to the individual.

Signature of Employer or Authorized Representative | Date (month/day/year)

LISTS OF ACCEPTABLE DOCUMENTS

LIST A

Documents that Establish Both Identity and Employment Eligibility

OR

1. U.S. Passport (unexpired or expired)

2. Certificate of U.S. Citizenship (INS Form N-560 or N-561)

3. Certificate of Naturalization (INS Form N-550 or N-570)

4. Unexpired foreign passport, with I-551 stamp or attached INS Form I-94 indicating unexpired employment authorization

5. Alien Registration Receipt Card with photograph (INS Form I-151 or I-551)

6. Unexpired Temporary Card (INS Form I-688)

7. Unexpired Employment Authorization Card (INS Form I-688A)

8. Unexpired Reentry Permit (INS Form I-327)

9. Unexpired Refugee Travel Document (INS Form I-571)

10. Unexpired Employment Authorization Document issued by the INS which contains a photograph (INS Form I-688B)

LIST B

Documents that Establish Identity

AND

1. Driver's license or ID card issued by a state or outlying possession of the United States provided it contains a photograph or information such as name, date of birth, sex, height, eye color and address

2. ID card issued by federal, state or local government agencies or entities, provided it contains a photograph or information such as name, date of birth, sex, height, eye color and address

3. School ID card with a photograph

4. Voter's registration card

5. U.S. Military card or draft record

6. Military dependent's ID card

7. U.S. Coast Guard Merchant Mariner Card

8. Native American tribal document

9. Driver's license issued by a Canadian government authority

For persons under age 18 who are unable to present a document listed above:

10. School record or report card

11. Clinic, doctor or hospital record

12. Day-care or nursery school record

LIST C

Documents that Establish Employment Eligibility

1. U.S. social security card issued by the Social Security Administration (other than a card stating it is not valid for employment)

2. Certification of Birth Abroad issued by the Department of State (Form FS-545 or Form DS-1350)

3. Original or certified copy of a birth certificate issued by a state, county, municipal authority or outlying possession of the United States bearing an official seal

4. Native American tribal document

5. U.S. Citizen ID Card (INS Form I-197)

6. ID Card for use of Resident Citizen in the United States (INS Form I-179)

7. Unexpired employment authorization document issued by the INS (other then those listed under List A)

Illustrations of many of these documents appear in Part 8 of the Handbook for Employers (M-274)

Form 2B: Partnership Agreement

1. Partners

_____

_____

_____

_____

(the Partners), agree to the following terms and conditions.

2. Partnership Name

The Partners will do business as a partnership under the name of _____

_____ .

3. Partnership Duration

The partnership ☐ began ☐ will begin on _____ .

It will continue

☐ indefinitely until it is ended by the terms of this agreement.

☐ until _____ , unless ended sooner by the terms of this agreement.

4. Partnership Office

The main office of the partnership will be at _____

_____ .

The mailing address will be

☐ the above address.

☐ the following address: _____

_____ .

5. Partnership Business

The primary business of the partnership is _____

_____ .

6. Capital Contributions

The Partners will contribute the following capital to the partnership on or before _____ .

A. Cash Contributions

Partner's Name	Amount
_____	$ _____
_____	$ _____
_____	$ _____
_____	$ _____

B. Non-Cash Contributions

Partner's Name	Description of Property	Value
_____	_____	$ _____
_____	_____	$ _____
_____	_____	$ _____
_____	_____	$ _____

7. Capital Accounts

The partnership will maintain a capital account for each Partner. The account will consist of the Partner's capital contribution plus the Partner's share of profits and less the Partner's share of losses and distributions to the Partner. A Partner may not remove capital from his or her account without the written consent of all Partners.

8. Profits and Losses

A. The net profits and losses of the partnership will be credited to or charged against the Partners' capital accounts

☐ in the same proportions as their capital contributions.

☐ as follows: _____.

B. The partnership will only make distributions to the Partners if all the Partners agree.

9. Salaries

No Partner will receive a salary for services to the partnership.

10. Interest

No interest will be paid on a Partner's capital account.

11. Management

Each Partner will have an equal say in managing the partnership.

☐ All significant partnership decisions will require the agreement of all the partners.

☐ Routine partnership decisions will require the agreement of a majority of the partners. The following partnership actions will require the agreement of all the Partners:

☐ borrowing or lending money

☐ signing a lease

☐ signing a contract to buy or sell real estate

☐ signing a security agreement or mortgage

☐ selling partnership assets except for goods sold in the regular course of business

☐ _____

_____

12. Partnership Funds

Partnership funds will be kept in an account at _____,
unless all Partners agree to another financial institution.

Partnership checks:

☐ may be signed by any Partner.

☐ must be signed by all the Partners.

☐ must be signed by _____ Partners.

13. Agreement to End Partnership

The Partners may unanimously agree to end the partnership.

14. Partner's Withdrawal

☐ The partnership will end if a Partner withdraws by giving written notice of such withdrawal to each of the other partners.

☐ Upon the withdrawal of a Partner, the other Partners will, within 30 days, decide either to end the partnership or buy out the withdrawing Partner's interest and continue the partnership. A decision to buy out the withdrawing Partner's interest and continue the partnership requires the unanimous consent of the remaining Partners.

15. Partner's Death

☐ The partnership will end if a Partner dies.

☐ Upon the death of a partner, the other Partners will, within 30 days, decide either to end the partnership or buy out the deceased Partner's interest and continue the partnership. A decision to buy out the withdrawing Partner's interest and continue the partnership requires the unanimous consent of the remaining Partners.

16. Buy-Out

If the remaining Partners decide to buy the interest of a withdrawing or deceased Partner under Paragraph 14 or 15, the remaining Partners, within _____ days after that Partner's withdrawal or death, will pay the withdrawing Partner or the deceased Partner's estate:

☐ The amount in the capital account of the withdrawing or deceased Partner as of the date of withdrawal or death.

☐ The fair market value of the interest of the withdrawing or deceased partner as determined by the partnership's accountant.

☐ _____

_____

17. Entire Agreement

This is the entire agreement between the parties. It replaces and supersedes any and all oral agreements between the parties, as well as any prior writings.

18. Successors and Assignees

This agreement binds and benefits the heirs, successors and assignees of the parties.

19. Notices

All notices must be in writing. A notice may be delivered to a party at the address that follows a party's signature or to a new address that a party designates in writing. A notice may be delivered:

(1) in person,
(2) by certified mail, or
(3) by overnight courier.

20. Governing Law

This agreement will be governed by and construed in accordance with the laws of the state of

_____.

21. Counterparts

The parties may sign several identical counterparts of this agreement. Any fully signed counterpart shall be treated as an original.

22. Modification

This agreement may be modified only by a writing signed by the party against whom such modification is sought to be enforced.

23. Waiver

If one party waives any term or provision of this agreement at any time, that waiver will only be effective for the specific instance and specific purpose for which the waiver was given. If either party fails to exercise or delays exercising any of its rights or remedies under this agreement, that party retains the right to enforce that term or provision at a later time.

24. Severability

If any court determines that any provision of this agreement is invalid or unenforceable, any invalidity or unenforceability will affect only that provision and will not make any other provision of this agreement invalid or unenforceable and such provision shall be modified, amended or limited only to the extent necessary to render it valid and enforceable.

Dated: _____

Signature: _____

Printed Name: _____

Address: _____

_____

Dated: _____

Signature: _____

Printed Name: _____

Address: _____

_____

Dated: _____

Signature: _____

Printed Name: _____

Address: _____

_____

Dated: _____

Signature: _____

Printed Name: _____

Address: _____

_____

Form 2C: Pre-Incorporation Agreement

1. Shareholders' Names

_____

_____

_____

_____

(the Shareholders), agree to the following terms and conditions.

2. Incorporation

The Shareholders will form a corporation under _____ law using

the Articles of Incorporation contained in Attachment _____.

☐ _____ will

sign the Articles of Incorporation as incorporator.

☐ All of the Shareholders will sign the Articles of Incorporation as incorporators.

3. Corporate Name

☐ The corporation will be called _____.

☐ The corporation may also do business under the assumed or fictitious name of _____

_____, which will be registered as required by law.

4. Corporate Purpose

The principal corporate purpose will be _____

_____

_____

5. Corporate Stock

The corporation will issue a total of _____ shares of common stock to the people listed in the next paragraph. All shares will have equal rights in voting on matters submitted to Shareholders. No additional shares will be authorized or issued unless all Shareholders agree in writing.

6. Stock Subscriptions

The Shareholders subscribe for the following shares of stock:

Name	Shares	Total Price
_____	_____	$ _____
_____	_____	$ _____
_____	_____	$ _____
_____	_____	$ _____

Payment is due upon incorporation. The corporation will issue a stock certificate to the shareholder as evidence of stock ownership.

7. Tax Status

The shares will be issued under Section 1244 of the Internal Revenue Code.

☐ The corporation will elect S Corporation status. Each Shareholder will sign the IRS election form consenting to such status.

8. Board of Directors

The Shareholders will constitute the initial Board of Directors.

9. Officers

The initial corporate officers will be:

_____ President

_____ Vice President

_____ Secretary

_____ Treasurer

10. Place of Business

The corporation's main office will be at: _____

_____.

11. Bylaws

The bylaws contained in Attachment _____ will be the bylaws of the corporation.

12. Entire Agreement

This is the entire agreement between the parties. It replaces and supersedes any and all oral agreements between the parties, as well as any prior writings.

13. Successors and Assignees

This agreement binds and benefits the heirs, successors and assignees of the parties.

14. Notices

All notices must be in writing. A notice may be delivered to a party at the address that follows a party's signature or to a new address that a party designates in writing. A notice may be delivered:

(1) in person,

(2) by certified mail, or

(3) by overnight courier.

15. Governing Law

This agreement will be governed by and construed in accordance with the laws of the state of

_____.

16. Counterparts

The parties may sign several identical counterparts of this agreement. Any fully signed counterpart shall be treated as an original.

17. Modification

This agreement may be modified only by a writing signed by the party against whom such modification is sought to be enforced.

18. Waiver

If one party waives any term or provision of this agreement at any time, that waiver will only be effective for the specific instance and specific purpose for which the waiver was given. If either party fails to exercise or delays exercising any of its rights or remedies under this agreement, that party retains the right to enforce that term or provision at a later time.

19. Severability

If any court determines that any provision of this agreement is invalid or unenforceable, any invalidity or unenforceability will affect only that provision and will not make any other provision of this agreement invalid or unenforceable and such provision shall be modified, amended or limited only to the extent necessary to render it valid and enforceable.

Dated: _____

Signature: _____

Printed Name: _____

Address: _____

_____

Dated: _____

Signature: _____

Printed Name: _____

Address: _____

_____

Dated: _____

Signature: _____

Printed Name: _____

Address: _____

_____

Dated: _____

Signature: _____

Printed Name: _____

Address: _____

_____

Form 2D: Corporate Bylaws

These are the bylaws of _____,

a _____ corporation.

Article I: Meetings of Shareholders

1.   The annual meeting of shareholders will be held on _____, _____.
     The annual meeting of shareholders will begin at _____ and will take place at the
     principal office of the corporation.

2.   At the annual meeting, the shareholders will elect a board of _____ directors and may take any other
     shareholder action permitted by state law.

3.   A special meeting of the shareholders may be called at any time by

     ☐   any shareholder

     ☐   _____ or more shareholders

     ☐   the president.

4.   At least 15 days before an annual or special meeting, the secretary will send a notice of the meeting to
     each shareholder. The notice must be sent by first-class mail and must state the time and place of the meet-
     ing. For a special meeting, the notice must also include the purposes of the meeting; no action can be taken
     at a special meeting except as stated in the notice, unless all shareholders consent.

5.   Shareholders may attend a meeting either in person or by proxy. A quorum of shareholders at any share-
     holders meeting will consist of the owners of a majority of the shares outstanding. If a quorum is present, the
     shareholders may adjourn from day to day as they see fit, and no notice of such adjournment need be
     given. If a quorum is not present, the shareholders present in person or by proxy may adjourn to such future
     time as they agree upon; notice of such adjournment must be mailed to each shareholder at least 15 days
     before such adjourned meeting.

6.   Each shareholder, whether represented in person or by proxy, is entitled to one vote for each share of stock
     standing in his or her name on the books of the company.

7.   Proxies must be in writing.

8.   Shareholders' actions require the assent of a majority of the corporate shares that have been issued, but if
     state law requires a greater number of votes, that law will prevail.

9.   Shareholders may, by written consent, take any action required or permitted to be taken at an annual or
     special meeting of shareholders. Such action may be taken without prior notice to shareholders. The written
     consent must:
     - state the action taken, and
     - be signed and dated by the owners of shares having at least the number of votes that would be
       needed to take such action at a meeting.

     If the written consent is not signed by all shareholders, the secretary will within 3 days send a copy of the
     written consent to the shareholders who did not sign it.

Article II: Stock

1. Stock certificates must be signed by the president and secretary of the corporation.

2. The name of the person owning shares represented by a stock certificate, the number of shares owned and the date of issue will be entered in the corporation's books.

3. All stock certificates transferred by endorsement must be surrendered for cancellation. New certificates will be issued to the purchaser or assignee.

4. Shares of stock can be transferred only on the books of the corporation and only by the secretary.

Article III: Board of Directors

1. The board of directors will manage the business of the corporation and will exercise all the powers that may be exercised by the corporation under the statutes of the State of _____
    _____, the articles of incorporation or the corporate bylaws.

2. A vacancy on the board of directors by reason of death, resignation or other causes may be filled by the remaining directors, or the board may leave the position unfilled, in which case it will be filled by a vote of the shareholders at a special meeting or at the next annual meeting. During periods when there is an unfilled vacancy on the board of directors, actions taken by the remaining directors will constitute actions of the board.

3. The board of directors will meet annually, immediately following the annual meeting of shareholders. The board of directors may also hold other regular meetings, at times and places to be fixed by unanimous agreement of the board. At annual or regular meetings, the board may take any actions allowed by law or these bylaws. Special meetings may be called by ☐ the president ☐ any director ☐ _____ or more directors, giving _____ days' written notice to all directors. A notice of a special meeting must be sent by first-class mail, and must state the time, place and purposes of the meeting; no action can be taken at a special meeting of directors except as stated in the notice, unless all directors consent.

4. A quorum for a meeting will consist of _____ directors.

5. Directors will act only by

    ☐ unanimous assent of the directors

    ☐ the assent of a majority of those directors present

    ☐ the assent of at least _____ directors.

6. The directors will not be compensated for serving as such. A director may, however, serve in other capacities with the corporation and receive compensation for such service.

7. Directors may, by written consent, take any action required or permitted to be taken at a directors' meeting. Such action may be taken without prior notice to the directors. The written consent must:
    *   state the action taken, and
    *   be signed and dated by at least the number of directors whose votes would be needed to take such action at a meeting.
    If the written consent is not signed by all directors, the secretary will within three days send a copy of the written consent to the directors who did not sign it.

8. Directors may meet or participate in meetings by telephone or other electronic means as long as all directors are continuously able to communicate with one another.

Article IV: Officers

1. The officers of the corporation will consist of a:

    ☐ president

    ☐ vice president

    ☐ secretary

    ☐ treasurer

    ☐ secretary-treasurer

    and such other officers as the board of directors may appoint.

2. The president will preside at all meetings of the directors and shareholders, and will have general charge of the business of the corporation, subject to approval of the board of directors.

3. In case of the death, disability or absence of the president, the ☐ vice president ☐ secretary will perform and be vested with all the duties and powers of the president.

4. The secretary will keep the corporate records, including minutes of shareholders' and directors' meetings and consent resolutions. The secretary will give notice, as required in these bylaws, of shareholders' and directors' meetings.

5. The treasurer will keep accounts of all moneys of the corporation received or disbursed, and will deposit all moneys and valuables in the name of the corporation in the banks and depositories that the directors designate. Checks against company accounts will be signed as directed by the board of directors.

6. The salaries of all officers will be fixed by the board of directors and may be changed from time to time by the board of directors.

Article V: Fiscal

1. The books of the corporation will be closed at a date to be selected by the directors prior to the filing of the first income tax return due from the corporation. The books will be kept on a ☐ cash ☐ accrual basis.

2. Within 75 days after the corporation's fiscal year ends, the treasurer will provide each shareholder with a financial statement for the corporation.

Article VI: Amendments

Any of these bylaws may be amended or repealed by a majority vote of the shareholders at any annual meeting or at any special meeting called for that purpose.

Adopted on: _____,

By: _____

Printed Name: _____

By: _____

Printed Name: _____

By: _____

Printed Name: _____

By: _____

Printed Name: _____

By: _____

Printed Name: _____

Form 2E: Stock Agreement

1. Names

_____

_____

_____

_____

_____

_____

(Shareholders), and _____

(Corporation) agree to the following:

2. Restrictions on Sale of Stock

Shareholders will sell their stock in _____

_____ only as stated in this agreement.

3. Offer to Corporation

A Shareholder who receives a good faith written offer to purchase all or part of his or her shares will offer the Corporation the opportunity to buy the shares on the same terms and will give the Corporation a copy of the offer he or she has received. The Corporation, through its board of directors, will have ten days from the time it receives written notice from a Shareholder to decide whether the Corporation will buy the shares.

4. Offer to Shareholders

If the Corporation does not buy the shares, the selling Shareholder will offer the remaining Shareholders (in writing and on a pro-rata basis) the opportunity to buy the shares on the same terms and will give the remaining Shareholders a copy of the offer he or she has received. The remaining Shareholders will have ten days from the time they receive written notice from the selling Shareholder to decide whether to buy the shares on a pro-rata basis or such other basis as the remaining Shareholders may agree upon.

5. Remaining Shares

If any shares are not bought by the Corporation or the remaining Shareholders, the selling Shareholder may sell those shares to the person who made the bona fide offer to purchase. The terms will be the same as offered to the Corporation and other Shareholders. Any sale to the person who made the bona fide offer must take place within 30 days after the procedures described in Sections 3 and 4 have been concluded, or such sale will be invalid.

6. Continuing Effect

Anyone who becomes an owner of shares of stock in the Corporation will be bound by this agreement. The following will be endorsed on all stock certificates:

"The transfer of shares represented by this certificate is subject to the terms of a stock agreement signed by the Shareholders and the Corporation, dated _____.

A copy is on file with the corporate Secretary."

7. Death of Shareholder

Upon the death of a Shareholder, the Corporation will, within 180 days, buy the deceased Shareholder's shares from the deceased Shareholder's estate. The amount to be paid will be:

☐ The fair market value of the deceased Shareholder's shares as determined by the Corporation's accountant.

☐ _____

_____

    The Corporation will buy and maintain insurance on the life of each Shareholder in an amount sufficient to pay for the shares of a Shareholder who dies. Life insurance proceeds that exceed the purchase price of the shares will belong to the Corporation.

8. Entire Agreement

This is the entire agreement between the parties. It replaces and supersedes any and all oral agreements between the parties, as well as any prior writings.

9. Successors and Assignees

This agreement binds and benefits the heirs, successors and assignees of the parties.

10. Notices

All notices must be in writing. A notice may be delivered to a party at the address that follows a party's signature or to a new address that a party designates in writing. A notice may be delivered:

(1) in person,

(2) by certified mail, or

(3) by overnight courier.

11. Governing Law

This agreement will be governed by and construed in accordance with the laws of the state of

_____.

12. Counterparts

The parties may sign several identical counterparts of this agreement. Any fully signed counterpart shall be treated as an original.

13. Modification

This agreement may be modified only by a writing signed by the party against whom such modification is sought to be enforced.

14. Waiver

If one party waives any term or provision of this agreement at any time, that waiver will only be effective for the specific instance and specific purpose for which the waiver was given. If either party fails to exercise or delays exercising any of its rights or remedies under this agreement, that party retains the right to enforce that term or provision at a later time.

15. Severability

If any court determines that any provision of this agreement is invalid or unenforceable, any invalidity or unenforceability will affect only that provision and will not make any other provision of this agreement invalid or unenforceable and such provision shall be modified, amended or limited only to the extent necessary to render it valid and enforceable.

Dated: _____

Signature: _____

Printed Name: _____

Address: _____

_____

Dated: _____

Signature: _____

Printed Name: _____

Address: _____

_____

Dated: _____

Signature: _____

Printed Name: _____

Address: _____

_____

Dated: _____

Signature: _____

Printed Name: _____

Address: _____

Dated: _____

Name of Business: _____

a _____

By: _____

Printed Name and Title: _____

Address: _____

_____

Form 2F: LLC Operating Agreement for Single-Member LLC

1. Names

This operating agreement is made by _____

_____, a _____ limited liability company, the Company,

and _____,

the Member.

2. Formation

The Company has been formed under the _____ statute authorizing the formation

of limited liability companies. The purpose of the Company is stated in the Articles of Organization.

3. Offices

The Company will have one or more offices at places the Member designates. The initial registered office

of the Company is located at _____

_____

and the Member is the resident agent.

4. Management

The Member has the right to manage the Company's business. The Member may delegate to another
person the authority to perform specified acts on behalf of the Company.

☐ If the Member dies or is unable to act, the Company will be managed by _____

_____ or by the person

the Member last designates in writing to manage the Company. That person will have full authority to

manage the Company until the Member can do so.

5. Capital Contributions

The Member will contribute

☐ $_____

☐ the following property: _____

_____

to the Company in exchange for the Member's interest in the Company. The Member will not be paid
interest on this capital contribution.

6. Taxes

For federal tax purposes, the Company will be taxed

☐ as a sole proprietorship, with profits and losses passing through to the Member.

☐ a corporation.

7. Funds

The Member will determine the financial institution that will hold Company funds and will determine the authorized signatures on Company accounts.

8. Additional Members

The Company may admit one or more additional members upon such terms as are determined by the Company and the Member. If new members are admitted, the Articles of Organization and the Operating Agreement will be appropriately amended.

9. Distributions

The Member will determine when and how cash and other assets of the Company will be distributed.

Dated: _____

Name of Business: _____,

a Limited Liability Company

By: _____, Member

Printed Name: _____

Title: _____

Address: _____

_____

Form 3A: Notice of Shareholders' Meeting

To the Shareholders of _____ :

A(n) ☐ annual ☐ regular ☐ special   meeting of shareholders will be held as follows:

1. Date: _____

2. Time: _____

3. Place: _____

4. Purposes: _____

_____

_____

_____

_____

_____

_____

_____

    ☐ To transact any other business that properly comes before the meeting.

5. This special meeting has been called by:

    ☐ the president: _____

    ☐ other authorized officer: _____

    ☐ the following shareholders: _____

_____

_____

_____

_____

Dated: _____

Signature: _____

Printed Name of Secretary: _____

Secretary of _____

Form 3B: Notice of Directors' Meeting

To the Directors of _____ :

A(n) ☐ annual ☐ regular ☐ special   meeting of directors will be held as follows:

1. Date: _____

2. Time: _____

3. Place: _____

4. Purposes: _____

_____

_____

_____

_____

_____

_____

_____

_____

   ☐ To transact any other business that properly comes before the meeting.

5. This special meeting has been called by:

   ☐ the president: _____

   ☐ other authorized officer: _____

   ☐ the following directors: _____

_____

_____

_____

_____

Dated: _____

Signature: _____

Printed Name of Secretary: _____

Secretary of _____

Form 3C: Shareholder Proxy

I appoint _____

as my proxy to vote all of my shares of stock of _____

_____ at the ☐ regular ☐ special ☐ annual   meeting of shareholders to

be held on _____.

Dated: _____

Signature: _____

Printed Name: _____

Address: _____

_____

Form 3D: Minutes of Shareholders' Meeting

The shareholders of _____

held a(n) ☐ annual ☐ special ☐ regular meeting on _____ at _____.

The meeting began at _____ and ended at _____.

Notice

A copy of the notice of the meeting sent on _____ to each director by

☐ first-class mail ☐ certified mail is attached.

Quorum

The following persons, constituting a quorum, were present in person or by proxy:

_____

_____

_____

_____

Actions Taken

The shareholders took the following actions:

1. The minutes of the ☐ annual ☐ special ☐ regular shareholders' meeting held on _____

   _____ were approved.

2. _____

   _____

   _____

3. _____

   _____

   _____

4. _____

   _____

   _____

Dated: _____

Signature: _____

Printed Name of Secretary: _____

Secretary of _____

Form 3E: Minutes of Directors' Meeting

The directors of _____

held a(n) ☐ annual   ☐ special   ☐ regular   meeting on _____ at _____.

The meeting began at _____ and ended at _____.

Notice

A copy of the notice of the meeting sent on _____ to each director by

☐ first-class mail   ☐ certified mail   is attached.

Quorum

The following directors, constituting a quorum, were present:

_____

_____

_____

_____

Actions Taken

The directors took the following actions:

1. The minutes of the directors' meeting held on _____ were approved.

2. _____

_____

_____

3. _____

_____

_____

4. _____

_____

_____

5. _____

_____

_____

Dated: _____

Signature: _____

Printed Name of Secretary: _____

Secretary of _____

Form 3F: Minutes of Telephone Conference Directors' Meeting

The directors of _____

held a meeting by telephone conference on _____.

    The meeting began at _____ and ended at _____. Throughout the meeting, the directors

could remain in voice contact with one another.

    The directors took the following actions:

_____

_____

_____

_____

_____

_____

_____

_____

_____

_____

_____

_____

_____

_____

_____

_____

_____

_____

_____

_____

Dated: _____

Signature: _____

Printed Name of Secretary: _____

Secretary of _____

Form 3G: Consent of Shareholders

The shareholders of _____
consent to the following:

_____

_____

_____

_____

_____

_____

_____

_____

_____

_____

_____

_____

_____

_____

_____

_____

_____

_____

_____

_____

Dated: _____

Signature: _____

Printed Name: _____

Signature: _____

Printed Name: _____

Signature: _____

Printed Name: _____

Signature: _____

Printed Name: _____

Form 3H: Consent of Directors

The directors of _____
consent to the following:

_____

_____

_____

_____

_____

_____

_____

_____

_____

_____

_____

_____

_____

_____

_____

_____

_____

_____

_____

_____

_____

_____

_____

_____

_____

_____

Dated: _____

Signature: _____

Printed Name: _____

Signature: _____

Printed Name: _____

Form 4C: Promissory Note
(Equal Monthly Installments; All Principal and Interest Paid)

1. Names

Borrower:_____

Lender: _____

2. Promise to Pay

For value received, Borrower promises to pay Lender $_____ and interest at the

yearly rate of _____% on the unpaid balance as specified below.

3. Monthly Installments

Borrower will pay _____ monthly installments of $_____ each.

4. Date of Installment Payments

Borrower will make an installment payment on the _____ day of each month beginning

_____ until the principal and interest have been paid in full.

5. Application of Payments

Payments will be applied first to interest and then to principal.

6. Prepayment

Borrower may prepay all or any part of the principal without penalty.

7. Loan Acceleration

If Borrower is more than _____ days late in making any payment, Lender may declare that the

entire balance of unpaid principal is due immediately, together with the interest that has accrued.

8. Security

☐ This is an unsecured note.

☐ Borrower agrees that until the principal and interest owed under this promissory note are paid in full,
this note will be secured by a security agreement and Uniform Commercial Code financing statement
giving Lender a security interest in the equipment, fixtures, inventory and accounts receivable of the

business known as _____

_____.

☐ Borrower agrees that until the principal and interest owed under this promissory note are paid in full,
this note will be secured by the

   ☐ mortgage

   ☐ deed of trust

covering the real estate commonly known as _____

and more fully described as follows: _____

_____

_____.

9. Collection Costs

If Lender prevails in a lawsuit to collect on this note, Borrower will pay Lender's costs and lawyer's fees in an amount the court finds to be reasonable.

10. Entire Agreement

This is the entire agreement between the parties. It replaces and supersedes any and all oral agreements between the parties, as well as any prior writings.

11. Successors and Assignees

This note binds and benefits the heirs, successors and assignees of the parties.

12. Notices

All notices must be in writing. A notice may be delivered to a party at the address that follows a party's signature or to a new address that a party designates in writing. A notice may be delivered:

    (1) in person,

    (2) by certified mail, or

    (3) by overnight courier.

13. Governing Law

This note will be governed by and construed in accordance with the laws of the state of _____

_____ .

14. Modification

This note may only be modified by a writing signed by the party against whom such modification is sought to be enforced.

15. Waiver

If one party waives any term or provision of this note at any time, that waiver will only be effective for the specific instance and specific purpose for which the waiver was given. If either party fails to exercise or delays exercising any of its rights or remedies under this note, that party retains the right to enforce that term or provision at a later time.

16. Severability

If any court determines that any provision of this note is invalid or unenforceable, any invalidity or unenforceability will affect only that provision and will not make any other provision of this note invalid or unenforceable and such provision shall be modified, amended or limited only to the extent necessary to render it valid and enforceable.

Signature

Dated: _____

Name of Business: _____

a _____

By: _____

Printed Name and Title: _____

Address: _____

Form 4D: Promissory Note
(Equal Monthly Payments; Large Final Balloon Payment)

1. Names

Borrower: _____

Lender: _____

2. Promise to Pay

For value received, Borrower promises to pay Lender $_____ and interest at the

yearly rate of _____% on the unpaid balance as specified below.

3. Monthly Installments

Borrower will pay _____ monthly installments of $_____ each.

4. Date of Payments

Borrower will make an installment payment on the _____ day of each month beginning

_____. On or before _____, Borrower will

make a lump-sum payment for the entire balance of accrued principal and interest.

5. Application of Payments

Payments will be applied first to interest and then to principal.

6. Prepayment

Borrower may prepay all or any part of the principal without penalty.

7. Loan Acceleration

If Borrower is more than _____ days late in making any payment, Lender may declare that the
entire balance of unpaid principal is due immediately, together with the interest that has accrued.

8. Security

☐ This is an unsecured note.

☐ Borrower agrees that until the principal and interest owed under this promissory note are paid in full,
this note will be secured by a security agreement and Uniform Commercial Code financing statement
giving Lender a security interest in the equipment, fixtures, inventory and accounts receivable of the
business known as _____.

☐ Borrower agrees that until the principal and interest owed under this promissory note are paid in full,
this note will be secured by the

   ☐ mortgage

   ☐ deed of trust

covering the real estate commonly known as _____

and more fully described as follows: _____

_____

9. Collection Costs

If Lender prevails in a lawsuit to collect on this note, Borrower will pay Lender's costs and lawyer's fees in an amount the court finds to be reasonable.

10. Entire Agreement

This is the entire agreement between the parties. It replaces and supersedes any and all oral agreements between the parties, as well as any prior writings.

11. Successors and Assignees

This note binds and benefits the heirs, successors and assignees of the parties.

12. Notices

All notices must be in writing. A notice may be delivered to a party at the address that follows a party's signature or to a new address that a party designates in writing. A notice may be delivered:

    (1) in person,

    (2) by certified mail, or

    (3) by overnight courier.

13. Governing Law

This note will be governed by and construed in accordance with the laws of the state of _____ _____.

14. Modification

This note may only be modified by a writing signed by the party against whom such modification is sought to be enforced.

15. Waiver

If one party waives any term or provision of this note at any time, that waiver will only be effective for the specific instance and specific purpose for which the waiver was given. If either party fails to exercise or delays exercising any of its rights or remedies under this note, that party retains the right to enforce that term or provision at a later time.

16. Severability

If any court determines that any provision of this note is invalid or unenforceable, any invalidity or unenforceability will affect only that provision and will not make any other provision of this note invalid or unenforceable and such provision shall be modified, amended or limited only to the extent necessary to render it valid and enforceable.

Signature

Dated: _____

Name of Business: _____

a _____

By: _____

Printed Name and Title: _____

Address: _____

Form 4E: Promissory Note
(Payments of Interest Only; Large Final Balloon Payment)

1. Names

Borrower:_____

Lender: _____

2. Promise to Pay

For value received, Borrower promises to pay Lender $_____ and interest at the

yearly rate of _____% on the unpaid balance as specified below.

3. Interest Payments

(Choose One)

☐ Borrower will pay interest on _____ of each year beginning in _____.

☐ Borrower will pay interest on the _____ day of each month beginning _____.

☐ Borrower will pay interest as follows: _____

_____

4. Principal Payment

Borrower will pay the principal in full on or before _____, together with any

accrued interest.

5. Prepayment

Borrower may prepay all or any part of the principal without penalty.

6. Loan Acceleration

If Borrower is more than _____ days late in making any payment, Lender may declare that the

entire balance of unpaid principal is due immediately, together with the interest that has accrued.

7. Security

☐ This is an unsecured note.

☐ Borrower agrees that until the principal and interest owed under this promissory note are paid in full,
this note will be secured by a security agreement and Uniform Commercial Code financing statement
giving Lender a security interest in the equipment, fixtures, inventory and accounts receivable of the

business known as _____.

☐ Borrower agrees that until the principal and interest owed under this promissory note are paid in full,
this note will be secured by the

   ☐ mortgage

   ☐ deed of trust

covering the real estate commonly known as _____

and more fully described as follows: _____

_____

8. Collection Costs

If Lender prevails in a lawsuit to collect on this note, Borrower will pay Lender's costs and lawyer's fees in an amount the court finds to be reasonable.

9. Entire Agreement

This is the entire agreement between the parties. It replaces and supersedes any and all oral agreements between the parties, as well as any prior writings.

10. Successors and Assignees

This note binds and benefits the heirs, successors and assignees of the parties.

11. Notices

All notices must be in writing. A notice may be delivered to a party at the address that follows a party's signature or to a new address that a party designates in writing. A notice may be delivered:

    (1) in person,

    (2) by certified mail, or

    (3) by overnight courier.

12. Governing Law

This note will be governed by and construed in accordance with the laws of the state of _____

_____.

13. Modification

This note may only be modified by a writing signed by the party against whom such modification is sought to be enforced.

14. Waiver

If one party waives any term or provision of this note at any time, that waiver will only be effective for the specific instance and specific purpose for which the waiver was given. If either party fails to exercise or delays exercising any of its rights or remedies under this note, that party retains the right to enforce that term or provision at a later time.

15. Severability

If any court determines that any provision of this note is invalid or unenforceable, any invalidity or unenforceability will affect only that provision and will not make any other provision of this note invalid or unenforceable and such provision shall be modified, amended or limited only to the extent necessary to render it valid and enforceable.

Signature

Dated: _____

Name of Business: _____

a _____

By: _____

Printed Name and Title: _____

Address: _____

_____

NOLO
www.nolo.com   **Form 4E: Promissory Note**
(Payments of Interest Only; Large Final Balloon Payment)   Page 2 of 2

Form 4F: Promissory Note
(Single Payment of Principal and Interest)

1. Names

Borrower:_____

Lender: _____

2. Promise to Pay

For value received, Borrower promises to pay Lender $_____ and interest at the

yearly rate of _____% on the unpaid balance as specified below.

3. Payment Date

Borrower will pay the entire amount of principal and interest on or before _____.

4. Prepayment

Borrower may prepay all or any part of the principal without penalty.

5. Security

☐ This is an unsecured note.

☐ Borrower agrees that until the principal and interest owed under this promissory note are paid in full, this note will be secured by a security agreement and Uniform Commercial Code financing statement giving Lender a security interest in the equipment, fixtures, inventory and accounts receivable of the business known as _____.

☐ Borrower agrees that until the principal and interest owed under this promissory note are paid in full, this note will be secured by the

   ☐ mortgage

   ☐ deed of trust

covering the real estate commonly known as _____

and more fully described as follows: _____

_____

_____

6. Collection Costs

If Lender prevails in a lawsuit to collect on this note, Borrower will pay Lender's costs and lawyer's fees in an amount the court finds to be reasonable.

7. Entire Agreement

This is the entire agreement between the parties. It replaces and supersedes any and all oral agreements between the parties, as well as any prior writings.

8. Successors and Assignees

This note binds and benefits the heirs, successors and assignees of the parties.

9. Notices

All notices must be in writing. A notice may be delivered to a party at the address that follows a party's signature or to a new address that a party designates in writing. A notice may be delivered:

(1) in person,

(2) by certified mail, or

(3) by overnight courier.

10. Governing Law

This note will be governed by and construed in accordance with the laws of the state of _____

_____.

11. Modification

This note may only be modified by a writing signed by the party against whom such modification is sought to be enforced.

12. Waiver

If one party waives any term or provision of this note at any time, that waiver will only be effective for the specific instance and specific purpose for which the waiver was given. If either party fails to exercise or delays exercising any of its rights or remedies under this note, that party retains the right to enforce that term or provision at a later time.

13. Severability

If any court determines that any provision of this note is invalid or unenforceable, any invalidity or unenforceability will affect only that provision and will not make any other provision of this note invalid or unenforceable and such provision shall be modified, amended or limited only to the extent necessary to render it valid and enforceable.

Signature

Dated: _____

Name of Business: _____

a _____

By: _____

Printed Name and Title: _____

Address: _____

_____

Form 4G: Security Agreement
(For Tangible Personal Property)

1. Names

This Security Agreement is between _____,

Borrower, and _____, Lender.

2. Grant of Security Interest

Borrower grants to Lender a continuing security interest in the following property (the "Secured Property"), the Secured Property which consists of:

☐ The tangible personal property owned by Borrower's business known as _____

_____, as listed in attached Attachment 1.

☐ Any additional tangible personal property that Borrower now owns or later acquires in connection with Borrower's business, including replacement inventory.

☐ _____

_____.

3. Security for Promissory Note

Borrower is granting this security interest to secure performance of a promissory note dated _____

_____ that Borrower executed in favor of Lender. The promissory note obligates Borrower

to pay Lender $_____ with interest at the rate of _____% a year, on the terms stated

in the promissory note.

4. Financing Statement

Concurrently with the execution of this Security Agreement, Borrower will sign a financing statement and other documents that Lender reasonably requests to protect Lender's security interest in the Secured Property.

5. Use and Care of the Secured Property

Until the promissory note is fully paid, Borrower agrees to:

A. Keep at _____

the Secured Property owned by the Borrower's business and use it only in the operation of the business.

B. Maintain the Secured Property in good repair.

C. Not sell, transfer or release the Secured Property unless Lender consents. Borrower may sell inventory in the ordinary course of Borrower's business, but will reasonably renew and replenish inventory to keep it at its current level.

D. Pay all taxes on the Secured Property as taxes become due.

E. Insure the Secured Property against normal risks, with an insurance policy that names Borrower and Lender as beneficiaries as their interests appear.

F. Deliver to Lender a copy of the insurance policy insuring the Secured Property and annual proof to Lender that Borrower has paid the premiums on the policy.

G. Allow Lender to inspect the Secured Property at any reasonable time.

6. Borrower's Default

If Borrower is more than _____ days late in making any payment required by the promissory note or if

Borrower fails to correct any violations of paragraph 5 of this Security Agreement within _____ days

of receiving written notice from Lender, Borrower will be in default.

7. Lender's Rights

If Borrower is in default, Lender may exercise the remedies contained in the Uniform Commercial Code for

the State of _____ and any other remedies legally available to

Lender. Lender may, for example:

    A. Remove the Secured Property from the place where it is then located.

    B. Require Borrower to make the Secured Property available to Lender at a place designated by Lender
       that is reasonably convenient to Borrower and Lender.

    C. Sell, lease or otherwise dispose of the Secured Property.

8. Notice to Borrower

Lender will give Borrower at least ten days notice of when and where the Secured Property will be sold,
leased or otherwise disposed of. Any notice required by this paragraph or by statute will be deemed given
to Borrower if sent by first-class mail to Borrower at the following address:

_____

_____

_____

9. Entire Agreement

This is the entire agreement between the parties. It replaces and supersedes any and all oral agreements
between the parties, as well as any prior writings.

10. Successors and Assignees

This agreement binds and benefits the heirs, successors and assignees of the parties.

11. Governing Law

This agreement will be governed by and construed in accordance with the laws of the state of _____

_____.

12. Counterparts

The parties may sign several identical counterparts of this agreement. Any fully signed counterpart shall be
treated as an original.

13. Modification

This agreement may be modified only by a writing signed by the party against whom such modification is
sought to be enforced.

14. Waiver

If one party waives any term or provision of this agreement at any time, that waiver will only be effective for
the specific instance and specific purpose for which the waiver was given. If either party fails to exercise or
delays exercising any of its rights or remedies under this agreement, that party retains the right to enforce
that term or provision at a later time.

15. Severability

If any court determines that any provision of this agreement is invalid or unenforceable, any invalidity or unenforceability will affect only that provision and will not make any other provision of this agreement invalid or unenforceable and such provision shall be modified, amended or limited only to the extent necessary to render it valid and enforceable.

Signatures

Dated: _____

LENDER

Name of Business: _____

a _____

By: _____

Printed Name and Title: _____

Address: _____

_____

BORROWER

Name of Business: _____

a _____

By: _____

Printed Name and Title: _____

Address: _____

_____

Attachment to Security Agreement

Attachment Number _____

1. Names

This attachment is made by _____,

Borrower, and _____, Lender.

2. Terms of Attachment

We agree that the tangible personal property covered by paragraph 2 of our Security Agreement dated

_____ includes the following:

_____

_____

_____

_____

_____

_____

_____

_____

_____

_____

_____

Dated: _____

Name of Business: _____

a _____

By: _____

Printed Name and Title: _____

Address: _____

_____

Name of Business: _____

a _____

By: _____

Printed Name and Title: _____

Address: _____

_____

Form 5A: Contract for Purchase of Business Assets From a Sole Proprietorship, Partnership or Limited Liability Company

1. Names

_____, Seller,

and _____,

Buyer, agree to the following sale.

2. Sale of Business Assets

Seller is selling to Buyer and Buyer is buying from Seller the assets of the business known as _____

_____ located at _____

_____.

3. Assets Being Sold

The assets being sold consist of:

☐ A. The goodwill of the business, including the current business name and phone number.

☐ B. The lease dated _____, between _____

_____, Seller, and _____

_____, Landlord, covering the premises at _____

_____.

☐ C. The inventory of goods.

☐ D. The furniture, fixtures and equipment listed in attached Schedule A.

☐ E. The equipment leases listed in attached Schedule B.

☐ F. Other: _____

4. Purchase Price

The purchase price is $_____, allocated as follows:

A. Goodwill $_____

B. Assignment of lease $_____

C. Furniture, fixtures and equipment $_____

D. Other: _____ $_____

Total $_____

☐ The total purchase price will be adjusted by prorating rent, taxes, insurance premiums, utility costs and security deposits as of the date of closing.

☐ The total purchase price will also be adjusted at closing by adding the price of the inventory as covered in paragraph 5.

NOLO
www.nolo.com

Form 5A: Contract for Purchase of Business Assets From a Sole Proprietorship, Partnership or Limited Liability Company Page 1 of 8

5. Price of Inventory *(Optional)*

At closing, in addition to the total purchase price listed in paragraph 4, Buyer will buy the inventory by paying Seller the amount Seller paid for those goods. A physical count of the goods will be made by:

☐   Seller and Buyer.

☐   an inventory service company mutually agreed upon by Seller and Buyer.

The count will be made _____ days before closing and will include only unopened and undamaged goods. If an inventory service company is used, Seller and Buyer will share the cost of the service equally.

☐   Buyer will pay no more than $ _____ for the goods.

6. Accounts Receivable

☐   Seller's accounts receivable will remain Seller's property. Buyer will within ten days send Seller the proceeds of any of Seller's accounts receivable that Buyer may collect after closing.

☐   At closing, Buyer will purchase all of Seller's accounts receivable that are no more than _____ days old. Buyer will pay Seller the balances owed on these accounts less _____%.

7. Deposit

Buyer will pay Seller a deposit of $_____ when Buyer and Seller sign this contract. This amount will be applied toward the amount listed in paragraph 4. Seller will return this deposit to Buyer if the purchase is not completed because Seller cannot or does not meet its commitments.

8. Payments at Closing

At closing, Buyer will pay Seller the following amounts, using a cashier's check:

☐ $_____ to be applied toward the amount listed in paragraph 4.

☐   The value of the inventory as determined under paragraph 5.

☐   The value of the accounts receivable as determined under paragraph 6.

9. Promissory Note

At closing, Buyer will give Seller a promissory note for the balance of the purchase price. The promissory note will be signed by Buyer.

☐   Buyer is a Sole Proprietor. _____ will sign the promissory note along with Buyer. Each signer will be jointly and individually liable for payment.

☐   Buyer is a Partnership. Each partner will co-sign the promissory note and will be jointly and individually liable for payment.

☐   Buyer is a Corporation or Limited Liability Company. The following people will personally guarantee the promissory note and will be jointly and individually liable for payment: _____

_____.

The promissory note will contain the following terms:

A.   The unpaid balance will be subject to interest at the rate of _____% a year.

B.   Buyer will pay $_____ on the _____ day of each month beginning one month after the closing until the principal and interest have been paid in full.

C.   The entire amount of principal and interest will be paid by _____.

D. Payments will be applied first to interest and then to principal.

E. Buyer may prepay all or any part of the principal without penalty.

F. If Buyer is more than _____ days late in making a payment, Seller may declare that the entire balance of the unpaid principal is due immediately, together with the interest that has accrued.

10. Security for Payment

At closing, to secure the payment of the promissory note, Buyer will sign a security agreement and UCC financing statement giving Seller a security interest in:

☐ The assets that Buyer is purchasing.

☐ The lease that is being assigned to Buyer.

11. Seller's Debts

Buyer is not assuming any of Seller's debts or liabilities. At or before closing, Seller will pay all debts and liabilities that are or may become a lien on the assets being bought by Buyer.

At closing, Seller will confirm in an affidavit (Attachment ____) that Seller has paid all debts and liabilities of the business, including those that are known and those that are in dispute.

12. Closing

The closing will take place:

Date: _____

Time: _____

Location: _____

At closing, Buyer and Seller will sign the documents specified in this contract and all other documents reasonably needed to transfer the business assets to Buyer. Buyer will pay Seller the amounts required by this contract and Seller will transfer the business assets to Buyer.

☐ **Spouse's Signature (Community Property States).** At closing, the spouse of the sole proprietor Seller will also sign the documents specified in this contract and all other documents reasonably needed to transfer the business assets to Buyer.

13. Documents for Transferring Assets

At closing, Seller will deliver to Buyer these signed documents:

☐ A. A bill of sale for the tangible assets being bought, with a warranty of good title.

☐ B. An assignment of the lease, with the landlord's written consent.

☐ C. Assignment of any other contracts that are being transferred to Buyer, with the written consent of the other contracting person, if such consent is required.

☐ D. Assignments of all trademarks, patents and copyrights that are part of this purchase.

Seller will also deliver to Buyer at closing all other documents reasonably needed to transfer the business assets to Buyer.

14. Seller's Representations

Seller warrants and represents that:

A. Seller has good and marketable title to the assets being sold. The assets will be free from encumbrances at closing.

B. At closing, Seller will have paid all taxes affecting the business and its assets.

C. There are no judgments, claims, liens or proceedings pending against Seller, the business or the assets being sold and none will be pending at closing.

D. Seller has given Buyer complete and accurate information, in writing, about the earnings of the business, its assets and liabilities, and its financial condition.

E. Until closing, Seller will not enter into any new contracts or incur any new obligations and will continue to conduct its business in a normal manner.

F. Other: _____

_____

_____ .

These warranties and representations will survive the closing.

15. Buyer's Representations

Buyer warrants and represents that:

A. Buyer has inspected the tangible assets that Buyer is purchasing and the premises covered by the lease, and is satisfied with their condition except for: _____

_____ .

B. Buyer has given Seller accurate information about Buyer's financial condition.
These warranties and representations will survive the closing.

16. Covenant Not to Compete

☐ **Seller Is a Sole Proprietor.** For _____ [years/months] following the closing, Seller will not directly or indirectly participate in a business that is similar to a business now or later operated by Buyer in the same geographical area. This includes participating in Seller's own business or as a co-owner, director, officer, consultant, independent contractor, employee or agent of another business.

In particular, Seller will not:

(a) solicit or attempt to solicit any business or trade from Buyer's actual or prospective customers or clients;

(b) employ or attempt to employ any employee of Buyer;

(c) divert or attempt to divert business away from Buyer; or

(d) encourage any independent contractor or consultant to end a relationship with Buyer. Seller acknowledges and agrees that if Seller breaches or threatens to breach any of the terms of this paragraph 16, Buyer will sustain irreparable harm and will be entitled to obtain an injunction to stop any breach or threatened breach of this paragraph 16.

Seller, by signing this agreement, accepts and agrees to be bound by this covenant not to compete.

At closing, Buyer will pay Seller $_____ for this covenant not to compete.

☐ **Seller Is a Partnership.** The partners named at the end of this contract are all of Seller's partners.

For _____ [years/months] following the closing, none of Seller's partners will directly or indirectly participate in a business that is similar to a business now or later operated by Buyer in the same geographical area. This includes participating in a partner's own business or as a co-owner, director, officer, consultant, independent contractor, employee or agent of another business.

In particular, none of the partners of Seller will:

NOLO
www.nolo.com

Form 5A: Contract for Purchase of Business Assets From a Sole Proprietorship, Partnership or Limited Liability Company Page 4 of 8

(a) solicit or attempt to solicit any business or trade from Buyer's actual or prospective customers or clients;

(b) employ or attempt to employ any employee of Buyer;

(c) divert or attempt to divert business away from Buyer, or

(d) encourage any independent contractor or consultant to end a relationship with Buyer. Each partner of Seller acknowledges and agrees that if any partner of Seller breaches or threatens to breach any of the terms of this paragraph 16, Buyer will sustain irreparable harm and will be entitled to obtain an injunction to stop any breach or threatened breach of this paragraph 16.

Each partner, by signing this contract, accepts and agrees to be bound by this covenant not to compete. At closing, Buyer will pay each partner $_____ for his or her covenant not to compete.

☐ **Seller Is a Limited Liability Company (LLC).** The members named at the end of this contract are all of Seller's members. For _____ [years/months] following the closing, none of Seller's members will directly or indirectly participate in a business that is similar to a business now or later operated by Buyer in the same geographical area. This includes participating in a member's own business or as a co-owner, director, officer, consultant, independent contractor, employee or agent of another business.

In particular, none of the members of Seller will:

(a) solicit or attempt to solicit any business or trade from Buyer's actual or prospective customers or clients;

(b) employ or attempt to employ any employee of Buyer;

(c) divert or attempt to divert business away from Buyer; or

(d) encourage any independent contractor or consultant to end a relationship with Buyer. Each member of Seller acknowledges and agrees that if any member of Seller breaches or threatens to breach any of the terms of this paragraph 16, Buyer will sustain irreparable harm and will be entitled to obtain an injunction to stop any breach or threatened breach of this paragraph 16.

Each member, by signing this contract, accepts and agrees to be bound by this covenant not to compete. At closing, Buyer will pay each member $_____ for his or her covenant not to compete.

17. Risk of Loss

If business assets are damaged or destroyed before closing, Buyer may cancel this contract, in which case Seller will promptly return the deposit.

18. Disputes

(Choose One)

☐ **Litigation.** If a dispute arises, any party may take the matter to court.

☐ **Mediation and Possible Litigation.** If a dispute arises, the parties will try in good faith to settle it through mediation conducted by:

☐ _____

☐ a mediator to be mutually selected.

Form 5A: Contract for Purchase of Business Assets From a Sole Proprietorship, Partnership or Limited Liability Company Page 5 of 8

NOLO
www.nolo.com

The parties will share the costs of the mediator equally. Each party will cooperate fully and fairly with the mediator and will attempt to reach a mutually satisfactory compromise to the dispute. If the dispute is not resolved within 30 days after it is referred to the mediator, any party may take the matter to court.

☐ **Mediation and Possible Arbitration.** If a dispute arises, the parties will try in good faith to settle it through mediation conducted by:

☐ _____ .

☐ a mediator to be mutually selected.

The parties will share the costs of the mediator equally. Each party will cooperate fully and fairly with the mediator and will attempt to reach a mutually satisfactory compromise to the dispute. If the dispute is not resolved within 30 days after it is referred to the mediator, it will be arbitrated by:

☐ _____ .

☐ an arbitrator to be mutually selected.

Judgment on the arbitration award may be entered in any court that has jurisdiction over the matter. Costs of arbitration, including lawyers' fees, will be allocated by the arbitrator.

19. Additional Agreements

Seller and Buyer additionally agree that: _____

_____

_____

_____

20. Required Signatures

This contract is valid only if signed by:

☐ all partners of Seller *(if Seller is a partnership)*.

☐ all members of Seller *(if Seller is an LLC)*.

☐ the spouse of Seller *(if Seller is a sole proprietorship)*.

21. Entire Agreement

This is the entire agreement between the parties. It replaces and supersedes any and all oral agreements between the parties, as well as any prior writings.

22. Successors and Assignees

This contract binds and benefits the heirs, successors and assignees of the parties.

23. Notices

All notices must be in writing. A notice may be delivered to a party at the address that follows a party's signature or to a new address that a party designates in writing. A notice may be delivered:

(1) in person,

(2) by certified mail, or

(3) by overnight courier.

24. Governing Law

This contract will be governed by and construed in accordance with the laws of the state of _____

_____ .

25. Counterparts

The parties may sign several identical counterparts of this contract. Any fully signed counterpart shall be treated as an original.

26. Modification

This contract may be modified only by a writing signed by the party against whom such modification is sought to be enforced.

27. Waiver

If one party waives any term or provision of this contract at any time, that waiver will only be effective for the specific instance and specific purpose for which the waiver was given. If either party fails to exercise or delays exercising any of its rights or remedies under this contract, that party retains the right to enforce that term or provision at a later time.

28. Severability

If any court determines that any provision of this contract is invalid or unenforceable, any invalidity or unenforceability will affect only that provision and will not make any other provision of this contract invalid or unenforceable and such provision shall be modified, amended or limited only to the extent necessary to render it valid and enforceable.

Dated: _____

SELLER

Name of Business: _____

a _____

By: _____

Printed Name and Title: _____

Address: _____

_____

BUYER

Name of Business: _____

a _____

By: _____

Printed Name and Title: _____

Address: _____

_____

☐ **SIGNATURES OF ALL PARTNERS OR MEMBERS** (For use where Seller is a partnership or LLC)

Signature: _____

Printed Name: _____

Signature: _____

Printed Name: _____

Signature: _____

Printed Name: _____

Signature: _____

Printed Name: _____

☐ **SIGNATURE OF SPOUSE OF SOLE PROPRIETOR SELLER** (For use in community property states)

Signature: _____

Printed Name: _____

Spouse of: _____

Form 5B: Contract for Purchase of Business Assets From a Corporation

1. Names

_____ ,

a _____ corporation, _____

_____ , Seller, and _____

_____ , Buyer, agree to the following sale.

2. Sale of Business Assets

Seller is selling to Buyer and Buyer is buying from Seller the assets of the business known as _____

_____ located at _____

_____ .

3. Assets Being Sold

The assets being sold consist of:

☐ A. The goodwill of the business, including the current business name and phone number.

☐ B. The lease dated _____ , between _____

_____ , Seller, and _____

_____ , Landlord, covering the premises at _____

_____

☐ C. The inventory of goods.

☐ D. The furniture, fixtures and equipment listed in attached Schedule A.

☐ E. The equipment leases listed in attached Schedule B.

☐ F. Other: _____

4. Purchase Price

The purchase price is $_____ , allocated as follows:

A. Goodwill $_____

B. Assignment of lease $_____

C. Furniture, fixtures and equipment $_____

D. Other: _____ $_____

Total $_____

☐ The total purchase price will be adjusted by prorating rent, taxes, insurance premiums, utility costs and security deposits as of the date of closing.

☐ The total purchase price will also be adjusted at closing by adding the price of the inventory as covered in paragraph 5.

5. Price of Inventory (Optional)

At closing, in addition to the total purchase price listed in paragraph 4, Buyer will buy the inventory by paying Seller the amount Seller paid for those goods. A physical count of the goods will be made by:

☐ Seller and Buyer.

☐ an inventory service company mutually agreed upon by Seller and Buyer.

The count will be made _____ days before closing and will include only unopened and undamaged goods. If an inventory service company is used, Seller and Buyer will share the cost of the service equally.

☐ Buyer will pay no more than $ _____ for the goods.

6. Accounts Receivable

☐ Seller's accounts receivable will remain Seller's property. Buyer will within ten days send Seller the proceeds of any of Seller's accounts receivable that Buyer may collect after closing.

☐ At closing, Buyer will purchase all of Seller's accounts receivable that are no more than _____ days old. Buyer will pay Seller the balances owed on these accounts less _____%.

7. Deposit

Buyer will pay Seller a deposit of $_____ when Buyer and Seller sign this contract. This amount will be applied toward the amount listed in paragraph 4. Seller will return this deposit to Buyer if the purchase is not completed because Seller cannot or does not meet its commitments.

8. Payments at Closing

At closing, Buyer will pay Seller the following amounts, using a cashier's check:

☐ $_____ to be applied toward the amount listed in paragraph 4.

☐ The value of the inventory as determined under paragraph 5.

☐ The value of the accounts receivable as determined under paragraph 6.

9. Promissory Note

At closing, Buyer will give Seller a promissory note for the balance of the purchase price. The promissory note will be signed by Buyer.

☐ Buyer is a Sole Proprietor. _____ will sign the promissory note along with Buyer. Each signer will be jointly and individually liable for payment.

☐ Buyer is a Partnership. Each partner will co-sign the promissory note and will be jointly and individually liable for payment.

☐ Buyer is a Corporation or Limited Liability Company. The following people will personally guarantee the promissory note and will be jointly and individually liable for payment: _____

_____.

The promissory note will contain the following terms:

A. The unpaid balance will be subject to interest at the rate of _____% a year.

B. Buyer will pay $_____ on the _____ day of each month beginning one month after the closing until the principal and interest have been paid in full.

C. The entire amount of principal and interest will be paid by _____.

D. Payments will be applied first to interest and then to principal.

E. Buyer may prepay all or any part of the principal without penalty.

F. If Buyer is more than _____ days late in making a payment, Seller may declare that the entire balance of the unpaid principal is due immediately, together with the interest that has accrued.

10. Security for Payment

At closing, to secure the payment of the promissory note, Buyer will sign a security agreement and UCC financing statement giving Seller a security interest in:

☐ The assets that Buyer is purchasing.

☐ The lease that is being assigned to Buyer.

11. Seller's Debts

Buyer is not assuming any of Seller's debts or liabilities. At or before closing, Seller will pay all debts and liabilities that are or may become a lien on the assets being bought by Buyer.

At closing, Seller will confirm in an affidavit (Attachment _____) that Seller has paid all debts and liabilities of the business, including those that are known and those that are in dispute.

12. Closing

The closing will take place:

Date: _____

Time: _____

Location: _____

At closing, Buyer and Seller will sign the documents specified in this contract and all other documents reasonably needed to transfer the business assets to Buyer. Buyer will pay Seller the amounts required by this contract and Seller will transfer the business assets to Buyer.

13. Documents for Transferring Assets

At closing, Seller will deliver to Buyer these signed documents:

☐ A. A bill of sale for the tangible assets being bought, with a warranty of good title.

☐ B. An assignment of the lease, with the landlord's written consent.

☐ C. Assignment of any other contracts that are being transferred to Buyer, with the written consent of the other contracting person, if such consent is required.

☐ D. Assignments of all trademarks, patents and copyrights that are part of this purchase.

Seller will also deliver to Buyer at closing all other documents reasonably needed to transfer the business assets to Buyer.

14. Seller's Representations

Seller warrants and represents that:

A. Seller has good and marketable title to the assets being sold. The assets will be free from encumbrances at closing.

B. At closing, Seller will have paid all taxes affecting the business and its assets.

C. There are no judgments, claims, liens or proceedings pending against Seller, the business or the assets being sold and none will be pending at closing.

NOLO
www.nolo.com
Form 5B: Contract for Purchase of Business Assets From a Corporation
Page 3 of 7

D. Seller has given Buyer complete and accurate information, in writing, about the earnings of the business, its assets and liabilities, and its financial condition.

E. Until closing, Seller will not enter into any new contracts or incur any new obligations and will continue to conduct its business a normal manner.

F. Other: _____
_____.

These warranties and representations will survive the closing.

15. Buyer's Representations

Buyer warrants and represents that:

A. Buyer has inspected the tangible assets that Buyer is purchasing and the premises covered by the lease, and is satisfied with their condition except for: _____

_____.

B. Buyer has given Seller accurate information about Buyer's financial condition.
These warranties and representations will survive the closing.

16. Covenant Not to Compete

The shareholders named at the end of this contract are all of Seller's shareholders. For _____ [years/months] following the closing, none of Seller's shareholders will directly or indirectly participate in a business that is similar to a business now or later operated by Buyer in the same geographical area. This includes participating in a shareholder's own business or as a co-owner, director, officer, consultant, independent contractor, employee or agent of another business.

In particular, none of the shareholders of Seller will:

(a) solicit or attempt to solicit any business or trade from Buyer's actual or prospective customers or clients;

(b) employ or attempt to employ any employee of Buyer;

(c) divert or attempt to divert business away from Buyer; or

(d) encourage any independent contractor or consultant to end a relationship with Buyer. Each shareholder of Seller acknowledges and agrees that if any shareholder of Seller breaches or threatens to breach any of the terms of this paragraph 16, Buyer will sustain irreparable harm and will be entitled to obtain an injunction to stop any breach or threatened breach of this paragraph 16.

Each shareholder of Seller, by signing this contract, accepts and agrees to be bound by this covenant not to compete. At closing, Buyer will pay each shareholder of Seller $_____ for his or her covenant not to compete.

17. Risk of Loss

If business assets are damaged or destroyed before closing, Buyer may cancel this contract, in which case Seller will promptly return the deposit.

18. Disputes

(Choose One)

☐ **Litigation.** If a dispute arises, any party may take the matter to court.

☐ **Mediation and Possible Litigation.** If a dispute arises, the parties will try in good faith to settle it through mediation conducted by:

☐ _____

☐ a mediator to be mutually selected.

The parties will share the costs of the mediator equally. Each party will cooperate fully and fairly with the mediator and will attempt to reach a mutually satisfactory compromise to the dispute. If the dispute is not resolved within 30 days after it is referred to the mediator, any party may take the matter to court.

☐ **Mediation and Possible Arbitration.** If a dispute arises, the parties will try in good faith to settle it through mediation conducted by:

☐ _____

☐ a mediator to be mutually selected.

The parties will share the costs of the mediator equally. Each party will cooperate fully and fairly with the mediator and will attempt to reach a mutually satisfactory compromise to the dispute. If the dispute is not resolved within 30 days after it is referred to the mediator, it will be arbitrated by:

☐ _____

☐ an arbitrator to be mutually selected.

Judgment on the arbitration award may be entered in any court that has jurisdiction over the matter. Costs of arbitration, including lawyers' fees, will be allocated by the arbitrator.

19. Additional Agreements

Seller and Buyer additionally agree that: _____

_____

_____

_____

_____

20. Required Signatures

This contract is valid only if signed by all of the shareholders of Seller.

21. Entire Agreement

This is the entire agreement between the parties. It replaces and supersedes any and all oral agreements between the parties, as well as any prior writings.

22. Successors and Assignees

This contract binds and benefits the heirs, successors and assignees of the parties.

23. Notices

All notices must be in writing. A notice may be delivered to a party at the address that follows a party's signature or to a new address that a party designates in writing. A notice may be delivered:

(1) in person,

(2) by certified mail, or

(3) by overnight courier.

24. Governing Law

This contract will be governed by and construed in accordance with the laws of the state of _____

_____.

25. Counterparts

The parties may sign several identical counterparts of this contract. Any fully signed counterpart shall be treated as an original.

26. Modification

This contract may be modified only by a writing signed by the party against whom such modification is sought to be enforced.

27. Waiver

If one party waives any term or provision of this contract at any time, that waiver will only be effective for the specific instance and specific purpose for which the waiver was given. If either party fails to exercise or delays exercising any of its rights or remedies under this contract, that party retains the right to enforce that term or provision at a later time.

28. Severability

If any court determines that any provision of this contract is invalid or unenforceable, any invalidity or unenforceability will affect only that provision and will not make any other provision of this contract invalid or unenforceable and such provision shall be modified, amended or limited only to the extent necessary to render it valid and enforceable.

Dated: _____

SELLER

Name of Business: _____

a _____

By: _____

Printed Name and Title: _____

Address: _____

_____

BUYER

Name of Business: _____

a _____

By: _____

Printed Name and Title: _____

Address: _____

Consent of Shareholders

To induce Buyer to buy the assets of _____

_____ we each represent and warrant that:

1. We are all of Seller's shareholders.
2. We consent to this contract.

3. We will each be personally bound by Seller's representations and warranties contained in this contract.

4. We will each be personally bound by the covenant not to compete contained in Paragraph 16.

5. We each personally guarantee the obligations of Seller contained in this contract.

Dated: _____ Shareholder: _____

Dated: _____ Shareholder: _____

Dated: _____ Shareholder: _____

Dated: _____ Shareholder: _____

Consent of Others to Covenant Not to Compete

☐ I   ☐ We   consent to and agree to be bound by the terms of the Covenant Not to Compete described in Paragraph 16 of the above Contract for Purchase of Business Assets and will sign the Covenant upon those terms.

Dated: _____

Signature: _____

Printed Name: _____

Dated: _____

Signature: _____

Printed Name: _____

Dated: _____

Signature: _____

Printed Name: _____

Dated: _____

Signature: _____

Printed Name: _____

Form 5C: Corporate Resolution Authorizing Sale of Assets

All of the shareholders and directors of _____

_____ , a _____

corporation, consent to the sale of the corporation's assets on the terms stated in the purchase agreement

attached to this resolution as Attachment _____ .

    The corporation's president is authorized to sign the purchase agreement on behalf of the corporation and to take such actions as the president deems necessary or appropriate to carry out the terms of the purchase agreement.

Dated: _____

Shareholder/Director: _____

Shareholder/Director: _____

Shareholder/Director: _____

Shareholder/Director: _____

Form 5D: Contract for Purchase of Corporate Stock

1. Names

Sellers _____   ☐ Spouses _____

_____   _____

_____   _____

_____   _____

_____   _____

_____   _____

Buyer: _____

The above-listed Sellers, ☐ their spouses, and Buyer agree to the terms of this contract.

2. Sale of Corporate Stock

Seller(s) is/are selling to Buyer and Buyer is buying from Seller(s) all the issued and outstanding stock of

_____,

a _____ corporation, free of encumbrances. The corporation has

issued _____ shares of stock, which are owned as follows:

Name of Shareholder	Shares of Stock Owned
_____	_____
_____	_____
_____	_____
_____	_____
_____	_____

3. Purchase Price

The purchase price is $_____ per share, for a total of $_____.
At closing, Buyer will pay the purchase price to each Seller by cashier's check.

Provision for Payment of Corporate Taxes

To provide for payment of corporate taxes incurred prior to closing but which have not yet been determined, at closing:

☐ A. Seller and Buyer will place an agreed-upon portion of the purchase price in escrow for 90 days with:

☐ _____.

☐ a person to be agreed upon.

☐ B. Seller will withhold an agreed-upon portion of the purchase price for 90 days.

Any portion of these funds not used to pay taxes will be returned to Seller at the end of the 90 days.

4. Closing

The closing will take place:

Date: _____

Time: _____

Location: _____

5. Documents for Buyer

At closing, Seller(s) will deliver these signed documents to Buyer:

A. Stock certificates for all the corporation's stock endorsed for transfer by Seller(s).

☐ **Community Property States.** Stock certificates will be co-endorsed by the spouse of each married Seller.

B. The resignations of the corporation's officers and directors.

C. The corporation's minute book and business records.

D. The corporation's contracts and leases.

E. The landlord's written consent to the assignment of the lease, if such consent is required.

F. The written consent of any other contracting party, if such consent is required.

G. All other documents reasonably needed to transfer the corporation to Buyer.

6. Sellers' Representations

Each Seller warrants and represents that:

A. Sellers own all of the issued and outstanding shares of the corporation's stock. The shares are free of any liens or encumbrances.

B. The corporation has good and marketable title to the assets listed in attached Schedule A. The assets will be free from liens and encumbrances at closing.

C. The debts and liabilities of the corporation are listed in attached Schedule B. There will be no other debts or liabilities at closing.

D. At closing, the corporation will have paid all taxes affecting the business and its assets, to the extent known at closing.

E. Any judgments, claims, liens or proceedings pending against the corporation or its assets have been disclosed to Buyer in writing. No others will be pending at closing.

F. Sellers have given Buyer, in writing, complete and accurate information about the earnings of the corporation, its assets and liabilities, and its financial condition.

G. The corporation is properly incorporated and is in good standing.

H. The corporation will not enter into any new contracts or incur any new obligations from now until closing and will continue to conduct its business in a normal manner.

I. The corporation owes no outstanding dividends and will declare no dividends from now until closing.

J. Between now and closing, the corporation will not increase the compensation of any employee, consultant, independent contractor, director or officer, or hire any new employee, consultant, independent contractor, director or officer.

These warranties and representations will survive the closing.

7. Covenant Not to Compete

For _____ [years/months] following the closing, none of Seller's shareholders will directly or indirectly participate in a business that is similar to a business now or later operated by Buyer in the same geographical area. This includes participating in a shareholder's own business or as a co-owner, director, officer, consultant, independent contractor, employee or agent of another business.

In particular, none of the shareholders of Seller will:

(a) solicit or attempt to solicit any business or trade from Buyer's actual or prospective customers or clients;

(b) employ or attempt to employ any employee of Buyer;

(c) divert or attempt to divert business away from Buyer, or

(d) encourage any independent contractor or consultant to end a relationship with Buyer. Each shareholder of Seller acknowledges and agrees that if any shareholder of Seller breaches or threatens to breach any of the terms of this paragraph 7, Buyer will sustain irreparable harm and will be entitled to obtain an injunction to stop any breach or threatened breach of this paragraph 7.

Each shareholder of Seller, by signing this contract, accepts and agrees to be bound by this covenant not to compete. At closing, Buyer will pay each shareholder of Seller $_____ for his or her covenant not to compete.

8. Risk of Loss

Until closing, Sellers assume the risk of loss or damage to the corporation's physical assets caused by fire or other casualty. If corporate assets are lost or destroyed by fire or other casualty before closing, Buyer may cancel this contract.

9. Disputes

(Choose One)

☐ **Litigation.** If a dispute arises, any party may take the matter to court.

☐ **Mediation and Possible Litigation.** If a dispute arises, the parties will try in good faith to settle it through mediation conducted by:

☐ _____.

☐ a mediator to be mutually selected.

The parties will share the costs of the mediator equally. Each party will cooperate fully and fairly with the mediator and will attempt to reach a mutually satisfactory compromise to the dispute. If the dispute is not resolved within 30 days after it is referred to the mediator, any party may take the matter to court.

☐ **Mediation and Possible Arbitration.** If a dispute arises, the parties will try in good faith to settle it through mediation conducted by:

☐ _____.

☐ a mediator to be mutually selected.

The parties will share the costs of the mediator equally. Each party will cooperate fully and fairly with the mediator and will attempt to reach a mutually satisfactory compromise to the dispute. If the dispute is not resolved within 30 days after it is referred to the mediator, it will be arbitrated by:

☐ _____ .

☐ an arbitrator to be mutually selected.

Judgment on the arbitration award may be entered in any court that has jurisdiction over the matter. Costs of arbitration, including lawyers' fees, will be allocated by the arbitrator.

10. Additional Agreements

Seller(s) and Buyer(s) additionally agree that: _____

_____

_____ .

11. Required Signatures

This contract is valid only if signed by all the persons owning shares in _____

_____ .

12. Entire Agreement

This is the entire agreement between the parties. It replaces and supersedes any and all oral agreements between the parties, as well as any prior writings.

13. Successors and Assignees

This contract binds and benefits the heirs, successors and assignees of the parties.

14. Notices

All notices must be in writing. A notice may be delivered to a party at the address that follows a party's signature or to a new address that a party designates in writing. A notice may be delivered:

(1) in person,

(2) by certified mail, or

(3) by overnight courier.

15. Governing Law

This contract will be governed by and construed in accordance with the laws of the state of _____

_____ .

16. Counterparts

The parties may sign several identical counterparts of this contract. Any fully signed counterpart shall be treated as an original.

17. Modification

This contract may be modified only by a writing signed by the party against whom such modification is sought to be enforced.

18. Waiver

If one party waives any term or provision of this contract at any time, that waiver will only be effective for the specific instance and specific purpose for which the waiver was given. If either party fails to exercise or delays exercising any of its rights or remedies under this contract, that party retains the right to enforce that term or provision at a later time.

19. Severability

If any court determines that any provision of this contract is invalid or unenforceable, any invalidity or unenforceability will affect only that provision and will not make any other provision of this contract invalid or unenforceable and such provision shall be modified, amended or limited only to the extent necessary to render it valid and enforceable.

Dated: _____

BUYER

Signature: _____

Printed Name: _____

Address: _____

SELLERS (Shareholders)

Signature: _____

Printed Name: _____

Address: _____

Signature: _____

Printed Name: _____

Address: _____

Signature: _____

Printed Name: _____

Address: _____

Signature: _____

Printed Name: _____

Address: _____

☐ SPOUSES OF SHAREHOLDERS (Community Property States)

Signature: _____

Printed Name: _____

Address: _____

Signature: _____

Printed Name: _____

Address: _____

Signature: _____

Printed Name: _____

Address: _____

Signature: _____

Printed Name: _____

Address: _____

Form 5E: Bill of Sale

1. Names

_____, Seller,

transfers to _____,

Buyer, full ownership of the property listed on Attachment to Bill of Sale.

2. Acknowledgment of Payment

Seller acknowledges receiving payment for this property in the form of:

☐ A cashier's check.

☐ A cashier's check and a promissory note secured by a security interest.

3. Warranty of Ownership

Seller warrants that Seller is the legal owner of the property and that the property is

☐ Free of all liens and encumbrances.

☐ Free of all liens and encumbrances except the security interest granted today by Buyer.

SELLER

Name of Business: _____

a _____

By: _____

Printed Name and Title: _____

Address: _____

BUYER

Name of Business: _____

a _____

By: _____

Printed Name and Title: _____

Address: _____

☐ Spouse of Sole Proprietor in a Community Property State

Signature: _____

Printed Name: _____

Personal Responsibility for Warranty

The following are all of Seller's ☐ Partners   ☐ LLC Members   ☐ Corporate Shareholders

Each will be personally responsible for the warranty in paragraph 3 of the Bill of Sale.

Signature: _____

Printed Name: _____

Address: _____

Signature: _____

Printed Name: _____

Address: _____

Signature: _____

Printed Name: _____

Address: _____

Signature: _____

Printed Name: _____

Address: _____

Attachment to Bill of Sale

This is an attachment to the Bill of Sale given by _____

_____, Seller, to

_____

Buyer.

    Seller is transferring to Buyer full ownership of the following property:

_____

_____

_____

_____

_____

_____

_____

_____

_____

_____

Dated: _____

SELLER

Name of Business: _____

a _____

By: _____

Printed Name and Title: _____

Address: _____

_____

Form 5F: Affidavit—No Creditors

State of _____)
)
County of _____)

I, _____, state under oath:

1. Entity Selling Assets

I make this affidavit on behalf of:

☐ myself, a sole proprietor of the business known as _____

_____

☐ _____ a partnership

☐ _____ a limited liability company

☐ _____ a corporation

as Seller of business assets to _____

_____, Buyer.

2. No Security Interests

The assets that Seller is transferring to Buyer today by a Bill of Sale are free of all security interests and other liens.

3. No Creditors

Seller has paid all debts and liabilities of Seller's business. There are no debts or liabilities of

☐ the owner of Seller's business (if Seller is a sole proprietor)

☐ Seller's partners (if Seller is a partnership)

☐ Seller's members (if Seller is a limited liability company)

☐ Seller's shareholders (if Seller is a corporation)

that affect Seller's assets or the right of Seller to transfer Seller's assets to Buyer.

4. No Claims

There are no claims or liens (either disputed or undisputed) against Seller, Seller's assets or

☐ the owner of Seller's business (if Seller is a sole proprietor)

☐ Seller's partners (if Seller is a partnership)

☐ Seller's members (if Seller is a limited liability company)

☐ Seller's shareholders (if Seller is a corporation)

that affect Seller's assets or the right of Seller to transfer Seller's assets to Buyer.

5. Indemnification

If, contrary to paragraphs 2, 3 or 4 of this Affidavit, there are any security interests or other liens, debts, liabilities or claims, Seller and the signer of this affidavit will immediately remove the encumbrances or liens, pay the debts, liabilities or claims, and indemnify, defend, hold harmless and protect Buyer from any loss or liability arising out of such security interest, lien, debt, liability or claim.

Signature

Dated: _____

SELLER

Name of Business: _____

a _____

By: _____

Printed Name and Title: _____

Address: _____

_____

Notarization

On this _____ day of _____ (month), _____ (year),

_____ (name of signer)

☐   whom I know personally to be the person who signed the above document

☐   whose identity was proved to me on the basis of _____

_____ (type of evidence, such as a driver's license)

to be the person who signed the above document appeared before me and acknowledged under oath that he/she signed the above document and that its contents are true to the best of his/her knowledge and belief.

_____

(signature of notary public)

_____

(typed, printed or stamped name of notary public)

Notary Public For

County of _____

State of _____

Residing at _____

_____

SEAL   _____

My commission expires: _____

Form 5G: Security Agreement

1. Names

_____, Buyer, grants to

_____, Seller,

a continuing security interest in the following property (the "Secured Property"), which consists of:

☐ The property listed in Attachment 1.

☐ Any additional tangible personal property that Buyer now owns or later acquires in connection with Buyer's business, including replacement inventory.

2. Security for Promissory Note

Buyer is granting this security interest to secure performance of a promissory note that Buyer executed on

_____ as partial payment for certain business assets. The promissory

note obligates Buyer to pay Seller $_____ with interest at the rate of _____% a

year, on the terms stated in the promissory note.

3. Financing Statement

Concurrently with the execution of this Security Agreement, Buyer will sign a financing statement and other documents that Seller reasonably requests to protect Seller's security interest in the Secured Property.

4. Use and Care of the Secured Property

Until the promissory note is fully paid, Buyer agrees to:

☐ A. Keep the Secured Property at _____

_____ and use it only in the _____

operation of the _____ business.

☐ B. Maintain the Secured Property in good repair.

☐ C. Not sell, transfer or release the Secured Property unless Seller consents. Buyer may sell inventory in the ordinary course of Buyer's business, but will reasonably renew and replenish inventory to keep it at its current level.

☐ D. Pay all taxes on the Secured Property as taxes become due.

☐ E. Insure the Secured Property against normal risks, with an insurance policy that names Buyer and Seller as beneficiaries.

☐ F. Deliver to Seller a copy of the insurance policy insuring the Secured Property and provide to Seller annual proof that Buyer has paid the premiums on the policy.

☐ G. Allow Seller to inspect the Secured Property at any reasonable time.

5. Buyer's Default

If Buyer is more than ten days late in making any payment required by the promissory note or if Buyer fails to correct any violations of paragraph 4 within ten days of receiving written notice from Seller, Buyer will be in default.

6. Seller's Rights

If Buyer is in default, Seller may exercise the remedies contained in the Uniform Commercial Code for the

State of _____ and any other remedies legally available to

Seller. Seller may, for example:

☐ A. Remove the Secured Property from the place where it is then located.

☐ B. Require Buyer to assemble the Secured Property and make it available to Seller at a place designated by Seller that is reasonably convenient to Buyer and Seller.

☐ C. Sell or lease the Secured Property, or otherwise dispose of it.

7. Notice to Buyer

Seller will give Buyer at least ten days notice of when and where the Secured Property will be sold, leased or otherwise disposed of. Any notice required here or by statute will be deemed given to Buyer if sent by

first-class mail to Buyer at the following address: _____

_____

8. Entire Agreement

This is the entire agreement between the parties. It replaces and supersedes any and all oral agreements between the parties, as well as any prior writings.

9. Successors and Assignees

This agreement binds and benefits the heirs, successors and assignees of the parties.

10. Governing Law

This agreement will be governed by and construed in accordance with the laws of the state of _____

_____.

11. Counterparts

The parties may sign several identical counterparts of this agreement. Any fully signed counterpart shall be treated as an original.

12. Modification

This agreement may be modified only by a writing signed by the party against whom such modification is sought to be enforced.

13. Waiver

If one party waives any term or provision of this agreement at any time, that waiver will only be effective for the specific instance and specific purpose for which the waiver was given. If either party fails to exercise or delays exercising any of its rights or remedies under this agreement, that party retains the right to enforce that term or provision at a later time.

14. Severability

If any court determines that any provision of this agreement is invalid or unenforceable, any invalidity or unenforceability will affect only that provision and will not make any other provision of this agreement invalid or unenforceable and such provision shall be modified, amended or limited only to the extent necessary to render it valid and enforceable.

Dated: _____

SELLER

Name of Business: _____

a _____

By: _____

Printed Name and Title: _____

Address: _____

_____

BUYER

Name of Business: _____

a _____

By: _____

Printed Name and Title: _____

Address: _____

Attachment to Security Agreement

This is an attachment to the Security Agreement given by _____,

_____, Seller to

_____,

Buyer.

The Secured Property consists of the following:

_____

_____

_____

_____

_____

_____

_____

_____

_____

_____

_____

Dated: _____

BUYER

Name of Business: _____

a _____

By: _____

Printed Name and Title: _____

Address: _____

_____

SELLER

Name of Business: _____

a _____

By: _____

Printed Name and Title: _____

Address: _____

_____

Form 6A: Gross Lease

1. Names

This lease is made by _____, Landlord,

and _____, Tenant.

2. Premises Being Leased

Landlord is leasing to Tenant and Tenant is leasing from Landlord the following premises:

_____

_____

☐ **Shared Facilities.** Tenant and Tenant's employees and customers may use the following additional facilities in common with other tenants, employees and customers:

☐ The adjacent parking lot.

☐ The parking lot located at _____.

☐ Restroom facilities.

☐ Storage areas.

☐ Hallways, stairways and elevators.

☐ Conference rooms.

☐ Other: _____.

3. Term of Lease

This lease is for _____ years beginning on _____ and ending

on _____.

4. Rent

Tenant will pay rent in advance on the _____ day of each month.

☐ Tenant will pay rent of $_____ per month for the entire term of the lease.

☐ Tenant will pay the following rent:

$_____ per month during the 12-month period beginning _____.

$_____ per month during the 12-month period beginning _____.

$_____ per month during the 12-month period beginning _____.

$_____ per month during the 12-month period beginning _____.

$_____ per month during the 12-month period beginning _____.

5. Option to Extend Lease

Landlord grants Tenant the option to extend this lease for an additional _____ years on the same

terms except as follows:

Tenant may exercise this option only if Tenant is in substantial compliance with the terms of this lease. To exercise this option, Tenant must give Landlord written notice on or before _____.

☐ **Additional Option**

If Tenant exercises the option granted above, Tenant will then have the option to extend this lease for _____ years beyond the first option period on the same terms except as follows: _____

_____

_____

_____

Tenant may exercise this additional option only if Tenant is in substantial compliance with the terms of this lease. To exercise this option, Tenant must give Landlord written notice on or before _____.

6. **Security Deposit**

Tenant has deposited $_____ with Landlord as security for Tenant's performance of this lease. Landlord will refund the full security deposit to Tenant within 14 days following the end of the lease if Tenant returns the premises to Landlord in good condition (except for reasonable wear and tear) and Tenant has paid Landlord all sums due under this lease. Otherwise, Landlord may deduct any amounts required to place the premises in good condition and to pay for any money owed to Landlord under the lease.

7. **Improvements by Landlord**

(Choose One)

☐ Tenant accepts the premises in "as is" condition. Landlord need not provide any repairs or improvements before the lease term begins.

☐ Before the lease term begins, Landlord (at Landlord's expense) will make the repairs and improvements listed in Attachment _____ to this contract.

8. **Improvements by Tenant**

Tenant may make alterations and improvements to the premises after obtaining the Landlord's written consent. At any time before this lease ends, Tenant may remove any of Tenant's alterations and improvements, as long as Tenant repairs any damage caused by attaching the items to or removing them from the premises.

9. **Tenant's Use of Premises**

Tenant will use the premises for the following business purposes:_____

_____

_____

and for purposes reasonably related to the main use.

10. Landlord's Representations

Landlord represents that:

A. At the beginning of the lease term, the premises will be properly zoned for Tenant's stated use and will be in compliance with all applicable laws and regulations.

B. The premises have not been used for the storage or disposal of any toxic or hazardous substance and Landlord has received no notice from any governmental authority concerning removal of any toxic or hazardous substance from the property.

11. Utilities and Services

Landlord will pay for the following utilities and services:

☐   Water

☐   Electricity

☐   Gas

☐   Heat

☐   Air-Conditioning

Any items not checked will be the responsibility of Tenant.

12. Maintenance and Repairs

A. Landlord will maintain and make all necessary repairs to: (1) the roof, structural components, exterior walls and interior common walls of the premises, and (2) the plumbing, electrical, heating, ventilating and air-conditioning systems.

B. Landlord will regularly clean and maintain (including snow removal) the parking areas, yards, common areas and exterior of the building and remove all litter so that the premises will be kept in an attractive condition.

C. Tenant will clean and maintain Tenant's portion of the building so that it will be kept in an attractive condition.

13. Insurance

A. Landlord will carry fire and extended coverage insurance on the building.

B. Tenant will carry public liability insurance; this insurance will include Landlord as an insured party. The public liability coverage for personal injury will be in at least the following amounts:

1. $_____ per occurrence.

2. $_____ in any one year.

C. Landlord and Tenant release each other from any liability to the other for any property loss, property damage or personal injury to the extent covered by insurance carried by the party suffering the loss, damage or injury.

D. Tenant will give Landlord a copy of all insurance policies that this lease requires Tenant to obtain.

14. Taxes

A. Landlord will pay all real property taxes levied and assessed against the premises.

B. Tenant will pay all personal property taxes levied and assessed against Tenant's personal property.

15. Subletting and Assignment

Tenant will not assign this lease or sublet any part of the premises without the written consent of Landlord. Landlord will not unreasonably withhold such consent.

16. Damage to Premises

A. If the premises are damaged through fire or other cause not the fault of Tenant, Tenant will owe no rent for any period during which Tenant is substantially deprived of the use of the premises.

B. If Tenant is substantially deprived of the use of the premises for more than 90 days because of such damage, Tenant may terminate this lease by delivering written notice of termination to Landlord.

17. Notice of Default

Before starting a legal action to recover possession of the premises based on Tenant's default, Landlord will notify Tenant in writing of the default. Landlord will take legal action only if Tenant does not correct the default within ten days after written notice is given or mailed to Tenant.

18. Quiet Enjoyment

As long as Tenant is not in default under the terms of this lease, Tenant will have the right to occupy the premises peacefully and without interference.

19. Eminent Domain

This lease will become void if any part of the leased premises or the building in which the leased premises are located are taken by eminent domain. Tenant has the right to receive and keep any amount of money that the agency taking the premises by eminent domain pays for Tenant's loss of business and for moving and relocation expenses.

20. Holding Over

If Tenant remains in possession after this lease ends, the continuing tenancy will be from month to month.

21. Disputes

(Choose One)

☐ **Litigation.** If a dispute arises, any party may take the matter to court.

☐ **Mediation and Possible Litigation.** If a dispute arises, the parties will try in good faith to settle it through mediation conducted by:

☐ _____

☐ a mediator to be mutually selected.

The parties will share the costs of the mediator equally. Each party will cooperate fully and fairly with the mediator and will attempt to reach a mutually satisfactory compromise to the dispute. If the dispute is not resolved within 30 days after it is referred to the mediator, any party may take the matter to court.

☐ **Mediation and Possible Arbitration.** If a dispute arises, the parties will try in good faith to settle it through mediation conducted by:

☐ _____

☐ a mediator to be mutually selected.

The parties will share the costs of the mediator equally. Each party will cooperate fully and fairly with the mediator and will attempt to reach a mutually satisfactory compromise to the dispute. If the dispute is not resolved within 30 days after it is referred to the mediator, it will be arbitrated by:

☐ _____

☐ an arbitrator to be mutually selected.

Judgment on the arbitration award may be entered in any court that has jurisdiction over the matter. Costs of arbitration, including lawyers' fees, will be allocated by the arbitrator.

Landlord need not participate in mediation or arbitration of a dispute unless Tenant has paid the rent called for by this lease or has placed any unpaid rent in escrow with an agreed-upon mediator or arbitrator.

22. Additional Agreements

Landlord and Tenant additionally agree that: _____

_____

_____

23. Entire Agreement

This is the entire agreement between the parties. It replaces and supersedes any and all oral agreements between the parties, as well as any prior writings.

24. Successors and Assignees

This lease binds and benefits the heirs, successors and assignees of the parties.

25. Notices

All notices must be in writing. A notice may be delivered to a party at the address that follows a party's signature or to a new address that a party designates in writing. A notice may be delivered:

(1) in person,

(2) by certified mail, or

(3) by overnight courier.

26. Governing Law

This lease will be governed by and construed in accordance with the laws of the state of _____

_____ .

27. Counterparts

The parties may sign several identical counterparts of this lease. Any fully signed counterpart shall be treated as an original.

28. Modification

This lease may only be modified by a writing signed by the party against whom such modification is sought to be enforced.

29. Waiver

If one party waives any term or provision of this lease at any time, that waiver will only be effective for the specific instance and specific purpose for which the waiver was given. If either party fails to exercise or delays exercising any of its rights or remedies under this lease, that party retains the right to enforce that term or provision at a later time.

30. Severability

If any court determines that any provision of this lease is invalid or unenforceable, any invalidity or unenforceability will affect only that provision and will not make any other provision of this lease invalid or unenforceable and such provision shall be modified, amended or limited only to the extent necessary to render it valid and enforceable.

Dated: _____

LANDLORD

Name of Business: _____

a _____

By: _____

Printed Name and Title: _____

Address: _____

_____

TENANT

Name of Business: _____

a _____

By: _____

Printed Name and Title: _____

Address: _____

_____

Form 6B: Net Lease for Entire Building

1. Names

This lease is made by _____, Landlord,

and _____, Tenant.

2. Premises Being Leased

Landlord is leasing to Tenant and Tenant is leasing from Landlord the following premises:

_____

_____

3. Term of Lease

This lease is for _____ years beginning on _____ and ending

on _____.

4. Rent

Tenant will pay rent in advance on the _____ day of each month.

☐ Tenant will pay rent of $_____ per month for the entire term of the lease.

☐ Tenant will pay the following rent:

$_____ per month during the 12-month period beginning _____.

$_____ per month during the 12-month period beginning _____.

$_____ per month during the 12-month period beginning _____.

$_____ per month during the 12-month period beginning _____.

$_____ per month during the 12-month period beginning _____.

5. Option to Extend Lease

Landlord grants Tenant the option to extend this lease for an additional _____ years on the same

terms except as follows:

_____

_____

_____

Tenant may exercise this option only if Tenant is in substantial compliance with the terms of this lease. To

exercise this option, Tenant must give Landlord written notice on or before _____.

☐ **Additional Option**

If Tenant exercises the option granted above, Tenant will then have the option to extend this lease for

_____ years beyond the first option period on the same terms except as follows: _____

_____

Tenant may exercise this additional option only if Tenant is in substantial compliance with the terms of this lease. To exercise this option, Tenant must give Landlord written notice on or before _____.

6. Security Deposit

Tenant has deposited $_____ with Landlord as security for Tenant's performance of this lease. Landlord will refund the full security deposit to Tenant within 14 days following the end of the lease if Tenant returns the premises to Landlord in good condition (except for reasonable wear and tear) and Tenant has paid Landlord all sums due under this lease. Otherwise, Landlord may deduct any amounts required to place the premises in good condition and to pay for any money owed to Landlord under the lease.

7. Improvements by Landlord

(Choose One)

☐ Tenant accepts the premises in "as is" condition. Landlord need not provide any repairs or improvements before the lease term begins.

☐ Before the lease term begins, Landlord (at Landlord's expense) will make the repairs and improvements listed in Attachment _____ to this contract.

8. Improvements by Tenant

Tenant may make alterations and improvements to the premises after obtaining the Landlord's written consent. At any time before this lease ends, Tenant may remove any of Tenant's alterations and improvements, as long as Tenant repairs any damage caused by attaching the items to or removing them from the premises.

9. Tenant's Use of Premises

Tenant will use the premises for the following business purposes:_____

and for purposes reasonably related to the main use.

10. Landlord's Representations

Landlord represents that:

A. At the beginning of the lease term, the premises will be properly zoned for Tenant's stated use and will be in compliance with all applicable laws and regulations.

B. The premises have not been used for the storage or disposal of any toxic or hazardous substance and Landlord has received no notice from any governmental authority concerning removal of any toxic or hazardous substance from the property.

11. Utilities and Services

Tenant will pay for all utilities and services, including water, electricity and gas, including the electricity or gas needed for heating and air-conditioning.

12. Maintenance and Repairs

A. Tenant will maintain and make all necessary repairs to: (1) the roof, structural components, exterior walls and interior walls of the premises, and (2) the plumbing, electrical, heating, ventilating and air-conditioning systems.

B. Tenant will clean and maintain (including snow removal) the parking areas, yards, common areas and exterior of the premises so that the premises will be kept in a safe and attractive condition.

13. Insurance

A. Tenant will carry fire and extended coverage insurance on the building in the amount of at least $_____; this insurance will include Landlord as an insured party.

B. Tenant will carry public liability insurance, which will include Landlord as an insured party. The public liability coverage for personal injury will be in at least the following amounts:

(1) $_____ per occurrence.

(2) $_____ in any one year.

C. Landlord and Tenant release each other from any liability to the other for any property loss, property damage or personal injury to the extent covered by insurance carried by the party suffering the loss, damage or injury.

D. Tenant will give Landlord a copy of all insurance policies that this lease requires Tenant to obtain.

14. Taxes

A. Tenant will pay all real property taxes levied and assessed against the premises during the term of this lease.

B. Tenant will pay all personal property taxes levied and assessed against Tenant's personal property.

15. Subletting and Assignment

Tenant will not assign this lease or sublet any part of the premises without the written consent of Landlord. Landlord will not unreasonably withhold such consent.

16. Notice of Default

Before starting a legal action to recover possession of the premises based on Tenant's default, Landlord will notify Tenant in writing of the default. Landlord will take legal action only if Tenant does not correct the default within ten days after written notice is given or mailed to Tenant.

17. Quiet Enjoyment

As long as Tenant is not in default under the terms of this lease, Tenant will have the right to occupy the premises peacefully and without interference.

18. Eminent Domain

This lease will become void if any part of the leased premises or the building in which the leased premises are located are taken by eminent domain. Tenant has the right to receive and keep any amount of money that the agency taking the premises by eminent domain pays for Tenant's loss of business and for moving and relocation expenses.

19. Holding Over

If Tenant remains in possession after this lease ends, the continuing tenancy will be from month to month.

20. Disputes

(Choose One)

☐ **Litigation.** If a dispute arises, any party may take the matter to court.

☐ **Mediation and Possible Litigation.** If a dispute arises, the parties will try in good faith to settle it through mediation conducted by:

☐ _____ .

☐ a mediator to be mutually selected.

The parties will share the costs of the mediator equally. Each party will cooperate fully and fairly with the mediator and will attempt to reach a mutually satisfactory compromise to the dispute. If the dispute is not resolved within 30 days after it is referred to the mediator, any party may take the matter to court.

☐ **Mediation and Possible Arbitration.** If a dispute arises, the parties will try in good faith to settle it through mediation conducted by:

☐ _____ .

☐ a mediator to be mutually selected.

The parties will share the costs of the mediator equally. Each party will cooperate fully and fairly with the mediator and will attempt to reach a mutually satisfactory compromise to the dispute. If the dispute is not resolved within 30 days after it is referred to the mediator, it will be arbitrated by:

☐ _____ .

☐ an arbitrator to be mutually selected.

Judgment on the arbitration award may be entered in any court that has jurisdiction over the matter. Costs of arbitration, including lawyers' fees, will be allocated by the arbitrator.

Landlord need not participate in mediation or arbitration of a dispute unless Tenant has paid the rent called for by this lease or has placed any unpaid rent in escrow with an agreed-upon mediator or arbitrator.

21. Additional Agreements

Landlord and Tenant additionally agree that: _____

_____

_____

22. Entire Agreement

This is the entire agreement between the parties. It replaces and supersedes any and all oral agreements between the parties, as well as any prior writings.

23. Successors and Assignees

This lease binds and benefits the heirs, successors and assignees of the parties.

24. Notices

All notices must be in writing. A notice may be delivered to a party at the address that follows a party's signature or to a new address that a party designates in writing. A notice may be delivered:

(1) in person,

(2) by certified mail, or

(3) by overnight courier.

25. Governing Law

This lease will be governed by and construed in accordance with the laws of the state of _____

_____.

26. Counterparts

The parties may sign several identical counterparts of this lease. Any fully signed counterpart shall be treated as an original.

27. Modification

This lease may only be modified by a writing signed by the party against whom such modification is sought to be enforced.

28. Waiver

If one party waives any term or provision of this lease at any time, that waiver will only be effective for the specific instance and specific purpose for which the waiver was given. If either party fails to exercise or delays exercising any of its rights or remedies under this lease, that party retains the right to enforce that term or provision at a later time.

29. Severability

If any court determines that any provision of this lease is invalid or unenforceable, any invalidity or unenforceability will affect only that provision and will not make any other provision of this lease invalid or unenforceable and such provision shall be modified, amended or limited only to the extent necessary to render it valid and enforceable.

Dated: _____

LANDLORD

Name of Business: _____

a _____

By: _____

Printed Name and Title: _____

Address: _____

_____

TENANT

Name of Business: _____

a _____

By: _____

Printed Name and Title: _____

Address: _____

_____

Form 6C: Net Lease for Part of Building

1. Names

This lease is made by _____, Landlord,

and _____, Tenant.

2. Premises Being Leased

Landlord is leasing to Tenant and Tenant is leasing from Landlord the following premises:

_____

_____

☐ **Shared Facilities.** As part of this lease, Tenant and Tenant's employees and customers may use the following additional facilities in common with other tenants, employees and customers:

    ☐ The adjacent parking lot.

    ☐ The parking lot located at _____.

    ☐ Restroom facilities.

    ☐ Storage areas.

    ☐ Hallways, stairways and elevators.

    ☐ Conference rooms.

    ☐ Other: _____.

3. Term of Lease

This lease is for _____ years beginning on _____ and ending

on _____.

4. Rent

Tenant will pay rent in advance on the _____ day of each month.

    ☐ Tenant will pay rent of $_____ per month for the entire term of the lease.

    ☐ Tenant will pay the following rent:

        $_____ per month during the 12-month period beginning _____.

        $_____ per month during the 12-month period beginning _____.

        $_____ per month during the 12-month period beginning _____.

        $_____ per month during the 12-month period beginning _____.

        $_____ per month during the 12-month period beginning _____.

5. Option to Extend Lease

Landlord grants Tenant the option to extend this lease for an additional _____ years on the same

terms except as follows:

_____
_____
_____

Tenant may exercise this option only if Tenant is in substantial compliance with the terms of this lease. To exercise this option, Tenant must give Landlord written notice on or before _____.

☐ **Additional Option**

If Tenant exercises the option granted above, Tenant will then have the option to extend this lease for

_____ years beyond the first option period on the same terms except as follows: _____

_____
_____
_____

Tenant may exercise this additional option only if Tenant is in substantial compliance with the terms of this lease. To exercise this option, Tenant must give Landlord written notice on or before _____.

6. Security Deposit

Tenant has deposited $_____ with Landlord as security for Tenant's performance of this lease. Landlord will refund the full security deposit to Tenant within 14 days following the end of the lease if Tenant returns the premises to Landlord in good condition (except for reasonable wear and tear) and Tenant has paid Landlord all sums due under this lease. Otherwise, Landlord may deduct any amounts required to place the premises in good condition and to pay for any money owed to Landlord under the lease.

7. Improvements by Landlord

(Choose One)

☐ Tenant accepts the premises in "as is" condition. Landlord need not provide any repairs or improvements before the lease term begins.

☐ Before the lease term begins, Landlord (at Landlord's expense) will make the repairs and improvements listed in Attachment _____ to this contract.

8. Improvements by Tenant

Tenant may make alterations and improvements to the premises after obtaining the Landlord's written consent. At any time before this lease ends, Tenant may remove any of Tenant's alterations and improvements, as long as Tenant repairs any damage caused by attaching the items to or removing them from the premises.

9. Tenant's Use of Premises

Tenant will use the premises for the following business purposes:_____

_____
_____

and for purposes reasonably related to the main use.

NOLO
www.nolo.com
Form 6C:
Net Lease for Part of Building
Page 2 of 7

10. Landlord's Representations

Landlord represents that:

A. At the beginning of the lease term, the premises will be properly zoned for Tenant's stated use and will be in compliance with all applicable laws and regulations.

B. The premises have not been used for the storage or disposal of any toxic or hazardous substance and Landlord has received no notice from any governmental authority concerning removal of any toxic or hazardous substance from the property.

11. Utilities and Services

A. **Separately Metered Utilities:** Tenant will pay for the following utilities and services that are separately metered or billed to Tenant:

☐ Water

☐ Electricity

☐ Gas

☐ Heating oil

☐ Trash collection

☐ Other: _____.

B. **Other Utilities.** Tenant will pay _____ % of the following utilities and services that are not separately metered to Tenant:

☐ Water

☐ Electricity

☐ Gas

☐ Heating oil

☐ Trash collection

☐ Other: _____.

Tenant will pay for these utilities in monthly installments on or before the _____ day of each month, in advance, in an amount estimated by Landlord. Every _____ months, Landlord will give Tenant copies of the bills sent to Landlord. If Tenant's share of the actual costs for utilities and services exceeds the amount paid in advance by Tenant, Tenant will pay Landlord the difference within 30 days. If Tenant has paid more than Tenant's share of the actual costs, Tenant will receive a credit for the overage which will be applied to reduce the next installments due from Tenant.

12. Maintenance and Repair of Common Areas

Landlord will maintain and make all necessary repairs to the common areas of the building and adjacent premises and keep these areas safe and free of trash. This includes:

☐ On-site parking areas

☐ Off-site parking areas

☐ Restroom facilities

☐ Storage areas

☐ Hallways, stairways and elevators

☐ Conference rooms

☐ Sidewalks and driveways

☐ Other: _____.

Tenant will pay Landlord _____ % of the cost of such maintenance and repairs. Tenant will pay these amounts in monthly installments on or before the _____ day of each month, in advance, in an amount estimated by Landlord. Within 90 days after the end of each lease year, Landlord will give Tenant a statement of the actual amount of Tenant's share of such costs for such period. If Tenant's share of the actual costs exceeds the amount paid in advance by Tenant, Tenant will pay Landlord the difference within 30 days. If Tenant has paid more than Tenant's share of the actual costs, Tenant will receive a credit for the overage which will be applied to reduce the next installments due from Tenant.

13. Maintenance and Repair of Leased Premises

Landlord will maintain and make all necessary repairs to the following parts of the building in which the leased premises are located:

☐ roof

☐ foundation and structural components

☐ exterior walls

☐ interior common walls

☐ exterior doors and windows

☐ plumbing system

☐ sewage disposal system

☐ electrical system

☐ heating, ventilating and air-conditioning systems

☐ sprinkler system.

Tenant will maintain and repair the leased premises and keep the leased premises in good repair except for those items specified above as being Landlord's responsibility.

14. Insurance

A. Tenant will carry fire and extended coverage insurance on the leased premises in the amount of at least $_____; this insurance will include Landlord as an insured party. Tenant will carry public liability insurance, which will include Landlord as a party insured. The public liability coverage for personal injury will be in at least the following amounts:

(1) $_____ per occurrence.

(2) $_____ in any one year.

B. Landlord will carry fire and extended coverage insurance on the building. Tenant will pay Tenant's proportionate share (_____%) of such insurance within ten days after receiving a statement from Landlord as to the cost.

C. Landlord and Tenant release each other from any liability to the other for any property loss, property damage or personal injury to the extent covered by insurance carried by the party suffering the loss, damage or injury.

D. Tenant will give Landlord a copy of all insurance policies that this lease requires Tenant to obtain.

15. Taxes

A. Tenant will pay _____% of all taxes and assessments that may be levied or assessed against the building and the land for the period of the lease. Tenant will pay these taxes and assessments in monthly installments on or before the _____ day of each month, in advance, in an amount estimated by Landlord. Landlord will give Tenant copies of the tax bills and assessments as Landlord receives them. If Tenant's share of the actual taxes and assessments exceeds the amount paid in advance by Tenant, Tenant will pay Landlord the difference within 30 days. If Tenant has paid more than Tenant's share of the actual taxes and assessment, Tenant will receive a credit for the overage which will be applied to reduce the next installments due from Tenant. Taxes and assessments to be paid by Tenant will be prorated on a due-date basis and will be assumed to cover a period of one year from the due date.

B. Tenant will pay all personal property taxes levied and assessed against Tenant's personal property.

16. Subletting and Assignment

Tenant will not assign this lease or sublet any part of the premises without the written consent of Landlord. Landlord will not unreasonably withhold such consent.

17. Damage to Premises

A. If the premises are damaged through fire or other cause not the fault of Tenant, Tenant will owe no rent for any period during which Tenant is substantially deprived of the use of the premises.

B. If Tenant is substantially deprived of the use of the premises for more than 90 days because of such damage, Tenant may terminate this lease by delivering written notice of termination to Landlord.

18. Notice of Default

Before starting a legal action to recover possession of the premises based on Tenant's default, Landlord will notify Tenant in writing of the default. Landlord will take legal action only if Tenant does not correct the default within ten days after written notice is given or mailed to Tenant.

19. Quiet Enjoyment

As long as Tenant is not in default under the terms of this lease, Tenant will have the right to occupy the premises peacefully and without interference.

20. Eminent Domain

This lease will become void if any part of the leased premises or the building in which the leased premises are located are taken by eminent domain. Tenant has the right to receive and keep any amount of money that the agency taking the premises by eminent domain pays for Tenant's loss of business and for moving and relocation expenses.

21. Holding Over

If Tenant remains in possession after this lease ends, the continuing tenancy will be from month to month.

22. Disputes

(Choose One)

☐ **Litigation.** If a dispute arises, any party may take the matter to court.

☐ **Mediation and Possible Litigation.** If a dispute arises, the parties will try in good faith to settle it through mediation conducted by:

☐ _____.

☐ a mediator to be mutually selected.

The parties will share the costs of the mediator equally. Each party will cooperate fully and fairly with the mediator and will attempt to reach a mutually satisfactory compromise to the dispute. If the dispute is not resolved within 30 days after it is referred to the mediator, any party may take the matter to court.

☐ **Mediation and Possible Arbitration.** If a dispute arises, the parties will try in good faith to settle it through mediation conducted by:

☐ _____.

☐ a mediator to be mutually selected.

The parties will share the costs of the mediator equally. Each party will cooperate fully and fairly with the mediator and will attempt to reach a mutually satisfactory compromise to the dispute. If the dispute is not resolved within 30 days after it is referred to the mediator, it will be arbitrated by:

☐ _____.

☐ an arbitrator to be mutually selected.

Judgment on the arbitration award may be entered in any court that has jurisdiction over the matter. Costs of arbitration, including lawyers' fees, will be allocated by the arbitrator.

Landlord need not participate in mediation or arbitration of a dispute unless Tenant has paid the rent called for by this lease or has placed any unpaid rent in escrow with an agreed-upon mediator or arbitrator.

23. Additional Agreements

Landlord and Tenant additionally agree that: _____

_____

_____

24. Entire Agreement

This is the entire agreement between the parties. It replaces and supersedes any and all oral agreements between the parties, as well as any prior writings.

25. Successors and Assignees

This lease binds and benefits the heirs, successors and assignees of the parties.

26. Notices

All notices must be in writing. A notice may be delivered to a party at the address that follows a party's signature or to a new address that a party designates in writing. A notice may be delivered:

(1) in person,

(2) by certified mail, or

(3) by overnight courier.

27. Governing Law

This lease will be governed by and construed in accordance with the laws of the state of _____

_____.

28. Counterparts

The parties may sign several identical counterparts of this lease. Any fully signed counterpart shall be treated as an original.

29. Modification

This lease may only be modified by a writing signed by the party against whom such modification is sought to be enforced.

30. Waiver

If one party waives any term or provision of this lease at any time, that waiver will only be effective for the specific instance and specific purpose for which the waiver was given. If either party fails to exercise or delays exercising any of its rights or remedies under this lease, that party retains the right to enforce that term or provision at a later time.

31. Severability

If any court determines that any provision of this lease is invalid or unenforceable, any invalidity or unenforceability will affect only that provision and will not make any other provision of this lease invalid or unenforceable and such provision shall be modified, amended or limited only to the extent necessary to render it valid and enforceable.

Dated: _____

LANDLORD

Name of Business: _____

a _____

By: _____

Printed Name and Title: _____

Address: _____

_____

TENANT

Name of Business: _____

a _____

By: _____

Printed Name and Title: _____

Address: _____

_____

Form 6D: Sublease

1. Names

This sublease is made by _____,

Sublandlord, and _____,

Subtenant.

2. Property Subleased

Sublandlord is subleasing to Subtenant, and Subtenant is subleasing from Sublandlord:

☐ All of the premises at _____.

☐ The following part of the premises at _____:

_____

_____

3. Original Lease

A. This subtenancy is subject to all the terms and conditions of the attached Original Lease dated

_____ between _____

_____, Landlord, and _____

_____, Tenant, except for the following:

_____

_____

_____

B. Except as specified in this Sublease, Subtenant will perform and observe all of the terms and conditions of the Original Lease as if Subtenant were named as Tenant in the Original Lease. Subtenant will do nothing that will create a breach by Sublandlord of any of the terms or conditions of the Original Lease.

4. Term of Sublease

This Sublease begins on _____ and ends on _____.

5. Rent

Subtenant will pay rent in advance on the _____ day of each month.

☐ Subtenant will pay rent of $_____ per month for the entire term of the Sublease.

☐ Subtenant will pay the following rent:

$_____ per month during the first year.

$_____ per month during the second year.

$_____ per month during the third year.

$_____ per month during the fourth year.

$_____ per month during the fifth year.

6. Option to Extend Sublease

Sublandlord grants Subtenant the option to extend this Sublease for an additional _____ (months/years) on the same terms except as follows:

_____

_____

_____

_____

_____

_____

Subtenant may exercise this option only if Subtenant is in compliance with the terms of this Sublease. To exercise this option, Subtenant shall give Sublandlord written notice at least _____ days before the expiration date of the original Sublease term.

7. Security Deposit

Subtenant has deposited $_____ with Sublandlord as security for Subtenant's performance of this Sublease. Sublandlord will refund the full security deposit to Subtenant at the end of the Sublease if Subtenant returns the premises to Sublandlord in good condition (except for reasonable wear and tear) and Subtenant has paid Sublandlord all sums due under this Sublease. Otherwise, Sublandlord may deduct any amounts required to place the premises in good condition and to pay for any sums due under the Sublease.

8. Notices From Landlord

If Landlord notifies Subtenant of any breach of the terms or conditions of the Original Lease which Subtenant is obligated to perform, Subtenant will immediately notify Sublandlord in writing. Subtent will promptly cure any breach.

If Landlord notifies Sublandlord of any breach of the terms or conditions of the Original Lease which Subtenant is obligated to perform, Sublandlord will immediately notify Subtenant in writing. Subtenant will promptly cure any breach.

9. Subletting and Assignment

Subtenant will not assign this Sublease or further sublet any part of the premises without the written consent of both Sublandlord and Landlord. Sublandlord will not unreasonably withhold such consent.

10. Indemnification

A.   Subtenant will indemnify Sublandlord and hold Sublandlord harmless from all claims and liabilities arising because of Subtenant's failure to meet the terms of the Sublease.

B.   Subtenant will arrange for Sublandlord and Landlord to be named as insured parties in all insurance policies required of the Tenant under the Original Lease.

11. Condition of Premises

Subtenant has inspected the premises and accepts the premises in as-is condition.

12. Landlord's Consent

This Sublease will not be effective unless Landlord signs the Landlord's Consent attached to this Sublease.

13. Disputes

(Choose One)

☐   **Litigation.** If a dispute arises, any party may take the matter to court.

☐ **Mediation and Possible Litigation.** If a dispute arises, the parties will try in good faith to settle it through mediation conducted by:

☐ _____.

☐ a mediator to be mutually selected.

The parties will share the costs of the mediator equally. Each party will cooperate fully and fairly with the mediator and will attempt to reach a mutually satisfactory compromise to the dispute. If the dispute is not resolved within 30 days after it is referred to the mediator, any party may take the matter to court.

☐ **Mediation and Possible Arbitration.** If a dispute arises, the parties will try in good faith to settle it through mediation conducted by:

☐ _____.

☐ a mediator to be mutually selected.

The parties will share the costs of the mediator equally. Each party will cooperate fully and fairly with the mediator and will attempt to reach a mutually satisfactory compromise to the dispute. If the dispute is not resolved within 30 days after it is referred to the mediator, it will be arbitrated by:

☐ _____.

☐ an arbitrator to be mutually selected.

Judgment on the arbitration award may be entered in any court that has jurisdiction over the matter. Costs of arbitration, including lawyers' fees, will be allocated by the arbitrator.

Sublandlord need not participate in mediation or arbitration of a dispute unless Subtenant has paid the rent called for by this lease or has placed any unpaid rent in escrow with an agreed-upon mediator or arbitrator.

14. Additional Agreements

Sublandlord and Subtenant additionally agree that: _____

_____

_____

_____

15. Entire Agreement

This is the entire agreement between the parties. It replaces and supersedes any and all oral agreements between the parties, as well as any prior writings.

16. Successors and Assignees

This sublease binds and benefits the heirs, successors and assignees of the parties.

17. Notices

All notices must be in writing. A notice may be delivered to a party at the address that follows a party's signature or to a new address that a party designates in writing. A notice may be delivered:

(1) in person,

(2) by certified mail, or

(3) by overnight courier.

18. Governing Law

This sublease will be governed by and construed in accordance with the laws of the state of _____

_____ .

19. Counterparts

The parties may sign several identical counterparts of this sublease. Any fully signed counterpart shall be treated as an original.

20 Modification

This sublease may only be modified by a writing signed by the party against whom such modification is sought to be enforced.

21. Waiver

If one party waives any term or provision of this sublease at any time, that waiver will only be effective for the specific instance and specific purpose for which the waiver was given. If either party fails to exercise or delays exercising any of its rights or remedies under this sublease, that party retains the right to enforce that term or provision at a later time.

22. Severability

If any court determines that any provision of this sublease is invalid or unenforceable, any invalidity or unenforceability will affect only that provision and will not make any other provision of this sublease invalid or unenforceable and such provision shall be modified, amended or limited only to the extent necessary to render it valid and enforceable.

Dated: _____

SUBLANDLORD

Name of Business: _____

a _____

By: _____

Printed Name and Title: _____

Address: _____

_____

SUBTENANT

Name of Business: _____

a _____

By: _____

Printed Name and Title: _____

Address: _____

_____

Form 6E: Landlord's Consent to Sublease

1. Names

_____, Landlord, gives this consent to

_____ Tenant, and

_____, Subtenant.

2. Consent to Sublease

Landlord consents to the attached Sublease dated _____, which has been signed by

Tenant and Subtenant for the following premises: _____

_____

_____

3. Status of Original Lease

A. The Original Lease referred to in the Sublease remains in full effect and has not been modified in any way.

B. Tenant has currently paid all rent due under the Original Lease.

C. Tenant is not in default under the Original Lease.

D. The Original Lease will not be modified without Subtenant's written consent.

4. Notice of Default

If Tenant or Subtenant defaults in the performance of any obligations under the Original Lease, Landlord will send a written notice to both Tenant and Subtenant by certified mail or overnight delivery (return receipt requested). Tenant and Subtenant will have _____ days after the notice is mailed or delivered to the overnight carrier to cure the default.

Dated: _____

TENANT

Name of Business: _____

a _____

By: _____

Printed Name and Title: _____

Address: _____

_____

SUBTENANT

Name of Business: _____

a _____

By: _____

Printed Name and Title: _____

Address: _____

_____

LANDLORD

Name of Business: _____

a _____

By: _____

Printed Name and Title: _____

Address: _____

_____

Form 6F: Assignment of Lease

1. Names

This lease assignment is made by _____,
Original Tenant, and _____, New Tenant,
with the consent of _____, Landlord.

2. Assignment

Original Tenant assigns to New Tenant all of Original Tenant's rights in the attached Lease dated
_____, which covers the premises located at _____
_____.

3. Effective Date

This assignment will take effect on _____.

4. Acceptance

New Tenant accepts this assignment and assumes the Lease. From the effective date of this assignment,
New Tenant will pay all rents and will perform all of Original Tenant's other obligations under the Lease.

5. Condition of Premises

New Tenant has inspected the premises and accepts the premises in as-is condition.

6. Landlord's Certification

Landlord certifies that:

    A.   Original Tenant has paid all rents through _____.

    B.   Landlord is holding a security deposit in the amount of $_____ , which Landlord
         will now hold for New Tenant under the terms of the Lease.

    C.   Original Tenant is not in default in performing any obligations under the Lease.

    D.   The Lease is unmodified and in full effect.

7. Reimbursement

New Tenant will immediately reimburse Original Tenant for:

☐   The security deposit that Original Tenant posted with Landlord under the Lease.

☐   Any rent and other items that Original Tenant has paid in advance under the Lease covering the
    period following the effective date of this assignment.

8. Landlord's Consent

Landlord consents to this assignment and to New Tenant's taking over Original Tenant's obligations.

9. Release

☐   Landlord releases Original Tenant from liability for the payment of rents and from the performance of all
    other Lease obligations from the effective date of this assignment.

10. Entire Agreement

This is the entire agreement between the parties. It replaces and supersedes any and all oral agreements between the parties, as well as any prior writings.

11. Successors and Assignees

This lease assignment binds and benefits the heirs, successors and assignees of the parties.

12. Notices

All notices must be in writing. A notice may be delivered to a party at the address that follows a party's signature or to a new address that a party designates in writing. A notice may be delivered:

(1) in person,

(2) by certified mail, or

(3) by overnight courier.

13. Governing Law

This lease assignment will be governed by and construed in accordance with the laws of the state of

_____.

14. Counterparts

The parties may sign several identical counterparts of this lease assignment. Any fully signed counterpart shall be treated as an original.

15. Modification

This lease assignment may only be modified by a writing signed by the party against whom such modification is sought to be enforced.

16. Waiver

If one party waives any term or provision of this lease assignment at any time, that waiver will only be effective for the specific instance and specific purpose for which the waiver was given. If either party fails to exercise or delays exercising any of its rights or remedies under this lease assignment, that party retains the right to enforce that term or provision at a later time.

17. Severability

If any court determines that any provision of this lease assignment is invalid or unenforceable, any invalidity or unenforceability will affect only that provision and will not make any other provision of this lease assignment invalid or unenforceable and such provision shall be modified, amended or limited only to the extent necessary to render it valid and enforceable.

Dated: _____

ORIGINAL TENANT

Name of Business: _____

a _____

By: _____

Printed Name and Title: _____

Address: _____

_____

NEW TENANT

Name of Business: _____

a _____

By: _____

Printed Name and Title: _____

Address: _____

_____

LANDLORD

Name of Business: _____

a _____

By: _____

Printed Name and Title: _____

Address: _____

_____

Form 6G: Notice of Exercise of Lease Option

To _____, Landlord:

1. Exercise of Lease Option

_____, Tenant,

exercises its option to extend through _____ its tenancy of the following premises:

_____

_____

_____

2. Notice to Landlord

This notice is given in accordance with the Lease dated _____ covering Tenant's current tenancy of the premises.

Dated: _____

Name of Business: _____

a _____

By: _____

Printed Name and Title: _____

Address: _____

_____

Form 6H: Extension of Lease

1. Names

This extension of lease is made by _____
_____, Landlord, and _____
_____, Tenant.

2. New Lease Term

The lease between Landlord and Tenant dated _____ for the following premises:
_____
_____ is extended through _____.

3. Modifications to Lease

The terms and conditions of the existing lease will apply during the extension period, except as follows:

_____
_____
_____

Dated: _____

LANDLORD

Name of Business: _____

a _____

By: _____

Printed Name and Title: _____

Address: _____

_____

TENANT

Name of Business: _____

a _____

By: _____

Printed Name and Title: _____

Address: _____

_____

Form 61: Amendment of Lease

Amendment Number _____

1. Names

This amendment of lease is made by _____, Landlord, and

_____, Tenant.

2. Terms Amended

The lease dated _____ covering the premises at _____

_____ is amended as follows:

_____

_____

_____

_____

_____

_____

3. Effective Date

This amendment will take effect on _____.

4. Other Terms of Lease

In all other respects, the terms of the original lease and any earlier amendments will remain in effect. If there is a conflict between this amendment and the original lease or any earlier amendment, the terms of this amendment will prevail.

Dated: _____

LANDLORD

Name of Business: _____

a _____

By: _____

Printed Name and Title: _____

Address: _____

_____

TENANT

Name of Business: _____

a _____

By: _____

Printed Name and Title: _____

Address: _____

_____

Form 6J: Attachment to Lease

Attachment Number _____

1. Names

This Attachment of lease is made by _____, Landlord, and

_____, Tenant.

2. Terms of Attachment

Landlord and Tenant agree to the following Attachment to the lease dated _____ covering

the premises at: _____.

_____

_____

_____

_____

_____

_____

_____

_____

_____

_____

_____

Dated: _____

LANDLORD

Name of Business: _____

a _____

By: _____

Printed Name and Title: _____

Address: _____

_____

TENANT

Name of Business: _____

a _____

By: _____

Printed Name and Title: _____

Address: _____

_____

Form 7B: Contract to Purchase Building

1. **Names**

    This contract is made by _____,

    _____ Seller, and _____

    _____, Purchaser.

2. **Purchase of Real Estate**

    Seller is selling and Purchaser is buying the property commonly known as _____

    _____.

    ☐ The legal description of the property is as follows: _____

    _____

    _____

    _____

    ☐ The legal description of the property is given in Attachment 1.

    Seller will transfer the property to Purchaser subject to easements and restrictions of record.

3. **Purchase Price**

    The purchase price is $_____. Seller acknowledges that Purchaser has deposited

    $_____ with _____

    as escrow agent upon the signing of this agreement. This deposit is to be credited against the purchase

    price. Purchaser will pay the balance of $_____ at closing in cash or by cashier's check.

4. **Financing Contingency**

    This contract is contingent upon Purchaser qualifying for and obtaining a commitment for a mortgage or

    deed of trust loan for _____% of the purchase price. Purchaser will apply for such financing within

    _____ business days from the date of this agreement and pursue the application in good faith.

    This financing contingency is to be removed by _____.

5. **Inclusions**

    This contract includes all improvements and fixtures (including lighting, plumbing, heating and cooling fix-

    tures) now on the property, and the following personal property: _____

    _____

    _____

    _____

    At closing, Seller will give Purchaser a bill of sale for the listed personal property.

6. **Exclusions**

    The following items are excluded from this contract: _____

    _____

    _____

    _____

7. Condition of Equipment

Seller warrants that all equipment will be in good working condition at the time of closing, except for:

_____

_____.

8. Physical Problems With Property

To the best of Seller's knowledge, there are no physical problems with the property that would not be

apparent upon inspection, except for the following:_____

_____

_____.

9. Cleaning of Premises

Seller warrants that the premises will be free of trash and will be left in broom-clean condition at the time of closing.

10. Special Assessments

Seller will pay any special assessments that are a lien on the property at the date of closing.

    Purchaser will pay any special assessments that become a lien on the property after the date of closing.

11. Utility Charges

Seller will pay any other charges made against the property by any government authority for installation or extension of water, sanitary or sewer service, if such charges have been incurred before the date of closing.

    Purchaser will pay for the charges incurred after the date of closing.

12. Real Estate Taxes

Real estate taxes will be prorated on a 30-day-month, 360-day-year basis to the date of closing based on the due date of the taxing authority. For proration purposes, these taxes will be deemed to be paid in advance.

13. Other Prorations

Rent, fuel and insurance, where applicable, will be prorated to the date of closing.

14. Closing and Possession

The purchase will be closed on _____. Possession will be given at closing.

15. Transfer of Title

Seller will transfer marketable title to the property to Purchaser by a warranty deed. Seller will pay any transfer tax when title passes.

16. Title Insurance

Seller, at Seller's expense, will provide an owner's policy of title insurance, including a policy commitment before closing, in the amount of the purchase price.

17. Additional Contingencies

This contract is contingent upon satisfactory completion of the following items:

☐   A **contractor's inspection** of the property at Purchaser's expense resulting in a report satisfactory

    to Purchaser. This contingency is to be removed by _____.

☐ An **architect's inspection** of the property at Purchaser's expense resulting in a report satisfactory to Purchaser. This contingency is to be removed by _____.

☐ An **environmental inspection** of the property at Purchaser's expense resulting in findings satisfactory to Purchaser. This contingency is to be removed by _____.

☐ A **review of public and private building and use requirements** affecting the property at Purchaser's expense resulting in findings satisfactory to Purchaser. This contingency is to be removed by _____.

☐ A **stake survey** or survey report at Purchaser's expense resulting in findings satisfactory to Purchaser. This contingency is to be removed by _____.

☐ Approval of the **title insurance** commitment by Purchaser's lawyer. This contingency is to be removed within _____ days after the title insurance commitment is received by Purchaser.

18. Removal of Contingencies

If any contingency in this contract is not removed in writing by the required date, this contract becomes voidable. After the required date and until the contingency is removed, either party may cancel this contract by written notice to the other. In that case, Seller will return the deposit to Purchaser or authorize the escrow agent to do so.

19. Loss Before Closing

Until the purchase is closed and the warranty deed delivered to Purchaser, the risk of loss by fire, windstorm, earthquake, flood or other casualty is assumed by Seller.

20. Default

If Purchaser defaults, Seller may (1) pursue legal remedies or (2) cancel this contract and claim the deposit as liquidated damages.

If Seller defaults, Purchaser may (1) enforce this contract, (2) demand a refund of the deposit in termination of this contract, or (3) pursue legal remedies.

21. Disputes

(Choose One)

☐ **Litigation.** If a dispute arises, any party may take the matter to court.

☐ **Mediation and Possible Litigation.** If a dispute arises, the parties will try in good faith to settle it through mediation conducted by:

    ☐ _____.

    ☐ a mediator to be mutually selected.

The parties will share the costs of the mediator equally. Each party will cooperate fully and fairly with the mediator and will attempt to reach a mutually satisfactory compromise to the dispute. If the dispute is not resolved within 30 days after it is referred to the mediator, any party may take the matter to court.

☐ **Mediation and Possible Arbitration.** If a dispute arises, the parties will try in good faith to settle it through mediation conducted by:

☐ _____.

☐ a mediator to be mutually selected.

The parties will share the costs of the mediator equally. Each party will cooperate fully and fairly with the mediator and will attempt to reach a mutually satisfactory compromise to the dispute. If the dispute is not resolved within 30 days after it is referred to the mediator, it will be arbitrated by:

☐ _____.

☐ an arbitrator to be mutually selected.

Judgment on the arbitration award may be entered in any court that has jurisdiction over the matter. Costs of arbitration, including lawyers' fees, will be allocated by the arbitrator.

22. Additional Agreements

Seller and Buyer additionally agree that: _____

_____

_____

23. Entire Agreement

This is the entire agreement between the parties. It replaces and supersedes any and all oral agreements between the parties, as well as any prior writings.

24. Successors and Assignees

This contract binds and benefits the heirs, successors and assignees of the parties.

25. Notices

All notices must be in writing. A notice may be delivered to a party at the address that follows a party's signature or to a new address that a party designates in writing. A notice may be delivered:

(1) in person,

(2) by certified mail, or

(3) by overnight courier.

26. Governing Law

This contract will be governed by and construed in accordance with the laws of the state of _____

_____.

27. Modification

This contract may be modified only by a writing signed by the party against whom such modification is sought to be enforced.

28. Waiver

If one party waives any term or provision of this contract at any time, that waiver will only be effective for the specific instance and specific purpose for which the waiver was given. If either party fails to exercise or delays exercising any of its rights or remedies under this contract, that party retains the right to enforce that term or provision at a later time.

29. Severability

If any court determines that any provision of this contract is invalid or unenforceable, any invalidity or unenforceability will affect only that provision and will not make any other provision of this contract invalid or unenforceable and such provision shall be modified, amended or limited only to the extent necessary to render it valid and enforceable.

Dated: _____

SELLER

Name of Business: _____

a _____

By: _____

Printed Name and Title: _____

Address: _____

_____

PURCHASER

Name of Business: _____

a _____

By: _____

Printed Name and Title: _____

Address: _____

_____

Form 7C: Option to Purchase Building

1. Names

This contract is made by _____,

Seller, and _____, Purchaser.

2. Option to Purchase Building

In exchange for $_____ that Purchaser has paid to Seller as an option fee, Seller grants to

Purchaser the option to purchase the property commonly known as _____

_____.

☐ The legal description of the property is as follows:

_____

_____

_____

☐ The legal description of the property is given in Attachment _____ to this contract.

3. Exercise of Option

Purchaser may exercise this option by delivering to Seller on or before _____

a written notice of exercise of option. Purchaser may deliver the notice by:

☐ Handing it to Seller.

☐ Sending it to Seller's office at _____

_____ by certified mail or

private overnight mail service, in which case the notice will be treated as delivered when placed

in the possession of the U.S. Postal Service or the private carrier.

4. Purchase Price

If Purchaser exercises the option, the purchase price is $_____. The option

fee ☐ will ☐ will not be applied toward the purchase price. The purchase price will be paid at

closing in cash or by cashier's check.

5. Inclusions

This contract includes all improvements and fixtures (including lighting, plumbing, heating and cooling fixtures)

now on the property, and the following personal property: _____

_____

_____

At closing, Seller will give Purchaser a bill of sale for the listed personal property.

6. Exclusions

The following items are excluded from this contract: _____

_____

_____

_____

7. Condition of Equipment

Seller warrants that all equipment will be in good working condition at the time of closing, except for:

_____

_____.

8. Access to Property

Upon reasonable notice to Seller, Purchaser and others chosen by Purchaser may enter the property at reasonable times to perform a contractor's inspection, an architect's inspection, an environmental inspection and a boundary line survey, as desired by Purchaser. Such inspections will be at Purchaser's expense.

9. Physical Problems With Property

To the best of Seller's knowledge, there are no physical problems with the property that would not be apparent upon inspection, except for the following: _____

_____.

10. Cleaning of Premises

Seller warrants that the premises will be free of trash and will be left in broom-clean condition at the time of closing.

11. Special Assessments

Seller will pay any special assessments that are a lien on the property at the date of closing.

Purchaser will pay any special assessments that become a lien on the property after the date of closing.

12. Utility Charges

Seller will pay any other charges made against the property by any government authority for installation or extension of water, sanitary or sewer service, if such charges have been incurred before the date of closing.

Purchaser will pay for the charges incurred after the date of closing.

13. Real Estate Taxes

Real estate taxes will be prorated on a 30-day-month, 360-day-year basis to the date of closing based on the due date of the taxing authority. For proration purposes, these taxes will be deemed to be paid in advance.

14. Other Prorations

Rent, fuel and insurance, where applicable, will be prorated to the date of closing.

15. Closing and Possession

The purchase will be closed on _____. Possession will be given at closing.

16. Transfer of Title

Seller will transfer marketable title to the property to Purchaser by a warranty deed. Seller will pay any transfer tax due when title passes.

17. Title Insurance

Seller, at Seller's expense, will provide an owner's policy of title insurance, including a policy commitment before closing, in the amount of the purchase price. The purchase is contingent upon Purchaser's lawyer approving:

☐ the title insurance commitment.

☐ a survey of the property to be provided by Seller.

Seller will deliver these documents to Purchaser on or before _____.

This contingency is to be removed within _____ days after Purchaser receives the documents called for above. If the contingency is not removed, Seller will refund the option fee to Purchaser.

18. Loss Before Closing

Until the purchase is closed and the warranty deed delivered to Purchaser, the risk of loss by fire, wind-storm, earthquake, flood or other casualty is assumed by Seller.

19. Default

If Purchaser defaults, Seller may (1) pursue legal remedies or (2) cancel this contract and claim the option fee as liquidated damages.

If Seller defaults, Purchaser may (1) enforce this contract, (2) demand a refund of the option fee in termination of this contract or (3) pursue legal remedies.

20. Disputes

(Choose One)

☐ **Litigation.** If a dispute arises, any party may take the matter to court.

☐ **Mediation and Possible Litigation.** If a dispute arises, the parties will try in good faith to settle it through mediation conducted by:

    ☐ _____.

    ☐ a mediator to be mutually selected.

The parties will share the costs of the mediator equally. Each party will cooperate fully and fairly with the mediator and will attempt to reach a mutually satisfactory compromise to the dispute. If the dispute is not resolved within 30 days after it is referred to the mediator, any party may take the matter to court.

☐ **Mediation and Possible Arbitration.** If a dispute arises, the parties will try in good faith to settle it through mediation conducted by:

    ☐ _____.

    ☐ a mediator to be mutually selected.

The parties will share the costs of the mediator equally. Each party will cooperate fully and fairly with the mediator and will attempt to reach a mutually satisfactory compromise to the dispute. If the dispute is not resolved within 30 days after it is referred to the mediator, it will be arbitrated by:

    ☐ _____.

    ☐ an arbitrator to be mutually selected.

Judgment on the arbitration award may be entered in any court that has jurisdiction over the matter. Costs of arbitration, including lawyers' fees, will be allocated by the arbitrator.

21. Additional Agreements

Seller and Buyer additionally agree that: _____

_____

_____

22. Entire Agreement

This is the entire agreement between the parties. It replaces and supersedes any and all oral agreements between the parties, as well as any prior writings.

23. Successors and Assignees

This contract binds and benefits the heirs, successors and assignees of the parties.

24. Notices

All notices must be in writing. A notice may be delivered to a party at the address that follows a party's signature or to a new address that a party designates in writing. A notice may be delivered:

    (1) in person,

    (2) by certified mail, or

    (3) by overnight courier.

25. Governing Law

This contract will be governed by and construed in accordance with the laws of the state of _____

_____.

26. Counterparts

The parties may sign several identical counterparts of this contract. Any fully signed counterpart shall be treated as an original.

27. Modification

This contract may be modified only by a writing signed by the party against whom such modification is sought to be enforced.

28. Waiver

If one party waives any term or provision of this contract at any time, that waiver will only be effective for the specific instance and specific purpose for which the waiver was given. If either party fails to exercise or delays exercising any of its rights or remedies under this contract, that party retains the right to enforce that term or provision at a later time.

29. Severability

If any court determines that any provision of this contract is invalid or unenforceable, any invalidity or unenforceability will affect only that provision and will not make any other provision of this contract invalid or unenforceable and such provision shall be modified, amended or limited only to the extent necessary to render it valid and enforceable.

Dated: _____

SELLER

Name of Business: _____

a _____

By: _____

Printed Name and Title: _____

Address: _____

_____

PURCHASER

Name of Business: _____

a _____

By: _____

Printed Name and Title: _____

Address: _____

_____

Form 7D: Contract to Purchase Vacant Land

1. Names

This contract is made by _____,

_____ Seller, and _____

_____, Purchaser.

2. Purchase of Real Estate

Seller is selling and Purchaser is buying the property commonly known as _____

_____.

☐ The legal description of the property is as follows:

_____

_____

_____

☐ The legal description of the property is given in Attachment _____.

Seller will transfer the property to Purchaser subject to easements and restrictions of record.

3. Purchase Price

The purchase price is $_____. Seller acknowledges that Purchaser has deposited

$_____ with _____

as escrow agent upon the signing of this agreement. This deposit is to be credited against the purchase

price. Purchaser will pay the balance of $_____ at closing in cash or by cashier's check.

4. Financing Contingency

This contract is contingent upon Purchaser qualifying for and obtaining a commitment for a mortgage or

deed of trust loan for _____% of the purchase price. Purchaser will apply for such financing within

_____ business days from the date of this agreement and pursue the application in good faith.

This financing contingency is to be removed by _____.

5. Special Assessments

Seller will pay any special assessments that are a lien on the property at the date of closing.
Purchaser will pay any special assessments that become a lien on the property after the date of closing.

6. Utility Charges

Seller will pay any other charges made against the property by any government authority for installation or
extension of water, sanitary or sewer service, if such charges have been incurred before the date of closing.
Purchaser will pay for the charges incurred after the date of closing.

7. Real Estate Taxes

Real estate taxes will be prorated on a 30-day-month, 360-day-year basis to the date of closing based on the
due date of the taxing authority. For proration purposes, these taxes will be deemed to be paid in advance.

8. Closing and Possession

The purchase will be closed on _____. Possession will be given at closing.

9. Transfer of Title

Seller will transfer marketable title to the property to Purchaser by a warranty deed. Seller will pay any transfer tax due when title passes.

10. Title Insurance

Seller, at Seller's expense, will provide an owner's policy of title insurance, including a policy commitment before closing, in the amount of the purchase price.

11. Additional Contingencies

This contract is contingent upon satisfactory completion of the following items:

☐ A **contractor's inspection** of the property at Purchaser's expense resulting in a report satisfactory to Purchaser. This contingency is to be removed by _____.

☐ An **architect's inspection** of the property at Purchaser's expense resulting in a report satisfactory to Purchaser. This contingency is to be removed by _____.

☐ An **environmental inspection** of the property at Purchaser's expense resulting in findings satisfactory to Purchaser. This contingency is to be removed by

_____.

☐ A **review of public and private building and use requirements** affecting the property at Purchaser's expense resulting in findings satisfactory to Purchaser. This contingency is to be removed by _____.

☐ A **stake survey** or survey report at Purchaser's expense resulting in findings satisfactory to Purchaser. This contingency is to be removed by _____.

☐ Approval of the **title insurance** commitment by Purchaser's lawyer. This contingency is to be removed within _____ days after the title insurance commitment is received by Purchaser.

12. Removal of Contingencies

If any contingency in this contract is not removed in writing by the required date, this contract becomes voidable. After the required date and until the contingency is removed, either party may cancel this contract by written notice to the other. In that case, Seller will return the deposit to Purchaser.

13. Default

If Purchaser defaults, Seller may (1) pursue legal remedies or (2) cancel this contract and claim the deposit as liquidated damages.

If Seller defaults, Purchaser may (1) enforce this contract, (2) demand a refund of the deposit in termination of this contract or (3) pursue legal remedies.

14. Disputes

(Choose One)

☐ **Litigation.** If a dispute arises, any party may take the matter to court.

☐ **Mediation and Possible Litigation.** If a dispute arises, the parties will try in good faith to settle it through mediation conducted by:

☐ _____.

☐ a mediator to be mutually selected.

The parties will share the costs of the mediator equally. Each party will cooperate fully and fairly with the mediator and will attempt to reach a mutually satisfactory compromise to the dispute. If the dispute is not resolved within 30 days after it is referred to the mediator, any party may take the matter to court.

☐ **Mediation and Possible Arbitration.** If a dispute arises, the parties will try in good faith to settle it through mediation conducted by:

☐ _____.

☐ a mediator to be mutually selected.

The parties will share the costs of the mediator equally. Each party will cooperate fully and fairly with the mediator and will attempt to reach a mutually satisfactory compromise to the dispute. If the dispute is not resolved within 30 days after it is referred to the mediator, it will be arbitrated by:

☐ _____.

☐ an arbitrator to be mutually selected.

Judgment on the arbitration award may be entered in any court that has jurisdiction over the matter. Costs of arbitration, including lawyers' fees, will be allocated by the arbitrator.

15. Additional Agreements

Seller and Buyer additionally agree that: _____

_____

_____

_____

_____

16. Entire Agreement

This is the entire agreement between the parties. It replaces and supersedes any and all oral agreements between the parties, as well as any prior writings.

17. Successors and Assignees

This contract binds and benefits the heirs, successors and assignees of the parties.

18. Notices

All notices must be in writing. A notice may be delivered to a party at the address that follows a party's signature or to a new address that a party designates in writing. A notice may be delivered:

(1) in person,

(2) by certified mail, or

(3) by overnight courier.

19. Governing Law

This contract will be governed by and construed in accordance with the laws of the state of _____

_____.

20. Counterparts

The parties may sign several identical counterparts of this contract. Any fully signed counterpart shall be treated as an original.

21. Modification

This contract may be modified only by a writing signed by the party against whom such modification is sought to be enforced.

22. Waiver

If one party waives any term or provision of this contract at any time, that waiver will only be effective for the specific instance and specific purpose for which the waiver was given. If either party fails to exercise or delays exercising any of its rights or remedies under this contract, that party retains the right to enforce that term or provision at a later time.

23. Severability

If any court determines that any provision of this contract is invalid or unenforceable, any invalidity or unenforceability will affect only that provision and will not make any other provision of this contract invalid or unenforceable and such provision shall be modified, amended or limited only to the extent necessary to render it valid and enforceable.

Dated: _____

SELLER

Name of Business: _____

a _____

By: _____

Printed Name and Title: _____

Address: _____

_____

PURCHASER

Name of Business: _____

a _____

By: _____

Printed Name and Title: _____

Address: _____

_____

Form 7E: Option to Purchase Vacant Land

1. Names

This contract is made by _____,

_____ Seller, and _____

_____ , Purchaser.

2. Option to Purchase Vacant Land

In exchange for $_____ that Purchaser has paid to Seller as an option fee, Seller grants to Purchaser the option to purchase the property commonly known as: _____

_____ .

☐ The legal description of the property is as follows: _____

_____

_____

_____

_____ .

☐ The legal description of the property is given in Attachment _____ to this contract.

If Purchaser exercises this option, Seller will transfer the property to Purchaser on the terms stated in this contract. The conveyance will be subject to easements and restrictions of record.

3. Exercise of Option

Purchaser may exercise this option by delivering to Seller on or before _____

a written notice of exercise of option. Purchaser may deliver the notice by:

☐ Handing it to Seller.

☐ Sending it to Seller's office at _____

by certified mail or private overnight mail service, in which case the notice will be treated as delivered when placed in the possession of the U.S. Postal Service or the private carrier.

4. Purchase Price

If Purchaser exercises the option, the purchase price is $_____ . The option fee ☐ will ☐ will not be applied toward the purchase price. The purchase price will be paid at closing in cash or by cashier's check.

5. Access to Property

Upon reasonable notice to Seller, Purchaser and others chosen by Purchaser may enter the property at reasonable times to perform a contractor's inspection, an architect's inspection, an environmental inspection and a boundary line survey, as desired by Purchaser. Such inspections will be at Purchaser's expense.

6. Special Assessments

Seller will pay any special assessments that are a lien on the property at the date of closing.

Purchaser will pay any special assessments that become a lien on the property after the date of closing.

7. Utility Charges

Seller will pay any other charges made against the property by any government authority for installation or extension of water, sanitary or sewer service, if such charges have been incurred before the date of closing. Purchaser will pay for the charges incurred after the date of closing.

8. Real Estate Taxes

Real estate taxes will be prorated on a 30-day-month, 360-day-year basis to the date of closing based on the due date of the taxing authority. For proration purposes, these taxes will be deemed to be paid in advance.

9. Closing and Possession

The purchase will be closed on _____. Possession of the premises will be given to Purchaser at closing.

10. Transfer of Title

Seller will transfer marketable title to the property to Purchaser by a warranty deed. Seller will pay any transfer tax due when title passes.

11. Title Insurance

Seller, at Seller's expense, will provide an owner's policy of title insurance, including a policy commitment before closing, in the amount of the purchase price. The purchase is contingent upon Purchaser's lawyer approving:

☐ the title insurance commitment.

☐ a survey of the property to be provided by Seller.

Seller will deliver these documents to Purchaser on or before _____.

This contingency is to be removed within _____ days after Purchaser receives the documents called for above. If the contingency is not removed, Seller will refund the option fee to Purchaser.

12. Default

If Purchaser defaults, Seller may (1) pursue legal remedies or (2) cancel this contract and claim the option fee as liquidated damages.

If Seller defaults, Purchaser may (1) enforce this contract, (2) demand a refund of the option fee in termination of this contract, or (3) pursue legal remedies.

13. Disputes

(Choose One)

☐ **Litigation.** If a dispute arises, any party may take the matter to court.

☐ **Mediation and Possible Litigation.** If a dispute arises, the parties will try in good faith to settle it through mediation conducted by:

☐ _____.

☐ a mediator to be mutually selected.

The parties will share the costs of the mediator equally. Each party will cooperate fully and fairly with the mediator and will attempt to reach a mutually satisfactory compromise to the dispute. If the dispute is not resolved within 30 days after it is referred to the mediator, any party may take the matter to court.

☐ **Mediation and Possible Arbitration.** If a dispute arises, the parties will try in good faith to settle it through mediation conducted by:

☐ _____.

☐ a mediator to be mutually selected.

The parties will share the costs of the mediator equally. Each party will cooperate fully and fairly with the mediator and will attempt to reach a mutually satisfactory compromise to the dispute. If the dispute is not resolved within 30 days after it is referred to the mediator, it will be arbitrated by:

☐ _____.

☐ an arbitrator to be mutually selected.

Judgment on the arbitration award may be entered in any court that has jurisdiction over the matter. Costs of arbitration, including lawyers' fees, will be allocated by the arbitrator

14. Additional Agreements

Seller and Buyer additionally agree that: _____

_____

_____.

15. Entire Agreement

This is the entire agreement between the parties. It replaces and supersedes any and all oral agreements between the parties, as well as any prior writings.

16. Successors and Assignees

This contract binds and benefits the heirs, successors and assignees of the parties.

17. Notices

All notices must be in writing. A notice may be delivered to a party at the address that follows a party's signature or to a new address that a party designates in writing. A notice may be delivered:

(1) in person,

(2) by certified mail, or

(3) by overnight courier.

18. Governing Law

This contract will be governed by and construed in accordance with the laws of the state of _____

_____.

19. Counterparts

The parties may sign several identical counterparts of this contract. Any fully signed counterpart shall be treated as an original.

20. Modification

This contract may be modified only by a writing signed by the party against whom such modification is sought to be enforced.

21. Waiver

If one party waives any term or provision of this contract at any time, that waiver will only be effective for the specific instance and specific purpose for which the waiver was given. If either party fails to exercise or delays exercising any of its rights or remedies under this contract, that party retains the right to enforce that term or provision at a later time.

22. Severability

If any court determines that any provision of this contract is invalid or unenforceable, any invalidity or unenforceability will affect only that provision and will not make any other provision of this contract invalid or unenforceable and such provision shall be modified, amended or limited only to the extent necessary to render it valid and enforceable.

Dated: _____

SELLER

Name of Business: _____

a _____

By: _____

Printed Name and Title: _____

Address: _____

_____

PURCHASER

Name of Business: _____

a _____

By: _____

Printed Name and Title: _____

Address: _____

_____

Form 7F: Attachment to Real Estate Purchase Contract

Attachment Number _____

_____, Seller,

and _____, Purchaser,

agree to the following Attachment to the real estate purchase contract dated _____

covering the property described as: _____

_____

_____

_____

[Describe what is agreed to.]

_____

_____

_____

_____

_____

_____

_____

_____

Dated: _____

SELLER

Name of Business: _____

a _____

By: _____

Printed Name and Title: _____

Address: _____

_____

PURCHASER

Name of Business: _____

a _____

By: _____

Printed Name and Title: _____

Address: _____

_____

Form 7G: Amendment of Real Estate Purchase Contract

Amendment Number _____

_____, Seller,

and _____, Purchaser,

agree to the following amendment of the real estate purchase contract dated _____

covering the property described as: _____

_____

_____

[Describe what is agreed to.]

_____

_____

_____

_____

_____

_____

    In all other respects, the terms of the original contract and any earlier amendments will remain in effect. If there is conflict between this amendment and the original contract or any earlier amendment, the terms of this amendment will prevail.

Dated: _____

SELLER

Name of Business: _____

a _____

By: _____

Printed Name and Title: _____

Address: _____

_____

PURCHASER

Name of Business: _____

a _____

By: _____

Printed Name and Title: _____

Address: _____

_____

Form 7H: Removal of Contingency

This contingency removal relates to the following real estate purchase contract:

Seller: _____

Purchaser: _____

Date of Contract Containing Contingency: _____

Location of Property: _____

_____

Purchaser removes the following contingencies:

☐   Contingency regarding financing (contract paragraph #_____).

☐   Contingency regarding satisfactory contractor's report (contract paragraph #_____).

☐   Contingency regarding satisfactory architect's report (contract paragraph #_____).

☐   Contingency regarding satisfactory environmental report (contract paragraph #_____).

☐   Contingency regarding satisfactory report on building and use requirements (contract paragraph #_____).

☐   Contingency regarding Purchaser's lawyer's approval of title insurance commitment, subject to a survey report or stake survey showing no encroachments objectionable to Purchaser (contract paragraph #_____).

☐   Other: _____

_____

Dated: _____

PURCHASER

Name of Business: _____

a _____

By: _____

Printed Name and Title: _____

Address: _____

_____

Form 71: Extension of Time to Remove Contingencies

This extension of time relates to the following real estate purchase contract:

Seller: _____

Purchaser: _____

Date of Contract Containing Contingency: _____

Location of Property: _____

_____

Purchaser and Seller agree that the dates for removal of contingencies are extended as follows:

☐ Contingency regarding financing (contract paragraph #_____) is extended to _____.

☐ Contingency regarding satisfactory contractor's report (contract paragraph #_____) is extended to _____.

☐ Contingency regarding satisfactory architect's report (contract paragraph #_____) is extended to _____.

☐ Contingency regarding satisfactory environmental report (contract paragraph #_____) is extended to _____.

☐ Contingency regarding satisfactory report on building and use requirements (contract paragraph #_____) is extended to _____.

☐ Contingency regarding Purchaser's lawyer's approval of title insurance commitment, subject to a survey report or stake survey showing no encroachments objectionable to Purchaser (contract paragraph #_____) is extended to _____.

☐ Other: _____

_____

_____

extended to _____.

Any contingency removal date not changed here will remain as previously agreed.

Dated: _____

SELLER

Name of Business: _____

a _____

By: _____

Printed Name and Title: _____

Address: _____

_____

PURCHASER

Name of Business: _____

a _____

By: _____

Printed Name and Title: _____

Address: _____

_____

Form 7J: Exercise of Option to Purchase Real Estate

To _____, Seller:

_____, Purchaser,

exercises its option to purchase the following property: _____

_____

_____

_____

This notice is given in accordance with the option contract dated _____.

Dated: _____

PURCHASER

Name of Business: _____

a _____

By: _____

Printed Name and Title: _____

Address: _____

_____

Form 7K: Renovation Contract

1. Names

This contract is made by _____, Owner,

and _____, Contractor.

2. Scope and Location

Contractor will provide renovation services to Owner's property located at _____

_____.

   Contractor will provide all of the materials, permits, plans, labor and supervision and insurance necessary for the renovation.

3. Plans, Specifications and Warranty

The plans and specifications dated _____ are stated in Attachment 1. Contractor's warranty is stated in Attachment 2.

4. Price

Owner will pay Contractor $_____ for the job. This price is subject to the additions and deductions described below.

☐ 5. Financing Contingency *(Optional)*

This contract is contingent upon Owner obtaining a renovation loan of $_____, for which Owner will apply within five business days. This contingency will be removed by _____

_____. If Owner does not remove the financing contingency in writing by the specified date, this contract will be void.

6. Payment Terms

(Choose One)

   ☐ Upon approval of Owner's financing, Owner will pay Contractor $_____ to be applied toward the price.

   ☐ Contractor has received $_____ from Owner to be applied toward the price.

   The balance of the price will be disbursed by Owner's renovation lender (if any) or by Owner according to the payment schedule in Attachment 3 of this contract. Disbursement of the final payment is covered in paragraph 14 of this contract.

   Upon completion of each construction stage, Contractor will submit to Owner and Owner's construction lender (if any) and title insurer an itemized application for payment, signed under penalty of perjury. Contractor will support each application for payment with such data substantiating Contractor's right to payment and the absence of construction liens as Owner and Owner's construction lender (if any) and title insurer may reasonably require.

   Owner will pay Contractor within seven days of receiving Contractor's application for payment. Owner, however, upon written notice to Contractor, may withhold a reasonable part of any payment for:

   A. Incomplete work

   B. Defective work not remedied

C. Claims filed against Owner's property by workers or suppliers or a reasonable likelihood of such claims being filed, or

D. Contractor's failure to pay for labor, materials or equipment.

When the grounds for withholding are removed, Owner will pay Contractor the amounts withheld. Contractor will promptly pay each subcontractor, material supplier and laborer for their services or materials.

7. Commencement of Renovation

Contractor will apply for building permits

(Choose One)

☐ when Owner's renovation loan has been verified.

☐ immediately.

☐ Other: _____

and, upon receiving the permits, will commence renovation.

8. Completion of Renovation

Contractor will complete the renovation by _____. If, however, Contractor cannot meet that deadline due to unanticipated weather conditions, strikes, fire or other causes beyond Contractor's control, the completion deadline will be extended for a period equal to the unavoidable delay if Contractor promptly notifies Owner in writing of the cause and length of the delay.

In any event, Contractor will complete the renovation by _____.

9. Change Orders

All changes to the job will be made through written change orders signed by Owner and Contractor.

10. Toxic Materials

Owner and Contractor are not aware of any toxic materials (such as asbestos, radon or lead-based paint) being present in the building. If during renovation any toxic materials or conditions are discovered, Contractor will immediately report the discovery to Owner and will safely handle the materials and deal with the conditions according to, and comply with, all local, state and federal laws and regulations. Owner will arrange and pay for the proper removal, containment or mitigation of the toxic materials or conditions.

11. Insurance

Contractor will maintain the following insurance:

A. Builder's Risk Insurance covering the theft of building materials, including building materials in transit to the site.

B. Worker's Compensation Insurance covering workers employed by Contractor.

C. Automobile Liability Coverage for owned, non-owned and hired vehicles with a $1,000,000.00 policy limit.

Contractor will require subcontractors to carry the same coverage specified in subparagraphs B and C, and will verify that subcontractors meet this requirement.

12. Indemnification

Contractor will indemnify and hold Owner harmless against all claims and expenses, including attorney fees, arising out of the performance of the renovation work and attributable to bodily damage or property damage caused by the act or omission of Contractor or any subcontractor, employee or anyone else for whose act Contractor is responsible.

13. Inspections

During the renovation, Owner, Owner's lender (if any) and all applicable public authorities will have the right to inspect the work and materials.

14. Final Payment

The renovation will be considered complete for final payment purposes when:

A. the municipality has issued a Certificate of Occupancy

B. the Owner's lender (if any) has approved the renovations as meeting the plans and specifications called for by this contract

C. all workers and suppliers have been paid, and

D. owner has determined that the renovation work meets the plans and specifications called for by this contract.

If the renovation is not complete at the time of final payment and a temporary Certificate of Occupancy has been issued, Owner will make the final payment but a portion of the payment will be placed in escrow with Owner's title insurance company equal to 150% of the estimated cost of completing the work. The escrow agreement will call for the escrow agent to release the escrowed funds to Contractor when Contractor has completed the renovation in a manner satisfactory to Owner and Owner's lender (if any).

15. Standards of Performance

The renovation work will comply with:

A. the plans and specifications set out in Attachment _____, and

B. the applicable laws, ordinances and building codes.

The renovation work will also meet the standards of workmanship prevailing in the community of

_____ for the renovation of

commercial buildings.

16. Contractor's Default

Contractor will be in default if Contractor:

A. does not have or maintain all legally required licenses

B. fails to supply enough properly skilled workers or proper materials

C. disregards laws, ordinances, building codes or orders of any public authority

D. violates any other provision of this contract

E. ceases work for more than seven consecutive days except for reasons beyond Contractor's control, or

F. becomes bankrupt or insolvent.

If Contractor defaults, Owner may give Contractor seven days written notice to cure the default. If Contractor fails to cure the default within that time, Owner may then terminate this contract, take possession of all materials at the site and finish the renovation work. Contractor will pay Owner any cost of finishing the renovation work in excess of the unpaid balance of the contract price as of the termination date.

Such action by Owner will not affect any other right or remedy available to Owner for Contractor's default.

17. Owner's Default

If Owner does not make timely payments as required by this contract, Contractor may give Owner seven days written notice to make all such payments. If Owner fails to make the payments after receiving the notice, Contractor may terminate this contract and recover from Owner payment for all work done through the termination date. Contractor may also pursue all remedies available under the lien laws of _____

_____.

Owner will not be in default for withholding payment or authorization for payment if:

A.   Contractor has materially defaulted on any obligations under this contract, or

B.   withholding of payments is based on a reason listed in paragraph 5 above.

18. Disputes

(Choose One)

☐ **Litigation.** If a dispute arises, any party may take the matter to court.

☐ **Mediation and Possible Litigation.** If a dispute arises, the parties will try in good faith to settle it through mediation conducted by:

☐ _____.

☐ a mediator to be mutually selected.

The parties will share the costs of the mediator equally. Each party will cooperate fully and fairly with the mediator and will attempt to reach a mutually satisfactory compromise to the dispute. If the dispute is not resolved within 30 days after it is referred to the mediator, any party may take the matter to court.

☐ **Mediation and Possible Arbitration.** If a dispute arises, the parties will try in good faith to settle it through mediation conducted by:

☐ _____.

☐ a mediator to be mutually selected.

The parties will share the costs of the mediator equally. Each party will cooperate fully and fairly with the mediator and will attempt to reach a mutually satisfactory compromise to the dispute. If the dispute is not resolved within 30 days after it is referred to the mediator, it will be arbitrated by:

☐ _____.

☐ an arbitrator to be mutually selected.

Judgment on the arbitration award may be entered in any court that has jurisdiction over the matter. Costs of arbitration, including lawyers' fees, will be allocated by the arbitrator.

19. Additional Agreements

Seller and Buyer additionally agree that: _____

_____

_____.

20. Entire Agreement

This is the entire agreement between the parties. It replaces and supersedes any and all oral agreements between the parties, as well as any prior writings.

21. Successors and Assignees

This contract binds and benefits the heirs, successors and assignees of the parties.

22. Notices

All notices must be in writing. A notice may be delivered to a party at the address that follows a party's signature or to a new address that a party designates in writing. A notice may be delivered:

(1) in person,

(2) by certified mail, or

(3) by overnight courier.

23. Governing Law

This contract will be governed by and construed in accordance with the laws of the state of _____ _____.

24. Counterparts

The parties may sign several identical counterparts of this contract. Any fully signed counterpart shall be treated as an original.

25. Modification

This contract may be modified only by a writing signed by the party against whom such modification is sought to be enforced.

26. Waiver

If one party waives any term or provision of this contract at any time, that waiver will only be effective for the specific instance and specific purpose for which the waiver was given. If either party fails to exercise or delays exercising any of its rights or remedies under this contract, that party retains the right to enforce that term or provision at a later time.

27. Severability

If any court determines that any provision of this contract is invalid or unenforceable, any invalidity or unenforceability will affect only that provision and will not make any other provision of this contract invalid or unenforceable and such provision shall be modified, amended or limited only to the extent necessary to render it valid and enforceable.

Dated: _____

OWNER

Name of Business: _____

a _____

By: _____

Printed Name and Title: _____

Address: _____

_____

CONTRACTOR

Name of Business: _____

a _____

By: _____

Printed Name and Title: _____

Address: _____

_____

Form 8A: Sales Contract (Lump Sum Payment)

1. Names

_____, Seller,

and _____, Buyer,

agree to the following sale.

2. Property Being Sold

Seller agrees to sell to Buyer, and Buyer agrees to buy from Seller, the following property:

_____

_____

_____

3. Condition of Property
(Choose One)

☐ **New Property.** The property is new.

☐ **Used Property.** Buyer has inspected the property and will accept it

    ☐ in "as is" condition.

    ☐ in "as is" condition except for the following modifications which Seller agrees to make before delivery:

    _____

    _____

    _____

☐ 4. Disclaimer of Warranties *(Optional)*

The property is being sold without any warranties, whether express or implied, including the implied warranties of merchantability and fitness for a particular purpose.

5. Purchase Price

The purchase price of the property is: $_____.

6. Down Payment
(Choose One)

☐ Buyer will make a down payment of $_____ when this contract is signed. This down payment will be applied toward the purchase price.

☐ Buyer will not make a down payment.

7. Time of Payment
(Choose One)

Buyer will pay Seller the purchase price (less any down payment) as follows:

☐ upon delivery of the property to Buyer in the condition called for in paragraph 3.

☐ the entire balance on _____.

8. Method of Payment

Buyer will pay Seller by:

☐ personal check.

☐ cashier's check.

☐ credit card issued by _____ .

9. Delivery

Seller will deliver the property to Buyer on _____ at _____

_____ .

10. Ownership

Seller has legal title to the property and is selling the property free of any liens or liabilities.

11. Transfer of Ownership

Seller will transfer ownership of the property to Buyer through:

☐ a bill of sale.

☐ such documents as may be required by the state of _____
to legally transfer the ownership of the property.

12. Other Terms and Conditions

_____

_____

_____

_____

_____

13. Entire Agreement

This is the entire agreement between the parties. It replaces and supersedes any and all oral agreements between the parties, as well as any prior writings.

14. Successors and Assignees

This agreement binds and benefits the heirs, successors and assignees of the parties.

15. Notices

All notices must be in writing. A notice may be delivered to a party at the address that follows a party's signature or to a new address that a party designates in writing. A notice may be delivered:

(1) in person,

(2) by certified mail, or

(3) by overnight courier.

16. Governing Law

This agreement will be governed by and construed in accordance with the laws of the state of _____

_____ .

17. Counterparts

The parties may sign several identical counterparts of this agreement. Any fully signed counterpart shall be treated as an original.

18. Modification

This agreement may only be modified by a writing signed by the party against whom such modification is sought to be enforced.

19. Waiver

If one party waives any term or provision of this agreement at any time, that waiver will only be effective for the specific instance and specific purpose for which the waiver was given. If either party fails to exercise or delays exercising any of its rights or remedies under this agreement, that party retains the right to enforce that term or provision at a later time.

20. Severability

If any court determines that any provision of this agreement is invalid or unenforceable, any invalidity or unenforceability will affect only that provision and will not make any other provision of this agreement invalid or unenforceable and such provision shall be modified, amended or limited only to the extent necessary to render it valid and enforceable.

Dated: _____

SELLER

Name of Business: _____

a _____

By: _____

Printed Name and Title: _____

Address: _____

_____

BUYER

Name of Business: _____

a _____

By: _____

Printed Name and Title: _____

Address: _____

_____

Form 8B: Sales Contract (Installment Payments)

1. Names

_____, Seller,

and _____, Buyer,

agree to the following sale.

2. Property Being Sold

Seller agrees to sell to Buyer, and Buyer agrees to buy from Seller, the following property:

_____

_____

_____

3. Condition of Property
(Choose One)

☐ **New Property.** The property is new.

☐ **Used Property.** Buyer has inspected the property and will accept it

    ☐ in "as-is" condition.

    ☐ in "as-is" condition except for the following modifications, which Seller agrees to make before delivery:

_____

_____

_____

_____

_____

_____

_____

_____

☐ **4. Disclaimer of Warranties** *(Optional)*

The property is being sold without any warranties, whether express or implied, including the implied warranties of merchantability and fitness for a particular purpose.

5. Purchase Price

The purchase price of the property is $_____ .

6. Down Payment
(Choose One)

☐ Buyer will make a down payment of $_____ when this contract is signed. This down payment will be applied toward the purchase price.

☐ Buyer will not make a down payment.

7. Time of Payment

Buyer will pay Seller the purchase price (less any down payment) in installments as follows:

_____

_____

_____

8. Delivery

Seller will deliver the property to Buyer on _____ at _____

_____.

9. Ownership

Seller has legal title to the property and is selling the property free of any liens or liabilities.

10. Transfer of Ownership

Seller will transfer ownership of the property to Buyer through:

☐ a bill of sale.

☐ such documents as may be required by the state of _____
to legally transfer the ownership of the property.

11. Security Interest

☐ Seller will not retain a security interest in the property.

☐ Seller will retain a security interest in the property. At the time the property is delivered to Buyer, Buyer will sign and deliver to Seller a security agreement and UCC financing statement giving Seller a security interest in the property until the purchase price has been paid in full.

12. Other Terms and Conditions

_____

_____

_____

_____

13. Entire Agreement

This is the entire agreement between the parties. It replaces and supersedes any and all oral agreements between the parties, as well as any prior writings.

14. Successors and Assignees

This agreement binds and benefits the heirs, successors and assignees of the parties.

15. Notices

All notices must be in writing. A notice may be delivered to a party at the address that follows a party's signature or to a new address that a party designates in writing. A notice may be delivered:

(1) in person,

(2) by certified mail, or

(3) by overnight courier.

16. Governing Law

This agreement will be governed by and construed in accordance with the laws of the state of _____

_____ .

17. Counterparts

The parties may sign several identical counterparts of this agreement. Any fully signed counterpart shall be treated as an original.

18. Modification

This agreement may only be modified by a writing signed by the party against whom such modification is sought to be enforced.

19. Waiver

If one party waives any term or provision of this agreement at any time, that waiver will only be effective for the specific instance and specific purpose for which the waiver was given. If either party fails to exercise or delays exercising any of its rights or remedies under this agreement, that party retains the right to enforce that term or provision at a later time.

20. Severability

If any court determines that any provision of this agreement is invalid or unenforceable, any invalidity or unenforceability will affect only that provision and will not make any other provision of this agreement invalid or unenforceable and such provision shall be modified, amended or limited only to the extent necessary to render it valid and enforceable.

Dated: _____

SELLER

Name of Business: _____

a _____

By: _____

Printed Name and Title: _____

Address: _____

_____

BUYER

Name of Business: _____

a _____

By: _____

Printed Name and Title: _____

Address: _____

_____

Form 8C: Bill of Sale

1. Names

Seller: _____

Buyer: _____

2. Transfer of Ownership

Seller sells and transfers to Buyer the following property:

_____

_____

   Seller acknowledges receiving $_____ and other consideration from Buyer as payment for this transfer of ownership.

3. Condition of Property

(Choose One)

☐ The property is new and Seller is transferring it to Buyer in new condition.

☐ The property is used and Seller is transferring it to Buyer in "as-is" condition.

4. Warranty of Ownership

Seller warrants that Seller is the legal owner of the property and that the property is free of all liens and encumbrances.

Dated: _____

SELLER

Name of Business: _____

a _____

By: _____

Printed Name and Title: _____

Address: _____

_____

Form 8D: Security Agreement

1. Names

Seller: _____

Buyer: _____

2. Grant of Security Interest

Buyer grants to Seller a continuing security interest in the following property (the "Secured Property") which

consists of: _____

_____

_____

and all proceeds, products and accessions of and to the Secured Property, including any money, property or insurance proceeds Buyer receives from the loss, sale, transfer or damage of or to the Secured Property.

3. Installment Payments

Buyer is granting this security interest to secure performance of Buyer's promise to make the following

installment payments on the Secured Property: _____

_____

_____

_____

4. Financing Statement

Concurrently with the execution of this Security Agreement, Buyer will sign and deliver to Seller a UCC financing statement to further protect Seller's security interest in the Secured Property.

5. Use and Care of the Secured Property

Until all installment payments have been made, Buyer agrees to:

A. Keep the Secured Property at _____

_____

B. Maintain the Secured Property in good repair.

C. Not sell, transfer or release the Secured Property unless Seller consents.

D. Pay all taxes on the Secured Property as taxes become due.

E. Insure the Secured Property against normal risks, with an insurance policy that names Buyer and Seller as beneficiaries based on their respective interests in the property.

F. Deliver to Seller a copy of the insurance policy insuring the Secured Property and provide annual proof to Seller that Buyer has paid the premiums on the policy.

G. Allow Seller to inspect the Secured Property at any reasonable time.

6. Default of Buyer

Buyer will be in default if:

A. Buyer is late in making any payment required by the promissory note and does not pay within ten days of Seller sending written notice of late payment, or

B. Buyer fails to correct any actual violations of paragraph 5 within ten days of receiving written notice from Seller.

7. Rights of Seller

If Buyer is in default, Seller may exercise the remedies contained in the Uniform Commercial Code for the State of _____ and any other remedies legally available to Seller.

Seller may, for example:

A. Remove the Secured Property from the place where it is then located.

B. Require Buyer to make the Secured Property available to Seller at a place designated by Seller that is reasonably convenient to Buyer and Seller.

C. Sell or lease the Secured Property, or otherwise dispose of it.

8. Notice to Buyer

Seller will give Buyer at least five days notice of when and where the Secured Property will be sold, leased or otherwise disposed of. Any notice required here or by statute will be deemed given to Buyer if sent by first-class mail to Buyer at the following address: _____

_____

9. Entire Agreement

This is the entire agreement between the parties. It replaces and supersedes any and all oral agreements between the parties, as well as any prior writings.

10. Successors and Assignees

This agreement binds and benefits the heirs, successors and assignees of the parties.

11. Governing Law

This agreement will be governed by and construed in accordance with the laws of the state of

_____.

12. Counterparts

The parties may sign several identical counterparts of this agreement. Any fully signed counterpart shall be treated as an original.

13. Modification

This agreement may only be modified by a writing signed by the party against whom such modification is sought to be enforced.

14. Waiver

If one party waives any term or provision of this agreement at any time, that waiver will only be effective for the specific instance and specific purpose for which the waiver was given. If either party fails to exercise or delays exercising any of its rights or remedies under this agreement, that party retains the right to enforce that term or provision at a later time.

15. Severability

If any court determines that any provision of this agreement is invalid or unenforceable, any invalidity or unenforceability will affect only that provision and will not make any other provision of this agreement invalid or unenforceable and such provision shall be modified, amended or limited only to the extent necessary to render it valid and enforceable.

Dated: _____

SELLER

Name of Business: _____

a _____

By: _____

Printed Name and Title: _____

Address: _____

_____

BUYER

Name of Business: _____

a _____

By: _____

Printed Name and Title: _____

Address: _____

_____

Form 8E: Contract for Manufacture of Goods

1. Names

_____, Seller,

and _____, Buyer,

agree to the following terms.

2. Property Description

Seller agrees to ☐ manufacture ☐ customize   and sell to Buyer, and Buyer agrees to buy from Seller, the following property:

_____

_____

Seller will ☐ manufacture ☐ customize   the property according to the specifications, which are designated Attachment 1 to this contract.

3. Purchase Price

The purchase price of the property is $_____.

4. Down Payment

(Choose One)

☐ Buyer will make a down payment of $_____ when this contract is signed. This down payment will be applied toward the purchase price.

☐ Buyer will not make a down payment.

5. Time of Payment

Buyer will pay Seller the purchase price (less any down payment) as follows:

☐ upon delivery of the property to Buyer.

☐ on _____.

☐ in installments according to schedule established in Attachment _____.

6. Method of Payment

Buyer will pay Seller by

☐ personal check.

☐ cashier's check.

☐ credit card issued by _____

☐ other _____

7. Delivery

Seller will deliver the property to Buyer by _____ at:

(Choose One)

☐ Seller's place of business, _____

☐ Buyer's place of business, _____

☐   Other: _____.

☐   **8. Disclaimer of Warranties** *(Optional)*

The property is being sold without any warranties, whether express or implied, including the implied warranties of merchantability and fitness for a particular purpose.

9. Bill of Sale

Concurrently with the delivery of the property to Buyer, Seller will execute and deliver to Buyer and transfer ownership of the property to Buyer through a bill of sale.

10. Security Interest

☐   Seller will not retain a security interest in the property.

☐   Seller will retain a security interest in the property. At the time the property is delivered to Buyer, Buyer will sign and deliver to Seller a security agreement and UCC financing statement giving Seller a security interest in the property until the purchase price has been paid in full.

11. Other Terms and Conditions

_____

_____

_____

_____

_____.

12. Entire Agreement

This is the entire agreement between the parties. It replaces and supersedes any and all oral agreements between the parties, as well as any prior writings.

13. Successors and Assignees

This agreement binds and benefits the heirs, successors and assignees of the parties.

14. Notices

All notices must be in writing. A notice may be delivered to a party at the address that follows a party's signature or to a new address that a party designates in writing. A notice may be delivered:

(1) in person,

(2) by certified mail, or

(3) by overnight courier.

15. Governing Law

This agreement will be governed by and construed in accordance with the laws of the state of

_____.

16. Counterparts

The parties may sign several identical counterparts of this agreement. Any fully signed counterpart shall be treated as an original.

17. Modification

This agreement may only be modified by a writing signed by the party against whom such modification is sought to be enforced.

18. Waiver

If one party waives any term or provision of this agreement at any time, that waiver will only be effective for the specific instance and specific purpose for which the waiver was given. If either party fails to exercise or delays exercising any of its rights or remedies under this agreement, that party retains the right to enforce that term or provision at a later time.

19. Severability

If any court determines that any provision of this agreement is invalid or unenforceable, any invalidity or unenforceability will affect only that provision and will not make any other provision of this agreement invalid or unenforceable and such provision shall be modified, amended or limited only to the extent necessary to render it valid and enforceable.

Dated: _____

SELLER

Name of Business: _____

a _____

By: _____

Printed Name and Title: _____

Address: _____

_____

BUYER

Name of Business: _____

a _____

By: _____

Printed Name and Title: _____

Address: _____

_____

Form 8F: Equipment Rental Contract

1. Names

_____, Owner,

and _____, Renter,

agree to the following rental.

2. Equipment Being Rented

Owner agrees to rent to Renter, and Renter agrees to rent from Owner, the following equipment:

_____

_____

_____ ("Equipment").

3. Duration of Rental Period

The rental will begin at _____ on _____ and will end at

_____ on _____.

4. Rental Amount

The rental amount is $_____ per ☐ day ☐ week ☐ month.

5. Payment

Renter has paid $_____ to Owner to cover the rental period specified in paragraph 3.

☐ Security Deposit *(Optional)*. In addition to the rent, Renter has deposited
$_____ with Owner. This deposit will be applied toward any additional rent
and any amounts owed for damage to or loss of the equipment, which Owner and renter agree
has the current value stated in paragraph 8. Owner will return to Renter any unused portion of the
deposit.

6. Delivery

Owner will deliver the equipment to Renter on _____ at:

☐ Owner's place of business

☐ Renter's place of business

☐ Other: _____

7. Late Return

If Renter returns the equipment to Owner after the time and date when the rental period ends, Renter will
pay Owner a rental charge of $_____ per day for each day or partial day beyond
the end of the rental period until the equipment is returned.

Owner can subtract these rental charges from the security deposit.

8. Damage or Loss

Renter acknowledges receiving the equipment in good condition, except as follows:

_____

_____

_____

Renter will return the equipment to Owner in good condition except as noted above. If the equipment is damaged while in Renter's possession, Renter will be responsible for the cost of repair, up to the current value of the equipment. If the equipment is lost while in Renter's possession, Renter will pay Owner its current value.

Owner and Renter agree that the current value of the equipment is $_____.

☐ **9. Use of Equipment** *(Optional)*

Renter acknowledges that use of the Equipment creates some risk of personal injury to Renter and third parties, as well as a risk of damage to property, and Renter expressly assumes that risk. Renter therefore agrees to use the Equipment safely and only in the manner for which it is intended to be used. Owner is not responsible for any personal injury or property damage resulting from Renter's misuse, unsafe use or reckless use of the Equipment. Renter will indemnify and defend Owner from and against any injury or damage claims arising out of Renter's misuse, unsafe use or reckless use of the Equipment.

10. Entire Agreement

This is the entire agreement between the parties. It replaces and supersedes any and all oral agreements between the parties, as well as any prior writings.

11. Successors and Assignees

This agreement binds and benefits the heirs, successors and assignees of the parties.

12. Notices

All notices must be in writing. A notice may be delivered to a party at the address that follows a party's signature or to a new address that a party designates in writing. A notice may be delivered:

(1) in person,

(2) by certified mail, or

(3) by overnight courier.

13. Governing Law

This agreement will be governed by and construed in accordance with the laws of the state of

_____.

14. Counterparts

The parties may sign several identical counterparts of this agreement. Any fully signed counterpart shall be treated as an original.

15. Modification

This agreement may only be modified by a writing signed by the party against whom such modification is sought to be enforced.

16. Waiver

If one party waives any term or provision of this agreement at any time, that waiver will only be effective for the specific instance and specific purpose for which the waiver was given. If either party fails to exercise or delays exercising any of its rights or remedies under this agreement, that party retains the right to enforce that term or provision at a later time.

17. Severability

If any court determines that any provision of this agreement is invalid or unenforceable, any invalidity or unenforceability will affect only that provision and will not make any other provision of this agreement invalid or unenforceable and such provision shall be modified, amended or limited only to the extent necessary to render it valid and enforceable.

Dated: _____

OWNER

Name of Business: _____

a _____

By: _____

Printed Name and Title: _____

Address: _____

_____

RENTER

Name of Business: _____

a _____

By: _____

Printed Name and Title: _____

Address: _____

_____

Form 8G: Storage Contract

1. Names

_____, Customer,

and _____,

Storer, agree to the following storage arrangements.

2. Property Being Stored

Storer agrees to store the following Property for Customer:

_____

_____

_____

_____

_____

_____

3. Storage Period

The storage will begin on _____ and continue until _____,
unless Customer takes back the Property before then.

4. Storage Fees

Customer has paid Storer $_____, which covers all storage fees through the storage
period set out in paragraph 3.

5. Additional Fees

If Customer does not take back the Property by the end of the stated storage period, Storer will continue to
store the Property until Customer does take back the property or Storer terminates the contract, if that occurs
sooner. The fee for storage beyond the stated storage period will be $_____ per

☐ week ☐ month, to be paid in advance by Customer.

6. Refunds

The unused portion of storage fees paid by Customer is not refundable, unless Storer terminates the storage
contract.

7. End of Storage

Following the end of the stated storage period, Storer may end this storage contract by sending written

notice to Customer at least _____ days in advance of the termination date. If Customer does not pay
any unpaid balance of storage fees and take back the Property by the termination date, the Property will be
treated as abandoned. Storer will sell the Property in a commercially reasonable manner and apply the
proceeds to the costs of sale and any unpaid storage fees. Storer will mail the balance of the proceeds to
Customer.

8. Storage Location

Storer will store the property at _____.

☐ 9. Value of Property *(Optional)*

Customer and Storer agree that the replacement value of the Property is $_____.

10. Condition of Property

The Property is in good condition except for the following:

_____

_____

_____

_____

11. Reasonable Care

Storer will use reasonable care to protect the Property. Customer will bear the expense of any damage to or loss of the Property not caused by Storer's actions or negligence.

12. Other Terms and Conditions

_____

_____

_____

13. Entire Agreement

This is the entire agreement between the parties. It replaces and supersedes any and all oral agreements between the parties, as well as any prior writings.

14. Successors and Assignees

This agreement binds and benefits the heirs, successors and assignees of the parties.

15. Notices

All notices must be in writing. A notice may be delivered to a party at the address that follows a party's signature or to a new address that a party designates in writing. A notice may be delivered:

(1) in person,

(2) by certified mail, or

(3) by overnight courier.

16. Governing Law

This agreement will be governed by and construed in accordance with the laws of the state of _____

_____ .

17. Counterparts

The parties may sign several identical counterparts of this agreement. Any fully signed counterpart shall be treated as an original.

18. Modification

This agreement may only be modified by a writing signed by the party against whom such modification is sought to be enforced.

19. Waiver

If one party waives any term or provision of this agreement at any time, that waiver will only be effective for the specific instance and specific purpose for which the waiver was given. If either party fails to exercise or delays exercising any of its rights or remedies under this agreement, that party retains the right to enforce that term or provision at a later time.

20. Severability

If any court determines that any provision of this agreement is invalid or unenforceable, any invalidity or unenforceability will affect only that provision and will not make any other provision of this agreement invalid or unenforceable and such provision shall be modified, amended or limited only to the extent necessary to render it valid and enforceable.

Dated: _____

STORER

Name of Business: _____

a _____

By: _____

Printed Name and Title: _____

Address: _____

_____

CUSTOMER

Name of Business: _____

a _____

By: _____

Printed Name and Title: _____

Address: _____

_____

Form 8H: Consignment Contract

1. Names

_____, Customer,

and _____,

Consignee, agree to the following consignment.

2. Property Consigned

Owner ☐ has delivered ☐ will deliver the following Goods to Consignee on consignment:

Goods _____ Sale Price _____

_____ _____

_____ _____

_____ _____

_____ _____

3. Efforts to Sell

Consignee will display the Goods and attempt to sell them at or above the prices listed in paragraph 2. Consignee will obtain the written consent of Owner before selling the Goods at prices lower than those listed in paragraph 2.

4. Proceeds of Sale

Following a sale, Consignee will retain from the sale proceeds a commission of _____% of the sale price. In computing the commission, sales tax will not be added to the sale price. Consignee will send the balance of the sale proceeds to Owner within five days of the sale.

5. Ownership Before Sale

Owner will retain ownership of the Goods until they are sold.

6. Risk of Loss

While the Goods are in Consignee's possession, Consignee will bear the risk of damage to or loss of the Goods. If the Goods are damaged or lost, Consignee will pay Owner the selling price listed above less the stated commission.

7. Termination of Consignment

Owner or Consignee may terminate this contract at any time. If either party terminates the agreement, Consignee will return the Goods to Seller at:

☐ Seller's place of business at _____.

☐ Consignee's place of business at _____.

☐ Other: _____.

8. Other Terms and Conditions

_____

_____

_____

_____

9. Entire Agreement

This is the entire agreement between the parties. It replaces and supersedes any and all oral agreements between the parties, as well as any prior writings.

10. Successors and Assignees

This agreement binds and benefits the heirs, successors and assignees of the parties.

11. Notices

All notices must be in writing. A notice may be delivered to a party at the address that follows a party's signature or to a new address that a party designates in writing. A notice may be delivered:

 (1) in person,

 (2) by certified mail, or

 (3) by overnight courier.

12. Governing Law

This agreement will be governed by and construed in accordance with the laws of the state of

_____ .

13. Counterparts

The parties may sign several identical counterparts of this agreement. Any fully signed counterpart shall be treated as an original.

14. Modification

This agreement may only be modified by a writing signed by the party against whom such modification is sought to be enforced.

15. Waiver

If one party waives any term or provision of this agreement at any time, that waiver will only be effective for the specific instance and specific purpose for which the waiver was given. If either party fails to exercise or delays exercising any of its rights or remedies under this agreement, that party retains the right to enforce that term or provision at a later time.

16. Severability

If any court determines that any provision of this agreement is invalid or unenforceable, any invalidity or unenforceability will affect only that provision and will not make any other provision of this agreement invalid or unenforceable and such provision shall be modified, amended or limited only to the extent necessary to render it valid and enforceable.

Dated: _____

CUSTOMER

Name of Business: _____

a _____

By: _____

Printed Name and Title: _____

Address: _____

_____

CONSIGNEE

Name of Business: _____

a _____

By: _____

Printed Name and Title: _____

Address: _____

_____

Form 9A: Employment Application

Full Name: _____

Address: _____

_____

Phone No. _____ Social Security No. _____

Are you legally entitled to work in the United States? ☐ Yes ☐ No

Are you 18 years old or older? ☐ Yes ☐ No

What position are you applying for? _____

If you are hired, when can you start work? _____

Education

High School

Name of School: _____

Location: _____

Number of years attended: _____ Did you graduate? ☐ Yes ☐ No

Trade School

Name of School: _____

Location: _____

Number of years attended: _____ Did you graduate? ☐ Yes ☐ No

College and Postgraduate

Name of School: _____

Location: _____

Number of years attended: _____ Did you graduate? ☐ Yes ☐ No What degree?

_____

Name of School: _____

Location: _____

Number of years attended: _____ Did you graduate? ☐ Yes ☐ No What degree?

_____

Employment History

Beginning with your most recent employment and working back in time, please give the following information:

Employer: _____

Address: _____

_____

Job Title: _____ Duties: _____

_____

Dates of Employment: _____ Supervisor: _____

Reason for Leaving: _____

Employer: _____

Address: _____

_____

Job Title: _____ Duties: _____

_____

Dates of Employment: _____ Supervisor: _____

Reason for Leaving: _____

Employer: _____

Address: _____

_____

Job Title: _____ Duties: _____

_____

Dates of Employment: _____ Supervisor: _____

Reason for Leaving: _____

Personal References

Please provide the names of two references who have not employed you and are not related to you.

Name: _____

Address: _____

Phone Number: _____ Relationship: _____

Name: _____

Address: _____

Phone Number: _____ Relationship: _____

Additional Qualifications

Please tell us about any other training, education, skills or achievements that you feel should be considered.

_____

_____

To _____ :

My answers are true and complete. I understand that if I am hired, any false or incomplete statements in this application will be grounds for immediate discharge.

Date: _____ Applicant's Signature: _____

Form 9B: Authorization to Release Information

I authorize _____
to obtain information about me from my previous employers, schools and credit sources.

I authorize my previous employers, schools that I have attended and credit sources to disclose such information
about me as _____
may request.

I authorize my previous employers to candidly disclose to _____
_____ all facts and opinions concerning my work performance,
cooperativeness and ability to get along well with others.

Dated: _____

Signature: _____

Printed Name: _____

Address: _____

_____

Form 9C: Offer of Employment

Date: _____

Dear _____:

    I am pleased to offer you a position with our company as _____

beginning _____. Your starting compensation will be $_____

to be paid _____.

    When you applied, I gave you a copy of our employee handbook. The handbook sets out our current employment policies and describes your job benefits. It also describes your responsibilities to the company. You may receive periodic updates.

    All the company's commitments to you and its other employees are stated in the handbook. Your employment is at will, meaning there is no promise of a job for any specific period of time. The company can terminate your employment at any time, for any reason or for no reason. This policy can be changed only by a written contract that I sign. No oral commitments to you regarding your employment are valid—whether made now or in the future.

    While I hope you enjoy working here, you of course have the right to terminate your employment at any time.

    If this offer of employment is acceptable to you, please sign a copy of this letter and return it to me within ten days. I look forward to having you join our staff.

Sincerely,

_____

Printed Name: _____

Title: _____

Acceptance:

I accept your offer of employment and acknowledge receiving and reading a copy of your current employee handbook.

Signature: _____

Printed Name: _____

Date: _____

Form 9D: Confidentiality Agreement

In consideration of _____,
Employer, hiring me as an Employee, I agree as follows:

1. Agreement Not to Disclose Confidential Information

I acknowledge that Employer may disclose to me or give me access to confidential information so that I may perform my employment duties. I agree that the confidential information includes Employer's trade secrets, sales and profit figures, customer lists, relationships with contractors, customers or suppliers, and opportunities for new or developing business. The confidential information may be contained in written materials such as computer hardware and software, disks, documents, files, drawings and product specifications. It may also consist of unwritten knowledge, including ideas, research, processes, practices or know-how. While I am employed by Employer, and afterward, I will not use or disclose to any other person or entity any confidential information or materials (either written or unwritten) except when I am required to do so to properly perform my duties to Employer or as required by law.

Information in the public domain, information generally known in the trade and information that I acquire completely independently of my services for Employer is not considered to be confidential.

2. Return of Confidential Information

While I am employed by Employer and afterward, I will not, except in performing my duties, remove or copy any confidential information or materials or assist anyone in doing so without Employer's written permission. Upon my termination by Employer, or at any time that Employer requests it, I will immediately return all confidential information and materials to Employer.

3. Right to an Injunction

I acknowledge that in addition to receiving or having access to confidential information as part of my employment, I will be in a position of confidence and trust with employees, clients and customers of Employer. I acknowledge and agree that if I breach or threaten to breach any of the terms of this Confidentiality Agreement, Employer will sustain irreparable harm and that Employer will be entitled to obtain an injunction to stop any breach or threatened breach of this Agreement.

4. Reasonableness

I acknowledge that the restrictions in this Agreement are reasonable and necessary to protect Employer and its confidential information.

5. Survivability

This agreement will survive the termination, for any reason, of my employment with Employer.

6. Entire Agreement

This is the entire agreement between the parties. It replaces any and all oral agreements between the parties, as well as any prior writings.

7. Successors and Assignees

This agreement binds and benefits the heirs, successors and assignees of the parties.

8. Notices

All notices must be in writing. A notice may be delivered to a party at the address that follows a party's signature or to a new address that a party designates in writing. A notice may be delivered:

(1) in person,

(2) by certified mail, or

(3) by overnight courier.

9. Governing Law

This agreement will be governed by and construed in accordance with the laws of the state of _____
_____.

10. Counterparts

The parties may sign several identical counterparts of this agreement. Any fully signed counterpart shall be treated as an original.

11. Modification

This agreement may only be modified by a writing signed by the party against whom such modification is sought to be enforced.

12. Waiver

If one party waives any term or provision of this agreement at any time, that waiver will only be effective for the specific instance and specific purpose for which the waiver was given. If either party fails to exercise or delays exercising any of its rights or remedies under this agreement, that party retains the right to enforce that term or provision at a later time.

12. Severability

If any court determines that any provision of this agreement is invalid or unenforceable, any invalidity or unenforceability will affect only that provision and will not make any other provision of this agreement invalid or unenforceable and such provision shall be modified, amended or limited only to the extent necessary to render it valid and enforceable.

Dated: _____

Signature: _____

Printed Name: _____

Form 9E: Covenant Not to Compete

In consideration of _____
Employer, hiring me as an Employee, I agree as follows:

1. Agreement Not to Compete

While I am employed by Employer, and for _____ [years/months] afterward, I will not directly or indirectly participate in a business that is similar to a business now or later operated by Employer in the same geographical area. This includes participating in my own business or as a co-owner, director, officer, consultant, independent contractor, employee or agent of another business.

In particular, I will not:

(a) solicit or attempt to solicit any business or trade from Employer's actual or prospective customers or clients;

(b) employ or attempt to employ any employee of Employer;

(c) divert or attempt to divert business away from Employer, or

(d) encourage any independent contractor or consultant to end a relationship with Employer.

2. Right to an Injunction

I acknowledge and agree that if I breach or threaten to breach any of the terms of this Agreement, Employer will sustain irreparable harm and will be entitled to obtain an injunction to stop any breach or threatened breach of this Agreement.

3. Reasonableness

I acknowledge that the restrictions in this Agreement are reasonable and necessary for the protection of Employer.

4. Survivability

This agreement will survive the termination, for any reason, of my employment with Employer.

5. Entire Agreement

This is the entire agreement between the parties. It replaces and supersedes any and all oral agreements between the parties, as well as any prior writings.

6. Successors and Assignees

This agreement binds and benefits the heirs, successors and assignees of the parties.

7. Notices

All notices must be in writing. A notice may be delivered to a party at the address that follows a party's signature or to a new address that a party designates in writing. A notice may be delivered:

(1) in person,

(2) by certified mail, or

(3) by overnight courier.

8. Governing Law

This agreement will be governed by and construed in accordance with the laws of the state of _____ _____.

9. Counterparts

The parties may sign several identical counterparts of this agreement. Any fully signed counterpart shall be treated as an original.

10. Modification

This agreement may only be modified by a writing signed by the party against whom such modification is sought to be enforced.

11. Waiver

If one party waives any term or provision of this agreement at any time, that waiver will only be effective for the specific instance and specific purpose for which the waiver was given. If either party fails to exercise or delays exercising any of its rights or remedies under this agreement, that party retains the right to enforce that term or provision at a later time.

12. Severability

If any court determines that any provision of this agreement is invalid or unenforceable, any invalidity or unenforceability will affect only that provision and will not make any other provision of this agreement invalid or unenforceable and such provision shall be modified, amended or limited only to the extent necessary to render it valid and enforceable.

Dated: _____

Signature: _____

Printed Name: _____

Form 9F: Contract With Employee

1. Names

This agreement is between _____ , Employer,

and _____ , Employee.

2. Job Duties

Employer hires employee for the position of _____ .

Employee agrees to perform the following services for Employer:

_____

_____

_____

_____

_____

_____

3. Duration of Employment

The employment will begin on _____ and end on _____
unless terminated sooner as specified in this contract.

4. Compensation

Employer will pay Employee $_____ per year. Employee's salary will be subject to all
normal state, federal and local withholding and will be paid in accordance with Employer's normal payroll
practices.

5. Other Benefits

Employer will provide the following additional benefits to Employee:

_____

_____

_____

6. Employer's Policies

Employee accepts Employer's policies as contained in the Employee Handbook which Employee acknowledges receiving.

7. Termination

If Employee does not satisfactorily perform the job duties described in paragraph 2 of this contract or substantially violates Employer's policies as set forth in its employee handbook, Employer may terminate
Employee's employment.

8. Agreement Not to Disclose Confidential Information

I acknowledge that Employer may disclose to me or give me access to confidential information so that I may
perform my employment duties. I agree that the confidential information includes Employer's trade secrets,
sales and profit figures, customer lists, relationships with contractors, customers or suppliers, and opportunities for new or developing business. The confidential information may be contained in written materials such

as computer hardware and software, disks, documents, files, drawings and product specifications. It may also consist of unwritten knowledge, including ideas, research, processes, practices or know-how. While I am employed by Employer, and afterward, I will not use or disclose to any other person or entity any confidential information or materials (either written or unwritten) except when I am required to do so to properly perform my duties to Employer or as required by law.

Information in the public domain, information generally known in the trade and information that I acquire completely independently of my services for Employer is not considered to be confidential.

9. Return of Confidential Information

While I am employed by Employer and afterward, I will not, except in performing my duties, remove or copy any confidential information or materials or assist anyone in doing so without Employer's written permission. Upon my termination by Employer, or at any time that Employer requests it, I will immediately return all confidential information and materials to Employer.

10. Agreement Not to Compete

While I am employed by Employer, and for _____ [years/months] afterward, I will not directly or indirectly participate in a business in a similar capacity that is similar to a business now or later operated by Employer in the same geographical area. This includes participating in my own business or as a co-owner, director, officer, consultant, independent contractor, employee or agent of another business.

In particular, I will not:

(a) solicit or attempt to solicit any business or trade from Employer's actual or prospective customers or clients;

(b) employ or attempt to employ any employee of Employer;

(c) divert or attempt to divert business away from Employer, or

(d) encourage any independent contractor or consultant to end a relationship with Employer.

11. Right to an Injunction

I acknowledge that in addition to receiving or having access to confidential information as part of my employment, I will be in a position of confidence and trust with employees, clients and customers of Employer. I acknowledge and agree that if I breach or threaten to breach any of the terms of paragraph 8, 9 or 10 of this Agreement, Employer will sustain irreparable harm and that Employer will be entitled to obtain an injunction to stop any breach or threatened breach of this Agreement.

12. Reasonableness

I acknowledge that the restrictions in this Agreement are reasonable and necessary for the protection of Employer.

13. Survivability

The provisions of Sections 8, 9 and 10 of this agreement will survive the termination, for any reason, of my employment with Employer.

14. Entire Agreement

This is the entire agreement between the parties. It replaces and supersedes any and all oral agreements between the parties, as well as any prior writings.

15. Successors and Assignees

This agreement binds and benefits the heirs, successors and assignees of the parties.

16. Notices

All notices must be in writing. A notice may be delivered to a party at the address that follows a party's signature or to a new address that a party designates in writing. A notice may be delivered:

    (1) in person,

    (2) by certified mail, or

    (3) by overnight courier.

17. Governing Law

This agreement will be governed by and construed in accordance with the laws of the state of _____

_____.

18. Counterparts

The parties may sign several identical counterparts of this agreement. Any fully signed counterpart shall be treated as an original.

19. Modification

This agreement may only be modified by a writing signed by the party against whom such modification is sought to be enforced.

20. Waiver

If one party waives any term or provision of this agreement at any time, that waiver will only be effective for the specific instance and specific purpose for which the waiver was given. If either party fails to exercise or delays exercising any of its rights or remedies under this agreement, that party retains the right to enforce that term or provision at a later time.

21. Severability

If any court determines that any provision of this agreement is invalid or unenforceable, any invalidity or unenforceability will affect only that provision and will not make any other provision of this agreement invalid or unenforceable and such provision shall be modified, amended or limited only to the extent necessary to render it valid and enforceable.

Dated: _____

EMPLOYER

Name of Business: _____

a _____

By: _____

Printed Name and Title: _____

Address: _____

_____

EMPLOYEE

By: _____

Printed Name: _____

Address: _____

_____

Form 9G: Contract With Independent Contractor

1. Names

This agreement is between _____ ,Client,

and _____ , Contractor.

2. Services to Be Performed

Contractor agrees to perform the following services for Client:

_____

_____

_____

_____

_____ .

3. Time for Performance

☐ Contractor will complete the performance of these services on or before _____ .

☐ Contractor will perform the services according to the following schedule:

_____

_____ .

4. Payment

Client will pay Contractor as follows: _____

_____ .

5. State and Federal Taxes

Client will not:

    a. withhold Social Security and Medicare taxes from Contractor's payments or make such tax payment on Contractor's behalf

    b. make state or federal unemployment contributions on Contractor's behalf, or withhold state or federal income tax from Contractor's payments.

Contractor will pay all applicable taxes related to the performance of services under this contract. This includes income, Social Security, Medicare and self-employment taxes. Contractor will also pay all unemployment contributions related to the performance of services under this contract. Contractor will reimburse Client if Client is required to pay such taxes or unemployment contributions.

6. Fringe Benefits

Neither Contractor nor Contractor's employee's are eligible to participate in any employee pension, health, vacation pay, sick pay or other fringe benefit plan of Client.

7. Invoices

Contractor will submit invoices to Client for all services performed.

8. Independent Contractor Status

The parties intend Contractor to be an independent contractor in the performance of the services. Contractor will have the right to control and determine the methods and means of performing the contractual services.

9. Other Clients

Contractor retains the right to perform services for other clients.

10. Assistants

Contractor, at Contractor's expense, may employ assistants as Contractor deems appropriate to perform the contractual services. Contractor will be responsible for paying these assistants as well as any expense attributable to them including income, Social Security and Medicare taxes, and unemployment contributions. Contractor will maintain workers' compensation insurance for all of its employees.

11. Equipment and Supplies

A. Contractor, at Contractor's expense, will provide all equipment, tools and supplies necessary to perform the contractual services, except for the following which will be provided by Client:

_____

_____

B. Contractor will be responsible for all expenses required for the performance of the contractual services, except for the following which will be paid for by Client: _____

_____

12. Disputes

(Choose One)

☐ **Litigation.** If a dispute arises, any party may take the matter to court.

☐ **Mediation and Possible Litigation.** If a dispute arises, the parties will try in good faith to settle it through mediation conducted by:

   ☐ _____

   ☐ a mediator to be mutually selected.

   The parties will share the costs of the mediator equally. Each party will cooperate fully and fairly with the mediator and will attempt to reach a mutually satisfactory compromise to the dispute. If the dispute is not resolved within 30 days after it is referred to the mediator, any party may take the matter to court.

☐ **Mediation and Possible Arbitration.** If a dispute arises, the parties will try in good faith to settle it through mediation conducted by:

   ☐ _____

   ☐ a mediator to be mutually selected.

   The parties will share the costs of the mediator equally. Each party will cooperate fully and fairly with the mediator and will attempt to reach a mutually satisfactory compromise to the dispute. If the dispute is not resolved within 30 days after it is referred to the mediator, it will be arbitrated by:

   ☐ _____

   ☐ an arbitrator to be mutually selected.

   Judgment on the arbitration award may be entered in any court that has jurisdiction over the matter. Costs of arbitration, including lawyers' fees, will be allocated by the arbitrator

13. Entire Agreement

This is the entire agreement between the parties. It replaces and supersedes any and all oral agreements between the parties, as well as any prior writings.

14. Successors and Assignees

This agreement binds and benefits the heirs, successors and assignees of the parties.

15. Notices

All notices must be in writing. A notice may be delivered to a party at the address that follows a party's signature or to a new address that a party designates in writing. A notice may be delivered:

(1) in person,

(2) by certified mail, or

(3) by overnight courier.

16. Governing Law

This agreement will be governed by and construed in accordance with the laws of the state of

_____.

17. Counterparts

The parties may sign several identical counterparts of this agreement. Any fully signed counterpart shall be treated as an original.

18. Modification

This agreement may only be modified by a writing signed by the party against whom such modification is sought to be enforced.

19. Waiver

If one party waives any term or provision of this agreement at any time, that waiver will only be effective for the specific instance and specific purpose for which the waiver was given. If either party fails to exercise or delays exercising any of its rights or remedies under this agreement, that party retains the right to enforce that term or provision at a later time.

20. Severability

If any court determines that any provision of this agreement is invalid or unenforceable, any invalidity or unenforceability will affect only that provision and will not make any other provision of this agreement invalid or unenforceable and such provision shall be modified, amended or limited only to the extent necessary to render it valid and enforceable.

Dated: _____

CLIENT

Name of Business: _____

a _____

By: _____

Printed Name and Title: _____

Address: _____

_____

CONTRACTOR

Name of Business: _____

a _____

By: _____

Printed Name and Title: _____

Address: _____

_____

Index

Here are answers to the most frequently asked questions about Registered Agent and ComplianceWatch®

What is a Registered Agent?

1. Q. *What is a Registered Agent?*

A. It is an "agent" of the corporation or Limited Liability Company (LLC) who is officially "registered" with the state to be responsible for receiving and forwarding vital legal documents, such as tax forms and notice of litigation (also known as service of process or SOP), on behalf of your corporation or LLC.

Most states require corporations and Limited Liability Companies (LLCs) to designate and maintain a Registered Agent to receive and forward this correspondence on behalf of your company. The Registered Agent for your corporation or LLC must be located at a legal address (not a PO Box) within that state, hence they are sometimes referred to as a "Resident" Agent.

2. Q. *What are the benefits of having a third party Registered Agent?*

A. Most business owners choose a third party to serve in this critical capacity. There are several good reasons for this, including:

◆ If you are frequently out of the office and no one is available during regular business hours to receive notice of litigation on your behalf, you could be defaulted for failing to answer a claim in a timely manner.

◆ If you aren't sure your address will stay the same in the future, having a Registered Agent allows you to change the location of your company easily without filing a costly change of address with the state.

◆ A third party Registered Agent offers a layer of privacy, protecting you from publicly being served litigation papers while in the presence of customers and employees.

---

3. Q. *Why choose The Company Corporation® for my Registered Agent Service?*

A. Most importantly, we will forward, via FedEx®, a notice of litigation when it arrives in our office. This notice details who is suing you, in what court, when process was served, the nature of the case and how much time you have to respond.

We also will receive and forward official state and federal documents as well as state franchise tax or annual reports when required.

The Company Corporation's® Registered Agent Service also includes ComplianceWatch®, a FREE online service that notifies you when critical corporate activities are due.

If you file a Change of Agent form with your state, you must send a copy of the document to The Company Corporation® to officially cancel your Registered Agent Service.

4. Q. *How does ComplianceWatch® help me maintain my corporate status?*

A. Other service companies simply help only with incorporating or forming the LLC. ComplianceWatch® helps manage the ongoing legal formalities associated with your corporate entity.

This service, offered exclusively by The Company Corporation®, helps protect your personal assets by keeping your business on track in a number of key ways:

◆ state-specific features help assure accurate record-keeping and reporting compliance

◆ automatic notification when it's time to file annual reports, pay franchise taxes and hold annual meetings

◆ convenient email messaging capabilities help you save time when communicating with your directors, officers and shareholders or LLC members

---

5. Q. *How do I register for ComplianceWatch®?*

A. It is easy to activate your ComplianceWatch® Service. Login to www.ComplianceWatch.com and take the "virtual tour" to learn about Compliance Watch features. Then, go to "Register for Compliance Watch," click on the link, fill in the User Information and you're on your way.

It's that easy!

6. Q. *My corporation or LLC is no longer active. What should I do now?*

A. There are benefits to officially terminating your corporation or LLC with your state. You avoid having to pay franchise taxes or file annual reports. In some states, there could be penalties involved should you try to restart your old company or even start a new one without having officially terminated the company with the appropriate Secretary of State's office. The Company Corporation® can provide the forms and assistance you need to dissolve or withdraw your company from the state.

Keep in mind that formal dissolution usually does not relieve the Registered Agent of its statutory responsibilities. For example, in Delaware, as your Registered Agent, we must continue to receive and forward your notice(s) of litigation for three years after a formal dissolution of a business.

If you wish to discontinue receiving invoices, you must complete certain business-closure activities, in writing, and signed by an authorized individual. You may not cancel over the phone. The document should state that you:

◆ have ceased operating your corporation or LLC

◆ are not going to pay for Registered Agent Service

◆ are instructing The Company Corporation® to reject any Service of Process

◆ are holding The Company Corporation® harmless in event of a default

7. **Q. What is the duration of Registered Agent Service?**

A. It is a 12-month service, annually renewed. Failure to renew your Registered Agent Service may affect your company's good standing with your state.

8. **Q. Is multi-year Registered Agent Service available?**

A. Absolutely! You can save money and time by choosing the two or three-year option for Registered Agent Service. Save up to 20% when you lock in today's prices and take advantage of the substantial two and three-year discounts. To learn more, just login to: www.aboutregisteredagent.com

9. **Q. How can I contact The Company Corporation® to pay the enclosed invoice to renew my Registered Agent Service?**

A. There are four easy ways to pay your annual invoice for Registered Agent Service - online, by phone, by mail, or by fax.

Direct online payment:
Click on:
www.aboutregisteredagent.com.

Direct phone payment:
Call toll-free:
1-800-792-2131

Direct mail payment:
Send completed invoice form to:
The Company Corporation
P.O. Box 13397
Philadelphia, PA 19101-3397

Direct fax payment:
Fax invoice with complete credit card information and length of service option selected to:
302-636-5454

Help ensure your good corporate standing. Don't delay. Renew your Registered Agent Service today!

The Company Corporation®
Incorporating Businesses Since 1899

The Company Corporation®
2711 Centerville Road, Suite 400
Wilmington, DE 19808
800-877-4224
www.incorporate.com

About
Registered Agent
and
ComplianceWatch®
Service

The Company Corporation®
Incorporating Businesses Since 1899

The Company Corporation® is an incorporation service company and does not offer legal or financial advice.

rev 3/03